Journalist Conor O'Clery holds a unique perspective on the last years of the Soviet Union, having opened the first foreign bureau in Moscow for *The Irish Times* in 1987. He was subsequently foreign correspondent in Washington, Beijing and New York (witnessing first hand the 9/11 attacks). One of the most respected journalists in Ireland, he twice won Irish Journalist of the Year. He has written eight previous books, including *Melting Snow: An Irishman in Moscow*; *The Greening of the White House*, about the Clinton presidency; *The Billionaire Who Wasn't*, a biography of philanthropist Chuck Feeney; and *May You Live in Interesting Times: Journals of a Foreign Correspondent*.

Other books by Conor O'Clery:

Melting Snow: An Irishman in Moscow
America: A Place Called Hope?
The Greening of the White House
Ireland in Quotes: A History of the Twentieth Century
Panic at the Bank
The Billionaire Who Wasn't
May You Live in Interesting Times

Moscow, December 25, 1991

The Last Day of the Soviet Union

CONOR O'CLERY

TRANSWORLD IRELAND

TRANSWORLD IRELAND
An imprint of The Random House Group Limited
20 Vauxhall Bridge Road, London SW1V 2SA
www.transworldbooks.co.uk

MOSCOW, DECEMBER 25, 1991
A TRANSWORLD IRELAND BOOK: 9781848271142

First published in 2011 in the United States
by PublicAffairs, a member of the Perseus Book Group

First published in Great Britain
in 2011 by Transworld Ireland
a division of Transworld Publishers
Transworld Ireland paperback edition published 2012

Addresses for Random House Group Ltd companies outside the UK
can be found at: www.randomhouse.co.uk
The Random House Group Ltd Reg. No. 954009

Penguin·Random House is committed to a sustainable future for
our business, our readers and our planet. This book is made from
Forest Stewardship Council® certified paper.

MIX
Paper from
responsible sources
FSC® C018179

Printed and bound in Great Britain by Clays Ltd, St Ives plc

Typeset in 11/14pt Sabon by Falcon Oast Graphic Art Ltd.

6 8 10 9 7 5

To Stanislav and Marietta

Goodbye our Red Flag.
You slipped down from the Kremlin roof
not so proudly
not so adroitly
as you climbed many years ago
on the destroyed Reichstag
smoking like Hitler's last fag.

Goodbye our Red Flag.
You were our brother and our enemy.
You were a soldier's comrade in trenches,
you were the hope of all captive Europe,
but like a Red curtain you concealed behind you
the Gulag
stuffed with frozen dead bodies.
Why did you do it,
our Red Flag?

I didn't take the Tsar's Winter Palace.
I didn't storm Hitler's Reichstag.
I'm not what you call a 'Commie'.
But I caress the Red Flag
and cry.

Yevgeny Yevtushenko

Contents

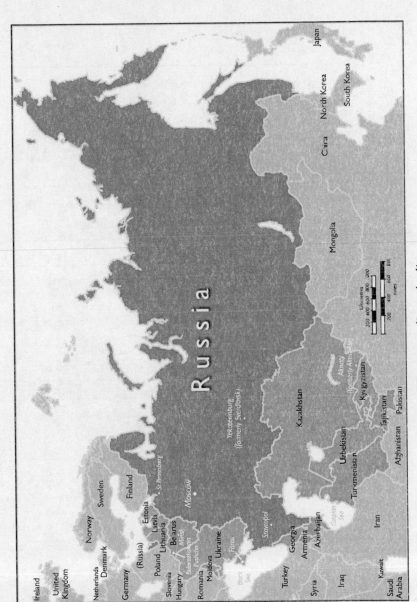

Russia, with the former Soviet republics in medium shading

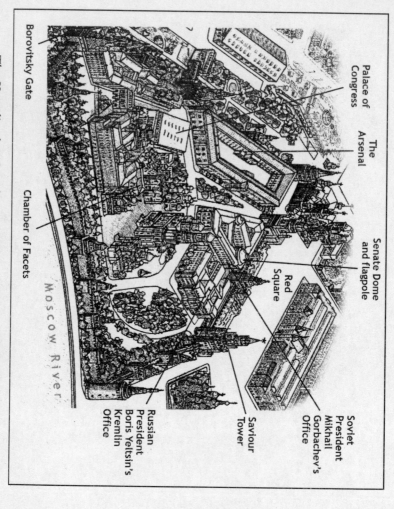

Palace of
Congress

The
Arsenal

Borovitsky Gate

Chamber of Facets

Senate Dome
and flagpole

Red
Square

Soviet
President
Mikhail
Gorbachev's
Office

Saviour
Tower

Russian
President
Boris Yeltsin's
Kremlin
Office

MOSCOW River

The Kremlin showing the proximity of Gorbachev's presidential
office and Yeltsin's temporary Kremlin office on December 25, 1991.

Preface

THIS BOOK IS A CHRONICLE OF ONE DAY IN THE history of one city. The day is Wednesday, December 25, 1991. The city is Moscow. It is the day the Soviet Union ends and the red flag comes down from the Kremlin. It is witness to a deeply personal and a politically charged drama, marked at the highest levels, and out of sight of the public, by shouts, tears, reminiscences and melodrama. It climaxes in a final act of surrender by Mikhail Gorbachev to Boris Yeltsin, two extraordinary men who despised each other and whose interaction shaped modern Russia.

In reconstructing the events of this mid-winter day, I have combined my interviews and my research in television and newspaper archives with material from over a hundred memoirs, diaries, biographies and other works that have appeared since the fall of the Soviet Union, in English and Russian. I have also drawn on my experience observing Gorbachev and Yeltsin up close in the last four years of Soviet rule, when I was a correspondent based in Moscow. During this period I frequented the Kremlin and the Russian White House where the fight between the two rivals played out. I hung around parliamentary and party meetings, grabbing every opportunity to question the two leaders when they appeared. I interviewed Politburo members, editors, economists, nationalists, Communist Party radicals and hardliners, dissidents, striking coal miners, and countless people just trying to get by. I was a face in the crowd at pro-democracy rallies, at Red Square commemorations and at the barricades in the Baltics. I travelled around Russia, from Chechnya to Yakutsk, and to the republics of Armenia, Azerbaijan, Belarus, Estonia, Kazakhstan, Latvia, Lithuania, Moldova, Tajikistan, Ukraine and Uzbekistan, observing the changes sweeping the USSR that would lead to the denouement on Christmas Day, 1991. And since then I have returned to Russia regularly, for both professional and personal reasons.

I was privileged to experience the last days of the Soviet Union and what came after not just as a foreign observer but as a member by marriage of a Russian-Armenian family. The Suvorovs live in Siberia where they experienced the excitement, hardships and absurdities of those turbulent years, and taught me the joys of summer at the dacha. My philologist wife, Zhanna, was a deputy in a regional soviet, and later, when we moved to Washington, she worked in the International Finance Corporation on the post-1991 project to privatize Russia. My father-in-law, Stanislav

Suvorov, a shoemaker now in his eighties and still working in a Krasnoyarsk theatre, suffered under the old system. He served five years in jail for a simple act of speculation – selling his car at a profit. He later prospered by providing hand-made shoes for top party officials. My mother-in-law, Marietta, a party member, welcomed the free market that came with the transition from Gorbachev to Yeltsin with the comment, 'At least now I don't have to humiliate myself to buy some cheese.' Nevertheless, I saw the pernicious effect on the family of economic and social chaos. My cousin-in-law Ararat, a police officer, was shot dead by the mafia in Krasnoyarsk. Marietta's savings disappeared overnight with hyperinflation. My sister-in-law Larisa, director of a music school, went unpaid for months in the post-communist economic turmoil, and one day received, in lieu of salary, a cardboard box of men's socks. All this, and an attempt by the KGB to compromise me by trying (and failing) to intimidate Zhanna into working for them shortly before the fall of the Soviet Union, has given me a unique insight into what was going on in the society that threw up Gorbachev and Yeltsin, and how it all came to a head.

In compiling the events of December 25, 1991, I have used only information that I have been able to source or verify. None of the dialogue or emotions of the characters has been invented. I have used my best judgement to determine when someone's recollection is misleading and self-serving, or simply mistaken, as the mind plays tricks with the past and witnesses sometimes contradict each other. One person in the Kremlin recalls that it snowed heavily in Moscow on December 25, 1991, others that it didn't (it was a dry mild day, confirmed by meteorological records). Some players have vivid recall, others do not: Andrey Grachev and Yegor Gaidar were able to provide me with detailed accounts of what went on inside the Gorbachev and Yeltsin camps respectively, but Yeltsin's collaborator Gennady Burbulis told me he simply did not have memories of that long-ago day.

A note on names and spelling: Russian names contain a first name, a patronymic and a surname, hence Mikhail Sergeyevich Gorbachev. The respectful form of address is the first name plus patronymic, which can cause confusion outside Russia – once after I politely addressed Gorbachev on television as 'Mikhail Sergeyevich', a friend complimented me for being on first-name terms with the Soviet leader. Among family and friends a diminutive form of the first name is common, such as Sasha for Alexander, Borya for Boris and Tolya for Anatoly. For the spelling of Russian names and words I have used the more readable system of transliteration, using -y rather than -i, -ii or -iy, thus Yury rather than Yuri. Different versions may appear in the bibliography where I have not changed publishers' spellings. For clarity I have included a list of the main characters at the end of the book.

Many people made this book possible by generously sharing their time and insights. I would especially like to acknowledge Jonathan Anderson, Ed Bentley, Stanislav Budnitsky, Charles Caudill, Giulietto Chiesa, Ara Chilingarova, Fred Coleman, Nikolay Filippov, Olga

Filippova, the late Yegor Gaidar, Ekaterina Genieva, Frida Ghitis, Martin Gilman, Svetlana Gorkhova, Andrey Grachev, Ron Hill, Steve Hurst, Gabriella Ivacs, Tom Johnson, Eason Jordan, Rick Kaplan, Ted Koppel, Sergey Kuznetsov, Harold Mciver Leich, Liu Heung Shing, Stuart H. Loory, Philip McDonagh, Lara Marlowe, Seamus Martin, Ellen Mickiewicz, Andrey Nikeryasov, Michael O'Clery, Eddie Ops, Tanya Paleeva, Robert Parnica, Claire Shipman, Olga Sinitsyna, Martin Sixsmith, Sarah Smyth, Yury Somov, Conor Sweeney, and the staff at the Gorbachev Foundation and the Russian State Library of Foreign Literature. A special thanks to Professor Stephen White of the University of Glasgow who provided me with some out-of-print Russian memoirs; John Murray, lecturer in Russian at Trinity College Dublin who read the first draft and made invaluable suggestions; Brian Langan of Transworld Ireland who edited and corrected the manuscript with forensic skill; and Clive Priddle of PublicAffairs who inspired and helped shape the concept. No words are adequate to acknowledge the research and editing talents of my wife, Zhanna, who travelled with me to Moscow a number of times to help track down archives and sources, and whose involvement at every stage in the composition and editing of the book made it something of a joint enterprise.

Introduction

'*During my tenure, I have been attacked by all those in Russian society who can scream and write ... The revolutionaries curse me because I have strongly and conscientiously favoured the use of the most decisive measures ... As for the conservatives, they attack me because they have mistakenly blamed me for all the changes in our political system.*'

Russian reformer Count Sergey Yulyevich Witte,
in his resignation letter as prime minister in 1906.

DURING HIS SIX YEARS AND NINE MONTHS AS LEADER OF the Soviet Union, Mikhail Gorbachev is accompanied everywhere by two plainclothes colonels with expressionless faces and trim haircuts. They are so unobtrusive that they often go unnoticed by the president's visitors, and even by his aides. These silent military men sit in the anteroom as he works in his office. They ride in a Volga saloon behind his ZiL limousine as he is driven to and from the Kremlin. They occupy two seats at the back of the aircraft when he travels out of Moscow and they sleep overnight at his dacha or city apartment, wherever he happens to be.

The inscrutable colonels are the guardians of a chunky black Samsonite briefcase with a gold lock weighing one and a half kilogrammes that always has to be within reach of the president. This is the *chemodanchik*, or 'little suitcase'. Everyone, even Gorbachev, refers to it as the 'nuclear button'. Rather it is a portable device that connects the president to Strategic Rocket Forces at an underground command centre on the outskirts of Moscow. It contains the communications necessary to permit the firing of the Soviet Union's long-range nuclear weapons, many of them pointed at targets in the United States. The job of the colonels – there are three assigned to guard the case, but one is always off duty – is to help the president, if ever the occasion should arise, to put the strategic forces on alert and authorize a strike.

There are three nuclear suitcases in total. One is with Mikhail Gorbachev, another is with the minister for defence and a third is assigned to the chief of the general staff. Any one of the devices is sufficient to authorize the launch of a missile, but only the president can *lawfully* order a nuclear strike. So long as Gorbachev possesses the *chemodanchik* he is legally the commander of the country's strategic forces, and the Soviet Union remains a nuclear superpower.

This all changes on December 25, 1991. At 7.00 p.m., as the world watches on television, Mikhail Gorbachev announces that he is resigning. The communist monolith known as the Union of Soviet Socialist Republics is breaking up into separate states. He has no further role. Immediately afterwards Boris Yeltsin, the president of newly independent Russia, is scheduled to come to his Kremlin office to take formal possession of the suitcase, whereupon the two colonels will say their goodbyes to Gorbachev and leave with Yeltsin. This will be the final moment in the disintegration of the superpower that has been ruled by Gorbachev since 1985, and that dominates a land mass stretching over eleven time zones and half the globe. Thereafter Russia, the largest of the fifteen republics, will be the sole nuclear power. Boris Yeltsin will acquire the legal capacity to destroy the United States several times over. It is an awesome responsibility. The Soviet arsenal consists of 27,000 nuclear weapons, of which 11,000 are on missiles capable of reaching the United States. One of these warheads alone could destroy a city.

The handover is to be the final act in a drama of Shakespearean intensity. Its major players are two contrasting figures whose baleful interaction has changed the globe's balance of power. It is the culmination of a struggle for supremacy between Mikhail Gorbachev, the urbane, sophisticated communist idolized by the capitalist world, and Boris Yeltsin, the impetuous harddrinking democrat perceived as a wrecker in Western capitals.

The ousted president and his usurper behave in a statesman-like manner before the cameras. Yet rarely in world history has an event of such magnitude been determined by the passionate dislike of two men for each other. Some years earlier, at the pinnacle of his power, Gorbachev humiliated Yeltsin publicly. The burly Siberian has never forgotten and in December 1991, the roles are reversed. Gorbachev is the one who is denigrated, reduced to tears as he and his wife, Raisa, are hustled out of their presidential residence. Even the carefully choreographed arrangements for the transfer of the nuclear communications and codes are thrown into disarray at the last minute through Yeltsin's petulance and Gorbachev's pride.

Nevertheless, the malevolence of Yeltsin and the vanity of Gorbachev do not stand in the way of something akin to a political miracle taking place. On December 25, 1991, a historical event on a par with the fall of the Austro-Hungarian Empire in 1918 or the collapse of the Ottoman Empire in 1923 occurs without a foreign war or bloody revolution as catalyst. Communist Yugoslavia disintegrates in flames but the Soviet Union breaks up almost impassively as the world looks on in disbelief. The mighty Soviet army relinquishes an empire of subject republics without firing a shot. It all happens very quickly. Few politicians or scholars predicted, even as the year 1991 began, the scale and scope of the historic upheaval at year's end.

The Soviet Union was born in the civil war that followed the 1917 October Revolution, when the Bolshevik faction led by Vladimir Ilyich Lenin seized control over most of the old Russian empire. Industrialized with great brutality under Josef Stalin, it repulsed invading Nazi forces in World War II and emerged as one of the world's two superpowers. The subsequent Cold War between East and West shaped international politics and assumptions for almost half a century.

But Lenin's great socialist experiment faltered. The economy stagnated and then collapsed. The centre lost control. On December 25, 1991, the country that defeated Hitler's Germany simply ceases to exist. In Mikhail Gorbachev's words, 'One of the most powerful states in the world collapsed before our very eyes.'

It is a stupendous moment in the story of mankind, the end of a millennium of Russian and Soviet empire, and the beginning of Russia's national and state renaissance. It signals the final defeat of the twentieth century's two totalitarian systems – Nazi fascism and Soviet communism – that embroiled the world in the greatest war in history. It is the day that allows American conservatives to celebrate – prematurely – the prophecy of the philosopher Francis Fukuyama that the collapse of the USSR will mark the 'end of history', with the universalization of Western liberal democracy as the final form of human government.

Mikhail Gorbachev created the conditions for the end of totalitarianism and Boris Yeltsin delivered the death blow. But neither is honoured in Russia in modern times as a national hero, nor is the date of the transfer of power formally commemorated in Moscow. Contemporary leaders discourage any celebration of December 25, 1991. What happened that day is viewed by many in Russia as, in Vladimir Putin's words, a 'great geopolitical catastrophe'. It is a reminder that the fall of their once-mighty superpower was celebrated in the United States as a victory in the Cold War, rather than as the triumph of a people who peacefully overthrew a totalitarian system to embrace democracy and free market economics. As a former Russian presidential chief of staff, Alexander Leontiyev, put it not long afterwards, 'Americans got so drunk at the USSR's funeral that they're still hung-over.'

Indeed, what is remarkable is the number of Americans who gather around the deathbed for the obsequies for communist power. Never before or since are Russian and American interests so intertwined. The distrust and enmity of the long Cold War dissolves into a remarkable dalliance between the competing nuclear powers. Americans from the International Monetary Fund and from the Chicago School of Economics are to be found in Moscow collaborating with Russian policymakers on a new direction for the Russian economy. Their guiding hands are at the elbow of Yeltsin's ministers as they embark on a mission unprecedented in economic history: the dismantling of the communist model and its replacement with the raw capitalism of neo-liberal economics.

During a visit to Russia just days before Gorbachev's resignation, US secretary of state James Baker marvels at how in all his meetings, one theme is uniform: 'the intense desire to satisfy the United States'. With each of the new republics trying to establish positive relations with America, he reckons that 'our ability to affect their behaviour' will never be greater than at this time. American president George H. W. Bush observes that the behaviour of the new states is 'designed specifically to gain US support for what they had done'. The deference to the United States is such that all the emerging new countries declare their adherence to a list of democratic principles laid down by the Bush administration to earn diplomatic recognition.

In the dying days of the Soviet Union, American diplomats and Russia's political figures enjoy such close relations that they consult each other almost on a daily basis. Gorbachev addresses the US ambassador as 'Comrade'. James Baker and his opposite number Eduard Shevardnadze dine in each other's homes and gossip about world affairs. Friendly contacts take place between the top agents of the CIA and the KGB who have spied on each other for decades. American evangelists show up in Moscow to rejoice and proselytize. A score of Christian leaders visit the Kremlin in the dying days of Soviet communism and the most ardent cleric among them tells Gorbachev, 'You are the person most prayed for in American churches; you are an instrument of God.' The Kremlin corridors echo during the last twenty-four hours with American accents as US television personnel crowd into the president's office to record the final hours. The only televised interviews given by the great Russian rivals are to US news channels.

Mikhail Gorbachev considers himself a personal friend of President Bush, who in the end tried to help him sustain a reformed Soviet Union. Boris Yeltsin courts the US president to gain his approval for breaking up that same entity. The former wants the approval of history; the latter craves international respect. Both measure their standing in the world by the quality of their relations with the United States. They are equally keen to assure Washington that the transfer of control over nuclear weapons will not endanger world peace. The Americans are just as anxious to maintain a friendship that advances their global interests and economic and political philosophy.

December 25, 1991, is therefore a high-water mark in Moscow's relations with the Western world, and in particular the United States. Only once before in history has Russia looked to the West with such enthusiasm for inspiration. That was three centuries earlier when Peter the Great introduced European reforms and moved the Russian capital from Moscow to St Petersburg as a window to the West. His legacy survived until 1917 and the triumph of the Bolsheviks.

Many notable events also take place in Moscow this day. The red flag with its hammer and sickle is hauled down from the Kremlin for the last time, and the white, blue and red tricolour of pre-revolutionary Russia is hoisted in its place. The Russian congress changes the name of the country from the Russian Soviet Federative Socialist Republic to the Russian Federation, or simply Russia.

At its close, the colonels say goodbye to Gorbachev and take the little suitcase to its new custodian.

Thus as many Westerners celebrate Christmas Day, 1991, the Soviet Union ceases to exist and Russia escapes from the cul-de-sac into which Lenin led it seventy-four years earlier, and a great country takes its place among the nations of Europe.

1

December 25: Before the Dawn

IN THE FIRST MOMENTS OF DECEMBER 25, 1991, THE midnight chimes ring out from the clock on the Saviour Tower inside the Kremlin. This is the signal for the hourly changing of the honour guard at the great red and black granite cubes that form the Mausoleum where lies the embalmed body of the founder of the Soviet Union, Vladimir Ilyich Lenin. Curious late-night strollers in Red Square, Russian and foreign, gather to watch as the greatcoated sentinels goose-step off to the Saviour Gate like marionettes, jerking their elbows high in the air. A new shift emerges to take over at what is officially known as the Soviet Union's Sentry Post No 1.

Many of the onlookers on this dry, still Wednesday morning are bare-headed. It is mild by mid-winter standards in Moscow, about 1 degree centigrade above freezing. The bitterly cold spell earlier in December when the temperature dipped to 17 degrees below zero ended with a heavy fall of snow three days ago. The vast cobbled square has since been swept clean, but the snow still gleams on the brightly lit onion domes of St Basil's Cathedral and on the swallow-tailed crenellations of the high brick Kremlin walls. It fringes the dome of the Senate Building inside the Kremlin, from which flies the red flag of the Soviet Union with its gold hammer and sickle emblem, clearly visible from Red Square. It has flown there since 1918, when the Russian capital was transferred from Petrograd back to Moscow.

A small group of people have assembled at the north-western end of Red Square, close by St Nicholas's Tower. Many of them hold flickering candles and press close to a group of American clerics who are conducting a midnight service. The minister, a middle-aged man in white robes, reads aloud from a large Bible. The preachers have travelled specially to Russia for this Christmas Day so that they can celebrate Christ's birthday in Red Square, in what is still officially the godless Soviet Union, something they could not dream of doing in past years.

Near the Arsenal Tower of the Kremlin stands a tall *yolka*, a New Year fir tree. Some foreigners mistake it for a Christmas tree. However, in Russia the Orthodox Christmas falls on January 7 in accordance with the old Julian calendar.

Even so, on Little Lubyanka Street, a fifteen-minute walk away past the yellow neo-renaissance façade of the feared KGB's headquarters, the strains of 'Oh Come All Ye Faithful' in Russian ring out in the night air. More than a thousand worshippers are celebrating midnight

Mass in the hundred-year-old Roman Catholic Church of St Louis, crushed into eighteen rows of wooden pews set among squat stone pillars that obstruct the views of the altar. By the door a notice states: 'If you are suffering, if you are tired of life, know that Christ loves you.' A priest conducting the service enthuses about the historical nature of the day, and 'the return of our government to a normal, Christian world'.

The congregation used to consist mainly of foreigners, says Sofia Peonkova, a regular attendee, but she has noticed that in the last two years many Russians have started coming. Yulia Massarskaya, aged eighty-two, tells a visitor that this is her first time in a Catholic church in Moscow since the 1917 October Revolution, when she was eight years old. 'I have never felt this good,' she whispers. 'It is like coming back home.'

The service ends, the worshippers disperse and the darkened streets of Moscow fall quiet for a few hours. But long before dawn many thousands of people begin emerging from the city's grim apartment blocks. Dressed in padded coats, scarves and fur hats, they make their way through the icy slush to catch the early trams and metro trains. It is the beginning of a daily search for food that has preoccupied Moscow's citizens for months. Their overriding goal is to find where deliveries have been made overnight. They form irritated lines in the darkness at grimy stores where the reward for waiting might be a loaf of bread, a scrawny chicken leg or a few wilted vegetables.

Shoppers in Moscow in December 1991 do not look for goods, they look for queues. They obey the advice of the Russian television programme *Vesti*: 'If you come across a queue, join it and count yourself lucky.'

Not since World War II has Moscow experienced such deprivation. The government has imposed rationing of 'meat products, butter, vegetable oils, grains, pasta products, sugar, salt, matches, tobacco products and household, bath and other soaps ... *where available*'. Three days ago the deputy mayor, Yury Luzhkov, admitted that three hundred and fifty stores in the city have run out of meat.

Everyone in Moscow – engineers, actors, professors, shoemakers, shop assistants, construction workers, poets – snaps up and hoards anything they can find to buy. If a consignment of cheese, or salami, or even just a batch of loaves, appears unexpectedly, people form a queue and take as much as they can carry. Starvation would be a reality for many families were it not for the buckets of potatoes and piles of cabbages kept in their apartments that were harvested in suburban plots before the snows of winter came.

As Moscow stirs to life, small covered trucks with canvas flaps splutter and cough their way along the city's potholed roads from the newspaper printing houses. They stop at street kiosks to dump parcels of newspapers on the ground. The bundles are much lighter than usual. Most dailies are reduced to four pages, as newsprint and printing ink are in short supply.

The concerns of the populace are reflected in stories about shortages and imminent price rises. A headline in *Komsomolskaya Pravda* says simply, 'Meat has arrived in Odessa'. At least it is more positive than 'No Bread in Krasnoyarsk' on *Pravda*'s front page. There is little in the skimpy newspapers to indicate that this will be a momentous day in the political history of the country, or indeed of the world. There is a clue, however, in *Pravda*. In a single paragraph on page one the Communist Party newspaper notes, without comment, that President Mikhail Gorbachev will make a major announcement, live on state television, before the day is out.

2

December 25: Sunrise

THE HEAVY SNOW ON THE SPRUCE AND FIR TREES THAT screen the large dacha west of Moscow has melted a little during the mild winter night. Water drips from the pine needles, and trickles out of the snow piled high along the driveway, giving the tarmacadam a dark sheen.

In an upstairs room, Mikhail Sergeyevich Gorbachev, president of the Soviet Union, commander-in-chief of the armed forces, puts on a starched white single-cuff shirt and a dark single-breasted navy wool suit with muted stripes, hand-made by his tailors on Kutuzovsky Prospekt. He selects from his large collection of silk ties a particular neckpiece, black with a red floral paisley design, which he often wears on important occasions.

Small in stature, with magnetic hazel eyes and silver hair that has long since receded to expose the purple birthmark on his head, Gorbachev this morning is exhausted and slightly hung-over. His duties as president are almost finished, but last night he lingered for a long time in his Kremlin office to reminisce with Moscow's police chief, Arkady Murashev, who called out of the blue to wish him well. Very few people have been taking the trouble to do that in the dying days of his reign, and on an impulse he had invited Murashev, a former political opponent, to join him for a glass or two of cognac. With the nuclear suitcase sitting an arm's length away on the table, the last Soviet president took great pains to impress upon his visitor that he had not made any mistakes in his quest to reform the Soviet Union. It was not his fault that it was falling apart.

There is nothing unusual in Gorbachev's staying late at the Kremlin. Work has always kept him in the office until ten or eleven o'clock. On arriving home, he and his wife Raisa have made it a practice to go for a walk together in the dark before retiring to bed. He tells her of the events of the day as they stroll along the paths around the dacha. He holds nothing back. He once caused a scandal among Russians by saying publicly that he even discussed matters of state with his wife. Gorbachev numbers the world's leading politicians as his friends, but his only really close ally in life is his companion and soulmate of thirty-eight years. They have always 'rejoiced at the successes and suffered the failures of the other', as he put it once, 'just as if they were our own'.

After breakfast in the morning – in winter it is always hot cereal, served in the upper-floor living quarters by their servant Shura, who wears a headscarf and no make-up, as Raisa requires of all the female staff – the president crosses the corridor to his library, where glass-fronted bookcases reach to the ceiling. In a space in the rows of bound volumes is a framed black-and-white photograph of Raisa, his favourite, taken when she was a rather prim-looking student at Moscow University. There is another of his father, Sergey, posing in simple military tunic decorated with three medals and two Orders of the Red Star for his service in the Great Patriotic War against Nazi Germany. These pictures, and a valuable icon embossed with gold leaf depicting the Archangel Mikhail which the head of the Russian Orthodox Church, Patriarch Alexey II, gave Gorbachev for his sixtieth birthday in March, will have to be packed with particular care when they leave.

Off the library is a small wood-panelled study with a desk of Karelian birch on which sit several white telephones and one red telephone beneath a transparent cover – the hotline for national emergencies, which the cleaners are instructed never to touch. Raisa has learned of late to dread these telephones ringing out, 'like a gunshot, destroying the peace of the night', bringing 'shouts of despair, entreaties, suffering and, sometimes, death'.

Petite and attractive at fifty-nine, Raisa too is show-ing the strain of this period of political upheaval. It has, as she puts it, tested her spirit, her mind and her will, and brought her incurable heartache and sleepless nights. Her health has been poor since she collapsed with a stroke during the attempted coup against Gorbachev in August. The stroke affected her power of speech and the movement in her right arm. The wrinkles on her once-porcelain complexion reveal the torment of watching her husband shrink in stature day by day.

To Raisa, Mikhail Gorbachev is a man of destiny. Indeed many superstitious people have interpreted the distinctive birthmark on his head as an omen. But Mikhail and Raisa themselves believe they were once given a sign that he is special. When they were in their twenties, both had the same dream. They were in a deep, black well from which they were trying to get out, and they kept falling back. Finally they succeeded in escaping and they saw in front of them a wide road and a huge bright sun. Raisa told her husband then, addressing him by his pet name, 'Misha, you are destined for greatness.'

Gorbachev has come to see himself as the embodiment of providence. He talks about his mission, of being *chosen* to carry out *perestroika* – a task that began as reconstruction of society and has come to mean for him the revival of his motherland. He sees his forced abdication as the outcome of an epic struggle 'between good and evil, loyalty and treachery, hope and disillusion, generosity and vengefulness'. To him the day of his downfall is 'a black page in the history of Russia'.

While in his study, the Soviet president has an opportunity to cast his eyes for the umpteenth time over his much-annotated resignation speech. It will be one of the most important pronouncements of his career. It will define him and his legacy, and put down a marker for the future of the country. He has little influence over that now of course. He is being forced to transfer power into the hands of 'incompetent, irresponsible people', ambitious and ruthless political adventurers, who he is firmly convinced are sacrificing the Soviet Union for the sake of their ardent desire to take over the Kremlin and push him out.

Less than two weeks ago, Gorbachev was telling George Bush on the telephone how confident he was that the Soviet Union would survive. At the time he had reason to believe that he would continue as president and that he would be residing indefinitely in the state dacha here in Razdory on the banks of the Moscow River. The successor to Lenin has done everything to keep the Union in existence since it started falling apart after the August coup four months ago, and the republics one after another began declaring their intention to break away. He has made himself hoarse trying to convince republic leaders, visiting statesmen, journalists and anyone else who would listen that the country should not be split up, that it was absurd, that it would lead to famine, civil war, blood.

The demise of the superpower he inherited finally became inevitable the previous Saturday, when all the republics ganged up to reject even a weakened central authority. Only on Monday, just two days ago, did he decide – he had little choice – that he would announce his resignation this evening. It was only on Monday afternoon that he established the terms for a peaceful transition with his hated rival. This was a painful experience. And he is not even being accorded the dignity of a solemn farewell ceremony.

At least he does not face the prospect of exile or death, the fate of two other recently deposed communist leaders in Europe, Erich Honecker of East Germany and Nicolae Ceauşescu of Romania. But he knows there are people only too eager to discredit him to justify what they are doing.

Under the transition agreement, the couple understand they have three days to leave the presidential dacha, their home for six years, after which they must give the keys to the new ruler of Russia. They will leave behind many memories, of entertaining world leaders around the dining table and talking long into the night about reshaping the world. There is much to do now of a more mundane nature. They have to sort through books, pictures and documents, and pack away clothes and private things to move to a new home. They have a similar task to perform at their city apartment on Moscow's Lenin Hills, which also belongs to the state.

When Gorbachev moved his family here they expected it would be for life. The dacha, called officially Barvikha-4, was the ultimate symbol of success for the top Soviet bureaucrat. They occupied smaller government dachas during Gorbachev's ascent to the pinnacle of Soviet power. As state-owned residences they were quite impersonal, and Raisa disliked that they were 'always on the move, always lodgers'. But this was to be their final stop. This dacha was different. It was their creation. The yellow three-storey complex was modelled in Second Empire style under Gorbachev's personal supervision after he became general secretary of the Communist Party in 1985. In those days the party leader had emperor-like powers of command, and it was built in six months by a special corps of the Soviet army, earning the generals a few Medals of Labour. This had been Raisa's first real home. 'My home is not simply my castle,' she once said. 'It is my world, my galaxy.'

Known by the security people as the *wolfschanze* (wolf's lair), the presidential dacha is serviced by a staff of several cooks, maids, drivers and bodyguards, all of whom have their quarters on the lower floor or in out-buildings. It has several living rooms with enormous fireplaces, a vast dining room, a conference room, a clinic staffed with medical personnel, spacious bath-rooms on each floor, a cinema and a swimming pool. Everywhere there is marble panelling, parquet floors, woven Uzbek carpets and crystal chandeliers. Outside large gardens and a helicopter landing area have been carved out of the 164 acres of woodland. The surround-ing area is noted for its pristine air, wooded hills and views over the wide, curving Moscow River.

For more than half a century Soviet leaders have occupied elegant homes along the western reaches of the river. This area has been the favoured retreat of the Moscow elite since the seventeenth century, when Tsar Alexey Mikhailovich expressly forbade the construction of any production facilities. Stalin lived in a two-storey mansion on a high bank in Kuntsevo, closer to the city. Known as Blizhnyaya Dacha (nearby dacha), it was hidden in a twelve-acre wood with a double perimeter fence, and at one time was protected by eight camouflaged 30-millimetre anti-aircraft guns and a special unit of three hundred interior ministry troops. At Gorbachev's dacha there is a military command post, facilities for the nuclear button and its operators, and a special garage containing an escape vehicle with a base as strong as a military tank.

Every previous Soviet leader but one left their dachas surrounded by wreaths of flowers. Stalin passed away in his country house while continuing to exercise his powers, and those who followed him, Leonid Brezhnev, Yury Andropov and Konstantin Chernenko, all expired while still in charge of the communist superpower. Only Stalin's immediate successor, Nikita Khrushchev, a reformer like Gorbachev, had his political career brought to a sudden end when he was ousted from power in 1964 for, as *Pravda* put it, 'decisions and actions divorced from reality'.

Today Gorbachev will suffer the same fate as Khrushchev. He will depart from the dacha as president of the Soviet Union. When he returns in the evening he will be *Gospodin* (Mister) Gorbachev, a pensioner, aged sixty – ten years younger than Khrushchev was when he was kicked out.

At around 9.30 a.m. Gorbachev takes his leave of Zakharka, as he fondly calls Raisa (he once saw a painting by the nineteenth-century artist Venetsianov of a woman of that name who bore a resemblance to Raisa). He goes down the wooden stairs, past the pictures hanging on the staircase walls, among them a multi-coloured owl drawn in a childish hand, sent to Raisa as a memento by a young admirer. At the bottom of the stairs there was, until recently, a little doll's house with a toboggan next to it, a reminder of plans for New Year's festivities with the grandchildren, eleven-year-old

Kseniya and four-year-old Nastya, that the family will now have to celebrate elsewhere. He spends a minute at the cloakroom on the right of the large hallway to change his slippers for outdoor shoes, then dons a fine rust-coloured scarf, grey overcoat and fur hat, and leaves through the double glass doors, carrying his resignation speech in a thin, soft-leather document case.

Outside in the bright morning light his driver holds open the front passenger door of his official stretch limousine, a ZiL-41047, one of a fleet built for party and state use only. Gorbachev climbs into the leather seat beside him. He always sits in the front.

Two colonels in plainclothes emerge from their temporary ground-floor lodgings with the little suitcase that accompanies the president everywhere. They climb into a black Volga sedan to follow the ZiL into Moscow. It will be their last ride with this particular custodian of the *chemodanchik*.

With a swish of tyres, the bullet-proof limousine – in reality an armoured vehicle finished off as a luxury sedan – moves around the curving drive, and out through a gate in the high green wooden fence, where a policeman gives a salute, and on to Rublyovo–Uspenskoye Highway. The heavy automobile proceeds for the first five miles under an arch of overhanging snow-clad fir trees with police cars in front and behind flashing their blue lights. It ponderously negotiates the frequent bends that were installed to prevent potential assassins from taking aim at Soviet officials on their way to and from the Kremlin. Recently some of the state mansions have been sold to foreigners by cash-strapped government departments, and many of the once-ubiquitous police posts have disappeared.

The convoy speeds up as it comes to Kutuzovsky Prospekt. It races for five miles along the centre lane reserved for official cavalcades, zooms past enormous, solid Stalin-era apartment blocks, and hurtles underneath Moscow's Triumphal Arch and across the Moscow River into the heart of the Russian capital. The elongated black car hardly slackens speed as it cruises along New Arbat, its pensive occupant unseen behind the darkened windows.

The seventh and last Soviet leader plans to explain on television this evening that he dismantled the totalitarian regime and brought the people freedom, *glasnost*, political pluralism, democracy and an end to the Cold War. For doing so, he is praised and admired throughout the world.

But here in Russia he is the subject of harsh criticism for his failure to improve the lot of the citizens. Few of the bleary-eyed shoppers slipping and sliding on the dirty, compacted snow outside the food stores will shed tears at his departure from office. They judge him through the prism of empty shop windows.

Gorbachev knows that. He has even repeated to foreign dignitaries a popular anecdote against himself, about a man in a long queue for vodka who leaves in frustration, telling everyone he is going to the Kremlin to shoot Gorbachev, only to return later complaining, 'There's a longer queue there.'

Self-criticism, however, is not a prominent part of his psychological repertoire. Gorbachev has, in fact, made many mistakes, but he will concede this only very grudgingly, as he looks back in his resignation speech on his service to the people.

Boris Nikolayevich Yeltsin almost always starts his day around two o'clock in the morning. The president of the Russian Federation suffers from acute insomnia. He doesn't like sleeping pills and finds they do not help him sleep anyway. He habitually gets out of bed a couple of hours after retiring in the late evening. Tall and awkward with small blue eyes set in a rough peasant face and a full head of silver hair, the sixty-year-old former construction engineer paces around the room on these occasions in his thin Japanese hotel robe, nursing his headache and stomach pains and drinking a little tea, before returning to bed an hour later. It is worse if he is afflicted by one of his periodic attacks of gout, which cause excruciating pain in his big toe.

Looking back at this time in his life Yeltsin will recall 'enervating bouts of depression, agonizing reflections late at night, insomnia and headaches, despair at the grimy and impoverished look of Moscow and other cities . . . the criticisms in the media, the badgering in the Russian parliament, the weight of decisions . . .' He is constantly dissatisfied with his work, 'and that is a frightful thing'. His mind is never at rest and he becomes more open with himself in the small hours than in the office during daylight, 'when all his buttons are buttoned'. He finds that at two in the morning 'you recall all sorts of things and mull over matters that are not always so pleasant'.

This December morning he has many matters to contemplate, some pleasant, some less so. Today he will
emerge triumphant from his long and nasty feud with
Mikhail Gorbachev. He acknowledges to himself that
the motivations for many of his actions are embedded in
his bitter conflict with the Soviet president. Just
recently his assistant Valentina Lantseva pleaded with
him to stop the love–hate relationship with the man in
the Kremlin. He retorted, 'Stop teaching me how to
live!' Never again will he have to negotiate with
Gorbachev, endure his windy lectures, put up with his
criticisms, take lashings from his profane tongue.
Gorbachev, the charming and sophisticated world
statesman, can turn the air blue with his profanity.
Yeltsin, the hard-drinking, backwoods Siberian, regarded as a buffoon in many international circles, never uses
swear words, and intensely dislikes those who do.

Today he must disport himself on global television as
a statesman, and show that the world has nothing to
fear from him and, indeed, owes him esteem. Before the
day is out, he will have his hands on the nuclear suitcase
now in Gorbachev's possession, and the world will
know that this is a safe pair of hands. He will appear
presidential, magisterial and generous to the man he is
casting into the political wilderness.

He will also have to deal in the next few hours with
a number of crises in his own ranks that threaten the
stability of his government and his radical plans for a
newly independent Russia.

Usually Yeltsin manages to snatch a few more hours'
sleep before rising, dressing in T-shirt and shorts, and

breakfasting in the kitchen on thin oatmeal porridge and tea followed by eggs, onions and tomatoes fried in butter. His wife Naina and thirty-year-old daughter Tanya prepare the meal. They have no servants in the state apartment they occupy on the fourth floor of a nine-storey block at 54 Second Tverskaya-Yamskaya Street in north-central Moscow, overlooking the abandoned monastery of the Transformation of the Saviour in a busy district near the Belarus Station. At its centre is a spacious sitting room with silver and grey striped wallpaper and floor-to-ceiling bookshelves weighed down with sets of blue, brown and green bound volumes of Russian classics, including Yeltsin's favourites, Chekhov, Pushkin and 'village writer' Sergey Yesenin, whose poetry no self-respecting Russian family would be without. The room has a large rubber plant and is decorated with landscapes from the Urals and a much-admired oil painting of wild daisies. There are piles of audiotapes of Yeltsin's favourite singer, Anna German. He likes the Polish artist so much that when he listens to her performing her popular number 'Once a Year Orchards Blossom', his normally stern face assumes a lyrical expression.

The apartment also has a roomy hallway, two large bedrooms with separate bathrooms, a tiny guest bedroom, a sizeable kitchen with balcony and a small office crammed with files from Yeltsin's time as Moscow party chief and with room only for an armchair and desk. A small heap of copies of his autobiography, *Notes of a President*, published the previous year in English as *Against the Grain*, sits on the floor.

The accommodation was allocated to Yeltsin when he came to Moscow from Sverdlovsk six years ago as a rising member of the *nomenklatura*, the subset of top communist cadres who ran the country until recently. Yeltsin and Naina share the space with Tanya, her second husband Leonid Dyachenko and their eleven-year-old grandson Boris, who sleeps on the living-room sofa when there is a guest staying. Yeltsin is proud of little 'Borka' because he is a real scrapper and a leader among his classmates.

The furniture is solid and durable, made in Sverdlovsk – or Yekaterinburg as it is now called since the pre-revolutionary name was restored three months ago. Yeltsin boasts that it is 'much better quality, and sturdier too, than Moscow-made junk'. Nonetheless Naina, or Naya as he calls her, has been known to give a cushion to visitors so they do not rip their clothes on the spring poking out through a hole in the sofa, and one of the kitchen stools has a nail protruding. They have three telephones in the apartment. The one for incoming calls is working again: it was turned off after the Yeltsins lost their phone bills in the confusion of the coup in August.

Alexander Korzhakov, Yeltsin's beefy security chief and drinking partner, constantly worries that Tverskaya Street is not a secure location for the president. 'It is easy to shoot at the entrance, easy to block his car, and easy for neighbours to see everything through the windows if the curtains are not drawn.' Tanya was once assaulted by a man who watched her dial the security code at the main door, then followed her inside and 'jumped at her'. Like Gorbachev, the Russian leader also has a state dacha, Arkhangelskoye-2, off the Rublyovo–Uspenskoye Highway, on the banks of the Moscow River some twenty miles outside Moscow. But he prefers to reside in the city apartment during the week, despite the limited space and the noisy polluted streets outside, and the family only goes to the dacha at weekends.

Yeltsin too is preparing to move. He and his family will take possession of the presidential dacha when the Gorbachevs move out, and give up their smaller country home, which belongs to the Russian Federation. He has decided that the Soviet leader's mansion should become the future residence of the Russian president. Not being on good social terms, Yeltsin has never been invited to the Gorbachevs' city apartment on Lenin Hills, a choice suburb next to Moscow University (since renamed Sparrow Hills), and he does not know whether he will appropriate it as well, until he makes an inspection and decides whether he would prefer it to the one he has now.

After Yeltsin showers, Naina blow-dries and combs his hair, and helps him dress in an expensive white shirt, blue patterned tie and smart, dark-coloured made-to-measure suit. He sits down for his wife to lace his shoes, a chore he finds difficult because of his bulk. His black shoes are, as always, buffed to a mirror-like sheen.

When Yeltsin was elected president in June of the Russian republic, the largest of the fifteen republics that made up the Soviet Union, his vice president Alexander Rutskoy, a former air force colonel, decided that

Russia's top official should dress with greater elegance. Rutskoy used his own military coupons to purchase for him an expensive new suit and several high-quality shirts. Yeltsin accepted the gifts but insisted on meeting the cost. Rutskoy used to embarrass him like that. One day he came into Yeltsin's office and said with a horrified look, 'Where did you get those shoes? You shouldn't be wearing shoes like that. You're the president.' And the next day he appeared with six pairs of Italian shoes.

Before going out into the hallway the bear-like Russian chieftain meekly subjects himself to a final inspection by his wife and daughter. Every morning Naina makes sure that her Borya's tie is straight, that there are no flecks of dust on his shoulders and that his splendid helmet of hair is perfectly in place. After the grooming, she always puts a ten-ruble note in his breast pocket so Yeltsin can pay for his own snacks or lunch.

Boris runs Russia but Naina runs the household. She is the *khozyaika*, the woman of the house, so much in charge at home that the most powerful man in the country hands over his pay packet every month as he has done since they were married thirty-five years ago in Sverdlovsk, and she gives him an allowance out of it. 'Without her,' Yeltsin admits, 'I would never have borne up under so many political storms . . . not in 1987, not in 1991.' But in all other matters Boris makes the decisions. 'He always has the last word,' she explained once, 'and he protects us like a stone wall.'

In the evening the ceremony is performed in reverse. The women line up to welcome him home, take off his clothes down to his underwear and put on his house slippers. 'The only thing he does is raise his arms and legs,' observed Korzhakov. In the opinion of his assistant, Lev Sukhanov, Naina is the most long-suffering wife in the country. 'What she had to experience in connection with her husband no one else has experienced. She felt all the effects of his struggle with the party machine, which I can affirm was absolutely ruthless, and fought dirty.'

At nine o'clock Yeltsin leaves the hallway, where a golf club rests among the umbrellas, given to him by the Swedish ice-hockey player Sven Tumba when he opened Moscow's first golf course two years ago. Yeltsin does not play golf but he is passionate about tennis and volleyball, and he likes to tell foreign visitors he was a member of the Russian Federation volleyball team. This isn't true but he has apparently come to believe it himself.

After descending in the small lift of the apartment block he steps outside and enters a black Niva with the engine running. Yeltsin used a modest Moskvich saloon when campaigning for votes seven months back – it was useful for his image as a man of the people – but since he was elected president, Korzhakov has insisted on the chunky four-wheel drive for better security. Yeltsin sits on the right-hand side in the back, with Korzhakov in the passenger seat in front of him, cradling an automatic weapon. Two other bodyguards in the car also nurse sidearms. The Niva is preceded and followed by cars carrying militia guards. The city has been awash with rumours of a second coup attempt by diehard pro-Soviet elements in the military, in a last-ditch effort to preserve the Soviet Union. As head of Yeltsin's personal security, Korzhakov is taking no chances.

The Niva crosses Tverskaya Street, where the police have stopped the traffic, and proceeds along Great Gruzinskaya Street, through the grounds of the decrepit city zoo and on to Kopushkovskaya Street. In five minutes it reaches its destination, the marble and concrete skyscraper on the Moscow River embankment known as the Russian White House. The car descends into the basement garage. For now, this is Yeltsin's power base. Very soon it will be the Kremlin.

3

Hiring the Bulldozer

THE RESIGNATION OF MIKHAIL GORBACHEV, ON December 25, 1991, will mark the end of a long-drawn-out and bitter struggle for power. It began soon after he was chosen as general secretary of the Communist Party of the Soviet Union on March 11, 1985, on the death of his predecessor Konstantin Chernenko. As it was the ruling party in a one-party state, the Communist Party's leader was the person who ran the country. Right away Gorbachev began putting together his own team to take charge. One of the first things he did was to recruit Boris Yeltsin.

The Soviet Union that Gorbachev inherited was a moribund, totalitarian society. Outwardly it appeared stable. The non-Russian republics acquiesced in rule from the Kremlin. Soviet engineers had sent the first man into space. Its military matched the West in weaponry. Soviet athletes were among the best in the world. The vast majority of its inhabitants were literate and higher education was within everyone's reach.

But thousands of political prisoners languished in detention camps, a legacy of the Stalin era. There was no independent media, no right of assembly, no free emigration, no democracy, limited freedom of religion and near zero tolerance for public criticism of those at the top. Corruption and alcoholism were a way of life. The courts did the bidding of the party, and the police and the KGB could arrest anyone without legal redress. The secret police stamped out unauthorized activities, from art shows to student discussion groups. Foreign books, journals and movies with unapproved content were banned.

By the mid-1980s the command economy imposed by Stalin was in crisis. City dwellers had a tolerable standard of living but most of the rural population endured wretched conditions. Lack of competition and dependence on world oil sales had stifled domestic manufacturing. The country was involved in a costly and dangerous arms race with the West and an unpopular war in Afghanistan, which Soviet troops had invaded in 1979.

It was a society pervaded by cynicism. Many people joked that they pretended to work and the government pretended to pay them, and that the four most serious problems facing agriculture were spring, summer, autumn and winter.

Things had to change. People were becoming aware of how the country was being left behind by the capitalist world in terms of freedoms and standard of living. A new generation of Russians was growing restless at censorship and travel restrictions. The ageing communist leaders sensed the dangers and the need for improvement. That was why they had turned to the youngest and most energetic comrade in the top ranks, Mikhail Gorbachev.

Born on March 2, 1931, in a village on the fertile steppes of southern Russia, Gorbachev was an earnest communist from his teenage days. In his formative years the country was in thrall to Stalin's cult of personality. At eighteen, he graduated from school with a silver medal for an essay entitled 'Stalin – Our Combat Glory; Stalin – the Elation of Our Youth'. He studied law at Moscow State University where he was open to new ideas, while aware that any deviation from the official line was, as he put it, 'fraught with consequences'. He was active in the university Komsomol, the young communist movement. There he met Raisa Maximovna Titorenko, an earnest student in the philosophy department and a convinced believer in Marxism-Leninism, though her thesis on collective farms gave her an insight into the miserable life of peasants under communism. They married in 1953, the year of Stalin's death. In later years Gorbachev would joke that she was the head of 'our family party cell'.

Conciliatory, smooth and garrulous, Gorbachev was noticed by his elders as a natural-born political leader. He joined the party at the age of twenty-one and slipped easily into the role of *apparatchik*, a professional party member who makes a career in administration. Exceptionally, for a careerist, he looked at things with a critical eye. He became convinced early on that 'there was something wrong in our country'. This was reinforced when he visited Czechoslovakia in 1969 with a party delegation and was met with rudeness by furious Czechs and Slovaks. The previous year Soviet tanks had crushed the communist reform movement that had led to the Prague Spring and the promise of a more prosperous and just society.

In 1970 he was appointed first party secretary – akin to governor – in the Stavropol region, a rich agricultural area almost the size of Ireland. Touring his fiefdom he found 'sheer misery and complete devastation' everywhere. He met and charmed important Soviet figures who vacationed in nearby Black Sea resorts and who would later sponsor his upward climb. Eight years later he was brought to Moscow and shortly afterwards appointed to the Politburo, the syndicate of a dozen senior communist officials who determined everything in Soviet life, from war and peace to the price of vodka and bread rolls. He stood out among his older comrades with his combination of youthful energy, toughness and effervescent optimism that problems could be solved with debate and imagination.

Though put in charge of agriculture, Gorbachev was sent abroad to get acquainted with foreign leaders. His suave manner and keen intellect charmed dignitaries more accustomed to impassive Soviet figures programmed to say *nyet*. He charmed Margaret Thatcher so much with his new thinking on international relations – consultation rather than confrontation – that the Iron Lady famously commented, 'I like Mister Gorbachev. We can do business together.' Foreigners found him to be almost subversive. When a French official visiting Moscow asked when an agriculture problem had arisen that had delayed their meeting, the future general secretary replied with a smile, 'In 1917.'

Gorbachev believed the country was in a parlous state and could only be saved by fundamental reforms and the end of the Cold War. His comrade Eduard Shevardnadze shared this view. Once while vacationing together in the Black Sea resort of Pitsunda in December 1984, the Georgian told him, 'Everything's rotten. It has to be changed.' It was almost heretical to utter such words aloud. Gorbachev now echoed them, in private, within hours of being given the top job by the Politburo. 'We can't go on living like this,' he told Raisa as they walked in their Moscow suburban garden, shivering in a temperature of minus 9 degrees after getting home at 4.00 a.m. from the Kremlin that March 12, 1985. Even the general secretary of the Communist Party would not risk saying such things indoors, for fear of KGB microphones.

Other influential voices urged him to make changes. Valery Boldin, a *Pravda* editor who had been his personal assistant for five years, warned him that a collapse in the economy could provoke a social explosion at any time.

When Gorbachev looked around for new blood in the party ranks, Yegor Ligachev, his silver-haired deputy, recommended Boris Yeltsin, the party chief in Sverdlovsk. 'This is our type of person – we have to pick him!' enthused Ligachev.

Boris Yeltsin was born on February 1, 1931, in the

impoverished western Siberian village of Butko in Sverdlovsk province. He started life with a splash. During his baptism, the drunken priest dropped him in the font and he had to be fished out by his mother. As a youth he was athletic, headstrong, outspoken and quarrelsome. He also had an exhibitionist urge. At a school assembly Yeltsin accused an unpopular class mistress of cruelty, which caused an uproar. She was eventually dismissed. Though he won his case, the school record stated his discipline to be 'unsatisfactory'. Always a ringleader and daredevil, he lost the thumb and index finger of his left hand when he and his pals experimented with a stolen hand grenade.

In college Yeltsin studied engineering, became a model construction specialist, and later won promotion to chief engineer and then to head of the House-Building Combine in Sverdlovsk, a heavily industrialized city closed to foreigners. In 1956 he married Naina Iosifovna Girina, who was studying to be a sanitary engineer.

Yeltsin did not apply to join the Communist Party until he was thirty, and then mainly to ensure his promotion to chief of the Sverdlovsk construction directorate. Through his force of character and organizational skills, he rose through the party ranks until in 1976 he was promoted to first secretary of Sverdlovsk region. This made him the boss of one of the most important industrial centres of the USSR, one and a half times the size of England and with a population of four and a half million.

Hard-driving and authoritarian, Yeltsin often

engaged in the old-style communist practice of 'storming' to get a job done in record time. He admitted once that he was a fairly well-known type of Russian who needed constantly to prove his physical strength and load himself up to complete exhaustion. He made unannounced visits to factories, walked in on school classes, went down mineshafts, tramped over fields and squeezed into decrepit buses to hear about problems first hand. He fired corrupt and incompetent managers and held televised meetings with citizens to answer their questions and complaints, which was daring for the time.

Despite his populist style, he nevertheless conformed to the prevailing orthodoxy and voiced ritual denunciations of Western imperialism. In September 1977, under instructions from Moscow, he ordered the bull-dozing of Ipatiev House in Sverdlovsk, the two-storey mansion in which the tsar's family had been murdered, to prevent it becoming an anti-Soviet shrine.

Gorbachev and Yeltsin first met in the early 1980s when the Sverdlovsk boss came to Moscow for sessions of the rubber-stamp Supreme Soviet parliament. They embraced in comradely fashion, but their personalities collided. They had different ways of getting things done. Where Gorbachev was spontaneous in speech, Yeltsin was ponderous. The man from Stavropol could be vain, voluble and at times charming, and as a natural insider he was adept at playing political games to get his way. The Sverdlovsk native, on the other hand, was an on-site boss with a strong physical presence, an outspoken grandstander who believed in hands-on management and was prepared to make huge bets on his political instincts. Where Gorbachev was perceived as a sophisticated and urbane Moscow University law graduate who liked to quote the revolutionary poetry of Vladimir Mayakovsky and pontificate endlessly at party meetings, driving his comrades to distraction, Yeltsin was a provincial from the hard-scrabble Urals whose preferred method of driving his comrades to distraction was by playing 'Kalinka' with wooden spoons, sometimes bouncing them playfully off the heads of aides, who learned to move away prudently when the spoons came out.

Yeltsin was at first enthusiastic about Gorbachev as a refreshingly open, sincere and frank leader. Gorbachev, on the other hand, had early misgivings about the stormer from the Urals. He would later describe how he recoiled from the sight of Yeltsin being helped from a session of the Supreme Soviet while his smiling Sverdlovsk comrades explained, 'It happens with our first secretary, sometimes he has a little too much to drink.'

For his part, the Sverdlovsk boss began to find the new general secretary patronizing when he attended party meetings in Moscow. He felt uneasy with the way Gorbachev addressed him. Gorbachev freely used *ty* instead of the more formal *vy*, and this to Yeltsin implied a lack of respect for his comrades. Like most Russian adults, Yeltsin only used the appellation *ty* with his family and most intimate friends.

The relationship cooled after Gorbachev received a critical report on the livestock industry in Sverdlovsk.

Yeltsin protested that the report was distorted, but Gorbachev dressed him down anyway. Nevertheless, on Ligachev's recommendation, Gorbachev sent him an invitation to come to Moscow and head up the Central Committee's construction department. It meant supervising building projects around the country. But Yeltsin was affronted, and declined the offer as too modest. His predecessors as party secretary in Sverdlovsk had been given higher posts when brought to the capital. Only after Ligachev phoned him, on April 4, 1985, and told him it was a matter of party discipline, did he agree to accept. Yeltsin moved to Moscow with his family. He arrived with a chip on his shoulder and inflated expectations. He was also somewhat jealous of Gorbachev, a party official of the same age, who had not managed a region as big or important as Sverdlovsk, but had been promoted faster.

Yeltsin went to pay his respects to Gorbachev in his fifth-floor cabinet in the Central Committee building in Moscow's Staraya Ploshchad, or Old Square. It was the practice at the time for Soviet leaders to have their administrative office in this rambling structure near Red Square, and to use the Kremlin only for party gatherings and for receiving important guests. The general secretary spoke to Yeltsin from behind an enormous writing table, under the watchful eyes of Lenin in a large portrait on the wall directly above him. Only high-ranking officials could sit beneath Lenin. For lesser bureaucrats the picture had to be placed to one side.

The protocol dispensed with, Yeltsin flung himself into his work as head of the party's construction department. He travelled around the Soviet Union inspecting major building projects. In Uzbekistan a KGB officer slipped him documents showing that the party boss there, Usmankhodzhaev, was on the take. He brought them to Gorbachev, who – by Yeltsin's account – blew up and accused him of allowing himself to be fooled. Ligachev himself had vouched for the honesty of the official, he said. But Yeltsin's source was right. Two years later the Uzbek boss was sacked, tried and convicted of crimes.

In December 1985, Gorbachev decided that Yeltsin's bull-headed and aggressive manner could be put to better use. Moscow needed a thorough clean-up. The capital city, run by the cocksure and grossly inefficient first secretary Viktor Grishin, was decaying from neglect and mired in corruption. Food supplies rotted in filthy depots. There was widespread graft and cheating and a black market in everything from cabbages to caviar. Many problems had piled up and Gorbachev believed they needed 'a large bulldozer to clear the way'. Yeltsin met all the requirements. Though blunt and quarrelsome, he was an apparently sincere communist with no connections to corrupt Moscow city officials. The new post also meant that Yeltsin would be elevated to candidate member of the Politburo, thereby satisfying his ambition for rapid promotion.

If he knew what opinions Yeltsin was expressing privately about some of the Communist Party leaders, Gorbachev might have had second thoughts about offering him the post. On a trip back to Sverdlovsk, Yeltsin voiced his contempt for the 'old fools' running the show, a term his rather horrified comrades took to mean the most important men in the Politburo, including Ligachev. But it was Ligachev who was most enthusiastic about promoting Yeltsin. He regarded his fellow Siberian as a good, honest party man with the force of personality to get things done, whether by bullying or storming. As a socialist puritan, Ligachev valued hard work in cadres as the ideal way of perfecting the worker-peasant state.

But Soviet prime minister Nikolay Ryzhkov, a dry, practical executive also from Sverdlovsk who knew Yeltsin of old, warned Gorbachev that while he was a builder by profession, Yeltsin was a destroyer by nature. 'You'll have trouble with him,' he said. 'I know him and I would not recommend him.'

Gorbachev stifled his doubts. On December 23, 1985, the Politburo assigned Yeltsin the post of first secretary of the country's corrupt capital city, with a mandate to clean it up and get things moving.

4

December 25: Morning

JUST BEFORE 10.00 A.M. ON DECEMBER 25, 1991, SLIGHTLY later than usual, Gorbachev's limousine comes within sight of the Kremlin, the 78-acre fortress inside one and a half miles of crenellated brick walls that has been the seat of communist government since 1918. The last Soviet leader can see the red flag with its hammer and sickle hanging limply in the soft breeze on the mast on top of the Senate Building. He expects it to remain there until the USSR expires at midnight on New Year's Eve. Then it is due to be replaced by the white, blue and red flag of independent Russia, with a grand display of fireworks. At least that is what he has been told.

Waiting inside the Kremlin walls for the presidential ZiL is Ted Koppel of ABC, with his executive producer Rick Kaplan and a camera crew. They are covering the last days of Gorbachev's presidency. The celebrated US television reporter, his fine silver-grey hair combed down over his forehead, is wearing a duffel coat with toggle fastenings, and is hatless in the chilly air.

Koppel and Kaplan are laughing at a misunderstanding that has just occurred in an exchange with a friendly Kremlin functionary. The official approached the Americans and wished them a Happy Christmas. With a straight face Kaplan, who is Jewish, replied, 'To me you will have to say "Happy Hanukkah".'

'Why would I have to say "Happy Honecker"?' asked the official, puzzled.

The Americans are amused at the official's assumption that Kaplan is referring to Erich Honecker, who fled to Moscow after the fall of the Berlin Wall two years earlier.

The mistake is understandable. The disgraced East German leader is in the news again this morning. The seventy-nine-year-old communist hardliner was given compassionate asylum in Moscow by Gorbachev, who privately regards him as an 'asshole' but who feels he should protect an old comrade. Fearing that after Gorbachev is no longer in power Yeltsin will send him back to Berlin, Honecker has claimed political asylum in the embassy of Chile. At about the same time as they joke about him, the Russian justice minister Nikolay Fyodorov is telling a press conference across town that Russia is washing its hands of the asylum seeker and his fate is now a matter between Germany and Chile. (Six months later Honecker is extradited to Germany but, too ill to stand trial, is allowed to emigrate to Chile, where he dies in 1994.)

Once through the Kremlin's Borovitsky Gate, Gorbachev's ZiL continues past the Great Kremlin Palace and the grandiose glass and concrete Palace of

Congresses, erected by Khrushchev for important Communist Party meetings, and on into the central Kremlin Square. As the driver spots Koppel and his camera crew, he brings the ZiL to a halt and by prior arrangement the Soviet president climbs out, adjusting his fur hat, to walk with the Americans the last bit of the way to his office.

As always with the Western media Gorbachev is engaging and courteous, and he greets the ABC television crew with a friendly smile. Koppel is struck by how calm he is, given the circumstances. 'He showed very little emotion throughout, he was very business-like, very self-contained and dignified.' The broadcaster likes Gorbachev. 'He reminded me of my father, an old-world European. When my father needed to get something notarized he dressed in a suit. I would tell him a notary public was some pimply-faced kid in a drugstore, but he would say, "No, a notary is important, he expects to be treated with dignity." That's what Gorbachev was like.'

The Soviet leader and the American reporter walk slowly towards Gorbachev's office building, with the camera crew recording their conversation, translated by a bulky female Russian interpreter walking close behind, her hair tied tightly in a bun. 'Today is a culmination of sorts. I'm feeling absolutely calm, absolutely free,' insists Gorbachev, when Koppel inquires how he is coping. 'Only my role is being changed. I am not leaving either political or public life. This [a peaceful transition] is happening probably for the first time here. Even in this I have turned out to be a pioneer. That is, the process we are following is democratic. My resignation from the office of the presidency doesn't mean political death.'

Was there perhaps a fable or parable that he might tell to a grandchild about what has happened in his country, Koppel asks. 'Here is a fable that I learned some years ago,' replies Gorbachev. 'A young ruler wanted to rule in a more humane way in his kingdom. And he asked the views of the wise men. And it took ten years to bring twenty volumes of advice. He said, "When am I going to read all that? I have to govern my country." Ten years later they brought him just ten volumes of advice. He said that is still too much. Five years later he was brought just one volume. But by then twenty-five years had passed and he was on his deathbed. And one of the wise men said, "All that is here can be summarized in a simple formula – people are born, people suffer and people die."' The message is clear: Gorbachev the reformer has suffered and done his best.

The Stavropol native likes to pepper his responses with such parables and anecdotes, especially for foreigners. At his last meeting with President Bush eight weeks ago he tried to convince him of the nobility of his efforts to create a new union by relating the story of a passer-by who asked construction workers what they were doing. 'We are breaking our backs,' replied one. But another said, 'Can't you see we are building a temple here?'

When Kaplan asks the Soviet president if it distresses him to be like Moses, led to the Jordan River but unable to cross, Gorbachev replies: 'A man is walking by the Moscow River. He falls in. He can't swim. He shouts "Help!" He is ignored. He thinks perhaps the people passing by don't understand Russian. He shouts for help in German. No good. He shouts for help in French and Spanish. He is about to go under when a man throws him a lifeline and says, "If you spent more time learning how to swim you wouldn't be in this trouble." '

Gorbachev also likes to compare his political trajectory and the fate of his reforms to that of the heroic airline pilot in the Soviet film *The Crew* who risks taking off during an earthquake saying, 'It's not safe to fly, but we can't stay here. So we're going to fly.'

The small procession comes to the Senate Building, the four-storey neo-classical citadel of Soviet power, built by Catherine the Great in the shape of a triangle, with its roof just visible from Red Square. The dome with the red flag once bore a statue of Justice, which was destroyed by Napoleon's troops in 1812. Today it is topped by a circular railed platform and a six-metre pole for the flag. At the entrance is a set of steps and a spectacular view of St Nicholas's Tower. In Stalin's day being 'summoned to the steps' meant being ordered to his office, a frightening prospect. Pausing at the door, Gorbachev quotes Winston Churchill about the difference between a politician and a statesman: 'The politician thinks about the next election – the statesman thinks about the next generation.' The message again is evident. He is a statesman. He is not a mere politician, like a certain other.

The president takes the lift to the third floor where his

office is situated along a dimly lit corridor with a high ceiling. There is a long red carpet down the middle and doors on either side. It smells of antiquity and fresh paint. Lenin lived in three large rooms with a kitchen along the same corridor. His former study is preserved as a museum, and contains a wicker-backed chair and desk with papers and appointment books arranged as they were on his last working day. It was from here that the founder of the Soviet Union gave the order for the liquidation of the tsar and his family in Ipatiev House in Sverdlovsk. Stalin also lived and worked in the Kremlin, though having been discredited by Khrushchev for his reign of terror, no museum was ever established in his name. Stalin's legacy is a series of five giant red stars made from stainless steel and ruby glass which are located on top of the Kremlin towers, replacing the copper two-headed eagles, symbols of Imperial Russia, which were there in pre-revolutionary times.

Before entering his office, Mikhail Gorbachev leaves the television crew and slips into a small room off the corridor, where his hairdresser, a young woman, is waiting to give him his daily grooming. It is a morning ritual of his, especially when something important is to take place, to make sure he looks presidential. The stylist gives his nape and sideburns a slight shave and combs and dries his hair. Today his appearance is more important than usual, because in a few hours he will make a televised address that will be seen by hundreds of millions of people around the world.

According to the transition agreement he made with Yeltsin on Monday, Gorbachev can continue to occupy his Kremlin office for another four days, until Sunday. This will allow him time to keep previously arranged appointments, grant a few final interviews and clear out his desk. Only yesterday Gorbachev assembled the staff in the Walnut Room close to his office and for the first time informed the forty or fifty men and women gathered there – advisers, assistants and heads of departments – that he was resigning within twenty-four hours and that they would all have to leave the Kremlin no later than December 29.

There is some evidence, however, that Yeltsin's Russian government is growing impatient and that the transition period may not be respected. The president's spokesman Andrey Grachev feels that the appropriate funeral rites for the deceased are being dispensed with, and that the new tenants are anxious to move in and are already 'pressing the relatives of the departed to vacate the premises'.

Yeltsin's guards have started to take over the checkpoints in the Kremlin and position themselves almost menacingly in the shadowy alcoves in the corridors. Until a few days ago, Officer Valery Pestov was head of Gorbachev's security service, but on December 16 he was informed that he had been transferred to Yeltsin's command. Gorbachev only found this out when told by a secretary. New security personnel and ushers have taken the place of the regular sentinels. The incoming masters have ordered Gorbachev's staff not to lock their office doors or their desk drawers, and to keep open the enormous burgundy-coloured filing cabinets in the corridor. They have begun stopping his officials to search their belongings and ascertain what is being carried in and out.

The Soviet president passes the checkpoints without hindrance but some of his aides and junior officials are regularly delayed and harassed. When an overeager sentry demands to inspect the briefcase of Ruslan Aushev, chairman of the Commission on Afghan Affairs and a Hero of the Soviet Union, later the president of Ingushetia, Aushev slaps him in the face. Stunned, the guard lets him pass. Vitaly Gusenkov, a Gorbachev aide, is detained for some time and only released when he threatens loudly to complain directly to the president.

Gorbachev's most senior adviser, Anatoly Chernyaev, is able to take his briefcase past the new guards without hindrance; he believes they respect him as a sort of elder statesman. By this means he manages to take some sensitive documents out of the Kremlin. But he has no illusions about what is going on. The Russian president wants to torture his predecessor with petty humiliations, he reckons. It all smacks of banditry in the spirit of Yeltsin, 'and Mikhail Sergeyevich still insists on a civilized transfer of power!'

The Kremlin receptionists have come in at their usual time but practically all that remains for them to do is to sort out the personal books Gorbachev is taking away and discard old papers. There are no longer any attendants in his cloakrooms. No telephones are ringing, insisting to be answered. Yeltsin has taken charge of all government communications and disconnected most lines. One of the five white phones by Gorbachev's desk is still connected but it too is mostly silent.

Chernyaev discovers that the dedicated telephone in his office along the corridor has been assigned to someone else. He can still use the telephone to dial out, 'but someone called, and it is not for me'. One message does get through to him. Yeltsin's deputy prime minister Gennady Burbulis calls to inform him, in his high-pitched, precise voice, that he must wind things down sharply. Burbulis, it seems, has earmarked Chernyaev's space for himself and is impatient to move in.

Shortly before 10.30 a.m., refreshed and slightly scented from his hairdresser's attention, Gorbachev enters the presidential office past the cramped reception area where the secretaries and bodyguards sit, and walks across the carpeted parquet floor to take his customary seat in the high-backed leather chair behind his desk. It is a big, gloomy room, twelve metres long and six metres wide, with wainscoting and a high ceiling. White damask drapes hang over the windows and a two-metre-high bookcase takes up half an adjoining wall. On one side are a work table, and a low coffee table with easy chairs where he relaxes with visitors. Gorbachev's desk of dark cherrywood with solid top and base is in the corner by the window. Behind it stands a ceiling-high red Soviet flag. In front of the desk are two adjacent leather armchairs which self-important visitors try to avoid. Sitting in them means having to look up at the president behind his desk. In the corner is a safe containing top-secret documents and some personal items, including a Makarov pistol with gold inlay that he received as a present from Viktor Chebrikov, head of the KGB from 1982 to 1988.

Off the anteroom is the Walnut Room, where major decisions were until recently made by Gorbachev and a select few communist leaders, often with no note-takers present, to be ratified in the adjoining Politburo Room. The Politburo Room was once Stalin's office. It is often referred to as the 'shoe room' because the table is shaped like the sole of a shoe. It has not been used since the party was outlawed and the Politburo disbanded after the August coup. On the table there is a control console that opens a special wall panel to expose a series of maps, which are also redundant. Many city and street names and even the titles of the fifteen Soviet-era republics have reverted to their pre-revolutionary forms in the past year, and from today the almost invisible dotted lines between the republics will become solid international borders with customs and immigration posts.

The two colonels with the nuclear suitcase have, as always, followed the president into the reception room attached to his office. They place the black object with sharp metal corners on a table so that it is in view. If there is a nuclear alert a light will flash. This has never happened since the *chemodanchik* was invented in 1983 in the final phase of the Cold War to provide Soviet leaders with a remote communications system to minimize reaction time should a missile be detected heading towards the USSR. The device has never left Gorbachev's side since 1985. In an emergency the top leaders can converse with each other and with the strategic forces command centre at Chekhov, a small town outside Moscow linked to the Kremlin by a secret

KGB subway known as Moscow Metro II. If one leader should be incapacitated by a nuclear strike, two others can authorize retaliatory action.

Occasionally the colonels have taken Gorbachev through the procedure, showing how in an emergency the president can monitor the trajectory of a suspect missile on a screen inside the case linked into the Soviet Union's command and control network, Kazbek. The system was designed to respond to the US Pershing medium-range ballistic missile, which has a seven-minute trajectory. By pressing one of a row of buttons inside the suitcase, the president can give the green light to different kinds of reactions, from a limited reprisal to nuclear Armageddon.

Contrary to popular belief, the three nuclear suitcases do not contain the codes necessary to unlock the safety mechanisms on nuclear missiles. The president can authorize access to these codes, however. If all the brief-case holders are killed in an attack, officers of the general staff have codes to launch counterstrikes on their own initiative.

Andrey Grachev notes that apart from the two colonels, the normally bustling anteroom is strangely empty. Not a single visitor is present, other than the Americans from ABC television. The appointments diary is blank.

Gorbachev's English-language interpreter, Pavel Palazchenko, finds the Kremlin corridors 'hushed, even more quiet than usual' as he arrives and walks along the corridor to his cubicle-sized office filled with dictionaries. The interpreter, whose bald head and moustache are often seen over Gorbachev's shoulder at international gatherings, senses an air of inevitability about what is happening in the Kremlin, where he has never felt at home since Gorbachev moved his presidential staff here from party headquarters in Old Square some months ago.

Palazchenko also senses something hostile in the building. It is as if, he feels, 'the environment itself is trying to eject us'.

5

The Storming of Moscow

LESS THAN A YEAR AFTER HE TOOK OFFICE, MIKHAIL Gorbachev summoned Communist Party leaders from all over the Soviet Union to a great congress in the Kremlin. As Moscow city boss, Boris Yeltsin saw to it that the streets of the capital were decorated with red banners for the occasion.

The day of the conference, February 25, 1986, was clear and bitterly cold, with the temperature not rising above minus 17 degrees. Inside the conference hall the new general secretary got a warm reception from the five thousand delegates. They expected much from the dynamic new leader after the stagnation of the previous two decades.

At this, the 27th Party Congress, Gorbachev launched his ambitious reform programme to revitalize the Soviet economy. He called it *perestroika*, or restructuring. Its aim was to renew Soviet-style socialism through greater freedom for initiative and to liberalize society through *glasnost*, or openness.

Gorbachev had worked on his speech to the Congress for several days at his holiday dacha in Pitsunda on the Black Sea, with the help of his close collaborator, Alexander Yakovlev. A heavy-jowled, balding man in his late sixties, with large plastic-rimmed glasses and his left knee stiff from a war wound, Yakovlev provided much of the intellectual drive for *perestroika*. Gorbachev had met him in May 1983 when he visited Canada, where Yakovlev was semi-exiled as Soviet ambassador after speaking out against Russian chauvinism.

In fact, *perestroika* could be traced back to a long and frank discussion Gorbachev and Yakovlev held in the back yard of a farm in Amherstburg, Ontario. The ambassador told him there how the Canadian system was superior because openness and democracy acted as a check on corruption. Yakovlev so impressed Gorbachev as a liberal but loyal party theoretician that he had him brought back to Moscow and made a candidate member of the Politburo. Behind the scenes the former ambassador urged his comrade to think dangerous thoughts, like splitting the party in two, holding elections and lifting censorship on the press.

Raisa listened to the discussions that day in Pitsunda and participated, chiding them for ignoring the plight of women and the family in Soviet society.

When he took the podium at the Congress, Gorbachev lectured the delegates on the need to combat corruption and inertia. He promised that with *perestroika* living conditions would improve and consumer goods would become more available. He spoke of 'new thinking' in international relations, meaning non-interference in other countries' domestic affairs, and said that Moscow must turn away from the policy of military confrontation with the West. He made it clear that everything which was not forbidden by law was to be allowed, reversing the unwritten rule that everything not expressly allowed was prohibited.

He also called a halt to the party habit of delivering panegyrics to the general secretary, and shortly afterwards cut short lavish words of praise from Eduard Shevardnadze, whom he had appointed foreign minister, earning a round of amused applause. Party hacks nevertheless queued at the microphone to herald the new leader's wisdom.

When Boris Yeltsin reached the podium, everyone expected another paean of praise for *perestroika*. However, like the schoolboy taking on the teacher, he criticized one of the 'zones beyond criticism' – the secret privileges enjoyed by party members. His few months in Moscow had made him aware of the level of public resentment over this system of lavish perks. 'Let a leader go to an ordinary store and stand in line there, like everyone else,' he boomed. 'Then perhaps the queues, of which everyone is sick and tired, will disappear sooner.'

There was consternation. This was a particularly sensitive subject. Many of the delegates had secured their high positions in the party specifically to improve the quality of their lives by *not* having to go to ordinary stores and queue with everyone else.

Special privileges for Communist Party members had long been a fixed part of Soviet society. The party compensated its leaders generously for their 'services to the people' according to a rigid system called the Table of Ranks, which mimicked a formal list of positions and ranks in tsarist Russia.

At the top, the members of the Politburo and the top party secretariat, some twenty-five in number, were free to use a special squadron of Ilyushin-62 long-range jet-liners and Tupolev-134 twin-engine airliners to fly anywhere they wanted. Each was allocated four personal bodyguards, a large ZiL limousine equipped with a radio telephone and a state-owned country house with cooks, waitresses and gardeners, as well as free time-shares in luxurious state holiday dachas at Black Sea resorts. Volga sedans were provided for wives, with drivers on twenty-four-hour call and Kremlin number plates that made militiamen snap to attention.

Everything was paid for by the KGB's Ninth Directorate, a forty-thousand-strong uniformed body-guard for party leaders and their families, which also operated a separate government-party telephone system. A spouse could order a bodyguard to get presents, pick up a tailor for a fitting or do the shopping. Other grades of party members received packages of choice foodstuffs delivered from 'special' shops closed to outsiders. Thousands of middle- and lower-ranking *apparatchiks* had access to different levels of supplies from private stores and to treatment in special medical clinics.

The system ensured loyalty. The fact that everything belonged to the state and could be withdrawn at a moment's notice was a disincentive for a cadre to express dissent.

Yeltsin himself gained from the fountain of party benefits. When he became a candidate member of the Politburo he was assigned a magnificent state dacha, Moskva-reka-5, situated by the river in the village of Usovo, northwest of the capital. It had just been vacated by Gorbachev, who had moved to an even more sumptuous country mansion built to his specifications. When Yeltsin went to inspect his new home, he was met by the commander of the bodyguard who introduced him to a bevy of cooks, maids, security guards and gardeners. The former provincial party chief was overwhelmed by the palatial rooms with marble panelling, parquet floors, crystal lighting, an enormous glass-roofed veranda, a home cinema, a billiards room and a 'kitchen big enough to feed an army'. The commander, beaming with delight, asked Yeltsin what he thought of it. The Moscow party chief would say later that he mumbled something inarticulate, while his wife and daughters Tanya, then aged twenty-five, and Yelena, twenty-eight, were too overcome and depressed to reply. 'Chiefly we were shattered by the senselessness of it all.' Nevertheless, he moved in right away, even before the nails were removed from the walls where Gorbachev's pictures had hung.

The former Sverdlovsk boss had plunged with zeal into the role of first secretary of the Moscow Communist Party. He believed Gorbachev 'knew my character and no doubt felt certain I would be able to clear away the old debris, to fight the mafia, and that I was tough enough to carry out a wholesale clean-up of the personnel'. During the first year of *perestroika*, he and Gorbachev spoke occasionally. They had a dedicated telephone line to each other. As one of the KGB officers assigned to guard the Moscow party chief, Alexander Korzhakov got the impression that Yeltsin 'worshipped' Gorbachev, noting how he would rush to pick up the special handset when it rang.

However, Yeltsin found that the task of reviving Moscow, the centre of the intellectual, cultural, scientific, business and political life of the country, was impossible under the failing command system. Moreover, he came to the conclusion that his predecessor Viktor Grishin had been an 'empty bladder' who had corrupted the Moscow party organization.

The city was in a wretched state. Everywhere there was 'dirt, endless queues, overcrowded public transport', he observed. The vegetable warehouses in particular were a scandal, full of rotting produce, rats and cockroaches. Sorting and packing was done by resentful squads of citizens dragooned into service.

At first Yeltsin was able to use *glasnost* as an instrument of reform in Moscow. He summoned a conference of one thousand members of the Moscow party where, with Gorbachev looking on, he berated them for being complacent and ostentatious and for exaggerating success while cooking the books. On his instructions, the proceedings were published, and caused a sensation. People queued at newspaper kiosks to read Yeltsin's outspoken remarks. Gorbachev himself had criticized 'bribery, inertia and complete unscrupulousness in party ranks' but Yeltsin was doing something about it. He was firing Moscow officials he found guilty of 'toadyism, servility and boot-licking'. These included one official called Promyslov, chairman of the city's executive committee, who spent so much time on foreign junkets that a joke which came to Yeltsin's ears ran that Promyslov made a short stopover in Moscow while flying from Washington to Tokyo. Yeltsin dismissed a party secretary who had the walls of his opulent home covered with animal hides, telling him, 'You are only a party leader, not a prince.' He set out to liquidate many of the city's redundant scientific research institutes, which had become the preserve of thousands of idle bureaucrats, something for which the faux members of the Soviet intelligentsia never forgave him. He tried to put a stop to enterprise managers exploiting workers from the countryside who lacked Moscow residency permits by hiring them as cheap labour.

The burly fire-breathing Siberian also took to barging unannounced into factories, hospitals, construction sites, schools, kindergartens, restaurants and shops as he had done in Sverdlovsk. He confounded managers with statistics. He had a gift for memorizing numbers. After studying documents en route in the car he would emerge and make a point of showing that he was no ignorant provincial and he knew a thing or two about their business. He took to riding in the crowded Moscow metro and on the city's ramshackle buses, particularly at rush hours. He joined queues at food stores to see for himself how people were treated. Unrecognized once in a meat shop, he ordered a cut of veal, knowing that a supply had just been delivered. Told there was none available, he charged behind the counter and found it being passed out through a back window. He had the management dismissed.

Yeltsin liked to reward those officials who met his high standards by giving them wristwatches. He would peel the watch from his arm for someone who pleased him, then a few minutes later produce an identical time-piece from his pocket to give to someone else. Once he made his assistant take off his precious Seiko to give to a builder. His bodyguard Korzhakov learned always to carry spare watches in his pocket.

This storming of the bureaucracy by Yeltsin at first suited Gorbachev's purposes in getting things moving. Gorbachev told him, without smiling, that he was a 'fresh strong wind' for the party. The country's new leader was doing his own round of inspections and meeting the public, but in the old style, giving advance notice that he was coming. On Gorbachev's first visit as general secretary to a Moscow hospital, the asphalt on the road outside was so fresh the steam was rising and, according to his aide, Valery Boldin, the beds in the wards to which he was directed were occupied by healthy, well-fed security officers with closely cropped hair who warmly recommended the medical staff and the food.

Politburo members, accustomed to diktat rather than dialogue, fretted about Yeltsin's populist forays around Moscow. In mid-1986 Gorbachev personally instructed Viktor Afanasyev, the editor of the party newspaper, *Pravda*, to downplay coverage of the publicity-seeking Yeltsin. At his urging the propaganda section of the Central Committee called in Mikhail Poltoranin, editor of the Moscow party newspaper, *Moskovskaya Pravda*, to dress him down for giving Yeltsin too much attention. In those days the party could have editors fired. Though Gorbachev occasionally spoke up in Yeltsin's defence, acknowledging that he was clearing the capital of 'dirt and crooks', he distanced himself from the Sverdlovsk 'stormer'. So too did Yeltsin's mentor, Yegor Ligachev, who did not like the way he was pushing party officials around. When Yeltsin shut down some special shops in Moscow, Ligachev lectured him for not making regular stores more efficient.

Resentment of Yeltsin among his comrades erupted in a confrontation on January 19, 1987, at a regular Thursday gathering of the Politburo in the Kremlin. Gorbachev was outlining an important speech he planned to make to the Central Committee on the next stage of reform. The content had been worked out privately in advance, as was usually the case. No one was expected to open their mouth at his presentation. But Yeltsin insisted on making a bellicose critique, raising about twenty comments on the text. In particular he challenged Gorbachev's assertion that the system was capable of renewal.

'The guarantees enumerated, the socialist system, the Soviet people, the party, have been around for all of seventy years,' he said. 'So none of them is a guarantee against a return to the past.' Yeltsin also urged Gorbachev to publicly name past Soviet leaders who were responsible for the country's stagnation, and he demanded a limit on the general secretary's term in office.

He had, he would later assert, become contemptuous of Gorbachev's 'self-delusions' and his alleged fondness for the perks of office, and his tolerance for officials continuing to live opulent lives during *perestroika*.

Gorbachev was livid. His prepared critique of the shortcomings of Soviet rule was already as severe as the party members could swallow. Furious, he got up and stalked out of the room. For thirty minutes the entire Politburo sat in silence, avoiding Yeltsin's eye.

The general secretary of the Communist Party had worked hard to get agreement from individual Politburo members on the propositions for reform in his speech. He considered these initiatives vital to his task of turning the ship of state around slowly and carefully without running it on to the rocks. He had taken risks with hardliners by loosening party control. He had eased the suppression of religion and set free scores of political prisoners. Just a month previously he had released the exiled Nobel Prize-winning scientist and dissident Andrey Sakharov from internal exile in Gorky (now Nizhny Novgorod). Editors were being allowed to hint at the truth about the terrors of the Stalin period, and to fill in the 'blank pages' of Soviet history. He was winding down the war in Afghanistan. He was about to announce the most radical reform in seventy years of totalitarian communism, the introduction of a form of managed democracy that would enable direct elections to a Congress of People's Deputies. He was doing this in the face of widespread resistance to *perestroika* by party *apparatchiks* who saw their sinecures threatened.

And here was this disrespectful braggart from Sverdlovsk accusing him of maintaining the old ways.

When he came back to the room, Gorbachev let fly at Yeltsin in a sustained harangue that lasted more than thirty minutes. Yeltsin's reproofs were 'loud and vacuous', he cried angrily. He never did anything but offer destructive criticism and many people in Moscow were complaining about his 'rudeness, lack of objectivity and even cruelty'. According to Yeltsin it was 'a tirade that had nothing to do with the substance of my comments, but was aimed at me personally', with the general secretary swearing at him in 'almost market porter's language'.

The tough construction engineer and scourge of Moscow's party hacks was crushed by Gorbachev's furious response. When the lecture was over, Yeltsin apologized lamely, saying, 'I've learned my lesson, and I think that it was not too soon.'

He later reflected, 'There can be no doubt that at that moment Gorbachev simply hated me.'

6

December 25: Mid-morning

IN CONTRAST TO THE KREMLIN, THE RUSSIAN WHITE House is already crackling with activity on the morning of December 25, 1991. The imposing ten-year-old edifice of marble and glass, constructed in the shape of a giant submarine with a fourteen-storey conning tower, is headquarters of the Russian government. The building has been a symbol of national resistance to totalitarianism since the failed August coup, when Yeltsin stood on a tank outside to defy the hard-line communists attempting to impose emergency rule and keep the Soviet Union intact. It contains the Russian Supreme Soviet, the parliament elected the previous year in the first free vote in Russia since the founding of the USSR. Before that the White House was dismissed by cynical Muscovites as a white elephant, housing a sham government and parliament whose members were hand-picked by the party and who rubber-stamped everything put in front of them. It is now home to a ively, fractious elected assembly that only two weeks ago voted, on Yeltsin's urging, to take Russia out of the dying Soviet Union by the end of the year.

Visitors climbing the terraced steps are greeted by a magnificent depiction of the imperial two-headed, red-tongued eagle of tsarist Russia rather than, as before, the giant statue of Lenin standing in a recess in the hall, which is still there but has been shrouded by curtains. In the reception rooms the large pictures of the Soviet founder that were once obligatory have been replaced with reproduction landscapes of silver birch and snow. The Russian tricolour flutters gaily from the roof, and little replica flags adorn the desks of the ministers inside. The cafeteria, so well stocked in the days before the party system of privileges broke down, still manages to supply deputies and parliamentary staff with bread and sausage. Even in the White House, however, the shortages are evident. The grand ornate blue-tiled bath-rooms on the fifth floor often do not have any lavatory paper; the parliamentary deputies are suspected of pocketing the toilet rolls that are installed first thing in the morning and taking them home.

Boris Yeltsin enters from the basement car park and takes the private lift to his spacious office on the fifth floor. There his aide Viktor Ilyushin has laid out on his desk the December 25 editions of the Russian news-papers. A dry *apparatchik* in his early forties, Ilyushin has been Yeltsin's assistant since Sverdlovsk days. Over the years he has learned to bear patiently the brunt of his boss's sometimes petulant outbursts. He always arrives first to prepare the day's schedule and present Yeltsin with the most important documents.

The broadsheets devote considerable space to a series of fresh presidential decrees, signed by Yeltsin the previous day, taking over departments and properties from the defunct Soviet government.

Where the Soviet Union was established by sword and gun, it is being dismantled by decree. In the previous two months Yeltsin has been appropriating Soviet assets, simply by signing one decree after another. He undermined the demoralized USSR government by first withholding Russian taxes, and then taking ownership of Soviet government ministries and the currency mint. All that Mikhail Gorbachev is left with are titles, a small staff and the nuclear suitcase.

Before Gorbachev's *glasnost* the newspapers were dull, mendacious and heavily censored. The main organs of information, the Communist Party newspaper *Pravda* and the government newspaper *Izvestia*, printed only what the party allowed. *Pravda* and *Izvestia* translate as 'truth' and 'news', and cynics would quip that 'in the *Truth* there is no news, and in the *News* there is no truth'. Today they are full of freewheeling reportage. It is the time of the greatest press freedom in Russian history, before or since. 'At the end of 1991 Russia had the most free press probably in the world,' in the opinion of Yegor Gaidar, Yeltsin's deputy prime minister. 'It was free from official control. It was free from censorship. It was free from the opinion of the readers. It was free from the owners. Of course it could not survive . . .' *Nezavisimaya Gazeta* (Independent Newspaper) is one of the most popular dailies for its investigative reporting, a great journalistic novelty for

Russian readers. *Kommersant* (Businessman) has re-appeared for the first time since the Bolsheviks seized power in 1917, its name deliberately spelt in pre-revolutionary style to show it has outlasted the communist era. *Pravda*, once the infallible mouthpiece of the Communist Party – it always had to be put on top of the pile of daily newspapers for sale – is struggling to survive and has seen its circulation drop from almost ten million to less than one million. Its youth equivalent, *Komsomolskaya Pravda*, previously the organ of the now-defunct Young Communist League, Komsomol, has transformed itself into a lively news-sheet. Its cheeky city counterpart, *Moskovsky Komsomolets*, has become so irreverent that a year ago it relegated the news of Gorbachev's Nobel Peace Prize to page three, below the fold. The other papers on Yeltsin's desk include the more solid *Izvestia*, now the most reliable high-circulation Russian daily; *Rossiyskaya Gazeta* (Russian Gazette), the organ of the Russian parliament; *Sovetskaya Rossiya* (Soviet Russia), the herald of the reactionaries, and *Trud* (Labour), the newspaper of the Soviet trade unions, which has seen its circulation collapse from a world record twenty-one million the year before to under two million.

All the newspapers report that the Russian parliament has the previous day approved a resolution freeing up prices on January 2. *Izvestia* warns in a headline: 'Prices for Bread, Milk, Sugar, Vodka, Medicine, Fuel, Electricity, Rents, Fares Can Rise by Three to Five Times.' Its report says: 'To use a well-known expression about democracy, free prices is the worst method of relations between buyers and sellers – if you disregard all the others.'

One of Yeltsin's decrees listed in *Rossiyskaya Gazeta* disbands the KGB, which is in the process of being transformed into the *Federalnaya Sluzhba Bezopasnosti*, or FSB, the federal security agency of Russia, which will be based, like its predecessor, in the Lubyanka. Another orders the conversion to Russian ownership of the communist-era USSR State Bank. *Izvestia* reports that the chief executive Vitaly Gerashchenko has submitted his resignation. 'It has not yet been accepted, but this is obviously only a matter of a few days, or maybe hours.' This cornerstone of the Soviet Union's economy will in future prop up a new Russian financial system.

The newspaper also reports that Yeltsin has ordered several iconic state properties to be transferred immediately from Soviet to Russian ownership. They are the Bolshoi Theatre, the Mali Theatre, the Tchaikovsky Conservatory, the Lenin Library, the Academy of Arts, Moscow State University, St Petersburg State University, the State Historical Museum, the Hermitage Museum, the Pushkin Museum of Arts, the Tretyakov Gallery, the Rublev Museum of Old Russian Culture and Arts, the Anthropological and Ethnographic Museum, the State Museum of Ethnography of the Peoples of the USSR, the State Museum of Eastern Art and the Polytechnic Museum. Until now all these institutions were as much the property of the other Soviet republics as that of Russia. The other republics can do little about their seizure by Russia, except to lay claim to Soviet property on their own territories. The list is topped by the most prestigious property in the whole of the Soviet Union. This is 'the Kremlin and all its contents including the architectural ensemble, the Moscow Kremlin State Historical and Cultural Museum Preserve and the Kremlin Palace of Congresses'. The symbol and heart of Soviet power for most of the century belongs to Russia now. The Soviet president is there today only on sufferance.

Outside its borders, the personnel and property of the USSR are also being transferred to Russia. Yury Vorontsov in New York wakes up this morning as the long-serving ambassador of the communist superpower to the United Nations, and will go to bed this evening as the ambassador of capitalist Russia. Vorontsov changes his status at midnight Moscow Time (4.00 p.m. the previous day in New York) by simply delivering to the UN secretary general, Javier Pérez de Cuéllar y de la Guerra, fax No. 2338 from the office of the Russian president in Moscow. It informs the secretary general that as the successor state to the USSR, Russia will take the Soviet Union's seat in the UN Security Council as one of the five permanent members with veto powers, and 'henceforth the name Russian Federation will be used in the United Nations instead of USSR'. It asks Pérez de Cuéllar to regard as official agents of the Russian Federation all the diplomats who until that day were Soviet representatives.

Only three years ago, Mikhail Gorbachev dazzled the General Assembly with his sweeping vision of a new world order for the twenty-first century that would be regulated by the two superpowers, the Soviet Union and the United States, which together would promote dialogue rather than confrontation and would work to eliminate nuclear weapons.

Yeltsin's team has already taken possession of the Soviet foreign ministry in Moscow, seized its bank accounts, evicted the last Soviet foreign minister of the Gorbachev era, Eduard Shevardnadze, and installed Yeltsin's foreign minister, Andrey Kozyrev. Throughout the day, Soviet embassies in different time zones around the world receive a communiqué from Kozyrev informing them that they all are about to become the foreign missions of Russia. Non-Russian Soviet diplomats will have to set up separate embassies for their own republics, which is the privilege and price of their independence. The communiqué instructs the diplomats that by December 31 the Soviet flag is to be lowered for the last time on every embassy building around the world and the Russian tricolour hoisted in its place. Some envoys are anxious to declare their allegiance to the new order without delay. Already the white, blue and red emblem is flying prematurely at the embassies in New Delhi, Teheran and Kabul.

In Washington, DC, on Christmas morning the red flag with hammer and sickle emblem is hanging listlessly on the mast above the first floor of the Soviet embassy on 16th Street. It is a still, mild day with the temperature rising to 8 degrees. Inside, the three hundred staff are dividing themselves into ethnic groups and claiming temporary diplomatic space by putting up the names of their republics on office doors. There is considerable chaos, compounded by a shortage of cash. Senior diplomats have had to give up comfortable homes in Maryland and Virginia and move into rooms in the embassy compound because there is no hard currency available from Moscow to pay their rents. Ambassador Viktor Komplektov has been in office only nine months and he knows that, unlike his counterpart at the United Nations, his days are numbered. He is not trusted by Yeltsin because of his failure to condemn the coup in August. For three days before it collapsed he enthusiastically disseminated the press releases of the putschists to the American media and peddled their lie to the US government that Gorbachev was ill and unable to continue his duties. The fifty-one-year-old ambassador decides to use the remains of his Soviet-era budget to hold the embassy's first-ever Christmas party as a 'last hurrah' for the USSR.

With caviar, sturgeon, champagne and vodka, the Soviet embassy in Washington goes down like the *Titanic*. 'Enjoy yourselves,' Komplektov tells the four hundred guests. 'This is the way we celebrate a grand occasion.' Afterwards the red flag is lowered and the Russian colours are raised in its place, signifying it is now the Russian embassy. Komplektov is recalled within three months.

Perversely, in Israel a new Soviet mission opens this morning. As if nothing has changed in Moscow, the first Soviet ambassador in thirty-four years presents his credentials to President Herzog, and the red flag with hammer and sickle is hoisted over the ancient Russian

Compound in Jerusalem. This anomaly arises from a promise Mikhail Gorbachev made two months previously, when he still had some authority, to his Israeli counterpart Yitzhak Shamir that he would restore Soviet–Israeli relations broken off at the time of the 1967 Middle East War. The credentials of the envoy, Alexander Bovin, are the last to be signed by a Soviet leader. Bovin's destiny is to be Soviet ambassador for a few hours, and then become ambassador of Russia, based in Tel Aviv, where he will remain in office for a further six years.

In Santa Cruz de Tenerife, the largest port of the Canary Islands, a Soviet cruise ship docks this Christmas morning. The passengers disembark for a day's sightseeing. When they return they find that the hammer and sickle on the side of the funnel has been prised off by the Russian crew and they sail away, citizens of a different country than when they boarded.

Approaching eleven o'clock, President Boris Yeltsin leaves his office in the White House and takes the lift down to the packed hall of the Russian Supreme Soviet. The two hundred and fifty-two members of the upper chamber of the Russian Congress of People's Deputies have been summoned there to make history. They take their places on polished wooden benches beneath an eggshell-blue ceiling and massive circular chandelier to decide whether or not to approve the final dismemberment of the Soviet Union.

7

A Bucketful of Filth

D ESPITE YELTSIN'S STRENUOUS EFFORTS, THE SITUATION
in Moscow did not noticeably improve throughout
1986 and 1987. His replacements in senior posts were
often just as corrupt or inefficient as those he fired. 'We
keep digging to get rid of all this filth but we still
haven't found the bottom of this black hole,' he complained in a talk with Moscow trade officials. The
research institutes ignored his demands for staff
reductions. Food continued to rot in railway yards. He
worked from 7.00 a.m. to midnight, his dissatisfaction
growing all the while. 'There were times when I would
drive home, my bodyguard would open the door and I
wouldn't have the strength to get out of the car.'

He grew more alienated from his comrades in the
Politburo. It rankled with Yeltsin that after nearly two
years in charge of Moscow he had still not been
elevated to full membership of the Politburo as his
predecessors in the Moscow post had been, and that he
was answerable to Yegor Ligachev, who believed that

instead of radical change, the party's goal should be the strengthening of the USSR's brand of socialism. Ligachev, the party puritan, saw him now as a dangerous populist.

After the fractious Politburo meeting of January 1987, Gorbachev began pointedly to shun the awkward Moscow party boss. He did his best to avoid shaking Yeltsin's hand or speaking with him at the Thursday Politburo sessions. Yeltsin's attack on party privileges had touched a raw nerve with him. Gorbachev did indeed like to live well. Besides building a palatial Moscow home, he had ordered the construction of an immense and architecturally tasteless summer residence for his exclusive use at Foros on the Black Sea. Even his most devoted aides were uneasy about his extravagant use of state funds. Georgy Shakhnazarov worried that it gave people reason to criticize him for his 'love of luxury'. When he first saw the great mansion, with its glass-enclosed escalator down to the beach, his loyal adviser Anatoly Chernyaev too began to have serious doubts about 'the perquisites attending his great historic mission'.

Yeltsin was a misfit in Gorbachev's otherwise obedient team. He began voicing opinions that were heretical at the time. In May 1987, when asked by Diane Sawyer, in Moscow for the CBS programme *60 Minutes*, if Russians thought capitalism worked, he said yes. 'Do you?' Sawyer asked. 'Of course I do!' He did not really know about capitalism then, but he knew that communism was not working and he was aware of the restless public mood.

Overworked, frustrated and sulking at being passed over for promotion, Yeltsin decided, on September 10, 1987, to quit the Politburo. The last straw was a lecture from Ligachev at a Politburo meeting for tolerating two small, unsanctioned demonstrations on Moscow streets. That evening the Moscow boss told Naina he would not work with 'this band' any more. He sat down and wrote a letter of resignation to Gorbachev, who was vacationing on the Black Sea.

In the letter, Yeltsin complained that his Politburo colleagues were indifferent to his problems in Moscow and were giving him the cold shoulder. He could no longer tolerate working for Ligachev whose methods were 'altogether unsystematic and crude'. He accused his comrades of paying lip service to *perestroika*. 'This suits them, and – if you will forgive me saying so, Mikhail Sergeyevich – I believe it suits you too.' He finished the communication by asking to be released from his duties as Moscow party chief and candidate Politburo member.

Gorbachev received the letter the next morning at his dacha on the Black Sea where he was working with aides. It came as a thunderbolt. Nobody in Soviet history had ever resigned voluntarily from the ranks of the Politburo. Chernyaev found him in a state of excitement.

'Here, read this!' said the party leader.

'What is it?'

'Read it! Read it!'

Chernyaev took the letter and looked through it.

'What should I do with this?' asked Gorbachev. Don't

take precipitate action, advised Chernyaev. Boldin read the epistle and thought Yeltsin had a point, as 'Gorbachev, for whom manoeuvring had become a habit, was really taking two steps forward, three to the side and one backward.'

The general secretary of the Communist Party was confronted with a dilemma. He didn't like the Moscow dynamo's 'overgrown ambition and lust for power'. Furthermore, a public split in the Politburo could damage the party. At the same time, it might strengthen his own hand with the conservatives if they saw how pressure was building up among the most impatient comrades. He called his subordinate in Moscow two days later and begged him, 'Wait, Boris, don't fly off the handle; we'll work this out.' He asked Yeltsin to hold off on his resignation and keep working for another two months, until after the seventieth anniversary of the October Revolution (which because of a later change in the Russian calendar fell on November 7), when Moscow would be celebrating and the city would be full of foreign dignitaries. Chernyaev recalled his chief saying, 'I managed to talk him into it. We agreed that he won't have an attack of nerves and rush around until after the celebrations.'

Yeltsin remembered the conversation differently. He believed Gorbachev had promised to respond to his letter when he came back from his vacation a few days afterwards. When weeks passed and nothing was said, he figured Gorbachev was quietly planning to make a show of him at a plenum of the Central Committee scheduled for October 21, 1987. This had been convened to hear the text of a ground-breaking speech on Soviet history that the general secretary was working on to commemorate the Revolution.

The three hundred members of the Central Committee converged on a rain-drenched Kremlin early that day without any sense that a blow-up was imminent. They stepped out of their ZiLs and Chaikas and hurried into the eighteenth-century Senate Building. The comrades assembled in St Catherine Hall, then known as Sverdlov Hall, named after Yakov Sverdlov, the Bolshevik leader who supervised the execution of Tsar Nicholas II and his family. Here in rows of ornate chairs beneath the stony gaze of eighteen pre-revolutionary poets in bas-relief sculptures among the white Corinthian columns and pilasters high above, they awaited the single item on the agenda: a reading by Gorbachev of his prepared speech. The fourteen Politburo members sat in a line behind a desk on a raised podium, facing the assembly.

Yeltsin took his place in the front row along with the half dozen other Politburo candidate members and various senior party officials. The meeting was closed to the media. By convention the advance speeches of the general secretary would be approved by acclamation and everyone would retire to enjoy a pleasant lunch.

Ligachev presided. He called upon Gorbachev to speak. The general secretary outlined his presentation. After thirty minutes he finished and Ligachev asked, 'If there are no questions . . . ?' Yeltsin hesitantly raised his hand, then took it down, as if he were in two minds. Gorbachev pointed him out to Ligachev, who asked if members wanted to open a debate on the speech. There were cries of 'No!' Slowly the big man from Sverdlovsk stood up, his intuition to speak out winning out over the pressure to conform. Ligachev signalled to him to sit down. But Gorbachev intervened. He would give Yeltsin enough rope to hang himself. 'I believe Boris Nikolayevich wishes to say something,' he remarked icily.

Yeltsin seemed nervous and ill prepared. He spoke for about seven minutes in a disjointed fashion, using notes jotted hastily on his voting card. Nevertheless, the thrust of his argument was clear. The promise of *perestroika* was raising unrealistic expectations that could give rise to disenchantment and bitterness. He was deeply troubled by 'a noticeable increase in what I can only call adulation of the general secretary by certain full members of the Politburo. I regard this as impermissible . . . This tendency to adulation is absolutely unacceptable . . . A taste for adulation, which can gradually become the norm again, can become a cult of personality. We cannot permit this.' Besides, the opposition to him from Comrade Ligachev was such that he must resign from the Politburo, he said. As for his leadership of the Moscow Communist Party 'that of course will be decided by a plenum of the city committee of that party'.

This was sensational. Besides the fact that no one had ever quit the Politburo, no one in the party had ever had the audacity to address a leader of the party in such a manner in front of the Central Committee since Leon Trotsky in the 1920s. In Chernyaev's opinion, 'Such a brazen attack on the holiest of holies – on the Central Committee secretariat, on the number-two person in the party, and on the general secretary himself – was truly scandalous.' Yeltsin rationalized later that 'Something had to be changed in that putrid system.' The general secretary had reverted to being equivalent to the tsar, father of the people, and to express the slightest doubt about his actions was an unthinkable act of sacrilege. 'One could express only awestruck admiration . . . or delight at being so fortunate as to be able to work alongside him.'

There was a stunned silence as Yeltsin sat down, his heart pounding 'ready to burst out of my ribcage'. He knew what would happen next. 'I would be slaughtered in an organized, methodical manner, and it would be done almost with pleasure and enjoyment.' It is doubtful, however, that he was ready for it.

Boldin saw Gorbachev's face go purple with rage. The suggestion that the general secretary aspired to greatness through a cult of personality had again hit a nerve.

'Perhaps it might be better if I took over the chair,' said Gorbachev.

'Yes, please do, Mikhail Sergeyevich,' said Ligachev hastily.

Gorbachev coldly summed up Yeltsin's speech, and suggested that their comrade was seeking to split off the Moscow party organization from the party as a whole. When Yeltsin tried to interject, Gorbachev told him brusquely to sit down and called for comments from the floor.

This was the signal for a sustained assault.

Sycophants and toadies, some of them victims of Yeltsin's purges in Moscow, took the microphone one after another to berate the heretic. Gorbachev watched his nemesis as the hammer blows descended. He reflected how Yeltsin himself had put people down meanly, painfully, often undeservedly. Now he read on Yeltsin's face a strange mixture of 'bitterness, uncertainty, regret; in other words, everything that is characteristic of an unbalanced nature'.

Some comments Yeltsin found especially hurtful. His one-time mentor in Sverdlovsk, Yakov Ryabov, who was then Soviet ambassador to France, doused him in what he later described as a bucketful of filth. The insults would have been part of the rough and tumble in some Western parliaments but they were damning in the context of a Central Committee plenum of the tightly disciplined Communist Party in 1987. Even the most progressive Politburo members, Eduard Shevardnadze and Alexander Yakovlev, rallied behind Gorbachev and spoke against the dissenter, something he found particularly painful. Some denunciations were predictable. Viktor Chebrikov, head of the KGB, berated him for blabbing to foreign journalists. He was dismissed by others as clueless, someone who distorted reality, who suffered delusions of grandeur and was guilty of political nihilism. A few speakers unwittingly proved his point about Gorbachev's cult of personality. 'As to the glorification of Mikhail Sergeyevich, I for one respect him with all my soul both as a man and as a party leader,' declared regional secretary Leonid Borodin, with no trace of irony.

Twenty-seven speakers spent a total of four hours hammering down the nail in the shoe before Gorbachev brought the vilification to an end. Yeltsin meekly asked for the floor again. As had happened before, he was utterly overwhelmed. All his bravado had evaporated. He tried to be conciliatory. He never had any doubts about *perestroika*, he stammered. He agreed with much of what had been said about him. He had only two or three comrades in mind who went overboard with praise for the general secretary.

Gorbachev cut in. 'Boris Nikolayevich, are you so politically illiterate that we must organize an ABC of politics for you here?'

'No, there is no need any more,' he replied.

Gorbachev twisted the knife. He accused his challenger of being 'so vain and so arrogant' that he put his personal pride above the party and of having a puerile need to see the country revolve around his persona. And at such a critical stage of *perestroika*!

When Gorbachev had finished Yeltsin mumbled, 'In speaking out today, and letting down the Central Committee and the Moscow city organization, I made a mistake.'

Unexpectedly Gorbachev offered Yeltsin a chance to undo the damage. 'Do you have enough strength to carry on with your job?' he asked.

'I can only repeat what I said,' replied Yeltsin, to catcalls. 'I still request that I be released.'

Gorbachev proposed that he be censured for his politically incorrect tirade. The motion was passed unanimously. Even Yeltsin voted in favour.

A few days later he wrote a letter to the general secretary expressing his wish to continue in the job as Moscow party chief. Chernyaev cautioned his boss: 'The stakes are high. The supporters of *perestroika* among the so-called general public are on Yeltsin's side.' But Gorbachev called his critic on the telephone to say bluntly, '*Nyet*!'

News of a rupture in the Politburo soon began to leak. Rumours about Yeltsin's 'secret speech' at the Central Committee spread throughout Moscow. Fabricated versions began appearing. One was concocted by his editor friend Mikhail Poltoranin. In this version Yeltsin complained that he had to take instructions from Gorbachev's wife, Raisa, though he had said no such thing. Poltoranin distributed hundreds of copies and they became part of *samizdat*, underground literature that the official media would not print.

On November 7, 1987, the seventieth anniversary of the October Revolution, Gorbachev and fellow members of the Politburo welcomed fraternal world leaders in Red Square to watch a military parade of goose-stepping soldiers and tanks belching diesel smoke.

Yeltsin was ignored by his comrades as they lined up on top of the Lenin Mausoleum, but diplomats, correspondents and foreign visitors could not take their eyes off him. The small revolt in the formidable ranks of Soviet communism was world news. Fidel Castro gave him a big hug, three times, and General Wojciech Jaruzelski of Poland embraced him, saying in fluent

Russian, 'Hang in there, Boris!' At a Kremlin reception for diplomats, American ambassador Jack Matlock noticed Yeltsin standing apart with a rather sheepish smile, shifting his stance from one foot to another 'like a schoolboy who has been scolded by his teacher'. The Moscow party chief smiled at him. The envoy kept his distance. The last thing Yeltsin needed was to be seen conversing with the American ambassador.

Political drama turned to ugly farce. Gorbachev called a meeting of the Moscow branch of the Communist Party for Wednesday November 11 to confirm Yeltsin's dismissal. Two days before the meeting, on November 9, Yeltsin apparently tried to kill himself. He was rushed to the special Kremlin hospital on Michurinsky Prospekt on the outskirts of Moscow, bleeding profusely from self-inflicted cuts to his chest. By his account, 'I was taken to hospital with a severe bout of headaches and chest pains . . . I had suffered a physical breakdown.' However, at his apartment, Naina took the precaution of removing knives, hunting guns and glass objects, as well as prescription medicines, in preparation for his return.

Gorbachev took the attitude that the Siberian rebel was faking to draw attention to himself and avoid the showdown. 'Yeltsin, using office scissors, had simulated an attempt at suicide,' he concluded. 'The doctors said that the wound was not critical at all; the scissors, by slipping over his ribs, had left a bloody but superficial wound.'

On the morning of the Moscow meeting he telephoned Yeltsin in his hospital room and told him to get dressed and come to the plenum of the Moscow city committee that would decide his future. 'I can't. The doctors won't even let me get up,' protested Yeltsin. 'That's OK, the doctors will help you,' replied Gorbachev.

Acting on party orders, a Kremlin physician, forty-one-year-old Dmitry Nechayev, gave his patient a strong dose of a pain-reliever and anti-spasm agent called baralgin. He 'started to pump me full of sedatives', recalled Yeltsin. 'My head was spinning, my legs were crumpling under me, I could hardly speak because my tongue wouldn't obey.' Yeltsin decided not to resist. He hoped that someone would speak up for him at the assembly.

Naina objected furiously to the head of security for Soviet politicians, General Yury Plekhanov, who was at the hospital, that discharging a sick man amounted to sadism. But Plekhanov answered to a higher authority.

Alexander Korzhakov assisted his charge, dazed, bandaged and with his face swollen, to a car, and drove him the six miles along Leninsky Prospekt and through the city centre to Old Square. The setting this time was not the grand rotunda of St Catherine Hall but the Hall of Meetings, a long, narrow whitewashed chamber in the Central Committee building. Yeltsin was brought barely conscious to an adjoining room where the Politburo members had gathered to make an impressive entrance.

When everyone else was seated they walked grimly on to the stage, like judges in a courtroom. Yeltsin trailed in behind them. The KGB had sealed off the front rows of seats for members who had put down their names to speak. They were, observed Yeltsin, mostly Moscow cadres who had been sacked in the previous year and a half, and were waiting like 'a pack of hounds, ready to tear me to pieces'. The Politburo members sat in three rows of chairs behind a long table, facing the hall.

Gorbachev got straight to the point. They were there to discuss whether to relieve their colleague of his duties as Moscow party chief. 'Comrade Yeltsin put his personal ambitions before the interests of the party,' he said. 'He made irresponsible and immoral comments at the Central Committee meeting.' He mouthed appeals and slogans but when things went wrong he manifested 'helplessness, fussiness and panic'.

One by one members of the Moscow party organization rose to follow Gorbachev's lead and accuse the drugged and dazed Yeltsin of everything from overweening ambition, demagoguery, ostentation and lack of ethics, to blasphemy, party crime and pseudo-revolutionary spirit. Twenty-three speakers once more savaged him over the course of four hours. Only the Moscow party second secretary, Yury Belyakov, praised the collegiality, open criticism and exchange of views that Yeltsin encouraged. One member sneered, 'We'll see people who will try to make Jesus Christ out of Boris Nikolayevich.' Another denounced him for treason to the cause of party unity. A third accused him of loving neither Moscow nor Muscovites. Their quarry only occasionally raised his eyes to look in disbelief as a former comrade abused him, and to shake his head when told he did not love Moscow.

Gorbachev grew uneasy at the fury he had unleashed.

'Some of the speeches were clearly motivated by revenge or malice,' he conceded in his memoirs. 'All of this left an unpleasant aftertaste. However, at the plenum Yeltsin showed self-control and, I would say, behaved like a man.'

In the tradition of show trials, the accused was permitted to display contrition after all the venom had been spat out and his morale demolished. He stumbled towards the microphone, his lips bluish, with Gorbachev holding his elbow, for the auto-da-fé. There were shouts of '*Doloi*' ['Down with him!'] from the front rows. Yeltsin mumbled incoherently and paused often to catch his breath. He would start a sentence, then lose his train of thought. He tried to salvage a shred of dignity, saying he believed in *perestroika*, but that its progress was patchy. He castigated himself for allowing 'one of my most characteristic personal traits, ambition' to manifest itself. He had tried to check it but regrettably without success. He concluded, abjectly, 'I am very guilty before the Moscow party organization . . . and certainly I am very guilty before Mikhail Sergeyevich Gorbachev, whose prestige in our organization, in our country and in the whole world is so high.'

But inside he felt only bitterness and wrath. Yeltsin would never forgive Gorbachev for his 'inhuman and immoral' treatment in dragging him from his hospital bed to be fired in disgrace. 'I was dismissed, ostensibly at my own request,' he recalled some years later, 'but it was done with such a ranting, roaring and screaming that it has left a nasty taste in my mouth to this day.'

Everyone shuffled off to the exits leaving their

wounded prey alone in the room, sick, exhausted and distraught, his head leaning on the presidium table. The last to leave the hall, Gorbachev glanced back as he crossed the threshold. He returned and put his arm under Yeltsin's and accompanied him from the room, prompted, Gorbachev's aide Andrey Grachev suspected, by pangs of conscience. The noble victor helped the vanquished off the field. Korzhakov got him into the car and rushed the stricken Yeltsin back to his hospital bed.

The job of Moscow party boss was given to Lev Zaikov, the Politburo member in charge of military industries, who boasted to Poltoranin, 'The Yeltsin epoch is over.'

Gorbachev hadn't finished with his troublesome protégé. He ordered that a version of the proceedings of the closed Moscow party meeting be published in *Pravda*. This piece of *glasnost* was clearly designed to display party disapproval of a maverick, in itself previously sufficient to achieve the demolition of a political career. But it backfired. Yeltsin attracted considerable sympathy from Moscow citizens who believed he really cared about improving their lives. Several hundred students demonstrated at Moscow University and crude notices appeared in the metro calling for publication of Yeltsin's secret speech in October.

Yeltsin waited in his hospital bed for a call from his party leader to find out his fate. He expected that he would be banished from Moscow. But that didn't happen. Perhaps unwilling to act in the old Brezhnev style, or because he felt that his bull-headed stormer still had a useful role to play, possibly even because he thought it was simply the right thing to do, Gorbachev rang the hospital a week later to offer him another job. Korzhakov brought the telephone to his bedside, and heard Yeltsin respond 'in a totally defeated voice'. Gorbachev suggested that he take the post of first deputy chairman of the state committee for construction. It was a desk job with no policy input, but he would remain a member of the Central Committee. Yeltsin accepted. Anything was better than to be made a pensioner at fifty-six.

Gorbachev had a warning for his adversary, however. 'I'll never let you into politics again,' he told Yeltsin, before putting down the receiver.

With the passage of time, some of Gorbachev's loyalists would complain that keeping his accuser in government was his biggest blunder. The general secretary would protest, however, that he had no hatred or feeling of revenge towards Yeltsin, and that despite their power struggles he never lowered himself to his level of 'kitchen squabbling'.

(Some years later, after Yeltsin has become president of post-Soviet Russia, he unexpectedly comes across Dmitry Nechayev, the doctor who injected him with drugs so he could be hauled before the Central Committee. He is astonished to learn that he is now personal physician to his prime minister, Viktor Chernomyrdin. According to Korzhakov in his memoirs, Yeltsin never forgave the doctor. 'Naina, unable to contain herself, went to get an explanation from the prime minister. Chernomyrdin acknowledged he had not heard of the doctor's injection of Yeltsin with baralgin but did not remove him from his service after this unpleasant conversation.' On April 7, 1996, the Interfax news agency reports that Dr Nechayev is shot dead early that morning by an unknown gunman outside the Kremlin hospital on Michurinsky Prospekt. It is one of two hundred and sixteen contract killings in Moscow that year. No one is ever arrested for the crime.)

8

December 25: Late Morning

APPROACHING MIDDAY IN THE WHITE HOUSE, BORIS Yeltsin takes the podium in the parliamentary chamber and informs the Russian Congress of People's Deputies that as a consequence of what happened four days ago the Soviet Union no longer exists and Mikhail Sergeyevich Gorbachev will announce his resignation as Soviet president later in the day. Immediately afterwards Gorbachev will sign a decree giving up his command of the Soviet armed forces, and Russia will assume full control of the 27,000 nuclear weapons based in the territories of Russia, Ukraine, Belarus and Kazakhstan.

The previous Saturday Yeltsin and the heads of ten other Soviet republics finalized the creation of a loose, ill-defined alliance, the Commonwealth of Independent States (CIS), to take the place of the Soviet Union on December 31. The ceremony was held in Alma-Ata, the ancient capital of Kazakhstan, almost two thousand miles southeast of Moscow, and today called Almaty.

He wants now to assure the world through his speech

to the deputies that there is no nuclear threat arising from what they are doing. The four nuclear republics, Yeltsin says, have signed a separate agreement, 'Joint Measures Regarding Nuclear Arms'. All Soviet tactical nuclear weapons – easy to move short-range missiles carrying low-yield warheads – will be transferred to Russia and put in storage within six months. The strategic warheads – intercontinental ballistic missiles held on land, planes and submarines – will be transported to Russian territory over a longer period of time. In the meantime, the four have pledged not to be the first to use nuclear weapons and not to transfer nuclear weapons or other nuclear explosive devices and technologies to any other entity whatsoever.

'There will be only a single nuclear button, and other presidents will not possess it,' Yeltsin declares. Moreover, to 'push it' will require the approval of himself and the leaders of the territories with nuclear stockpiles. 'Of course, we think this button must never be used.'

The fact that Gorbachev is voluntarily handing over the nuclear communications equipment is, in Yeltsin's mind, the most significant thing that will happen today after the ratification of the Alma-Ata agreements and Gorbachev's resignation. It will of course make official what is already a reality: the president of the Russian Federation is the person with ultimate power in Moscow. Just as importantly, it will undermine the case being put about by Gorbachev's associates that Yeltsin's actions in breaking up the Soviet Union amount to a coup against the legitimate president.

Though at the time officially still president and commander-in-chief of the Soviet armed forces, Gorbachev was not invited to give his views to the leaders of those countries that formed the commonwealth – namely Armenia, Azerbaijan, Belarus, Kazakhstan, Kyrgyzstan, Moldova, Russia, Tajikistan, Turkmenistan, Ukraine and Uzbekistan. (The four remaining former republics of the disintegrating USSR – Estonia, Lithuania, Latvia and Georgia – want nothing to do with the commonwealth and are looking instead to the West for future alliances.) Nor did the gathering of presidents pay any attention to a letter Gorbachev had sent them offering to play a role. They have no time for their former overlord now, or for his delusions and conceits.

There is applause for Yeltsin's announcement. He has many opponents in the assembly, some of them staunch communists, some vociferous critics like his own vice president Alexander Rutskoy, who deeply regret the demise of the great superpower in which they were born, but everyone realizes that a point has been reached where practically every single republic believes it will be better off on its own.

Vladimir Isakov from Yekaterinburg, one of the few parliamentarians who openly supported the failed putsch in August, is among the small minority who voice opposition to the agreement. He rises on a point of order. He observes that when Yeltsin was elected president of Russia, he swore an oath to the constitution of the Soviet-era 'Russian Soviet Federative Socialist Republic (RSFSR)'. He has now

'high-handedly violated it'. Yeltsin signed the docu-
ments in Alma-Ata as the president of the 'Russian
Federation' but it is still legally the RSFSR, he protests.
Therefore the agreement is illegal.

There is consternation. Yeltsin and his followers
ceased using the Soviet title after the coup, but had not
got around to formally altering the name. They look
completely nonplussed and a brief silence falls until the
dilemma is resolved by the parliament's speaker. 'Well,
before the president answers the question, how about
we change the name now?' suggests Ruslan
Khasbulatov, an academic of Chechen descent who
made his name by bravely defending the White House
at Yeltsin's side in August. 'A congress will later
establish whether it indeed conforms to the text of the
new constitution.'

Khasbulatov proposes a motion changing the title of
the assembly to which they were elected from 'The
Congress of People's Deputies of the Russian Soviet
Federative Socialist Republic (RSFSR)' to 'The Congress
of People's Deputies of the Russian Federation
(Russia)'. The measure is carried on a roll-call vote.
Izvestia's reporter Ivan Yelistratov, watching from the
gallery, sees only two votes against.

The deputies in the hall burst into applause as the
Soviet republic created by the Bolsheviks in 1917 as
the USSR's biggest and most powerful constituent, an
enormous territory consisting of 6,592,800 square miles
and covering more than a ninth of the earth's land
surface, ceases to exist as a legal entity. Other republics
of the Soviet Union have already made similar changes

in their designations but the Russian Federation is the last to dump socialism from its official title. Shortly afterwards an excited newsreader on Radio Moscow reports that the removal of the words 'Soviet' and 'Socialist' reflects the official demise of the Soviet Union.

Yeltsin has another cause for satisfaction this day. Outside the chamber several deputies rush to a conference room after hearing that a 'sensational' press conference – as a reporter from *Sovetskaya Rossiya* describes it – is being given by an expert from a parliamentary commission investigating the August coup. The expert, Alexander Kichikhin, confirms what everyone suspected, that Vladimir Zhirinovsky, the leader of the tiny Liberal Democratic Party, who often rambles round the White House corridors, showering listeners with spittle during half-crazed rants about the evils of Russia's enemies, ranging from Jews to the CIA, is a stooge of the KGB. His phoney party has no branches, and was recruited solely to oppose Boris Yeltsin in Russia's first ever presidential election in June. To Yeltsin's satisfaction Zhirinovsky had got only 8 per cent of the vote, despite the support of much of the official media.

The Russian president returns to his fifth-floor cabinet and wolfs down a quick lunch. He regularly has meat pies and apples delivered from the self-service cafeteria. Out of his window he can see the wide Moscow River as it begins a loop southwest like a horseshoe, past the Kievsky railway station, around Luzhniki sports stadium, back northeast by Gorky Park and around the ramparts of the Kremlin two miles distant, where Mikhail Gorbachev is also grabbing a quick lunch and fighting fatigue and the onset of influenza as he prepares for the speech that will mark his transition from presidential to civilian life.

Yeltsin will take Gorbachev's place there behind the Kremlin's high red-brick walls, completing the remarkable resurrection that began four years ago when he was left a broken man, physically and psychologically, and demoted from Moscow party chief to the junior post of first deputy chairman of the state committee for construction.

9

Back from the Dead

MIKHAIL GORBACHEV'S WARNING TO BORIS YELTSIN IN November 1987 that he would never let him into politics again left the former Moscow party chief with a sense of despair. He felt that 'where my heart had been was a burnt-out cinder'.

Nevertheless, Gorbachev had given him a secure job in Moscow and allowed him to remain a member of the Central Committee, when he could have banished him to the provinces and got rid of him once and for all.

Yeltsin surmised sourly that if Gorbachev didn't have a Yeltsin he would have to invent one. However much Gorbachev disliked him, he reckoned he was useful to the general secretary, who could play the role of wise, omniscient hero pitted against 'Ligachev who plays the villain' on one side and, on the other, 'Yeltsin the bully boy, the madcap radical'.

Gorbachev also had to protect his own reputation as a reformer. It would not have enhanced his growing standing abroad as an enlightened progressive if he had treated his political opponent in the old way. He had to show that he could be magnanimous even to an irresponsible wrecker who he was sure could not rise above street-level politicking.

Yeltsin spent several weeks in the hospital before being discharged. At home he endured crushing headaches and deep depression. 'I felt like crawling up the wall and could hardly restrain myself from crying out loud. It was like the tortures of hell.' He couldn't sleep and vented his feelings of rage on his family.

He began work in the state construction ministry in Pushkin Street on January 8, 1988, a mild day with snow drifting down in large flakes, arriving in a ZiL with four KGB bodyguards, as he was still a candidate member of the Politburo. He was formally relieved of this post by the Central Committee on Thursday, February 17, and that evening had to go home from work in a mid-sized Chaika, without a security escort. The demotion was automatic but left him terribly distressed. According to his assistant Lev Sukhanov it plunged him into psychological turmoil, and the inner conflict between the two sides of his character, the party boss and the rebel, began to tear him apart.

While Yeltsin was allowed to keep his apartment at 54 Second Tverskaya-Yamskaya Street, he had to move his belongings from Moskva-reka-5 dacha in Usovo to a more cramped country home. His security agents from the KGB's Ninth Directorate were removed. One of them, Alexander Korzhakov, volunteered to stay on as a personal bodyguard and was consequently fired by the KGB. He was soon earning ten times more than he had been before. Korzhakov was taken on as a ghost employee by three sympathetic businessmen who were running cooperative enterprises that had been permitted to operate under *perestroika*. He did nothing except call round to each once a month to collect his 'salary'. Korzhakov's act of loyalty to Yeltsin marked the start of an intense friendship that saw the two men play tennis together and stay up drinking late at night. They became so close that they exchanged blood from their fingers, twice, to pledge eternal loyalty as 'blood brothers'.

Yeltsin used his savings to buy a sturdy Moskvich car the colour of an aluminium saucepan. Korzhakov tried to teach him to drive, an experience that he claimed made his hair turn grey, especially after his chief crashed into and seriously injured a motorcyclist.

The restless Siberian had little to do in his new job and was closely monitored in case he got up to political mischief. Every morning, shifts of barely disguised KGB agents arrived to loiter in the corridor outside his office and observe who was coming in and out. His room and telephones were bugged. Lev Sukhanov called someone in Perm one day and complained about their working conditions and a friendly KGB source told him the call to Perm had been noted and he should be careful.

The Moscow newspapers, still under party sway, were not permitted to publish anything positive about the former city boss. He went to Central Committee meetings where he was ignored. In February the Paris newspaper *Le Monde* published Mikhail Poltoranin's colourful account of Yeltsin's secret speech, including the allegation that Raisa Gorbacheva interfered with his work. Gorbachev instructed foreign ministry spokesman Gennady Gerasimov to tear a strip off *Le Monde* at a press briefing for publishing the fabrication. He was furious that Yeltsin himself did not refute the charge.

Gradually Yeltsin's anguish abated. He began to go for walks alone in the street. People who recognized him stopped to smile and shake his hand. Here were the first hints that the long-apathetic masses were becoming politicized, and that Yeltsin had acquired a popular base outside the party structures by giving voice to people's resentments.

The following month it was Yegor Ligachev who overreached. When Gorbachev was on a trip abroad, the party's number two instructed newspapers to publish a lengthy letter from a Leningrad schoolteacher, Nina Andreyevna, which defended Stalinist values and called for a halt to democratic reforms. Ligachev had sent a team to Leningrad to beef up the letter and he pushed it as a manifesto of a new party line. No newspaper editor had the courage to refuse publication, though it was clearly a mutiny against *perestroika*. The country held its breath to see which way things would go.

When Gorbachev returned to Moscow he and Alexander Yakovlev composed a lengthy response condemning the letter as an attack on his reforms, and ordered the editor of *Pravda* to publish it. The reform policy was seen to be on course again and the radicals surged back out of the trenches. Gorbachev did not dump Ligachev but the bone-headed zealot's influence was diminished.

In the following months newspaper editors became more daring. Books and plays challenging communist orthodoxy began to appear. The ringing of long-silent church bells was permitted. Informal meetings at Pushkin's statue in central Moscow were allowed so that disgruntled members of the populace could let off steam. At these ad hoc gatherings the chant of 'Yeltsin! Yeltsin!' began to be heard. The former Moscow chief was becoming a lightning rod for discontent.

In his absence, the standard of living had if anything deteriorated. A popular anecdote described a dog praising *perestroika* saying, 'My chain is a little longer, the dish is further away, but I can now bark all I want.' A well-motivated but disastrous anti-drinking campaign by the Politburo resulted in an acute shortage of vodka and a collapse in government revenues. Sugar became *deficit* as it was bought up to make bootleg spirits called *samogon*. Gorbachev had promoted the crusade, declaring that communism should not be built on vodka taxes, but Ligachev took it to the point of absurdity, at one point ordering the uprooting of hundred-year-old vines in the Crimea. Another anecdote described how an American and a Russian tested the echo on a mountaintop. The American shouted 'Bourbon' and heard the word 'bourbon' echo several times. The Russian called out 'Vodka', and the echo came back, 'Where? Where? Where . . . ?'

Yeltsin's growing street profile and renewed self-confidence intrigued the media at home and abroad. In

April Yegor Yakovlev, editor of the weekly *Moscow News* (and no relation to Alexander Yakovlev), plucked up the courage to ask Yeltsin to tell the story of how he was drugged and hauled before the Moscow party. They did the interview in the Kremlin Palace of Congresses. Yakovlev suggested they take a picture of Yeltsin in his Moskvich parked outside.

In a frolicsome mood, Yeltsin posed at the wheel of the boxy automobile with Korzhakov beside him and Sukhanov in the back, then on a whim he turned the ignition key and started steering the car towards the exit. Knowing how bad a driver he was, his passengers were terrified. 'He mixed up the pedals and it was jumping around like a kangaroo,' recalled Korzhakov. 'I swear to God I never felt such fright,' said Sukhanov. 'We went through Manezh Square and past the Exhibition Hall. We were trying to get him to stop. He said, "Those who are afraid, get out!" We were hostages to the unpredictability of our chief. He drove all the way to his apartment block. We were so nervous, our shirts were soaking wet.'

Yegor Yakovlev was hesitant about publishing the interview in contravention of the Kremlin's gagging order. He let it appear only in the German language edition of *Moscow News*, but it still caused a stir among the Russian intelligentsia. A month later Yeltsin gave an interview to the BBC in which he called for Ligachev to be sacked and, at last, denied that he had criticized Raisa in his 'secret speech'.

Yeltsin's opportunity to be heard again in Russia came at a special Communist Party conference in June

1988 – the nineteenth, but the first since 1941 –
convened by Gorbachev to push through more new
reform policies. As distinct from regular party
congresses, such conferences were called only rarely to
resolve urgent policy matters. In the spirit of *glasnost*
the television cameras were allowed in. Yeltsin, a semi-
outcast, was not invited but was slipped a ticket as a
member of the delegation from Karelia, a region on the
Finnish border, where he was admired. Arriving at the
Kremlin's Palace of Congresses he found himself an
object of curiosity among the five thousand delegates,
making him feel like an elephant in the zoo. He sent a
written request to the platform to address the conference, but he was confined to a seat at the back of the
balcony from where no one was ever called.

On the fifth and last day, sure that he was being overlooked, Yeltsin walked down the hall staircase to the
lower floor, persuaded the KGB guards to admit him
and marched to the platform holding aloft his red
conference-mandate card. A delegate from Tajikistan
who was speaking broke off in mid-sentence and the
hall fell silent as Yeltsin lumbered towards the rostrum,
all the time staring Gorbachev in the eye. Reaching the
presidium he demanded the right to speak. Politburo
members on the stage held a whispered consultation,
following which Gorbachev sent Valery Boldin down to
ask him quietly to go to the anteroom – he would have
the floor later.

As Yeltsin began to walk back up the aisle some
sympathetic delegates and journalists whispered loudly
to him not to leave the hall. Realizing he might not be

readmitted, he stopped and marched back to the front row and took an empty seat there. Gorbachev had little option but to call him to the microphone.

With delegates on the edge of their seats, Yeltsin began by asserting that he was proud of what socialism had achieved but there must be an analysis of the cause of the stagnation that still pervaded society. There should be no forbidden topics. The salaries and perks of the leadership should be made public. If there were shortages everyone should feel them. This last remark drew a scattered round of applause; there were some in the hall who felt as he did. He concluded by asking for his political rehabilitation. This provoked boos and shouts. Gorbachev intervened. 'Speak on, Boris Nikolayevich,' he said. 'They want you to have your say. I think we should stop treating the Yeltsin case as secret.' Yeltsin responded that his only political mistake was to deliver his controversial speech at the wrong time, just before the seventieth anniversary of the October Revolution, but that the party should tolerate opponents as Lenin did. He left the podium to applause from some and hisses from others, and went outside where he was surrounded by a crush of journalists and camera crews.

In the hall some delegates rose to pillory their impulsive comrade all over again. Yegor Ligachev indignantly uttered a line that would haunt him: 'Boris, you are wrong!' Within days people in Moscow were wearing lapel buttons saying, 'Yegor, you are wrong!'

As the conference was about to end, Gorbachev introduced his most far-reaching domestic reform yet.

During his closing speech he produced a piece of paper from his pocket. On it was written a resolution to fast-track the creation of a new Congress of People's Deputies of two thousand two hundred and fifty members, of whom two-thirds would be directly elected from all across the Soviet Union and a third chosen by party-approved public bodies. It would replace the rubber-stamp Soviet parliament which met only eight days a year without ever hearing a dissenting voice. It was a giant leap towards democracy.

Already looking at their watches and preparing to leave for the railway stations and airports, many loyal delegates raised their cards to vote for this sensational resolution without realizing what they were doing.

This was the high point of Gorbachev's reforms, achieved by sleight of hand. He had got support from the ruling Communist Party for the first multiple-candidate elections in seven decades of Soviet power. His scheme was a masterly combination of democracy and party management. The party would automatically have a hundred seats. This meant that Gorbachev and his Politburo comrades would safely include themselves in this 'red hundred' to avoid any risk of being rejected by the people. Gorbachev dared not seek popular support in an electoral district. Yeltsin's celebrity was growing and he might oppose him and win.

As the election laws were being drawn up, Gorbachev moved faster to push Soviet society to break with the past. *Glasnost* flowered as never before. The ban on the sale of foreign newspapers was lifted. Andrey Sakharov was permitted to travel abroad. Newspaper editors published scathing accounts of mismanagement and shortages. In November Gorbachev declared that 'only the democratization of our entire life can guarantee to overcome stagnation'. It was springtime for *glasnost*. 'There is no alternative to Gorbachev,' enthused Vitaly Korotich, editor of the avant-garde magazine *Ogonyok* (Little Flame), which had become so popular it was sold out every week within hours of going on sale. 'The bureaucrats who oppose him are the usual "fat cats", people with no idealism, people who believe in nothing.'

Gorbachev's stock rose internationally. In February 1989 the last Soviet troops left Afghanistan. US–Soviet talks on nuclear disarmament gathered pace. He created the conditions for the freedom of East European countries that had been in thrall to Moscow since World War II. Gorbachev made it clear that the communist regimes there could no longer count on Soviet tanks to prop them up. At a foreign ministry briefing Gerasimov called this the Frank Sinatra doctrine – they could do it their way. It led to a series of counter-revolutions throughout 1989, in which one communist regime after another in Eastern Europe was ousted. They began in Poland and spread to Hungary, East Germany, Bulgaria, Czechoslovakia and Romania. The Berlin Wall fell in November, leading to German reunification a year later.

Aware that if Yeltsin won a contested seat in the new Congress of People's Deputies he would have a popular mandate, the Soviet leader set a trap for his most strident critic. He fixed the rules so that government ministers could stand for election only if they resigned their posts. If his tormentor did run, and if he were defeated, he would be out of a job.

Yeltsin did decide to run when the election was called for March 26, 1989. He put his name forward as a candidate in Moscow's District No. 1, a constituency encompassing the whole city. The Politburo agreed to the novel proposal of holding a 'selection meeting' at which a thousand party members would choose two out of three prospective candidates to represent the capital. Eight hundred of the party members given permission to take part were, by Yeltsin's reckoning, carefully chosen as obedient, brainwashed card-carriers, who had been instructed to favour Yury Brakov, general manager of the ZiL plant. After a meeting that went on until 3.00 a.m., Yeltsin was nominated with more than 50 per cent support and Brakov came second. The card-carriers were not so obedient after all.

His vigour restored, Yeltsin raced around Moscow to crowded election rallies, capitalizing on his underdog status to whip up support. He advocated ending party privileges and allowing people to decide issues by referendum. The party inadvertently added to his mystique by instructing editors to ignore his campaign. A more effective telegraph agency was at work on his behalf – the rumour circuit, which for decades had been the conduit for hard news in the Soviet capital. When a worried Gorbachev approved a Politburo commission to censure Yeltsin for anti-party activities, tens of thousands of outraged voters poured into the streets for the biggest unsanctioned public gathering in Moscow since the Revolution, and the idea was quickly dropped.

Having set democracy and *glasnost* in motion, Gorbachev had to agree to allow a debate on state television between Yeltsin and Brakov, representing the progressive and conservative wings of the Communist Party. The evening it was shown millions tuned in to watch. But not everything was above board. The 'ordinary citizens', who allegedly telephoned the studio and whose questions were passed on to the candidates, were set up. The man who supposedly posed the most hostile question to Yeltsin told reporters next day that he was unaware his name had been used. 'Tell Yeltsin not to worry,' he said. 'I'm going to vote for him anyway.'

On election day candidate Boris Nikolayevich Yeltsin, riding a wave of popular affection, got six million votes, almost nine out of every ten votes cast. Eighty-five per cent of the newly elected deputies to the Congress were members of the party, but it was not much of a party victory. A sizeable minority were disillusioned party radicals like Yeltsin who could not be relied upon to vote in divisions according to the instructions of the Central Committee as in the past. Gorbachev acknowledged that 'the election has shown for whom the bell tolls'. But ungraciously he did not congratulate Yeltsin for three days, and his rival's triumph was barely mentioned in *Pravda*.

Yeltsin had to admit that he had Gorbachev to thank for his political resurrection. Stalin shot awkward comrades, Khrushchev pensioned them off, Brezhnev sent them as ambassadors to distant countries. 'Gorbachev's *perestroika* set a new precedent,' he conceded later. 'A dismissed politician was given the chance to return to political life. New times were on the way, unpredictable and unfamiliar, in which I had to find a place for myself.'

In four years Gorbachev had presided over an extraordinary liberalization of Soviet society. People could march, demonstrate, vote in elections, criticize the party and enjoy a much freer press. By doing so he had, however, unleashed forces that threatened to destroy the party he led. Elected deputies would inevitably respond to the people who voted for them rather than to members of an increasingly unpopular Communist Party apparatus. The conservatives trying to hold him back had no alternative policy, other than a return to the old ways, which meant repression and stagnation.

The People's Congress opened on May 25, 1989, in the Palace of Congresses in the Kremlin. The ten days of debates were televised live, on Gorbachev's orders. He was stunned by the anger and vitriol that poured forth. On the first day viewers heard attacks on the KGB, criticism of Raisa and calls for the removal of Lenin's body from the Red Square Mausoleum. Siberian writer Valentin Rasputin electrified everyone by suggesting that Russia should one day leave the Union.

Deprived for so long of the right to even listen to such criticisms without risking arrest, people across the eleven time zones of the Soviet Union could not tear themselves away from their radio and television sets. Three years after emerging from exile as a dissident, Andrey Sakharov, selected as a deputy for the Academy of Sciences, was able to broadcast to the nation his call for a federal structure to replace the Soviet Union, in order to end the oppression suffered under the Stalinist model. There was outrage across the country when Gorbachev cut off the microphone as Sakharov was calling for a repeal of Article 6 of the Soviet constitution, which guaranteed the leading role of the Communist Party. Though Sakharov had run well over his time, many never forgave Gorbachev this one act of censorship, stilling the voice of conscience that had been silenced for years.

Gorbachev had nevertheless achieved a truly amazing feat in liberalizing debate about the future in a country where people had been gagged for most of the century. For the first time all the opposing and disparate elements of Soviet political life gathered in one place, free to say what they liked: hard-line communists, dissidents, military officers, workers, scientists, academics and intellectuals, not to mention a few Orthodox bishops and Muslim muftis.

Deputies and journalists mixed freely in the huge airy foyer draped with hanging ferns, and at a gigantic buffet with one hundred and forty tables laden with savouries and attended by two hundred and eighty waiters in identical white suits and bow ties. Dazed Politburo members found themselves besieged when they appeared among the crowd. The secretive Soviet leadership was suddenly accessible, and diminished by being seen in the flesh.

The Congress was still subservient to the party and its leader, however. Hundreds of old-style communists had got themselves elected by posing as democrats.

Historian Yury Afanasyev termed the body 'Stalinist-Brezhnevite' in its overall make-up. Yeltsin preferred to term it 'Gorbachevian, faithfully reflecting our chairman's inconsistency, timidity, love of half measures and semi-decisions.'

When it came to the election by the Congress members of a Supreme Soviet, a smaller body that would meet regularly to consider legislation, Yeltsin was consequently overlooked. Crowds came out on the streets of Moscow in a spontaneous protest. A deputy from Siberia, Alexey Kazannik, offered to give up his Supreme Soviet place to make way for Yeltsin. In the end, Gorbachev realized that denying the politician with the biggest single electoral mandate would make the Congress look ridiculous, and ultimately bent the rules to allow him to take his seat in the upper body.

Nothing was the same for Soviet citizens after the *Sturm und Drang* of the Kremlin sessions. 'On the day the Congress opened they were one sort of people,' observed Yeltsin. 'On the day it closed, they were a different people. However negatively we assess the final result ... the most important thing was achieved. Almost the entire population was awakened from its lethargy.'

Yeltsin himself became a different person through his exposure to the radical reformers who gathered around him in the Kremlin foyer. Andrey Sakharov especially made a strong impression. Sakharov did not like Yeltsin but he saw in him a leader for the emerging democrats, one who had a level of support among the proletariat to which members of the intelligentsia could not aspire.

The Congress marked the real start of Yeltsin's political evolution from communist 'stormer' to anti-communist democrat.

Gorbachev noted how unhappy his Politburo comrades were about the whole exercise. 'How could it be otherwise, when it was already clear to everybody that the days of party dictatorship were over!'

From his exile in Vermont, Alexander Solzhenitsyn, the chronicler of the gulag, saw a flicker of hope for his native land. 'Russia lies utterly ravaged and poisoned; its people are in a state of unprecedented humiliation, and are on the brink of perishing physically, perhaps even biologically,' he noted. Now, however, 'having lived through these seventy lethal years inside communism's iron shell, we are crawling out, though barely alive'.

When he went for his summer vacation at Foros on the Black Sea, Mikhail Gorbachev mused aloud to Raisa about his future, wondering whether he should step aside. Now that people had got such a great measure of freedom, let others show that they know how to use it, he suggested. He was not serious, but Raisa was, perhaps sensing what lay ahead. 'It's time, Mikhail Sergeyevich,' she said, 'to devote yourself to private life, to retire and write your memoirs. You've done your job.'

10

December 25: Midday

IN THE KREMLIN, AFTER HIS LUNCH OF SMALL OPEN sandwiches with salami, and cottage cheese with sour cream, Mikhail Gorbachev is overwhelmed with tiredness and the enormity of what he has to do in a few hours. At the back of his office, behind the work table, is a door leading to a small resting room. Inside are a bed and washing facilities. Gorbachev goes in, shuts the door and lies down to rest.

Anatoly Chernyaev and Andrey Grachev find the president's office empty when they enter shortly afterwards with a sheaf of farewell letters for him to sign. They have been dictated by Gorbachev and are addressed to foreign presidents, prime ministers and royalty. The recipients comprise an A list of current and former world leaders whom he has met and befriended during his years in office: George H.W. Bush, Helmut Kohl, François Mitterrand, John Major, Giulio Andreotti, Brian Mulroney, King Juan Carlos and Queen Sofia of Spain, Lech Wałęsa, Václav Havel,

Ronald Reagan, Margaret Thatcher, and the heads of the governments of Korea, Finland, Egypt, Syria, Israel, Iran and Norway. Gorbachev has worked hard to get the tone and content of the letters right. The warm relationship with his counterparts abroad is most important to the Soviet president. It is a measure of his international standing, a recognition of what he has achieved in reforming the Soviet Union, and an assurance of global approval for lessening world tensions, reversing the nuclear arms race, allowing the Berlin Wall to fall and letting Eastern European countries have their freedom.

Chernyaev knocks on the door of the resting room. It takes Gorbachev five minutes to compose himself and come out. He looks fresh and fit but his eyes are teary. Grachev notes a slight redness, caused either by lack of sleep or perhaps the shedding of a few tears provoked by 'the tension of the final days'. The president settles into his high-backed leather chair and carefully reads the letters one by one before signing each with a felt pen. Chernyaev leaves to have them dispatched.

Grachev takes the opportunity to show Gorbachev the front page of *Moskovsky Komsomolets*. It has a headline quoting an 1836 verse by the poet Alexander Pushkin, 'Exegi Monumentum': 'I shall not wholly die.' Gorbachev's eyes light up. He finishes the quotation triumphantly: 'In my sacred lyre, my soul shall outlive my dust and escape corruption.' In common with most Russians, Gorbachev can recite Pushkin and other national poets at length. A few days ago he recalled for some American visitors a narrative by the revolutionary poet Vladimir Mayakovsky, in which one of his characters didn't like the United States and wanted to close it down. Gorbachev wanted to make the point that the Soviet republics had no right to say the USSR was dead. When he is in a mellow mood after a good dinner he is known to entertain guests by declaiming lines from Mayakovsky in a quiet voice – though it is some time since he quoted the famous phrase, 'Lenin lived, Lenin lives and Lenin will live' from Mayakovsky's elegy, 'Vladimir Ilyich Lenin'.

Like many world leaders, Gorbachev has got out of the habit of reading the newspapers himself, preferring that his subordinates provide him with what he needs to know, thus protecting him from negative coverage. Under *glasnost*, censorship was relaxed and newspapers became more daring. Now they provide freewheeling news and commentary, much of it insulting to the outgoing president.

Gorbachev has not yet been shown that day's editions and Chernyaev decides not to upset him by disclosing that they reveal in humiliating detail several aspects of his personal affairs. A report in *Rossiyskaya Gazeta* discloses that at Alma-Ata four days ago Yeltsin and the presidents of the republics discussed Gorbachev's material and financial terms after he steps down as Soviet president.

'Regarding Gorbachev's conditions of retirement,' the writer states, 'Yeltsin announced the following: he will be given a pension equivalent to today's salary, indexed for inflation; he will be given a state dacha but not the one he is in; he will have two state cars and a 20-strong staff, including security, drivers and service. After a vacation he will start his activities in the Gorbachev fund.'

A commentary in the newspaper rubs it in: 'Gorbachev induced chaos, which destroyed the doomed empire . . . and has to pay for it by being withdrawn from the post without pity or sorrow from his fellow politicians and the Soviet people.'

Chernyaev is furious that Yeltsin has leaked – and distorted – the details of his private dealings with Gorbachev. The Russian president has blabbed to editors to let the world know how generous and considerate his behaviour is towards his defeated adversary, and how 'civilized' his last meeting with Gorbachev had been – a nine-hour session on Monday at which they hammered out the terms of Gorbachev's departure from political life. The reports say that Gorbachev was too demanding and Yeltsin had to reduce 'by ten times', from two hundred to twenty, the number of staff he wanted to retain. The claim 'is a lie because Gorbachev didn't ask for two hundred people', Chernyaev writes in his diary. There are other things 'in the same nasty style'. It adds insult to injury, he feels, that the amount of Gorbachev's pension has been bandied about, apparently with unconcealed relish, among the leaders of the republics, former allies who used to show Gorbachev deference, but who now regard him with contempt. Some wanted to give him nothing.

He is also privately dumbfounded by the way Gorbachev too is portraying his last conversation with Yeltsin on Monday as civilized. It is an illusion,

Chernyaev believes, to talk about that meeting, as Gorbachev does, as if it had been conducted in a normal fashion, as if between comrades, and '*as if nothing happened*', when it was in fact an exercise in condescension and triumphalism on Yeltsin's part. Chernyaev admires 'the unrivalled courage and self-control that Gorbachev has demonstrated in situations of premeditated humiliation and disrespect towards his achievements and his name, all under an avalanche of disgusting mendacity and mockery'. At the same time he is somewhat resentful of the president's obsession with his own fate. He helped Gorbachev draw up the terms for his retirement. 'But what about me? He didn't even take care of my pension. Tomorrow Mikhail Sergeyevich will deliver his farewell and we will be out of our posts. Where should I go to apply for my pension, which district office? Mikhail Sergeyevich is talking about his "RAND-type corporation" and says, don't worry, there will be a place for everyone. He was very cheerful and optimistic. Money will flow, he says. I don't believe this and I don't want it. I would like to feel free but what money will I live on? I don't have any savings.'

The 'RAND-type corporation' is the foundation that Gorbachev plans to set up after retirement and that will in fact provide jobs for Chernyaev and other senior members of his staff after they leave the Kremlin.

The Kremlin staff know that Gorbachev is already a wealthy man. One day last week he stunned Chernyaev and Alexander Yakovlev by confiding to them that he had received an $800,000 advance from a German publisher for his autobiography, *Memoirs*. 'You know, Anatoly,' Gorbachev had said. 'I want to keep $200,000 for myself and give you $30,000 to $40,000.'

'There's no need to do that, I don't need that,' Chernyaev had replied.

Yakovlev counselled Gorbachev to put aside about $600,000 for establishing the Gorbachev fund and to attract matching contributions from other donors. He and Chernyaev 'with one voice' advised him not to give anything to various hospitals as it would be wasted, and to hold on to a substantial sum as 'you have to live in dignity further on without going to Yeltsin asking for money'.

Gorbachev, however, is well aware of his money raising powers. On a visit to South Korea in April, President Roh Tae-woo proffered, and he accepted, an envelope containing $100,000, an extraordinary act on both their parts at a first meeting. Gorbachev gave the money to his chief of staff Valery Boldin for transfer to a children's hospital. He knows that after his retirement there will be an avalanche of requests for well-paid appearances and lectures from around the world.

Chernyaev, a war veteran with full moustache under a pudgy nose, feels the indignities of being forced from office as much as Gorbachev. He believes that, like his boss, he is also about to become unemployed. The ultimate loyal insider, he sees Gorbachev every day, plying him with memos on personnel and policy matters, sitting in on meetings with foreign leaders and taking notes, free to speak his mind and criticize. Always cheerful, never ruffled, he is the only official whom the very private Gorbachevs have taken regularly to their vacation dacha at Foros on the Black Sea, where he has ghost-written much of Gorbachev's books and essays extolling his reforms. The president's English-language interpreter, Pavel Palazchenko, regards Chernyaev as the 'unsung hero' of *perestroika*. Chernyaev's pro-reform views were shaped during three years working in Czechoslovakia where he saw Soviet tanks turning back the tide of reform in 1968.

Leaving his Kremlin post means losing much more than income for the seventy-year-old Chernyaev. He no longer will have the opportunity to combine family life at his home in Vesnina Street near Moscow University on the city's western outskirts with visits to his mistress, Lyudmila Pavlovna, who lives conveniently close to the Kremlin in Malaya Gruzinskaya Street. Late in the evening, 'having dropped off milk at home and having lied about where I was going', Chernyaev would regularly hurry off to be with his beloved Lyuda. All he ever wanted, he notes in his diary, was really just to have a good life.

He sees an irony in the fact that the coming of political freedom for Russia means a loss of his personal freedom to spend time with his lover. 'I have to get used to "freedom",' he writes in his diary. 'But you can't be free when you have family . . . Would that I had enough strength to spit at everything and go to the woman I love, but the woman would want me always to be cheerful and assured, she would want me to have a good job, she would not want me to be like a dependant, or a poor person who comes for consolation.' He is also wary of competition for his mistress. Alexander Bovin, just dispatched to Israel by Gorbachev as the last Soviet ambassador, also tried to court Lyuda but, writes Chernyaev with satisfaction, 'with little success'.

Chernyaev is as licentious as his master is prudish. In 1972 he accompanied Gorbachev, then a young regional party secretary, on a trip to Amsterdam and dragged him to sex shops and an adult cinema to watch an X-rated movie. Gorbachev 'was embarrassed by what he saw, perhaps even revolted'. The future party leader kept tugging his aide's sleeve, and insisted instead on talking about how to fix the problems in Stavropol.

Lyuda is the final passion of the lothario who works with Gorbachev, the last woman who, as he puts it, graciously allows him one-night stands. Several years after leaving the Kremlin, the ageing mandarin with high testosterone levels will publish a treatise about his obsession with the opposite sex, called *Eternal Woman*. In its pages Chernyaev muses among other things about how he could get an erection at some times and at other times not. 'Now in the 77th year of life, this (penis) can give up any time,' he ruminates in the book. 'And then that's it. The old man is finished! Lyuda is gone! Love, happiness and the meaning of life all disappear. That's it! Close the shop!' The publication earns him the title of 'Playboy in the Kremlin' in a review by Gennady Gerasimov, published in *Sovetskaya Belorussiya*.

Yegor Yakovlev arrives in the Senate Building to help supervise the media coverage of Gorbachev's resignation address. The former editor of *Moscow*

News and now head of the state television and radio company, Gosteleradio, Yakovlev has a notorious temper but around Gorbachev his avuncular face with arched eyebrows, white hair and outsize spectacles is a comforting presence on the final day.

Aware of the historical importance of recording Gorbachev's last hours as president, Yakovlev has brought veteran Russian writer and filmmaker Igor Belyaev into the Kremlin to make his own documentary alongside the small ABC television crew.

Belyaev and Gorbachev have known each other since they were at Moscow State University together. The documentary-maker is deeply appreciative of what his fellow alumnus has achieved in liberalizing the communist state. He is close to Gorbachev and feels 'like his ally, that I was helping him'. It occurs to him that they are both part of a lost generation, born too late to become war veterans, and too early to become cosmonauts, for whom Gorbachev is 'the figurehead, the main representative of our views, of what we essentially are'. He tells Gorbachev that he remembers him as little short of a dissident at university, though the president thinks this is overstating it. 'Obviously I was not a dissident at all,' Gorbachev protests, 'although I already felt a burgeoning criticism of our reality.'

Gorbachev tells his old friend, 'At this important point in history, the most important thing is to overcome it without blood, without reds fighting whites. Society is pregnant with an explosion. If, God forbid, there is political madness and score-settling when people are suffering so much, there will be huge consequences.'

Yegor Yakovlev fears, however, that the Belyaev narrative has little chance of being shown on Russian television, because the pro-Yeltsin executives at Gosteleradio are highly sensitive to the perils of paying special attention to Gorbachev. 'Television is being taken away from me,' Yakovlev complains helplessly to Gorbachev's aides. 'I am no longer master there. Yeltsin's people are ruling the roost.'

It was Yegor Yakovlev who recommended that ABC be brought into the heart of the Kremlin in the final days. He advised the president to 'pick one foreign network from all those demanding access to a moment of world history'. They settled on ABC *Nightline* as one of the most respected and influential US television news programmes. ABC also has a record of connecting Soviet leaders to American audiences, and Ted Koppel, who speaks Russian, has got to know Gorbachev and his aides quite well.

For his part Gorbachev appreciates how popular he is in the United States and how useful it will be to have the world watching, via the lens of an American television camera, how the transition is being conducted. Who knows how the unpredictable Boris Yeltsin would behave otherwise.

Both Gorbachev and Yeltsin, from their different perspectives, see the United States as their ally in the dying days of the Soviet Union. Gorbachev has been cheered on by US president George H. W. Bush, who would prefer the devil he knows – an intact and supplicant Soviet Union – to a chaotic group of new countries, some with nuclear weapons on their territory. Yeltsin is anxious to present the responsible face of the new Russia to the United States, as he needs its assistance to make the historic switch from communism to capitalism. Both are vying to influence American and global opinion for their own purposes and standing.

No one is more surprised than Koppel himself that he has been allowed into the heart of the Kremlin, free to roam around and film in a sanctum of power to which correspondents rarely if ever got access. The chairman of ABC News, Roone Arledge, had sent him to Moscow in mid-December to try to grab an interview with Gorbachev before he resigned, if that was to be his fate. Instead Koppel had been offered exclusive foreign rights to record the last days in office of the Soviet president.

Chernyaev encounters the ABC crew in Gorbachev's outer office. He thinks how 'shameful for us that only foreign television journalists were running around us representing the significance of Gorbachev for the whole world, a significance which the Western public fairly gives him . . . If it wasn't for Yegor Yakovlev bringing in ABC during those last days, who literally lived in the corridors filming everything they came across, there would have been an information blackout up to the very end of his presence in the Kremlin.'

Grachev believes that the president is also very conscious that these last days in the Kremlin are part of world history, and 'that's why he accepted the argument it should be recorded for history'. The fifty-year-old silver-haired veteran of the Communist Party's international department has been by Gorbachev's side since

1985, first as a foreign policy adviser and since the attempted coup in August as his press secretary. He sees a comparison between Koppel and the American communist writer John Reed, who chronicled the 1917 October Revolution in his book *Ten Days That Shook the World*. According to Grachev, 'The intention was that Koppel should be the John Reed of the day. Some seventy-four years earlier Reed witnessed the birth of Soviet Russia from the inside. Koppel came to witness the final hours of that Revolution.'

After a couple of days, observed Grachev, Kaplan and Koppel 'blended into the walls of the Kremlin so completely that even the guards stopped paying attention to them'. The two Americans are surprised to find that Russian journalists are showing scant interest in Gorbachev's departure. 'They were really nervous being around Gorbachev,' recalled Kaplan. 'They knew the Soviet Union was ended. The Soviets were leaving the Kremlin and the Russians were getting ready to march in and they wanted to show allegiance to the next government.'

They are also surprised at how little the Soviet president has to do of an official nature in his last days. Once when Kaplan was in the Kremlin with associate ABC producer Holly Petersen, Gorbachev said to them, 'Come in, meet my cabinet.' They were brought into a big room to find his ministers sitting there, and Gorbachev gave him a two-hour interview in their presence. None of it ever got shown on television.

The Americans at first reckoned on being back in the United States for the holidays, but having accepted the Kremlin's offer of unlimited access, they are at the mercy of history's timetable. The *Nightline* presenter swore to his family he would be home by Christmas Day and when he broke the news that they were stuck in Moscow, 'my wife didn't speak to me for a day!' Kaplan too finds himself in his family's bad books. At one point he calls home using the satellite phone with unfolding dish he carries in a little briefcase. 'My wife is yelling at me – it's Christmas time, holidays, children on vacation!'

Gorbachev overhears and offers to take the phone, saying in English, 'I talk.'

'You don't want to do this!' replies Kaplan.

Gorbachev asks, 'Why is she angry?'

Kaplan explains, 'I am a week here and I am still not going home.'

Gorbachev laughs and says, 'If it was me, Raisa would kill me!'

Gorbachev later borrows the satellite phone to call his own wife. Kaplan thinks that he takes it because he is wary about using his own telephone in the Kremlin. The Soviet president can trust no one now.

11

Knee-deep in Kerosene

WITH HIS NAME DOMINATING GLOBAL HEADLINES after his election to the Soviet Congress, Boris Yeltsin decided in late summer 1989 that it was time for him to see the world and look at how other systems worked. He accepted an invitation to go on a lecture tour sponsored by the secretive Esalen Institute, a Californian non-profit foundation 'dedicated to the exploration of human potential' whose leaders were close to the US administration.

Visiting America for the first time turned out to be a life-changing experience for Yeltsin, revealing to him the human potential and dynamism of a different ideology.

He was astonished by New York. As a construction expert he was awed at the majestic skyscrapers, and he marvelled at the cheapness, quality and speed of service in the restaurants. He found Americans 'wonderfully open, sincere and friendly, industrious and intelligent'. He was mesmerized by the cornucopia of food in

Randall's Grocery store, a supermarket in Houston, Texas, which he dropped into unannounced with his assistant Lev Sukhanov on his way to the airport after visiting the Lyndon B. Johnson Space Center. They had never seen such a place. It had 30,000 items, countless varieties of sausage, no queues and a woman at the checkout reading the prices with a device like a hairdryer. There he had an epiphany. He concluded that the sole purpose of the Iron Curtain was to prevent Soviet citizens knowing what was on the other side, as it would be too much for them to endure.

'Look to what limits we have brought our people,' he complained to Sukhanov as they flew on to Miami, deeply depressed at what he had seen. 'We were told fables!' Sukhanov observed that 'after Houston, in a plane provided by a millionaire, Yeltsin's belief in the Bolshevik idea was finally destroyed. During those minutes he decided to leave the party and start fighting for supreme power in Russia.'

Yeltsin's public lectures in the United States were well received, except the one scheduled at Johns Hopkins University in Baltimore on September 12. The Russian was drunk when he arrived late on September 11 aboard a private plane supplied by David Rockefeller. 'It was the most astonishing scene I have ever witnessed,' recalled his US host, Jim Garrison, executive director of Esalen's Soviet–American Exchange Program, which engaged in non-governmental diplomacy with Soviet counterparts. Garrison, an admirer of Gorbachev, came to dislike Gorbachev's 'forceful, primitive and highly erratic' rival, who was 'completely consumed with a dark passion' for overthrowing the Soviet leader. 'The president of Johns Hopkins was there to greet Yeltsin, and a young lady with a bunch of roses. When he came down the steps, Yeltsin turned round and urinated on the back tyre of the plane.' Yeltsin was bundled into his hotel where he spent the night drinking Jack Daniel's. He was so intoxicated the next morning he could hardly stand, said Garrison. Yeltsin managed to give his lecture but 'with the students laughing at him, not with him'.

As Yeltsin was struggling through his speech at Johns Hopkins, the White House called to say that the Soviet deputy, who had requested a meeting with President Bush, would be granted a session at 11.30 a.m. in the White House with national security adviser Brent Scowcroft, with the possibility that Bush might 'drop by'. Bush did not want to offend Gorbachev by giving his fiercest critic anything resembling a summit meeting in Washington, particularly at a time when he and the Soviet leader were working together to achieve a number of American goals, such as the withdrawal of Soviet troops from Eastern Europe. The party drove at speed to Washington and arrived at 12.15 p.m.

'Jim, you are late,' said Bush's special assistant Condoleezza Rice.

'Condi, you have no idea,' replied Garrison.

Yeltsin at first refused to enter the White House unless Bush would guarantee to meet him. He protested, 'I am an important man in my country.' But when told Scowcroft would not wait, he crossed the threshold.

The national security adviser greeted him truculently with the question, 'What is the meaning of your trip to Washington?'

Yeltsin retorted, 'You want to know the meaning of life?'

The White House official and his deputy Robert Gates were treated to what Gates later described as an 'excruciatingly monotonous presentation' from the boorish visitor. Scowcroft at one point closed his eyes as if sleeping. When Vice President Dan Quayle dropped by, Yeltsin stared at him hard and long without speaking until Quayle left, crushed. Bush at last appeared in the room. The Russian, suddenly stone-cold sober, proceeded to give an earnest account of the situation back home. Later White House sources told reporters that the visitor was a lightweight with no political future, who had made 'off-the-wall' predictions about the Soviet Union's collapse.

Tipped off about the Russian's behaviour, the *Washington Post* published a colourful account of 'Yeltsin's Smashing Day'. It was lifted by Italian journalist Vittorio Zucconi and embellished for an article that appeared in the Italian tabloid newspaper *La Repubblica* on September 14. Zucconi wrote that, for Yeltsin, America was a bar five thousand kilometres long and that he had drunk six bottles of spirits and numerous cocktails and embarked on a wild shopping spree. It was partly an invention, based on the *Post* article and the correspondent's conception of how a full-blooded Russian might behave on his first visit to the United States. The *La Repubblica* article was brought to the attention of

Gorbachev who encouraged *Pravda* to republish it. It duly appeared on September 18 in the party organ, complete with every lurid detail.

This latest attempt to discredit the people's hero again backfired. Copies of *Pravda* were burned in Red Square by irate Muscovites who saw it as another dirty trick to pull down the one politician they felt they could trust. Three days later, after *Pravda* editorial staff had checked out the story themselves and found it to be partly invented, the paper was forced to apologize – the first ever retraction by the communist flagship.

Subsequently, however, after Yeltsin returned to Moscow, Soviet television obtained footage of him slurring his words at the Baltimore event. Under orders from Gorbachev's aides, the progressive head of state television Mikhail Nenashev was forced to broadcast it nationwide at prime time, though he was against putting it on air at all and took care to include shots of Yeltsin arriving home with a gift of 100,000 disposable syringes for hospitals. Yeltsin claimed the tape was deliberately slowed down by the KGB to make him look intoxicated, though even his supporters inside Soviet television doubted that this was true. Nevertheless, the episode deepened Yeltsin's hatred for Gorbachev and Gorbachev's contempt for his adversary.

A week after the *Pravda* story appeared, Yeltsin found himself at the centre of another embarrassing controversy. Some time after ten o'clock on the exceptionally cold, dry evening of September 28, he appeared soaking wet at the guard post of the Uspenskoye government dacha compound. He told the militiamen there that he had dismissed his driver and was walking the last three hundred metres to visit an old friend, carrying a bunch of flowers, when unidentified men threw him off a bridge into the Moscow River. Alerted by one of the militiamen, his daughter Tanya telephoned Alexander Korzhakov, who grabbed some warm clothes, a bottle of spirits and some apples and drove to the militia post in his Niva. Yeltsin's security chief found his boss lying motionless by an electric heater. He was blue with cold 'as if ink was poured over him', and wearing only wet briefs. His suit was hanging on a nail with blood and grass stains.

Yeltsin told him that after his official car was driven off, four big men shoved him into the back of a red Zhiguli and dropped him from the bridge with a sack tied over his head. He would have drowned if he had not managed to free himself.

The guards made a report, and interior minister Vadim Bakatin took note of Yeltsin's statement. Two weeks later Bakatin recounted the story to the Supreme Soviet, with Gorbachev in the chair. There was a flurry of press interest, with speculation ranging from the possibility that Yeltsin was visiting his mistress – a cook in a dacha whose occupant was away – and that she had doused him with a bucket of water (the cook denied an affair), or that there was a KGB plot to kill or embarrass him, or even that he had showed up un-invited at a birthday party in Nikolay Ryzhkov's nearby dacha which Gorbachev was attending and KGB guards had been told to teach him a lesson. Looking back years later, Korzhakov was still at a loss about what happened. The river was only a metre deep, he recalled. 'It was a joke to think he would have drowned, and Yeltsin was telling me the water was over his head.'

Gorbachev taunted Yeltsin about the incident in a televised exchange at the Supreme Soviet. But most people in Moscow preferred again to give Yeltsin the benefit of the doubt. He was a flesh-and-blood Russian, one of them, who drank hard, fell into rivers, spoke out and took the consequences. The more he was attacked by the organs of communism, the more were ordinary Muscovites convinced that he was their man.

On the evening of December 14, 1989, Andrey Sakharov, the intellectual force for change in Russia who complemented Yeltsin's crude political force, died from a heart attack. The former dissident was eulogized by a guilty nation that realized it had lost its moral compass. His body was laid out in the Academy of Sciences building and tens of thousands of mourners queued in heavy snow to file past the bier. Gorbachev and other Politburo members came and stood briefly to pay their respects to the honest scientist whom they had kept in internal exile as a dissident. Boris Yeltsin stood motionless for several minutes by his body, as if absorbing his spirit and acknowledging his new role as undisputed leader of the opposition in a fast-changing Russia. Yeltsin was now the most prominent member of the loose collection of radicals known as the Interregional Group of Deputies, which had held some chaotic, freewheeling sessions since it was formed in a Moscow hotel lobby during the summer to press for speedier reform.

Before Sakharov was interred in the Vostryakovskoye Cemetery, over one hundred thousand people attended a funeral rally in a slushy car park at which calls for the end of the Communist Party's monopoly predominated. Commuters in a passing train opened windows to shout and wave encouragement. The public mood was becoming more defiant of authority. Such displays boded ill for a party that relied on control of an apathetic people to remain in power.

Gorbachev pressed on with the reform process. He encouraged the fifteen republics of the Soviet Union to hold their own democratic elections to make their leaders more accountable to the people. Parliaments already existed in each republic, but the poll results were always fixed by the communist bosses and the legislatures had little power to legislate.

Individual elections for all the republics were scheduled for March 4, 1990. The campaign in Russia was marked by enormous pro-democracy rallies in support of Yeltsin as a candidate for the Russian Congress of People's Deputies. For the first time, pre-revolutionary Russian flags and anti-communist slogans appeared among the demonstrators. Fear of the KGB and police was rapidly evaporating. Things had gone too far for repression of political views, especially when the electoral process bore the stamp of party approval.

Over eight thousand candidates stood for one thousand and sixty-eight seats in the Russian Congress. Gorbachev joked as he and Raisa cast their ballots that he had set up a party committee at his home to decide whom to support. He also warned reporters that the process had its limits. To split up the Soviet Union would risk the type of chaos that accompanied the Cultural Revolution in China.

Boris Yeltsin ran in Sverdlovsk District No. 74. He advocated an elected president, a multi-party system, and a separate central bank and military units for the Russian republic. As for other republics like Lithuania, which were pressing for secession, let them leave the Union if they wished, he declared. This would weaken the centre and give the Russian people a greater ability to decide their own fate. It would also weaken Gorbachev, who commanded the centre, an outcome that Yeltsin found equally, if not more, attractive.

Greeted by wildly enthusiastic fans everywhere he went, Yeltsin was elected with 84 per cent of the vote in his constituency, defeating eleven other candidates. He had drawn on a deep well of discontent with the failure of communism to feed and clothe its people decently, and on the perception that Russia was exploited by the other fourteen republics, where people lived better lives.

In response, Gorbachev resolved to strengthen and secure his own power and ward off his increasingly menacing rival. He persuaded the Soviet Congress of People's Deputies to select by secret ballot a president of the Soviet Union for a five-year term – himself, of course – followed by direct nationwide elections for future presidents. Gorbachev got himself elevated to the presidency at a special session in the Kremlin Palace of Congresses on March 15, 1990, but with only 59 per cent support, mainly due to a partial boycott. The narrowness of the vote drew gasps of astonishment.

Vitaly Korotich speculated in an editorial in *Ogonyok* that in the secret ballot many party *apparatchiks* who paid lip service to *perestroika* had ganged up with radicals to vote against Gorbachev. 'The former see Gorbachev as Allende, the latter as Pinochet,' he said.

The day after the vote, Gorbachev returned to the Congress and took an oath to the constitution of the USSR at a table flanked by a three-metre-long red flag with a golden hammer and sickle and a gold-bordered red star in its upper canton, the official emblem of the USSR. He got the briefest of standing ovations and retreated upstairs for a quiet glass of champagne with Raisa and aide Georgy Shakhnazarov. He was now President Gorbachev, head of state, the leader of the party in what was still a one-party state, commander-in-chief of the armed forces, and the chief executive of one of the world's two superpowers. He ordered the KGB security service to ensure that in future a red flag be placed in a special floor holder next to him wherever he might be, in the manner of American presidents. He had the words *Sovetsky Soyuz* (Soviet Union) painted on the side of the presidential plane. He set up a presidential council to which he appointed long-time aides, including Valery Boldin, whom he also promoted to chief of staff.

Paradoxically Gorbachev had less authority than ever. He was tainted now by retaining the leadership of the discredited Communist Party, whose Stalinist institutions were proving allergic to change, and this deepened his unpopularity. He was becoming isolated in a shrinking middle ground. He was even under surveillance from his own secret police, a conclusion reached by Korotich after a bizarre incident in the Kremlin. Gorbachev summoned the editor to his office and threw a tantrum about *Ogonyok*'s 'unfair' coverage of Ligachev, 'but as he screamed, his eyes remained calm and benign, and Alexander Yakovlev sat by, grinning'. It was done for show. 'I'm convinced he was bugged,' said Korotich, 'and that he knew it.'

Gorbachev's popularity had suffered the previous year when Soviet troops used sappers' spades and gas to attack a peaceful nationalist demonstration in the Georgian capital, Tbilisi, resulting in twenty deaths. Gorbachev claimed that the decision to use force was made by the Georgian leadership without consulting him, and years later he would blame Soviet defence minister Dmitry Yazov for giving the order to a local general. Many did not believe him, and now in April 1990 in Sverdlovsk he hardened his stance against nationalism, vowing that he would never let the Baltics leave the Soviet Union. He also blustered in the same speech that Yeltsin was finished as a politician.

However, it was Gorbachev who was in decline. The new Soviet president was humiliated on May 1, 1990, when the pro-reform Moscow Club of Electors joined the end of the official May Day parade in Red Square. After the usual disciplined march-past of grateful workers chanting official slogans, thousands of raucous, angry, disrespectful Muscovites appeared carrying banners reading 'Gorbachev, resign' and 'Down with the cult of Lenin'. Marchers with Lithuanian and Ukrainian flags stopped in front of Gorbachev to whistle and jeer. The benign expressions on the faces of the Politburo members on the Lenin Mausoleum turned to granite.

State television always continued live coverage of Red Square parades as long as the leaders remained on the Mausoleum. Now, these mortifying scenes were being broadcast to 150 million viewers across the USSR. The transmission was only stopped when a television director ran screaming into the studio to shut it down. After a few minutes of confusion, Gorbachev led his comrades off the platform, his shoulders hunched and his fedora hat pulled down, and ordered an investigation of the 'political hooligans'. His flirtation with the democrats was over.

Raisa Gorbacheva felt the anger not just of the democrats but of the party conservatives who believed her husband was destroying their careers. When she went to the district party committee to pay her dues she was appalled at the local party secretary's spiteful attitude towards her. 'I really feel he hated us,' she confided to Pavel Palazchenko. 'They will never forgive Mikhail Sergeyevich.'

Yeltsin meanwhile was being carried forward on a wave of pro-Russian nationalism. On May 17, 1990, a damp, overcast late spring day, the first freely elected Russian Congress since before the Revolution met in the Great Kremlin Palace. The interior was dominated by the immense, theatrical picture by Boris Ioganson of *Lenin's Speech at the Third Congress of the Komsomol*. The white, blue and red flag of the provisional government of Alexander Kerensky which briefly ruled Russia in 1917 was carried into the debating chamber, and deputies responded with a standing ovation of several minutes. The tricolour, which originated as a naval and military ensign at the end of the seventeenth century in imitation of the Dutch colours, and was first recognized as the flag of Russia in 1896, was banished after the October Revolution. More than anything else, its reappearance symbolized the beginning of the end of the seven-decades-long experiment in social engineering based on Karl Marx's idea of a workers' state. A couple of years earlier people would have been arrested for displaying it.

Most of the deputies were party members, with views ranging from neo-Stalinist to radical democrat, but almost all were united in a desire to carve out greater sovereignty for Russia within the Soviet Union.

Yeltsin put himself forward for election as chairman of the presidium, in effect Russia's head of state. Gorbachev let it be known he favoured Alexander Vlasov, an uninspiring government functionary who was less threatening as a political rival. Though not an elected member, Gorbachev came to the Russian chamber to intimidate the deputies by his presence. He insisted that the president's flag of the Union be placed beside him to symbolize his new status. The only seat where the flag could be accommodated was in the balcony perched high above the chamber like a royal box. From there Gorbachev descended at intervals to lecture deputies on the risks of voting for his former comrade. From the podium he accused Yeltsin of abandoning socialist principles and working for the destruction of the Soviet Union.

In the Congress 40 per cent of deputies were solidly for Yeltsin and 40 per cent against. The remaining 20 per cent – known as the 'swamp' – resented Gorbachev's interference and leaned towards Yeltsin. On May 29 the Siberian won a secret ballot with five hundred and thirty-five votes, four more than the absolute majority required. For the first time Gorbachev had failed to get his preferred candidate elected for a leadership post in the Soviet Union.

Gorbachev learned the result while reclining in one of the leather seats in the blue and white Soviet presidential airliner midway across the Atlantic, en route to Ottawa and a summit meeting in Washington with President Bush. His aides drafted a conciliatory telegram of congratulations, acknowledging, 'You have shown yourself to be a real fighter.' Gorbachev rejected it, saying Yeltsin didn't need that kind of backhanded compliment. Though he conceded that they were now going to have to negotiate with Yeltsin, he didn't congratulate the winner for a week.

In the United States, President Bush received Gorbachev at the White House, and they travelled together by helicopter the fifty miles to Camp David. They were hemmed in by two plainclothes officers: an American air force major with a metallic Zero Halliburton briefcase in a black leather casing strapped to his wrist, and a Russian colonel with a little black suitcase also attached to his forearm – the respective doomsday devices for the two presidents to launch nuclear war against each other.

At Camp David Gorbachev drove Bush around in a golf cart. His driving on a par with Yeltsin's, he almost overturned it to avoid a tree, as the colonels careened along behind them. Over a lunch of hot sorrel soup, Bush asked Gorbachev about Yeltsin's new role in Soviet politics. Yeltsin is not a 'serious person', retorted the Soviet president. 'He's become a destroyer.'

The destroyer was meanwhile enjoying his spoils. After his election as chairman of the Russian parliament, Yeltsin and his loyal sidekick Lev Sukhanov took the lift to the fifth floor of the Russian White House to occupy the office of the previous title-holder. They were amazed to find it was as big as a dance hall. 'I have seen many an office in my life,' Yeltsin related, 'but I got a pleasant tingle from the soft modern sheen, all the shininess and comfort.' Sukhanov said in wonderment, 'Look, Boris Nikolayevich, what an office we've seized!' Yeltsin had a subversive thought that frightened him. 'We haven't just seized an office. We've seized an entire Russia!' His campaign against perks notwithstanding, he soon took over for his own use a well-staffed mansion previously used as a vacation retreat of the Russian Council of Ministers in Arkhangelskoye.

On settling into work, Yeltsin dismissed the KGB guards assigned to the office and installed his ex-KGB pal Alexander Korzhakov at the head of a new security unit. For the first few days the corridors outside his vast office were strangely quiet. The staff of the old administration went into hiding, expecting that Yeltsin would fire them too and put in his own people. Yeltsin called the employees together and told them he would keep them on if they wished. Most stayed.

There was a whiff of cordite in the air as the confrontation with Gorbachev sharpened. Yeltsin and his staff began acquiring weapons for personal protection, helped by sympathizers in the Soviet defence and interior ministries. Within a year, he later reckoned, his security directorate had collected sixty assault rifles, a hundred pistols, two bullet-proof jackets and five Austrian walkie-talkies.

Though leader of a country almost twice the size of the United States, Yeltsin had little power. He could not raise taxes. He had no army. He was unable to speak to the people on state television, which was still controlled by the Kremlin. *Glasnost* had not advanced to the point at which political opponents of the USSR leadership could command time on the airwaves. The Russian Supreme Soviet remained what it had always been – a decoration, part of a Soviet-era fiction that republics governed themselves, whereas in reality they had no control over people or resources.

Yeltsin and his deputies were determined to change that. They hoped to take some power away from the centre, and establish enough sovereignty to get Russia out of its economic crisis. He proposed that Russia's laws should be made superior to Soviet laws, and take precedence on the territory of Russia, a popular move even with the conservative Russian deputies. 'There were numerous options,' Yeltsin recounted, 'but we had only one – to win!'

On June 12, 1990, the parliament adopted a Declaration of Sovereignty of the RSFSR by a vote of nine hundred and seven votes to thirteen against and nine abstentions. The vote was greeted by a standing ovation. The date would be celebrated in future as Russia Day. Yeltsin would reflect in time that 'as soon as the word *sovereignty* resounded in the air, the clock of history once again began ticking and all attempts to stop it were doomed. The last hour of the Soviet empire was chiming.'

All over the USSR in the weeks that followed, other republics took their cue from Russia and proclaimed their sovereignty in a wave of nationalism. In many republics the campaign for greater independence was supported not just by nationalists but by hard-line members of the communist *nomenklatura*, who fretted about Gorbachev's threatening reform policies and wanted to grab power for themselves.

Gorbachev's *perestroika* had by now created a situation in which the USSR could be preserved only by a new union treaty, or by military force.

The immensity of what was happening gave Yeltsin 'a bad case of the shakes'. The system could no longer crush him openly, he believed, but 'it was quite capable of quietly eating us, bit by bit'. It could sabotage his actions, and him. Gorbachev still controlled the KGB, the interior ministry, the foreign ministry, the Central Bank, state television and other instruments of control. He was commander of the armed forces, the ultimate arbiter in a physical struggle for power.

But Gorbachev was losing the people. By

mid-summer 1990, most Russians had stopped paying heed to his speeches. Life was not improving. After five years waiting for a 'crucial turning point' that was never reached, people were dismissing his lectures as *mnogo slov*, so many words, a lot of hot air. Behind his back, party secretaries were calling him *Narciss*, the Narcissist. (Gorbachev's secretaries termed Yeltsin *Brevno*, or the Log, the Russian equivalent of 'thick as a plank'.) The shops and liquor stores were still empty.

When Gorbachev made a typical long-winded address to the 28th Congress of the Communist Party in the Kremlin Palace of Congresses on July 2, 1990, almost nobody was listening. 'There are voices which say that in all our failures *perestroika* is to blame – this is simply rubbish,' he said, his eyes glinting behind steel-rimmed spectacles as he surveyed the rows of fidgeting party officials and hard-jawed military generals among the delegates. 'The abandoned state of our farms . . . the massive ecological problems . . . the national and ethnic problems . . . have not arisen yesterday but have their roots in the past . . . We must continue with *perestroika*.' He got five seconds of desultory applause.

It was Gorbachev's turn to sit stone-faced as Yegor Ligachev, defence minister Dmitry Yazov and KGB chief Vladimir Kryuchkov – whom Gorbachev had appointed in the belief that he was a reformer – won thunderous applause as one after another they denounced 'anti-socialist elements' in the party. Their real target was Gorbachev himself, who had privately admitted to Shakhnazarov not long before that he was 'close to social democracy'. For communists, there was nothing worse than a social democrat.

The most 'anti-socialist element', Boris Yeltsin, instinctively knew that power was draining away from the ruling party. He staged yet another dramatic démarche. He went to the podium to declare that as chairman of the Russian parliament he preferred 'to bow to the will of all the people' rather than follow the instructions of the party. He was therefore suspending his membership. He made a show of turning in his red cardboard party card, No. 03823301, issued by the Sverdlovsk party committee on March 17, 1961. To shouts of 'Shame!' Yeltsin strode from the hall. He was convinced he had inflicted a severe blow against Gorbachev, who watched his 'ostentatious exit' from the platform.

The Russian leader was followed out by several radicals, including Anatoly Sobchak, soon to be mayor of Leningrad, whose staff included the future president of Russia, Vladimir Putin. Still at that time an officer of the KGB, Putin would not turn in his party card for another year and a half.

Gorbachev had few illusions about the calibre of the party hacks left behind after the walkout or about their hatred of him. Following a meeting with regional party secretaries he privately cursed the 'self-interested scum that don't want anything except a feeding trough and power'. But he resisted the urging of Alexander Yakovlev and Anatoly Chernyaev to resign as general secretary and follow Yeltsin out of the party, fearing this could split society and risk civil war. As Chernyaev later put it, 'Only Yeltsin, with his animal instinct, heard the distant thunder of history.'

'You must understand me,' Gorbachev explained to Chernyaev. 'I can't let this lousy, rabid dog off the leash. If I do that, all this huge structure will be turned against me.' He had to keep the colossus of conservatism under control or it would overthrow *perestroika*. The alternatives were to cooperate with the power-hungry Yeltsin in administering a dose of shock therapy to the economy, which would involve giving the republics more freedom and risk a coup by empire loyalists, or to throw in his lot with the conservatives and try to coerce the Soviet republics into the kind of submission that Stalin had achieved. Whatever option he chose, it was clear that the USSR was in deep crisis.

The Soviet president was also painfully aware of the problem in having so many nationalities to govern. He once cited to Margaret Thatcher the well-known quip by Charles de Gaulle about the difficulty of governing a country with more than one hundred and twenty different kinds of cheese. How much harder it was to run a country with one hundred and twenty different nationalities, Gorbachev said. 'Yes, especially if there is no cheese,' ad-libbed one of his aides.

Gorbachev wanted to proceed slowly, bringing the hardliners with him. He summoned newspaper editors for a private meeting at which he blasted the radicals in the Soviet Congress, singling out Yeltsin by name, and referring with contempt to their programme of 'a multi-party system, the right to leave the USSR, a market economy, free press, everyone doing whatever they please . . .'. Such concepts, less than two years before they all came to pass, were still unthinkable, even outrageous, to rank and file members of the party. 'We are knee-deep in kerosene,' Gorbachev warned the editors. 'And some people are tossing matches.'

12

December 25: Early Afternoon

ALONE WITH ANDREY GRACHEV IN HIS KREMLIN OFFICE, and with just over four hours remaining before he is to deliver his resignation speech, Mikhail Gorbachev takes a pen and begins rehearsing it aloud. He asks his aide for his opinion as he goes through it, marking points where he has last-minute queries about the precise wording. Since his appointment as presidential spokesman in September, Grachev has become one of the small inner circle around Gorbachev. The president has grown to appreciate his sure touch and smooth, sophisticated approach to public relations.

Gorbachev cannot bring himself to say he is *resigning*. He decides to insert instead, 'I hereby *discontinue my activities* at the post of president of the Union of Soviet Socialist Republics.'

Having gone through several rewrites, the speech is a balance between a justification of the policies Gorbachev pursued in power and a statement of his dismay at how history has played out. It betrays just a little of the bitterness he feels about the way Yeltsin and the republic presidents trumped him in the political games of the last few weeks. However, he has indicated to Yeltsin he will not use the occasion to make an outright attack on him or what he has done. It would not in any case be dignified to do so.

Gorbachev makes one substantial amendment nevertheless to prick his opponent. In the text he notes that it is vitally important to preserve the democratic achievements of the last few years, 'and they are not to be abandoned, whatever the circumstances, and whatever the pretexts'. It can be taken as a warning that Yeltsin and his successors might seek undemocratic ways to consolidate their power. The final version also contains a small segment from an earlier draft that Gorbachev dropped and then decided to put back in. It states that the decisions taken by Yeltsin and his fellow conspirators 'should have been made on the basis of popular will'. That too is likely to irritate Yeltsin.

The bulk of the 1,200-word address is the final contribution to the Gorbachev presidency by Anatoly Chernyaev, who has drafted practically every important speech delivered by the Soviet leader. He has been working on the valediction since Gorbachev asked him to start composing a text two weeks earlier. That was when the president acknowledged for the first time that the end might be near. Other aides provided drafts, but they were for the most part rejected. Four days ago Chernyaev thought he had completed his task but Gorbachev twice went back to the basic text and twice got his adviser to completely rework it. Even now the president is still tinkering. Alexander Yakovlev produced his own draft, which was conciliatory to Yeltsin and contained frank admissions of mistakes. Gorbachev was tempted to adopt much of Yakovlev's apologia but Chernyaev categorically rejected it as 'a capitulation and a whining', and the president in the end agreed.

A week ago, when Eduard Shevardnadze was asked to come to the Kremlin and provide input, he also took issue with Yakovlev's version. The Georgian was in a foul temper when he arrived and was in no mood for making any concessionary gestures or for kowtowing to Yeltsin. He had just been told brusquely by a clerk in the foreign ministry building in Smolenskaya-Sennaya Street that Yeltsin had liquidated the Soviet foreign ministry and claimed its personnel and assets for Russia. Shevardnadze had to leave his seventh-floor minister's office immediately as Russian foreign minister Andrey Kozyrev wanted to move in.

Yeltsin's people are cynical and ill-mannered, he complained in his thick Georgian accent. 'Their main purpose is to get armchairs; they all look at each other and boast about the offices they got in Smolenskaya-Sennaya . . .' He never liked Kozyrev, the nondescript but ambitious Russian foreign minister, called the 'Whisperer' behind his back because of his soft voice. Shevardnadze resents that neither Yeltsin nor Kozyrev had the decency to tell him to his face that his ministry was being whipped out from under his feet. He and his closest aide Sergey Tarasenko are also fearful for their lives and those of Gorbachev and other Kremlin officials. 'We don't know who is going to shoot whom,'

Tarasenko confided to Jim Garrison, the former Esalen executive now heading the International Foreign Policy Association, an organization sponsored by former US secretary of state George Shultz and Shevardnadze to mobilize aid for Soviet children, and who happened to be visiting Shevardnadze the day he was ejected from his office.

Shevardnadze had glumly forecast to Gorbachev's aides that there would be a new putsch and an explosion of violence and repression on a mass scale as a result of Yeltsin's actions in dismantling the Soviet Union. Alexander Yakovlev echoed his pessimism. He predicted that, '*Dai Bog*' (Please God), Yeltsin wouldn't last longer than the spring.

The final version of the farewell address, Chernyaev notes, is 'born of Gorbachev's suffering through this excruciating December'. In the place of Yakovlev's 'whining' he has made sure that it includes a measure of defiance and self-justification and that it blames Yeltsin by implication for ending the Soviet Union. The draft portrays Gorbachev as the principled player in the political drama taking place, though he has no control over the fast-moving events now. It proclaims that he has fulfilled the historical task of leading a totalitarian country towards democracy. It includes a passing acknowledgement by Gorbachev of his own failings, though he distances himself from self-blame by using the royal 'we', with the formula, 'We certainly could have avoided certain errors.'

As the final draft of the address is being typed up, Pavel Palazchenko comes to the anteroom of

Gorbachev's office. He reminds Chernyaev that George Bush expects a final call from President Gorbachev. 'Well, I guess today is the day,' Chernyaev tells him.

But it is Christmas Day in the Western world and everyone is on holiday. When Palazchenko calls the American embassy in Moscow to request a connection to Washington, no one is there to take the call. The embassy is closed. A voice on the answering machine gives only the number of the marine on duty in case of an emergency concerning an American citizen. He could turn for help to the foreign ministry in Moscow, which has the capacity to organize a call to the American president through the embassy in Washington, but these diplomatic assets are in the hands of Yeltsin's team, whose members are not to be trusted.

The interpreter goes through his notebook and finds the Moscow home number of Jim Collins, the US deputy head of mission, to whom he explains his predicament. Collins gives him the number in Washington of the State Department operations desk, which Palazchenko calls on an open line through the Moscow operator. At the State Department, the duty officer advises him that President Bush is spending Christmas Day at Camp David. He patches Palazchenko through to the marine on duty at the forest retreat. The US president is still asleep – it is early morning in America – but the officer says Bush will take the call after he wakes up. They fix a time for the connection: 5.00 p.m. in Moscow, 9.00 a.m. in Washington.

Fully recovered from his after-lunch bout of

depression, Gorbachev invites Ted Koppel and Rick Kaplan into his office to continue filming their historical record for ABC television. He makes a point of emphasizing the peaceful nature of the transition and that nothing like this has ever happened in Russian history. 'The process, after all, is a democratic one.'

Koppel asks if Gorbachev could retain power if he wanted, given that he is still head of the Soviet armed forces. 'There are people who change their positions to make sure they keep power,' replies Gorbachev coyly. 'To me that is unacceptable. If what is happening didn't matter to me and if I wanted to remain in government more than anything else, then that would be not too difficult to achieve.'

It is a vain boast. The moment has passed when Gorbachev could achieve such a goal, though he will never concede that. Years later, putting a gloss on his ousting, he claims that sometimes his hands were itching to use force, but that he realized such a course of action could lead to a civil war and even a global nuclear conflict.

Gorbachev emphasizes to Koppel the most important message he wants to get across to the Americans, that there will be no nuclear crisis. He draws attention to the portion of the speech containing his assurance to the world that he has done everything in his power during the transitional period to ensure safe control over nuclear weapons.

The American journalists are once more impressed at the calmness of the president. He is more relaxed than some days ago, Gorbachev tells them, as 'the psychological stress is hardest until you make the decision'. Kaplan is struck too by his proud demeanour. 'The one word I would use is dignified,' he recalled. 'It was evident he wanted to be perceived as in control, not in control of the Soviet Union or Russia, but in control of himself.'

13

Dictatorship on the Offensive

IN THE WAKE OF THE RUSSIAN PARLIAMENT'S declaration of sovereignty in June 1990, Mikhail Gorbachev and Boris Yeltsin had the option of trying to destroy each other, or of entering into a political alliance. Something drastic had to be done. The Soviet economy was on the point of collapse. There were now chronic shortages of everything in the Russian capital. Even cigarettes had become scarce and there were minor 'tobacco riots' in several cities. The longest queues that summer were at photographers' studios, as Muscovites were obliged to apply for identity cards for city stores to prevent country people stripping the shelves bare. Ration coupons were issued for clothes, shoes and domestic appliances. Sugar was restricted to two kilograms per month per person. Butter was rarely seen. Flour and salt disappeared from the shops and bread ran out daily. Meat was only available in expensive markets. Consumers were hoarding, making the shortages worse.

People told bitter anecdotes about how bad things had become. A forgetful old man stands outside a supermarket with an empty shopping bag, wondering if he has done his shopping or not. Many jokes were aimed at party privileges. In Congress a deputy complains to the presidium, 'I want to work like I do under communism and live like under capitalism,' and is told, 'No problem! Join us on the platform.' A Russian moves to Latvia in the hope that one day he will wake up abroad (he soon does). Another anecdote doing the rounds goes: 'How does a clever Russian Jew talk to a foolish Russian Jew? By telephone from New York.'

The humiliation of Russians at their degraded state was compounded by the arrival of food parcels from Germany, the country the Soviet Union defeated in World War II. Praskoviya Fyodorovna, aged seventy-eight, who had served as a wireless operator in the war, wept as she opened a cardboard box sent by a family in Düsseldorf. It contained a tin of cocoa, three slim bars of milk chocolate, two bulky slabs of Edel marzipan, a packet of wafer biscuits, a kilo of Diamant flour and packages of sugar and rice. 'And now they help the victorious,' she sobbed.

In Moscow the people standing in line reacted with indifference, even anger, when on October 15, 1990, Gorbachev was awarded the Nobel Peace Prize for his leading role in the easing of tensions between East and West and the freedoms gained by Eastern Europe. As far as they were concerned, their lot had worsened while their leader was feeding his ego on the back-slapping international circuit. In an extraordinary swipe at his president, Soviet foreign ministry spokesman Gennady

Gerasimov told reporters, 'We must remember this certainly was not the prize for economics.'

At first the rivals chose to enter into an alliance to meet the crisis. The command system having failed so catastrophically, Gorbachev and Yeltsin agreed to co-operate on a crash programme to create a market economy. The task of drawing up a blueprint was given to a joint working group led by radical economist Stanislav Shatalin, a balding adviser to Gorbachev with a quick sense of humour who referred to himself as the Diego Maradona of economics, and Yeltsin's deputy prime minister, Grigory Yavlinsky. Gorbachev and Yeltsin at last had a civilized meeting. For five hours in late August, as the rain beat down incessantly outside the Kremlin, they agreed to implement the forthcoming economic plan together. The Russian leader felt Gorbachev treated him as an equal for the first time. He mollified the Soviet president by declaring that for Russia to go it completely alone would mean destroying the Union and 'we have rejected that notion'.

The accord between Gorbachev and Yeltsin didn't last. Gorbachev balked when Shatalin and Yavlinsky produced a 500-day plan similar to the shock therapy applied in Poland earlier in the year. It involved the step-by-step lifting of price and currency controls, withdrawal of state subsidies, and large-scale privatiz-ation, with October 1, 1990, as the starting date. The Soviet leader caved in to ferocious pressure from the military and industrial sectors, which feared losing their generous subventions, and from party hardliners who saw in the plan the disintegration of the Soviet Union if the centre lost its ability to issue commands to the republics. In mid-October, unable to give up the old Bolshevik notion of the leader as the ultimate social designer, or of himself as the wise compromiser, he reconciled Shatalin's plan with a reform programme drawn up earlier by Soviet prime minister Nikolay Ryzhkov. A vain *apparatchik* known as the 'Weeping Bolshevik' for his emotional outbursts, Ryzhkov proposed keeping much of the old system intact and maintaining Kremlin control over all the rights designated for the republics. Gorbachev considered, then ruled out, holding a referendum on his half measure.

The radical reformers were furious. Feeling betrayed, Yeltsin called the compromise a blueprint for chaos, like 'trying to cross a hedgehog with a grass snake'. In a speech he threatened that Russia would go ahead and implement the 500-day plan on its own. Outraged, Gorbachev called an emergency meeting of his presidential council in the Kremlin. There was near-hysteria over Yeltsin's threat and the possibility that other republics would follow in defying the centre. Chernyaev found the room filled with fear and hatred. Ryzhkov screamed that they would all be shot or hanged, that everything was out of control. At one point Gorbachev left the room briefly to greet a US delegation led by Dick Cheney, switching as he did to the role of garrulous and charming master-statesman, then as soon as the Americans had gone, continuing his outburst in the corridor against Yeltsin's people, 'who all deserve a good punch in the face'.

Yeltsin, however, had as yet no way of carrying out his threat to go it alone. His departments had little or no resources to implement any economic plan. His industry minister, Viktor Kisin, complained that at the time 'there was only one person in the ministry – the minister himself; there was no office, no chair, no telephone'. Yeltsin's helplessness was exposed when his officials placed an order for two armoured limousines with the Gorky factory in Moscow in October. The order was refused, on directions from the Kremlin.

The rivals met again but another five hours of discussion led nowhere. At the meeting Yeltsin asked, 'Why are you moving to the right so sharply?'

'Because society is moving to the right,' replied Gorbachev.

'You then simply do not know what is happening in society,' retorted Yeltsin.

Next day Yeltsin reported the conversation to the Russian parliament, in what Chernyaev described as his usual rude and insulting manner. Gorbachev complained to his aides he would be forced to declare war on Yeltsin.

But Gorbachev was indeed becoming isolated from Soviet society and Yeltsin had the backing of the people. On November 7, after Gorbachev and his comrades had reviewed the annual military parade in Red Square commemorating the October Revolution, Yeltsin appeared at the head of an anti-communist crowd organized by the radical group Democratic Russia. They carried pictures of the last tsar and banners displaying black humour, such as '1917 the crime – 1990 the punishment'.

Gorbachev's knowledge of what was happening at this time in society came principally from his aide, Valery Boldin, who was secretly scheming to subvert his boss. The blandest of bureaucrats, with a square face and outsize horn-rimmed spectacles, Boldin wielded great influence over Gorbachev's diary and routine. Anyone who wanted to see the president had to go through the dogmatic *apparatchik* whom Gorbachev had recruited from *Pravda*'s editorial team in 1981. Besides being Gorbachev's gatekeeper, he was head of the General Department of the Communist Party, which gave him control over archives and documents circulated by the Central Committee. Even Gorbachev's close aide Anatoly Chernyaev only learned much later that Boldin had a secret information department that supplied Gorbachev with, in Chernyaev's words, a 'tendentious concoction' of negative materials designed to poison him against his pro-reform friends.

Boldin in time would admit that he despised Gorbachev 'for his lordly manner and contempt for his subordinates'. He had never forgotten the humiliating way his position had been confirmed six years before, when he was summoned into the presence of Mikhail and Raisa Gorbachev and told that he had lived up to their expectations. An important party official in his own right, Boldin felt he was treated as a servant. Yet he was so successful at hiding the rancour he felt that Raisa was fooled into thinking he was her loyal ally. She would find out before long how wrong she was. Boldin was unpopular with Gorbachev's staff for his oily attitude towards Gorbachev. Chernyaev never spoke warmly of Boldin, and senior secretariat member Olga Lanina couldn't stand him. Grachev thought he was obsessed with the power he wielded. One of Boldin's quirks was collecting books bound in fine-tooled leather that 'exposed' convoluted Masonic conspiracies favoured by right-wing extremists. But Boldin lived up to his Bolshevik ideals. He refused the perks of his status, declining a Chaika, access to a special clinic and a larger dacha, and was contemptuous of the Gorbachevs' taste for the lavish benefits of office.

The alarmist information that Boldin fed his master came from KGB chief Vladimir Kryuchkov, a sixty-seven-year-old admirer of Stalin who was also posing as a reformer. The short, baby-faced Kryuchkov, nick-named Cherub by his staff, was a conspiracy theorist with a taste for Chivas Regal who wore a cardigan under his jacket and looked more like a college professor than a Soviet spymaster. Operating from a cavernous oak-panelled office on the fourth floor of the KGB building, with a portrait of Gorbachev on the wall, he produced a stream of reports claiming that Western intelligence agencies were intent on the destruction of the Soviet Union as a great power. Kryuchkov's agents tapped the telephones of the leading reformers, including Yeltsin and Alexander Yakovlev, and provided the transcripts, via Boldin, to their most avid reader – Gorbachev. Every day the Soviet president would go through hundreds of pages of these reports compiled secretly on his closest colleagues.

On December 11, 1990, in a chilling throwback to darker days, the head of the KGB appeared on the main evening television news to warn, 'at the president's request', that the pro-democracy movements in the republics were the creatures of foreign money and intelligence, and that 'we in the security forces have made our choice: we stand for the flowering of our socialist homeland'.

A horrified Eduard Shevardnadze thought Kryuchkov's rhetoric smacked of the 1930s. It seemed to Palazchenko that the hawks wanted to welcome Gorbachev back as a prodigal son who had sown his wild oats and was now returning to the fold. It was evident to Chernyaev that his boss had reached the limit of his reform capacity and was retreating, confused, before an onslaught of the reactionaries. He found it sad to see Gorbachev swaggering and acting superior. He and Alexander Yakovlev listened together on radio one day as Gorbachev made a 'disastrous' speech to the Supreme Soviet. Yakovlev muttered in some distress, 'He's done for, now I'm sure of it.' Gorbachev, as Russian journalist Leonid Nikitinsky put it, had looked back at the Central Committee and turned into a pillar of salt.

The Soviet leader abruptly dissolved his presidential council, rather than heed its more progressive members. As a gesture to his old comrade, he kept Alexander Yakovlev on as a special adviser, though he cut him out of decision-making. Kryuchkov and Boldin partly succeeded in poisoning Gorbachev against Yakovlev. Together they came to Gorbachev's office to warn the incredulous president that the former ambassador to Canada was in reality an agent of the CIA.

As he hardened his position Gorbachev fired the head of state television, Mikhail Nenashev, a protégé of Alexander Yakovlev, and put the more subservient director general of the official Soviet news agency TASS, Leonid Kravchenko, in charge. After four years of *glasnost*, television had become daring and hard-hitting, and Gorbachev now saw it as a threat to the system rather than an instrument of reform.

A charming hardliner with a boyish face, Kravchenko told state television editorial staff, 'I am the president's man and I have come to carry out the president's will.' Gorbachev thereafter called Kravchenko several times a day to instruct him on what political material was suitable viewing for the masses. He ordered Kravchenko to exclude opposition voices, in particular Boris Yeltsin's. Popular broadcaster Vladimir Pozner had to resign after earning Kravchenko's disapproval for saying on *The Late Show Starring Joan Rivers* on Fox Television in the United States that Yeltsin was more popular than Gorbachev.

The next to go was fifty-two-year-old Vadim Bakatin, the respected police chief. An enlightened reformer and talented artist, Bakatin was dedicated to getting Soviet interior ministry police to obey the law rather than the party. He was detested by a bloc of communists calling themselves *Soyuz* (Union). Their leader Viktor Alksnis, a colonel-deputy who strutted around in a black leather jacket even on hot days, had called for his sacking, claiming he was not tough enough on separatists. Gorbachev stunned his dwindling corps of reformers by meekly obeying. He replaced Bakatin on December 2 with Boris Pugo, a soft-spoken balding Latvian with tufts of hair sticking up on each side in clown-like fashion. As head of the KGB in Riga, Pugo had ruthlessly kept the lid on the Latvian independence movement.

The Congress of People's Deputies started its fourth session on December 16, with Gorbachev a prisoner of its conservative majority. Another *Soyuz* leader, Colonel Nikolay Petrushenko, who resembled Sergeant Bilko from the CBS comedy series, boasted in the foyer that they would get rid of Shevardnadze next, because of his role in the loss of Eastern Europe. Deeply disillusioned with Gorbachev, Shevardnadze was already determined to quit.

The white-haired foreign minister shocked the deputies, and Gorbachev, by announcing from the podium that he was resigning. 'Comrade democrats,' he said, 'you have scattered. Reformers have taken to the hills. Dictatorship is on the offensive.' With that he walked from the hall.

Next day Gorbachev nominated the least effectual member of the Politburo, Gennady Yanayev, to the new post of vice president, in a further attempt to co-opt the conservatives. Standing at the rostrum with large bags under his eyes and an unconvincing hairpiece, Yanayev declared with all the sincerity of the privileged *apparatchik*, 'I am a convinced communist to the depths of my soul.' Even the Congress majority did not want this hard-drinking, chain-smoking propagandist. They rejected him on the first ballot. Gorbachev angrily made his confirmation a vote of confidence and got his vice-presidential nominee accepted on a second ballot.

Three weeks later, Gorbachev appointed another backstabber as prime minister. Valentin Pavlov, a rotund economist who liked loud silk ties and giggled a lot, concealed a hatred for Gorbachev whom he regarded as a man with two faces. Gorbachev claimed later that he did not know that this crew-cut xenophobe, known contemptuously as 'Porcupig', was a drunkard and a die-hard communist. Pavlov almost immediately outraged the population by withdrawing all large banknotes from circulation overnight, wiping out the savings of millions of people. He justified this by citing an outlandish conspiracy theory, peddled by Kryuchkov, that private banks in Austria, Switzerland and Canada planned to dump a large amount of money on the Soviet market with the goal of producing political instability.

Completing the group encircling Gorbachev was defence minister Dmitry Yazov. A corpulent and salty tongued World War II veteran with a florid complexion, ham-like hands and a bent for English and Russian poetry, Field Marshal Yazov was a true communist, who lived modestly and believed that private property was the root of all evil, and that only incompetence and corruption had prevented the Soviet Union enjoying prosperity.

Everything was in place for what this motley and sinister assortment of hardliners wanted – a bloody crackdown on the independence movements that were fracturing the Soviet Union. The most assertive of these were in the Baltic republics, which had been annexed by Stalin half a century earlier and longed for their pre-war freedoms. Gorbachev never understood Baltic nationalism. He used a chopping motion of his hand to express his contempt for the 'secessionists and political adventurers' making trouble on the Soviet Union's western flank.

Nine months before, after Sąjūdis, the anti-Moscow national front of Lithuania, won the state election, the country bordering Poland had become the first Soviet republic to declare independence. The Soviet emblem on the parliament building in the capital, Vilnius, had been chiselled off and replaced with a canvas depicting a knight with a sword in hand, the emblem of free Lithuania. The new government had taken over public buildings and dropped Russian as an official language.

The conservatives in Moscow were appalled at this. Gorbachev himself never intended that his changes should go so far. He warned the Lithuanian parliament to submit to Soviet power and imposed an economic blockade. Troops staged provocative parades in Vilnius and military helicopters dropped leaflets over the city, urging the Russian and Polish minorities to join pro-Soviet rallies. The intimidation had no effect.

On January 12, 1991, a shadowy pro-Soviet 'committee for national salvation' announced in Vilnius that it was taking power. This committee 'requested' Soviet units to seize the television tower in Vilnius, which was broadcasting pro-independence material. Unarmed Lithuanians had gathered outside the tower fearing it would be taken over by pro-Moscow forces. In the early hours of January 13, troops from the KGB Alpha Group, trained especially to fight terrorists, arrived and fired live bullets into the crowd. Thirteen civilians were killed and several hundred injured. One KGB officer was accidentally shot dead by his own men. Gorbachev at first voiced support for the faceless committee of national salvation. He did not disown the KGB assault on the civilians at the TV tower but blamed everything on the Lithuanian declaration of independence, which he called 'a virtual night-time, constitutional coup'.

In Moscow *glasnost* was suspended and news of the massacre was suppressed. Central television gave only the military version of events in Vilnius. The lively late-night programme *Vzglyad* (Glance) was taken off the air and an independent news agency, Interfax, was silenced. TASS described the nationalist defenders of the television tower as 'intoxicated youths . . . singing pro-fascist songs'. It seemed as if the totalitarian past had returned.

Knowing that if sovereignty could be crushed in the Baltics it could be crushed in Russia too, Yeltsin acted quickly. He flew to Tallinn, capital of Estonia, the most northerly of the three Baltic republics, to meet the defiant elected presidents of Lithuania, Latvia and Estonia. There in the barricaded parliament, protected by Estonian youths with hunting guns, he signed an agreement with them to recognize each other's sovereignty. Yeltsin's prestige stiffened the nationalists' resolve to resist, infuriating Gorbachev. A friendly KGB source advised Yeltsin not to take a flight back to Moscow, as it might be sabotaged. He was driven instead the two hundred and seventeen miles from

Tallinn to Leningrad (now St Petersburg) and from there flew back to the Russian capital.

An energized Yeltsin reported to deputies packing a committee room in the White House that the military crackdown in the Baltics was 'the start of a powerful offensive against democracy in the Soviet Union, and Russia's turn will come'. He was applauded by adoring Russian journalists. Commanding, self-assured and red-eyed with exhaustion, he urged Russian soldiers not to fire on unarmed civilians, saying it would be unlawful under the new Russian constitution. 'You are a pawn in a dirty game,' he told them. An army paratroop unit in the Belarusian city of Vitebsk subsequently refused to deploy to Latvia. Yeltsin also announced that the presidents of Russia, Belarus, Ukraine and Kazakhstan had decided to draw up a treaty to replace the old Soviet Union. 'I think I may now say where – in Minsk,' said Yeltsin, slyly, 'but I can't tell you when.'

'That son of a bitch! What's to be done about him?' cried Gorbachev to his advisers when he got a report of Yeltsin's remarks. They listened to him in silence, aghast at the turn of events. Chernyaev later composed an anguished, 2,000-word letter of resignation, saying he was tortured by burning shame over events in Lithuania. 'You've told me and others many times that the Russian people would never permit the destruction of the empire. But now Yeltsin is impudently doing just that – in the name of Russia! And very few Russians are protesting,' he wrote. 'As a result, you chained yourself to policies that you can only continue by force . . .' He did not deliver the letter, however, and stayed on with

Gorbachev, as he saw no proof of his boss's complicity in planning the bloodshed. He confided to diplomats that General Valentin Varennikov, commander of land forces in the USSR and an admirer of Stalin, had ordered in the troops on his own initiative. Chernyaev also concluded that Gorbachev genuinely believed misleading reports from Kryuchkov and Pugo that people in the Baltics were being intimidated by a minority of separatists. In private, however, the loyal aide berated Gorbachev for allowing the military to send in the tanks, saying, 'This is the demise of your great undertaking!' Gorbachev protested that 'I couldn't simply dissociate myself from the army and express my disapproval after all the insults there to soldiers, officers, their families [calling them] occupiers and pigs.'

Outside the Kremlin, the Russian capital was in uproar. Muscovites took to the streets to show that they had had enough of totalitarian methods. Some carried placards insulting the president as 'Gorbaty', the Hunchback. The non-state media gave graphic accounts of the killings.

Yegor Yakovlev, the editor who had toed the Gorbachev line in *Moscow News* and taken his side in the power struggle with Yeltsin, was deeply disillusioned. The journal's thirty directors, a who's who of the liberal Russian intelligentsia, expressed their bitter loss of faith in the president and announced they were quitting the party. All signed their names to a devastating editorial accusing 'a regime in its death throes' of committing a criminal act. 'After Bloody Sunday in Vilnius, what is left of our president's favourite topics of "humane socialism", "new thinking" and "our European home" – virtually nothing!'

This charge from intellectuals whom he had encouraged and protected would rankle with Gorbachev for years. Infuriated, he demanded the Supreme Soviet suspend a recently adopted law on press freedom – which he had promoted – and assign a censor to each media organization. Even conservative deputies found this too much in the face of public outrage.

On Sunday, January 20, Yeltsin addressed a Moscow protest rally of one hundred thousand people. He warned that the danger of dictatorship had become a reality. International leaders harboured similar fears. Several days later, after Soviet black berets in Latvia's capital, Riga, shot dead two militiamen, a television cameraman and two civilians, President Bush put off a summit meeting with Gorbachev scheduled for mid-February. The United States, Canada and the European Parliament delayed implementing aid programmes.

Under such internal and international pressure, and with his own innate revulsion for bloodshed, Gorbachev pulled back. He adopted a more conciliatory tone to the Baltics. He went on television on January 22 to say that he was deeply moved by the deaths, declared the use of armed force inadmissible, and denied that the military activity was a prelude to direct rule. Belatedly Gorbachev would claim that the hardliners' plan was 'to establish a blood bond with me, to subordinate me to a kind of gangsters' mutual protection society'.

But the damage had been done. Making things worse,

no one was ever punished for the slaughter in Vilnius. In July 1991 Gorbachev's chief law officer, Soviet Prosecutor Nikolay Trubin, exonerated Soviet forces, finding, grotesquely, that all the casualties were shot by Lithuanian nationalists.

In the Kremlin, Gorbachev continued to rage about the 'illogical' behaviour of Yeltsin, who was 'infatuated with sovereignty'. He telephoned his minion in state television, Leonid Kravchenko, and instructed him to close down Radio Rossiya, the voice of Yeltsin's parliament, which had been granted a frequency in December. It had carried factual reports from Lithuania that infuriated Mikhail Gorbachev personally, according to Yeltsin's radio controller Oleg Poptsov. Kravchenko protested that shutting it down would cause a scandal. Gorbachev insisted that it be restricted then to a much weaker frequency, in 'the back of beyond'.

Kravchenko denied repeated requests from Yeltsin for airtime on state television in the weeks after Vilnius. Every appearance of Yeltsin made Gorbachev crazy, he recalled. 'It looked childish, like little boys battling for domination, but it was based of course on the instinctive fear that Yeltsin was acquiring an authority with the people which threatened Gorbachev's own survival.'

He finally bowed to enormous public pressure and agreed to broadcast a live interview with Yeltsin on February 19. Gorbachev insisted that one of the two interviewers should be Sergey Lomakin, a good-looking young favourite of Raisa. Gorbachev sent Lomakin a list of hostile questions and Lomakin asked even tougher ones. But Yeltsin managed to create a sensation for the millions of viewers who tuned in across the USSR. He called for the immediate resignation of Gorbachev, who was 'lying to the people and was smeared with the blood of ethnic conflicts', and demanded the transfer of all power to the leaders of the fifteen Soviet republics.

Gorbachev recalled Yeltsin's behaviour with disgust. 'His speech teemed with rude and offensive remarks about me,' he complained. 'His hands were trembling. He was visibly not in control of himself and laboriously read out a prepared text.' In Washington, Bush watched the Russian leader's performance on a news report and remarked to his aides in the Oval Office, 'This guy Yeltsin is really a wild man, isn't he!'

Despite everything, President Bush and other Western leaders wanted the Soviet Union to stay intact under its current leader. They preferred dealing with the sophisticated and amenable Gorbachev than the unpredictable Yeltsin. Robert Gates, deputy national security adviser and future head of the CIA, who in the early days wrote off Gorbachev as an aberration, now saw him doing 'what we wanted done on one major issue after another'. With some justification Yeltsin complained that Americans didn't get it. They saw only one figure in Moscow and that figure was surrounded by so much foreign euphoria they couldn't see the truth.

On a second trip to the United States that spring Yeltsin, with his increased stature as leader of the Russian republic, asked for an official invitation to the White House. Bush hesitated, commenting to Brent Scowcroft that such a step would 'drive Gorbachev nuts'. That might be just why Yeltsin wanted it, suggested his national security adviser. 'Well that's also why I *don't* want to do it,' replied Bush. They agreed they would see him, but would get Congress rather than the White House to issue the official invitation to Washington.

Yeltsin's call for the resignation of the Soviet president overshadowed Gorbachev's sixtieth birthday on March 2, 1991. He celebrated in the Kremlin with Yazov, who presented him with a sabre with inlaid sheath, Pugo who gave him an inscribed Makarov pistol, and Kryuchkov and others who sent expensive presents straight to his dacha. Kravchenko arranged for Soviet television to broadcast a sycophantic documentary called 'Our First President'.

The best birthday present he got, however, came from six pro-Gorbachev communist deputies in Yeltsin's parliament, who secured enough votes to call a special session of the Russian Congress for March 28 to have Yeltsin impeached for his television outburst. Gorbachev clutched at this straw. He told Chernyaev, 'Boris Nikolayevich is done for, he's starting to toss and turn, he's afraid of being held responsible for what he has and hasn't done for Russia.'

Yeltsin raised the stakes at a vast outdoor assembly in Moscow on March 9 by declaring war on the leadership in the Kremlin, an intemperate remark he withdrew a week later.

The hardliners around Gorbachev decided on a

display of military might to intimidate the restless populace. When the Russian Congress convened on March 28 to debate Yeltsin's future, demonstrations were banned and armoured vehicles, tanks and several hundred troop carriers filled with conscripts were deployed nose-to-tail in streets around the Kremlin. Kryuchkov and Pugo had fed Gorbachev ridiculous warnings that radical democrats were preparing to storm the ancient fortress using ropes and grappling irons. These deployments only ensured that a pro-Yeltsin rally in the streets outside became an anti-Gorbachev demonstration. Inside, the deputies refused to debate in a state of siege and voted to adjourn. Tens of thousands of demonstrators milled around military barricades in the streets near the Kremlin as a heavy, fluffy snow coated everyone in white. The confrontation brought the country to the brink of civil conflict. Gorbachev was stunned when Alexander Yakovlev asked him to think of how Moscow would turn out for a funeral if a demonstrator should be killed. The tension was defused when Yeltsin's collaborator, Ruslan Khasbulatov, persuaded Gorbachev at a tense meeting in the Kremlin that the idea of people scaling the Kremlin walls was outlandish. (Aides were joking among themselves that it would not be possible as there was a shortage of rope in the shops.) The president ordered Yazov to take the troops out of the city.

Khasbulatov would later identify the day the state powers blinked as the day the defeat of the reactionary forces began. Alexander Yakovlev told a visiting

American senator, David Boren, that mobilizing the armed forces against the people was Gorbachev's single biggest mistake.

For three days the Russian Congress was deadlocked over whether to censure Yeltsin. In the end the 'swamp' of undeclared deputies rejected impeachment rather than side with the unpopular Gorbachev. They were also alarmed by a spreading coal-miners' strike in support of Yeltsin, which began when miners coming off a shift at one mine shaft found there was no soap. Even Ivan Polozkov, leader of the communist faction, stated from the rostrum that the time was not right to destroy Yeltsin because of the ferocious backlash this could provoke.

Fearful of the gathering momentum towards the disintegration of the Soviet Union, Gorbachev organized a referendum throughout the USSR to restore popular support for stability and a new union treaty. It asked for a yes or no to the question: 'Do you consider necessary the preservation of the USSR as a renewed federation of equal sovereign republics in which the rights and freedom of an individual of any nationality will be fully guaranteed?' The referendum was held on March 16. Six of the fifteen Soviet republics had become so independent-minded they boycotted the poll, but in the remaining nine, 76 per cent of voters responded yes. Gorbachev took this majority as a mandate to negotiate a new union treaty that would give republics a measure of sovereignty, but preserve the Union of which he was president.

Yeltsin cleverly turned the plebiscite to his advantage.

On the referendum paper distributed in Russia he added an extra question – do people support the idea of a directly elected president for Russia. The voters gave their approval. The Russian Congress agreed to hold the first free presidential election in Russia, on June 12, 1991.

Yet, while his popularity swelled at home, Yeltsin found to his dismay that his high profile in Moscow did not impress world leaders. Dignitaries who arrived in Russia on fact-finding missions came with perceptions of an unstable and vodka-loving bully. On the other hand, they liked Gorbachev personally and felt protective towards him. When Yeltsin asked US secretary of state James Baker to call on him during such a visit to the Soviet president in mid-March, Baker saw it as an effort to 'drive Gorbachev up the wall'. The American declined after consulting Gorbachev, who 'naturally went through the roof' and raved about how unstable Yeltsin was and how he would use populist rhetoric to become a dictator. Gorbachev displayed similar childishness, forbidding his associates to attend a dinner Baker hosted at the embassy in protest at the presence of some of Yeltsin's team.

The effete British foreign secretary Douglas Hurd took a dislike to the ponderous, blunt-talking nonconformist when they met in Moscow. He suggested to Ambassador Braithwaite as they left the meeting that the Russian was a dangerous man barely under control. However, Braithwaite concluded that Yeltsin's analysis was correct and that Gorbachev was by now 'living almost entirely in cloud-cuckoo land'. Richard Nixon, visiting Yeltsin in Moscow as an unofficial envoy of the White House, cursed the media for giving him the impression of an 'incompetent, disloyal boob'. Yeltsin might not have the 'grace and ivory-tower polish of Gorbachev', he reported to Bush on his return to the United States, 'but he inspires the people nevertheless'.

Yeltsin went to France where he believed he would at least be respected by the democratic parliamentarians of Europe. He got an unpleasant surprise. *Le Monde* lectured him that in Europe 'only one Russian is recognized – Gorbachev'. He was greeted with an 'icy shower' at the European Parliament in Strasbourg where Jean-Pierre Cot, chairman of the group of socialists, reproached him publicly as a demagogue and an irresponsible politician for opposing Gorbachev, 'with whom we feel more assured'. These remarks caused outrage among ordinary Russians – even *Pravda* called them an insult – and only served to increase Yeltsin's popularity.

The Russian populist returned home chastened by the 'terrible blow' of Western reaction. But there was a surprise in store for him. Gorbachev invited him to a meeting of the heads of all the Soviet Union's republics at a dacha on the outskirts of Moscow, and what the Soviet leader had to say to him there, Yeltsin found, 'exceeded all my expectations'.

14

December 25: Mid-afternoon

BY THREE O'CLOCK IN THE AFTERNOON OF DECEMBER 25, 1991, Mikhail Gorbachev is able at last to relax. Everything is ready. There is nothing more to be done in preparation for his farewell address. Ted Koppel and Rick Kaplan are brought into the office to film more presidential thoughts for their ABC documentary. Anatoly Chernyaev and Andrey Grachev are there too.

One of the white telephones on the desk rings and Gorbachev picks up the receiver. It is his wife calling from the presidential dacha. This is not unusual. Raisa has long been in the habit of ringing her husband or his officials to involve herself in events. But this time it is different. She is in great distress.

The president makes a signal to the Americans that this is a private matter. 'He got a call from Raisa,' Rick Kaplan would recall. 'We were ordered to leave the room.'

Raisa is in tears. She tells her husband in considerable agitation that several of Yeltsin's security men have arrived at their dacha to serve them notice to quit immediately. They have also ordered the family to vacate the president's city apartment at Kosygin Street on Lenin Hills within two hours. The men said they had been authorized to take this action by a decree signed by the president of Russia that morning privatizing the apartment. They have orders 'to remove her personal belongings from the premises of the government representative' – the bureaucratic term for the president's official residences. The unwelcome visitors have already started moving some of the Gorbachevs' family possessions out of the mansion.

Gorbachev is livid over the impudence and lack of courtesy Yeltsin's security staff are showing his wife. It was only decided two days ago that he would discontinue his activities as president of the Soviet Union this evening, and there has been no time to prepare for moving. Moreover he was specifically given a grace period of three more days by Yeltsin to vacate the country residence and the presidential apartment after his resignation. He does not even know if he will have the services of the Ninth Department of the KGB to provide a crew for packing and transport. The unit has been renamed and has come under Yeltsin's control.

Previously he could always rely on Colonel Vladimir Redkoborody to protect them from any intrusions, but the former KGB intelligence officer, who was last week responsible for the security of both presidents, is now answerable only to Yeltsin.

This 'especially vindictive act' against Raisa strikes Chernyaev as a boorish effort by Yeltsin to make the final day miserable for both Gorbachev and his wife. Grachev too is outraged. 'Can you imagine! He was still acting president.'

Gorbachev tries to calm Raisa and promises to sort things out right away. Red blotches appear on the president's cheeks as his fury mounts. He starts making angry calls, cursing and swearing as he demands to speak to the security officials responsible. He eventually gets Colonel Redkoborody on the line. 'You're really out of line and you'd better straighten up,' Gorbachev cries, lacing his words with profanities. 'You're talking about somebody's home here. Do I have to report all this to the press? Please, what are you doing? Stop this madness.'

Redkoborody blusters and promises to talk to the security men. He blames excessive zeal at lower levels but at the same time mentions he has orders from higher up. Yeltsin's chief bodyguard Alexander Korzhakov later discloses that the command came directly from his boss, who ordered him to mount a campaign of daily harassment of Gorbachev's staff at the dacha so he could move in himself right away. Korzhakov sees his task as making life difficult for the Gorbachevs, but observes that they are 'not in any rush to leave'.

Gorbachev's anger has some effect. After his heated conversation with Redkoborody he is given more time to vacate the dacha. But Yeltsin's security men have also arrived at the Gorbachevs' state apartment in Lenin Hills where they are now rummaging around and removing their personal effects. 'Everything had to be done in a rush,' Gorbachev complains, after finding the mess the next day. 'We were forced to move to different lodgings within twenty-four hours. I saw the results in the morning – heaps of clothes, books, dishes, folders, newspapers, letters and God knows what lying strewn on the floor.'

Yeltsin has as little respect for Raisa's feelings as he has for Gorbachev's. Raisa was hostile to him from the start, he believes, and this played a role in her husband's attitude towards him. Yeltsin was among the first to criticize Raisa's high profile as Gorbachev's wife, complaining that 'she unfortunately is unaware how keenly and jealously millions of Soviet people follow her appearances in the media'. When he began highlighting Gorbachev's privileges as Communist Party chief, Yeltsin blamed Raisa for encouraging his expensive tastes. 'He likes to live well, in comfort and luxury,' he noted. 'In this he is helped by his wife.' Yeltsin once tackled Gorbachev to his face at a Politburo meeting about Raisa's 'interference'. This impertinence deepened the rift between them.

Slight and always elegantly dressed, Raisa is admired and envied by members of the Russian intelligentsia, and by quite a few ordinary Russians, as the first Soviet leader's wife to show a sophisticated and humanizing face to the world. She swept away the image of Politburo wives as tongue-tied women whose qualifications, it was said, were to be heavier than their husbands. Anatoly Sobchak's wife, Lyudmila, considered that, while she lectured people like a schoolteacher, Raisa was 'the first woman who dared to violate the Asiatic custom where the wife sits at home and doesn't show her face'. Chernyaev thought she made the Gorbachevs look like 'normal people' in the West. Gorbachev would say in later years that taking his educated, energetic wife with him on trips was a second revolution in addition to *perestroika*.

No leader's spouse played a public role in Soviet life before, except Lenin's wife, Nadezhda Krupskaya, who was a revolutionary and a member of the Politburo in her own right. Yeltsin trumpeted to aides that Raisa had no business going with Gorbachev on foreign trips and playing a high-profile role on the international stage. When US ambassador Jack Matlock inquired of the Russian leader if he intended bringing Naina on a trip to the United States, he retorted, 'No. Absolutely not! I'll not have her acting like Raisa Maximovna!' It might be acceptable in a rich, prosperous and contented society but 'not in our country, at least not at this time'. Gorbachev caused a rumpus years earlier when he told NBC's Tom Brokaw that he discussed everything, including national affairs at the highest level, with his wife. As far as Yeltsin was concerned Raisa's influence had an adverse effect on Gorbachev's attitude towards people, towards staff appointments and towards politics in general, and that she was 'standoffish and puts on airs'.

There have been several instances of Raisa taking an interest in affairs of state. Most criticism was aired in private but at the Congress of People's Deputies a delegate from Kharkov once told an outraged Gorbachev from the podium that he was incapable of escaping the 'vindictiveness and influence' of his wife.

On one occasion she took it upon herself to explain to Fyodor Burlatsky, editor of *Literaturnaya Gazeta*, that the people were not ready for the free market. Gorbachev's wife is still dabbling in policy matters in the final months of the Soviet Union. Congress speaker Ivan Laptiev complained to Rodric Braithwaite that he was rung by Raisa and it was forty-five minutes before he could get off the phone, leading the British ambassador to conclude that Gorbachev couldn't get in a word edgeways at home.

Raisa was seen as rather frosty by the tradition-bound Kremlin wives, whom she in turn found to be 'full of arrogance, suspicion, sycophancy and tactlessness'. Korzhakov claimed – in his tell-all memoirs – that Raisa once ordered, in front of his subordinates, the head of the KGB security department, General Plekhanov, who later became one of the August coup participants, to move a heavy bronze lamp standard. 'When I heard that, I thought, that's why he betrayed Gorbachev.'

By contrast Boris Yeltsin boasted that he never discussed work with the family. If his wife and daughters bombarded him with questions about the events of the day when he came home from work he would tell them to be quiet, saying, 'I don't need politics at home.' Naina concurred in a comment she once made to the Novosti news agency: 'He didn't like it when someone began discussing political or economic issues at home. That is why we refrained from giving him advice, although we were certainly concerned over the situation in the country and wanted it to improve fast.' If she voiced an opinion he didn't like, Yeltsin would tease Naina, a qualified sanitary engineer, by saying, 'Just concern yourself with the plumbing!' She would retort, 'If there was no plumbing, where would you go?'

The novelty of dealing with Raisa created a problem for the Soviet media. The liberal head of Soviet television from 1989 to 1990, Mikhail Nenashev, said she spoiled the mood of everyone when she became involved in a programme. He perceived her as unhealthily ambitious and he resented having to broadcast her speeches, which, like those of most spouses in her position, were often filled with empty banalities. If he cut them back, Gorbachev's aides gave him a hard time. Her favourite correspondent, Sergey Lomakin, believed Raisa did a lot of good, such as recruiting musicians and doctors she met abroad to come to Russia. But from the beginning Yegor Ligachev warned Gorbachev about the negative effect of her over-exposure on television, and even the submissive Kravchenko, who succeeded Nenashev, told Gorbachev that the shorter any item about her on television the better. When Gorbachev protested in a pained way that other world leaders travelled with their wives, Kravchenko responded that as a rule they didn't make declarations on television.

Gorbachev knew well from the start that some people made negative comments at seeing Raisa by his side, such as, 'Who does she think she is, a member of the Politburo?' Nevertheless, he valued her both as a close companion and a considerable political asset on his international travels. When he made a speech to French legislators in Paris on one of his first visits abroad, he glanced at Raisa in the audience and gave her what *Paris Match* described as a look full of tenderness. She made a stunning impression in London in 1984 when she appeared at an evening function in a stylish white satin dress and gold lamé sandals with chain straps, and held forth on English literature with British ministers. In Washington she discussed world affairs with prominent American women at the Washington home of socialite Pamela Harrison. *Woman's Own* magazine in the United Kingdom made her 'Woman of the Year' in 1987.

The masses inevitably resented her celebrity. The Russian women who endured harsh living conditions and had no access to haute couture disliked her as much as the Russian men reared in the domestic tradition of *domostroi*, the practice dating back to Ivan the Terrible under which husbands dominated and wives obeyed. Her elegance was a reminder that special shops with luxury clothes existed that were inaccessible to ordinary citizens. She became the subject of frequent gossip. Gorbachev complained in his memoirs that she supposedly went shopping with an American Express card when they didn't know what an American Express card was, and that she allegedly spent large sums on fashion to compete with Nancy Reagan, when all her clothes were made by seamstress Tamara Makeeva in Moscow. He raged in particular about Yeltsin spreading the 'lie' that he and Raisa had use of a gold credit card as a Politburo member. 'It was a disgrace to read all this nonsense.'

This story originated, however, in the Western media.

On June 6, 1988, *Time* magazine reported that after admiring Margaret Thatcher's diamond earrings on the trip to London four years earlier, Raisa 'dropped into Cartier on New Bond Street to buy a pair ($1,780) for herself, paying with the American Express card'. *Time* also claimed she owned four fur coats, and wore three of them in one day in Washington, and it made the unlikely allegation that Mikhail Gorbachev was once overheard quipping, 'That woman costs me not only a lot of money but also a lot of worry.'

Raisa was deeply offended by the many articles about her in Russia and abroad in which 'accuracy was totally absent, and invention, myths and even slander became the "basis" of what was written . . . If it had not been for my name appearing in the text I would never have believed they were writing about me.' Gorbachev blamed Western 'centres of psychological warfare' out to undermine him, and 'political riff-raff' in Russia who stirred up a campaign of innuendo against Raisa to discredit his reforms.

Much was also made in the American media of a cold war between Raisa and Nancy Reagan, wife of President Reagan. The former actress found the Marxist-Leninist lady hard going. 'She never stopped talking. Or lecturing, to be more accurate.' Nancy was taken aback when Raisa 'snapped her fingers to summon her KGB guards' to get a different chair. 'I couldn't believe it. I had met first ladies, princesses and queens, but I had never seen anybody act this way.'

Raisa developed a much warmer relationship with Barbara Bush, though George Bush had difficulty appreciating her deadpan humour. At a dinner in the Soviet embassy in Washington, the US president joked to Raisa, as they were being entertained by a very over-weight and unpretty Russian opera singer, 'I think I'm falling in love.' 'You'd better not,' she scolded him. 'Remember Gary Hart!' Bush concluded she had been briefed on the scandal surrounding the former senator, and that she was not kidding. Bush invited Jane Fonda, Van Cliburn, Douglas Fairbanks Jr, Dizzie Gillespie and other celebrities to a lunch in the White House after the Soviet embassy made it known Raisa wanted to meet stars of show business.

Raisa broke new ground by becoming the first Soviet leader's wife to engage in charitable work. She notably donated $100,000 in royalties from her husband's books in 1990 to improve Russia's treatment of child-hood leukaemia and she became an active patron of a children's hospital in Moscow. But she always main-tained a reserve about her private life and endured the negative press in dignified silence. 'Why should I talk about myself?' she told family friend Georgy Pryakhin, who was engaged to record a series of conversations with her for a short sentimental book called *I Hope*. 'I am not a film star or a writer or an artist or a musician or a fashion designer. And I am not a politician . . . I am the wife of the head of the Soviet state, supporting my husband as far as I can and helping him as I have always done ever since our young days when we linked our lives together.'

The book has just been published and no doubt has come to the attention of the Russian president, which goes some way to explaining his harsh actions towards her just when her husband is about to resign. Without naming him, she singles out Yeltsin and his acolytes for particular scorn in its pages. They are party men who for thirty years expounded the merits of 'barrack-room socialism' and were in charge of building society, and then announced that 'they will gladly destroy it all, and set about its destruction'. She is scathing about how easily some former comrades have changed their coats, and how 'yesterday's energetic propagandist for atheism today vows eternal loyalty to Christian dogmas'.

Valery Boldin would later characterize Raisa as tough, harsh, domineering and fussy, an imperious first lady who delivered barbs and humiliating lectures to those working for her. According to him she had no qualms about issuing orders over the phone to the general secretary's aides and to several members of the government. He seemed to enjoy her company at times, however, and related how they shared the pleasure of surreptitiously sipping red wine together on an international flight at the height of the anti-alcohol campaign. But he wrote that he recoiled when on the same flight she tried to order Gorbachev's aides, whose allegiance was first and foremost to the party, to swear an oath of loyalty to her husband. They all declined.

In the opinion of the president's interpreter, Pavel Palazchenko, who helped her with the English-language edition of I Hope, Raisa is not at all the aloof and didactic woman she often seems on television, but is an authentic person. Georgy Shakhnazarov believes Gorbachev would have benefited if he had listened to her advice more often, and that Raisa fulfilled her mission honourably and set a precedent for future spouses of Russian leaders.

Gorbachev's distress at Yeltsin's treatment of his wife on their last day as the Soviet Union's first couple is deepened by his knowledge of a truth they have obscured from the world: that Raisa is at the end of her tether. The drama of their life is something that 'ultimately she is not able to bear'. He acknowledges in time that she is a very vulnerable person. 'She was strong but she had to endure a great deal.' Only two decades later does he disclose how ill she is at the time. After the August coup 'she had a massive fit, or rather a micro stroke', he tells the newspaper *Novaya Gazeta*. 'Then she had a haemorrhage in both eyes. Her eyesight deteriorated dramatically. And the incredible stress continued.'

Gorbachev calls Raisa back and assures her that no one will intrude further into their state dacha that day. Still red in the face with anger after he replaces the receiver, he laments to his colleagues, 'What a disgrace! Can you imagine, it was the living space for the family for seven years. We have several hundred if not thousands of books there. We would need time to pack them all.' He has little but contempt for the people around Yeltsin, and for those who denounced the communists for their system of privileges and are now jostling each other 'like hogs at a trough'.

The eviction orders, delivered even before he has stepped down, make it clear to Gorbachev that he can no longer trust Yeltsin to honour the commitments in the transition package negotiated between them two days ago. He has to be prepared for more humiliations before the day is out.

It takes some minutes for him to calm down over the action of 'those jerks' and turn his mind again to the farewell address he is to give in three and a half hours. When he recovers his composure, Gorbachev turns to Grachev and says, 'You know, Andrey, the fact that they're acting this way makes me certain that I am right.'

15

Hijacking Barbara Bush

After the debacle in the Baltics in January 1991, Gorbachev realized he had to compromise with the republics if he was to have any chance of saving the Soviet Union. Force would not work. It only fuelled nationalist sentiment, went against his nature and threatened to destroy his legacy as a democratic reformer – not to mention slamming the door on the billions of dollars in international credits he was seeking to restructure the economy.

Therefore he invited Yeltsin and the leaders of the other fourteen Soviet republics to meet him on April 23 at Novo-Ogarevo, an estate with several fine buildings set in a pine grove high on the banks of the Moscow River. The aim would be to discuss a future union with more power devolved to the republics. Nine of them accepted his invitation, including Yeltsin.

The 'nine plus one' group – nine republic leaders plus Gorbachev – gathered in a second-floor room of a reception house constructed in the style of a nineteenth-century manor. Gorbachev sat at the top of a long table on which were placed four slim microphones to amplify his voice. Behind him the Soviet flag hung from a three-and-a-half-metre-high stand and a heavily bearded Karl Marx observed the proceedings from a portrait on the wall over Gorbachev's shoulder. The Soviet president was in a conciliatory mood. He said that he was ready to sign a draft union treaty giving real sovereignty to the republics, and that after a new Soviet constitution was adopted, he would dissolve the Congress of People's Deputies and hold direct elections for the post of Soviet president.

Now in a position to make, rather than demand, concessions, Yeltsin responded in kind, and dropped his insistence on full Russian sovereignty – which he was as yet unable to implement in any case. After a day-long discussion, Gorbachev dictated a statement which the nine presidents signed, noting that they were all prepared to work together on a new union treaty. They retired for dinner and toasts to a new beginning. For Gorbachev it was a load off his mind 'and a glimmer of hope emerged'. Yeltsin felt 'warmed and excited' after the lengthy session.

However, the new civility between Gorbachev and Yeltsin did not extend beyond the drawing rooms and lawns of Novo-Ogarevo. Yeltsin's political ambitions were soaring. To no one's surprise he announced that he would run for president of the Russian republic in the ground-breaking election for which he had got a mandate on the back of Gorbachev's referendum. Gorbachev professed to be neutral, but took steps to undermine Yeltsin's chances. Oleg Shenin, a Central Committee secretary, claimed that Gorbachev, who often referred to Yeltsin as unbalanced, repeatedly gave him an assignment to locate some documentation about Yeltsin's health. During the campaign the KGB provided Gorbachev with transcripts of Yeltsin's conversations with his security chief Alexander Korzhakov at a Moscow tennis club. The pleasant lady at the club who insisted on giving them post-match refreshments in her office ensured that they lingered within range of the KGB microphones installed there.

Yeltsin realized that without access to television he was at a disadvantage compared to a candidate with the backing of Gorbachev's Kremlin. Of all the republics, Russia was the only one without its own television channel. In those days Soviet television had two channels, Channel 1 for news and major events, and Channel 2 for sports and cultural and educational programmes. Both were broadcast throughout the Soviet Union. As the campaign got under way, the Russian parliament pressurized Kravchenko to cede its control of Channel 2 to the Russian government. The television chief gave in, for once without consulting Gorbachev. The president was furious, and raged at Kravchenko, 'How dare you help my opponents like this!'

Gorbachev correctly saw that a Russian channel would not only help Yeltsin but would become a propaganda tool against him. It went on air under its new masters on May 13, 1991, with fast-paced news and satirical sketches, including one of an old woman singing a song with the words, 'Gorbachev first banned vodka. Now he is banning food.'

In advance of the June election Yeltsin chose as his running mate Alexander Rutskoy, a former combat pilot and Afghan War hero whom he described as a real tiger, a macho man who would make middle-aged matrons swoon with delight. His only problem with the deputy was that he used expletives all the time, something Yeltsin abhorred. The straight-laced provincial was intolerant of the bad habits of others. Yeltsin also detested smoking and would take a cigarette from the fingers of a smoker sitting near him – on one occasion it was Hannelore Kohl, the wife of Chancellor Kohl of Germany – and stub it out.

His principal opponent was Nikolay Ryzhkov, but the humourless bureaucrat had only a record of failed economic reforms to show. The ebullient mood of the Yeltsin campaign was conveyed in an anecdote about a military helicopter pilot saying, 'Welcome aboard, future president of Russia,' and Yeltsin replying: 'Thank you, future general!'

Yeltsin won handily with his platform of radical economic reform and privatization in a more sovereign Russia. He received forty-six million votes compared to thirteen million for Ryzhkov and six million for the extreme nationalist Vladimir Zhirinovsky. Gorbachev's preferred runner, Vadim Bakatin, got fewer than three million votes. Yeltsin believed he won because the other candidates represented the old failed order while he embodied a yet non-existent country that everyone was waiting impatiently to appear. He had also shown that it was possible to be a Russian patriot while supporting greater freedom for the other republics. Their common enemy was the centre, representing Soviet imperialism. And at the heart of the centre was Gorbachev.

The inauguration of President Boris Nikolayevich Yeltsin as the first freely elected leader in Russia's thousand-year history took place on July 10, 1991, in the Kremlin Palace of Congresses, beneath a giant replica of a double-headed eagle. The pompous ceremony was designed to evoke the colour and majesty of pre-revolutionary Russia, and boost Yeltsin's national credentials and his political legitimacy. President Gorbachev was in attendance as the red RSFSR flag with hammer and sickle and blue stripe was hoisted into the azure summer sky over the building. When Yeltsin made his appearance a fanfare of trumpets rang out and the chimes of the Spassky Tower played the national anthem. Yeltsin had wanted a twenty-four-gun salute and a giant screen on Red Square to relay the scene to the masses but Gorbachev, still master of the Kremlin, vetoed this as over the top. Patriarch Alexey II of Moscow and all Russia, resplendent in jewelled cloak and crown, made a sign of the cross over Yeltsin, the first occasion on which the Orthodox Church had given a Russian leader its blessing since the time of the tsars. A full chorus performed the 'Glory' chorus from Glinka's *A Life for the Tsar*.

'Great Russia is rising from its knees,' declared Yeltsin. 'We shall surely transform it into a prosperous, law-based, democratic, peaceful and sovereign state.' In front of the television cameras Gorbachev reached out to shake Yeltsin's hand. The new Russian president deliberately stayed back, forcing Gorbachev to walk towards him.

After the inauguration Gorbachev assigned Yeltsin a ceremonial office in the Kremlin. It was located in the neo-classical mansion Building 14, erected by Stalin in the 1930s on the site of a convent and a small palace. It was a cobblestone's throw across a narrow courtyard from the much superior two-hundred-year-old Senate Building, listed as Building 1, where Gorbachev had his own suite of presidential offices. Gorbachev joked that there were two bears inhabiting the same den. That was when he thought the arrangement would endure.

Ten days later Yeltsin used his authority as elected president to make a bold move. He banned all political parties – there was only one – from organizing cells in farms, factories, colleges and military units and state bodies on the territory of Russia. Yury Prokofyev, first secretary of the Moscow Communist Party, rushed to Gorbachev's Kremlin office in a panic to demand he issue a decree countermanding Yeltsin. Gorbachev declined, partly to avoid a fight that would scupper the talks on a union treaty. In a single stroke, the Communist Party ceased to have a role in the Russian workplaces it had dominated for most of the century. By then Moscow had elected a radical Congress deputy, Gavriil Popov, as mayor, and the days when a party official ran the city, as Yeltsin once had, were at an end.

Observing what was going on, Gorbachev's doctrinaire aide Valery Boldin concluded that by letting Yeltsin get away with it, Gorbachev had like a coward abandoned and betrayed the Communist Party of the

Soviet Union of which he was still general secretary. In truth the great monolith created by Lenin was a fast-diminishing political force. Membership had declined by a quarter through resignations in the previous year, and the Politburo met only every few weeks, no longer a ruling body since Gorbachev had assumed the USSR presidency and chosen to rule by presidential decree from his Kremlin office.

The prospect of a new union treaty that would weaken the Soviet Union threw the revanchist forces in the USSR Supreme Soviet into a panic. They were on the brink of losing power. There was concern that Gorbachev was planning a party congress in the autumn of 1991 to create a new party of democratic socialism. On June 17, while Gorbachev was at Novo-Ogarevo and Yeltsin was absent in Washington, a small group of Gorbachev's disloyal ministers made their first move to turn back the tide. Prime Minister Valentin Pavlov put forward a resolution in the USSR Supreme Soviet to transfer many of Gorbachev's powers to himself, supposedly to deal with the critical economic situation. He demanded the authority to impose a ban on strikes, mobilize students and workers to save the harvest, and end moves to a market economy.

Stunned at his audacity the parliament went into a brief private session. Behind closed doors KGB chief Kryuchkov warned deputies that Western intelligence agents, planted inside the Kremlin and helped by Harvard economists, were plotting to destabilize the Soviet Union. Thus alarmed, the deputies continued their debate in open session for four days in an atmosphere of growing crisis. Gorbachev was nowhere to be seen, nor did he designate anyone to oppose this threat to his authority.

At midday on the third day of debate, June 20, Mayor Popov turned up at the US embassy and asked the ambassador Jack Matlock for an urgent meeting. In the embassy library, the former economics professor with a distinctive mop of white hair and bristling moustache put his finger to his lips and jotted a message on Matlock's spiral notebook in Russian: 'A coup is being organized to remove Gorbachev. We must get word to Boris Nikolayevich in Washington.' Matlock took the notebook and scrawled in Russian, 'Who is behind this?' Popov wrote, 'Pavlov, Kryuchkov, Yazov, Lukyanov.' Anatoly Lukyanov was the slippery speaker of the Supreme Soviet and a friend of Gorbachev since university days.

Matlock relayed Popov's message to Washington using a secure telephone system called STU-3. President Bush instructed him to warn Gorbachev personally, without mentioning the source. At eight o'clock in the evening the ambassador went to the Kremlin. He found the Soviet president alone with Chernyaev and in a mellow mood. They sat at the long table in his office. Gorbachev chuckled when Matlock told him of the warning. 'I have everything well in hand,' he said. 'We'll see tomorrow.' After Matlock departed, Gorbachev poked fun at American gullibility, but he stopped smiling when Chernyaev casually mentioned that he had heard a rumour about suspicious troop movements outside Moscow.

The Popov warning came as Yeltsin was getting the Rose Garden treatment at the White House as the elected president of Russia, though the Americans were still holding their nose. In his speech of welcome Bush managed to mention Gorbachev favourably more times than he mentioned his guest. In the Oval Office Bush told Yeltsin of Popov's warning. He jumped at the Russian's suggestion that they should call Gorbachev to reinforce the urgency of the warning. CIA director Robert Gates was struck by the strange picture of 'the presidents of the United States and Russia calling the president of the Soviet Union from the White House to warn him of a possible coup attempt'.

When Bush called Gorbachev he inadvertently named Popov as the source – even worse, he did so over a line known to be monitored by the KGB. Matlock was furious when he heard. He saw this careless intimacy as a measure of how deep Bush's infatuation with Gorbachev had become.

After leaving the White House, Yeltsin remarked caustically on how keen Bush was to get on the phone with his friend and that he was acting as if he were under Gorbachev's spell, like an adherent of Anatoly Kashpirovsky, a popular Russian faith healer.

Rather than thank Popov for the warning, or ask him for the source and reliability of his information, the Soviet leader, when he next met the Moscow mayor, shook his finger at him and said, 'Why are you telling tales to the Americans?'

Gorbachev reimposed his will on the Supreme Soviet the next day with a sustained and wrathful broadside, ending what he called the 'great scandal' created by Prime Minister Pavlov's irresponsible behaviour. After he harangued the cowering deputies, Pavlov's resolution was shelved. The Soviet president told reporters with a grin, 'The putsch is over!' Astonishingly Gorbachev did not fire his comic-opera prime minister, just as he failed to dismiss the bloodstained KGB chief and ministers of the interior and defence when they lied to him about Vilnius, though he privately lambasted them as 'scoundrels and bastards'.

At a subsequent meeting of the Central Committee, hardline communists raged at Gorbachev about his inadequacy in dealing with the crisis in party authority. 'All right,' he said. 'I'm quitting.' He walked out. Seventy-two of the three hundred members, among them Andrey Grachev, signed a statement saying they would leave the ranks of the party also. It was a ploy by Gorbachev and it worked. The challengers backed down. Gorbachev returned. Chernyaev gleefully noted how the gutless rabbits among Gorbachev's most trenchant critics who longed for a return to totalitarianism 'shit in their pants' and begged him to stay as head of the party. The Stalinists were trapped. If they lost him as general secretary, they lost any hold over the presidency, and Gorbachev as president could claim the loyalty of state structures.

Gorbachev, however, in his desire to hold his enemies close, missed an opportunity to divest himself of a thoroughly discredited ideology. This deepened his unpopularity with the reformers. On a visit to the Bolshoi Theatre that summer, Gorbachev was criticized from the stage by Yelena Bonner, widow of Andrey Sakharov, for his role in the Baltics crackdown. 'They celebrate Sakharov's legacy but they radiate hate, anger and revenge,' fumed the president to Chernyaev afterwards. 'How can one deal with these people? They have already forgotten who released Sakharov.'

Meanwhile negotiations for a new union treaty between Gorbachev and the republics' leaders continued over several sessions at the Novo-Ogarevo mansion during July 1991. Yeltsin would normally arrive last to underline his importance and his driver and security agent Korzhakov would make sure his limousine was manoeuvred to the front of the line of cars parked by the entrance – once infuriating the gardener by ploughing up the lawn to get into position. Typically Gorbachev made some introductory remarks as each session began and invited responses, whereupon the republic presidents averted their eyes like schoolboys and waited to see how Yeltsin would react. Gorbachev became embarrassingly supplicant and Yeltsin more bullying. Once the Russian president told Gorbachev bluntly to allow him to continue speaking. Boldin described Gorbachev 'looking at the protestor apologetically with his big, moist brown eyes'. On another occasion Gorbachev said that if the centre's ability to levy taxes was not maintained, 'I might as well go home.' Yeltsin responded by saying, 'Don't force us to decide the matter without you.' After a long silence Gorbachev called for a break and the issue was shelved.

A new structure for the Soviet Union emerged. The centre would retain foreign policy, defence and much financial authority, and the republics would otherwise govern themselves and gain control of their own resources and state security. The country would no longer bear the titles 'Soviet' or 'Socialist'. Gorbachev insisted, however, on a federal tax. Without it he would have no country.

Agreement was finally reached after a twelve-hour session that went on until 2.00 a.m. on July 29. A new union treaty, to be signed on August 20, would replace the 1922 treaty establishing the Soviet Union. Under it the republics would have sovereign control over their own political systems and the right to negotiate secession in the future.

But at its heart was a virus that could destroy the USSR. Gorbachev had yielded on the single tax issue. He had agreed that the levels of taxes to finance the institutions of the centre would be determined 'in consultation with the republics'. This meant that Russia and the other republics would have a veto on federal taxes. Western leaders had warned Gorbachev not to surrender on tax. Jacques Delors, President of the European Economic Commission, told him bluntly that he could only win the struggle if he insisted on a federal tax to finance a single armed force.

Gorbachev's concession, in the opinion of economist Yegor Gaidar, signalled the moment the Soviet Union fell apart. 'In essence this was the decision to dissolve the empire, raising hopes that it could be transformed into a soft confederation . . . it ended the history of the USSR as a single state.'

After the other presidents left at 3.30 a.m.,

Gorbachev and Yeltsin stayed behind with Nursultan Nazarbayev, president of the second-biggest Soviet republic, Kazakhstan, who strongly supported a continued union. They began to discuss what they would do after the new treaty came into effect. At one point Yeltsin stopped talking. 'What's up, Boris?' asked Gorbachev. The Russian president made a sign and indicated they should retire to the balcony. He had a feeling that the KGB might be listening.

Sitting on wicker chairs they continued their discussion in the unseasonably chilly night air. Yeltsin said he would nominate Gorbachev for the post of elected president of the new union of sovereign states. However, he must get rid of his 'odious entourage' in the cabinet – KGB chairman Kryuchkov, defence minister Yazov and interior minister Pugo, and other notorious hardliners – before the republics would sign up to a new centre. Gorbachev replied: 'We'll remove Kryuchkov and Pugo.' He would ditch his unpopular prime minister Valentin Pavlov and Nazarbayev could take his place. He would also get rid of the vice-presidency, held by the lacklustre Yanayev.

Only much later would they discover, from KGB transcripts found in Boldin's safe, that hidden microphones, placed on the balcony by Gorbachev's KGB chief of security, General Medvedev, had picked up every word. Kryuchkov – though he would later deny it – had put Gorbachev himself under close surveillance. Copies of the Soviet president's most intimate conversations were kept in a KGB file marked Subject No. 110. Raisa too was monitored. She was Subject

No. 111. There was even a microphone at the hairdresser's salon she frequented.

Though they had negotiated in a reasonably civil fashion, Gorbachev and Yeltsin still vied to upstage each other in front of the world. When George Bush arrived in Moscow for a summit with Gorbachev on July 30, Yeltsin demanded a separate meeting with him. The US president agreed to give him ten minutes, but stipulated that there would be no joint press conference afterwards.

Nevertheless, Yeltsin was on his home ground. The more he forced the Americans to pay attention to him, the greater his prestige in the eyes of Russians. He made Bush and Brent Scowcroft wait seven minutes outside his Kremlin office, kept them talking inside for forty minutes while he pressed Russia's case for aid, and facilitated a media ambush of the US president by allowing reporters to gather outside. 'Yeltsin's really grandstanding, isn't he?' complained Bush to Scowcroft as he left. Yeltsin subsequently declined to turn up at a separate meeting between Bush and the presidents of the Soviet republics hosted by Gorbachev so as not to be seen as a member of his rival's 'entourage'.

Yeltsin then telephoned Gorbachev before a Soviet state dinner for George and Barbara Bush and demanded that both of them escort the Bushes to their seats to demonstrate the new balance of power between the Russian and Soviet presidents. Gorbachev indignantly refused, saying this was his function as host. Yeltsin had other ideas. As Gorbachev and Raisa stood with George and Barbara Bush at the entrance to the dining hall in the Kremlin's Chamber of Facets to welcome the guests, they were puzzled to see Yeltsin's wife, Naina, arrive on the arm of Gavriil Popov. At the last minute Yeltsin turned up in majestic solitude and with elaborate courtesy offered to escort Barbara Bush to her table as if he were the host. 'Is that really all right?' asked Barbara, with a steely smile. The American First Lady kept Raisa between herself and the lumbering Russian as they walked to the tables. Gorbachev asked Yeltsin sarcastically why he had entrusted his wife to the Moscow mayor, to which Yeltsin replied cheerfully, 'Oh, he is no longer a danger!'

George Bush later described Yeltsin as a real pain for hijacking Barbara, and Matlock thought his behaviour boorish and childish. 'Everyone was dumbfounded except me,' noted Gorbachev. 'I knew Boris too well.'

Next day, at a dinner hosted by the Americans in the US embassy, Yeltsin and Nazarbayev found themselves seated some distance from the head table. They simply got up and walked to Bush's place and engaged him in lengthy conversation. No one dared tell them they were out of line. 'Our heroes experienced no embarrassment,' observed a disgusted Gorbachev. 'Of course this behaviour went beyond all bounds of protocol.'

Everyone saw that the dinner seating arrangements reflected Bush's preference for his friend Mikhail and his continued support for his efforts to hold the Soviet Union together. But the grandstanding served Yeltsin's purpose. It exposed the uncomfortable fact for the Americans that their hero Gorbachev was losing control over the previously subservient republics, and most importantly, Russia.

On July 31 Mikhail and Raisa Gorbachev entertained George and Barbara Bush and James Baker at a state dacha on the western outskirts of Moscow. They relaxed on wicker chairs on the sunlit veranda; Gorbachev in a grey shirt, sweater and slacks, Bush in a polo shirt. This was Gorbachev in his element, re-shaping the world with his international friends. But they were rudely interrupted.

An American official, John Sununu, intruded to give Baker a note: the Associated Press was reporting that armed men had attacked a Lithuanian border post. Seven customs officials had been killed, execution-style. Bush noted how Gorbachev visibly paled when told what was in the note. Deeply embarrassed at being informed first by the Americans, Gorbachev sent Chernyaev off to call Kryuchkov. The KGB chief dismissed the killings as an act of organized crime, or 'an internal Lithuanian thing'. It would later be established that it was a covert operation by the Soviet special police force, OMON, to teach the separatists a lesson, and most likely to compromise Gorbachev during his summit.

In the course of their conversation, Bush told Gorbachev that he did not think the collapse of the Soviet Union was in America's interests. He dismissed as extremists those in his own Republican Party who wanted the Soviet Union to break up, though the most prominent was his defence secretary, Dick Cheney. He promised to oppose separatist tendencies on his trip to Ukraine the following day.

On August 1 in the Ukrainian capital of Kiev, Bush

warned in a public speech that Americans would not aid those 'who promote a suicidal nationalism based upon ethnic hatred'. Bush's 'Chicken Kiev' speech, as it was dubbed by American columnist William Safire, delighted Gorbachev and infuriated Ukrainians who were moving fast towards a break with Moscow. It was widely seen as evidence that Bush was as seriously out of touch about what was happening in the Soviet Union as Margaret Thatcher, who a year before had said she could no more open an embassy in Kiev than she could in San Francisco.

With the Americans heading home, Gorbachev prepared to depart for a vacation at his presidential dacha at Cape Foros on the Black Sea. He told Chernyaev, using the diminutive of his aide's first name, 'I'm tired as hell, Tolya. Everywhere you look things are in a bad way . . . Everything has become so petty, vulgar, provincial. You look at it and you think, to hell with it all! But who would I leave it to? I'm so tired.'

He had everything riding on the new union treaty now. Before leaving on vacation, the Soviet president personally supervised preparations for a grand signing ceremony in the Kremlin's St George's Hall on August 20, the day after he was due back from Foros. He spent hours with staff discussing the placing of flags, the arrangement of chairs for the republic presidents and diplomats, the state banners to be displayed behind them, the delicacies and champagne to be served, and even the typeface for the treaty document.

Before he set off for the three-hour flight to Crimea on August 4, Gorbachev had a visit from his disillusioned old friend, Alexander Yakovlev, who informed him he was quitting as his adviser. He warned Gorbachev that if he didn't get rid of the 'dirty circle' around him, they would seize power. 'You exaggerate,' replied Gorbachev dismissively.

A few days later a KGB source tipped off Yakovlev that hardliners were conspiring to take control, and that he and Shevardnadze were on a death list. Yakovlev sought out a radical ex-KGB officer, Oleg Kalugin, for advice. They met in a busy street to avoid listening devices. Would the security organs really try to kill them, he asked. 'Kryuchkov is a madman, he might resort to anything,' replied Kalugin. KGB archives would later reveal that their conversation in the roadway was monitored by more than a dozen agents.

On August 16 Yakovlev resigned from the Communist Party and wrote an explanation for his action in the newspaper *Izvestia*. He had evidently got wind of the same information that Popov had. An 'influential Stalinist group', he warned in the article, 'is planning an imminent coup'.

16

December 25: Late Afternoon

'*D*OROGOI (DEAR) GEORGE, HAPPY CHRISTMAS TO you and Barbara!' Gorbachev cries.

It is late afternoon in the Kremlin, early morning in Camp David. His interpreter Pavel Palazchenko has succeeded at last in making the connection between the two presidents. Gorbachev takes the call at his office desk as Palazchenko listens on a separate handset. Ted Koppel and his ABC crew are seated in front of him, their sensitive microphone picking up both ends of the conversation. The president's press secretary Andrey Grachev has brought them into the office to witness the historic exchange.

Speaking in Russian and addressing the US president as *ty*, the form used for family and close friends, Gorbachev says, 'George, let me say something to you that I regard as very important. I have here on my desk a decree as the president of the USSR on my resignation. I will also resign my duties as commander-in-chief and will transfer authority to use nuclear weapons to the president of the Russian Federation. So I am conducting affairs until the completion of the constitutional process. I can assure you that everything is under strict control. As soon as I announce my resignation, I will put these decrees into effect. There will be no disconnection. You can have a very quiet Christmas evening.'

Gorbachev's translator is painfully aware that he is facilitating the last formal consultation between the two presidents, for whom he has interpreted many times. He cannot help wondering what is going through their minds. 'Was Gorbachev perhaps thinking that Bush could have done more for him? Was Bush trying to rationalize some of his decisions?' Was the American president concluding that he has 'done his best', but that things in Russia are 'beyond his control'?

Speaking as if he still has influence over events, Gorbachev tells the US president, 'The debate on our (new) union (treaty), on what kind of state to create, took a different tack from what I thought right. But let me say that I will use my political authority and role to make sure that this new commonwealth will be effective.'

It is important to promote cooperation rather than disintegration and destruction, Gorbachev adds. 'That is our common responsibility. I emphasize this point.'

Knowing of Bush's concern about the security of the USSR's nuclear arsenal, Gorbachev promises him again that he will ensure the safe transfer of the nuclear suitcase to the president of the Russian republic this evening, immediately after he has left office.

'I am pleased that already at Alma-Ata the leaders of the commonwealth worked out important and strategic agreements . . . I attach great importance to the fact that this aspect is under effective control. I've signed a decree on this issue that will come into effect immediately after my final statement. You may therefore feel at your ease as you celebrate Christmas, and sleep quietly tonight.'

Unable to bring himself to mention Yeltsin by name, Gorbachev promises to support the new administration in Moscow. 'But watch out for Russia,' he says. 'They will zig and zag. It won't all be straightforward.' As for himself, 'I do not intend to hide in the taiga. I will be active in political life. My main intention is to help all the processes here, begun by *perestroika* and new thinking in world affairs.'

Glancing at the ABC crew, he adds, 'Your people, the media here, have been asking me about my personal relationship with you. I want you to know at this historic time that I value greatly our cooperation together, our partnership and friendship. Our roles may change, but I want you to know that what we have developed together will not change. Raisa and I send to you and Barbara our best wishes.'

Bush reassures Gorbachev that their friendship is as strong as ever, 'No question about that.' He lavishes praise on his Kremlin counterpart. 'What you have done will go down in history, and future historians will give you full credit for your accomplishments.'

He is also delighted to hear that his friend does not plan to 'hide in the woods' and will stay involved politically and publicly. 'I am totally confident that will benefit the new commonwealth.'

The American president recalls a visit Gorbachev made to Camp David the previous year and how to everyone's amazement the Soviet leader tossed a ringer at his first try at the horseshoe pit where the president played one of his favourite games. Bush had presented Gorbachev with a horseshoe as a keepsake and Gorbachev had given him in turn a map of US military bases compiled by the KGB.

'You have found me up at Camp David once again,' he says. 'We're here with Barbara and with three of our children's families . . . The horseshoe pit where you threw that ringer is still in good shape . . . I hope that our paths will cross again soon. You will be most welcome here. And indeed I would value your counsel after you have had a little time to sort things out. And perhaps we could do it right back up here at Camp David.'

Out of deference to Gorbachev, Bush also avoids mentioning the Russian president by name. He indicates that the White House's relationship with Yeltsin will be cautious but not quite as friendly. 'I will of course deal with respect – openly, forcefully and hopefully pro-gressively – with the leader of the Russian republic and the leaders of these other republics . . . but none of that will interfere with my desire to stay in touch with you, to welcome suggestions from you as you assume whatever your new duties will be, and furthermore to keep intact the friendship that Barbara and I value very, very much.

'And so at this special time of year and at this historic

time, we salute you and thank you for what you have done for world peace. Thank you very much.'

'Thank you, George,' replies Gorbachev, his hazel eyes growing misty. 'I am glad to hear all of this today. I am saying goodbye and shaking your hands.'

Bush is deeply affected by the exchanges and the expressions of endearment. He senses that Gorbachev is drained of energy and uncertain about the future of the country he loves. He is taken aback later, when watching an account of the last day on ABC television news, to learn that his exchanges with Gorbachev were picked up by the camera crew. Normally conversations between himself and Gorbachev are private, overheard only by the interpreters and stenographers. 'However, I could hear Bush clearly,' recalled Koppel. 'It was one of those truly bizarre moments. Bush did not know I was listening and recording.'

After putting down the phone at Camp David and ending the telephone connection with Moscow, the US president switches on a little tape recorder in which he sometimes confides his private thoughts after encounters with world figures. Gorbachev's 'was the voice of a good friend', he murmurs into the machine. 'It was the voice of a man to whom history will give enormous credit. There was something very moving about this phone call . . . I don't want to get too maudlin or too emotional, but I literally felt like I was caught up in real history with a phone call like this. It was something important. Some enormous turning point.' Before switching off the recorder, he adds, 'God, we're lucky in this country! We have so many blessings.'

Anatoly Chernyaev feels that the ending of the Gorbachev–Bush tandem is an enormous loss to the world and that it is 'ridiculous, provincial and unworthy of Russia to ignore Gorbachev's contribution'. After the call he wonders if the rest of the world knows better Gorbachev's contribution to the advance of civilization than the Russians themselves. 'There has been an unwavering, genuine respect (abroad) for Gorbachev and gratitude for what he did. This is simply a matter of historical fact, and his epoch stands out as one of the most remarkable of the centuries.'

Andrey Grachev too has mixed feelings. He ponders how George Bush and James Baker wasted valuable time after coming to office in 1988 before engaging with Gorbachev, and convinces himself that they must share some of the blame for what is happening. 'To Gorbachev the value of historic time was different. The balloon was losing air, approaching the earth. While the drama in the Soviet Union was Shakespearean, Baker's reaction was methodical, calculated in America's interest.'

Gorbachev takes one more international call – his last as president – from Hans-Dietrich Genscher, foreign minister and vice-chancellor of Germany. Genscher wishes him well, a gesture that pleases Gorbachev as their relationship had become frosty over what he thought was Genscher's shabby treatment of him on a visit to Moscow in the autumn.

As Koppel begins another taped interview with Gorbachev for his documentary, Yegor Yakovlev asks Palazchenko in a whisper what the interpreter will do for a job, now that Gorbachev is resigning. Palazchenko tells Yakovlev that he hasn't figured anything out yet. He has been offered employment in the Russian foreign ministry but when Chernyaev had asked him if he had accepted he had replied indignantly, 'You can't think I would do anything other than leave government.' He mutters to Yakovlev, 'I know I just can't go over to work for the new boss, like the staff of the Kremlin cafeteria.'

'That is my problem too,' confesses the Russian television chief, who seems to Palazchenko to be on the verge of tears.

At that moment Gorbachev looks over and notices how distressed Yegor Yakovlev is. Finishing his remarks to the ABC camera, he comes to commiserate with his old friend, like a bereaved person who finds the strength to comfort someone grieving on his behalf. 'Well, Yegor, keep your chin up,' says the soon-to-be ex-president. 'Everything is only just beginning.'

As the weak winter sunshine fades and the lights start coming on in the Russian White House on the other side of the city centre, Boris Yeltsin decides that the time has come for him to talk to the world on television, to display his responsibility and statesmanship, before Gorbachev gives his farewell speech. He instructs his information minister Mikhail Poltoranin to call CNN and tell them the moment has arrived.

The CNN television crew come hurrying from their office in Building 7/4 on Kutuzovsky Prospekt, just across Novo-Arbatsky Bridge from the White House.

They are immediately let through security at the entrance and admitted to an ornate marble-walled banquet room.

Yeltsin has chosen this grand auditorium with massive chandeliers and large tapestries portraying pastoral scenes as an imposing backdrop for the big occasion. The crew arrange camera, lights and chairs. They get a two-minute warning that Yeltsin is on his way.

For CNN this is an outstanding triumph. The transition of power in the Soviet Union is the most important world story since the Gulf War ten months back, when the network scored a spectacular success with its coverage of the bombing of Baghdad. The Atlanta-based outfit has not only secured the sole television interview with Boris Yeltsin on his day of triumph. It has also acquired exclusive rights to broadcast live Gorbachev's farewell speech to the globe from the Kremlin later in the evening. Ted Koppel and Rick Kaplan of ABC are already in the Kremlin but have nothing like the personnel and equipment needed for such a major television operation.

Founded by Ted Turner in Atlanta in 1980 as the world's first round-the-clock television news service, CNN has invested heavily in the Soviet Union during its first decade. It located one of its pioneer foreign bureaux in the Russian capital. Turner brought the Goodwill Games to Moscow in 1986 to encourage competition between US and Soviet athletes, after the United States boycotted the 1980 Olympic Games over the Soviet Union's invasion of Afghanistan. On a trip to

Russia during the early days of Gorbachev's reforms, the CNN founder was so impressed by the new Communist Party general secretary that he suggested to a bewildered Soviet official that he should be made an honorary member of the party. The official politely demurred, and offered him instead membership in the Soviet Union of Journalists, which Turner in turn declined, citing his distaste for trade unions of any kind.

In 1989 CNN became the first non-Soviet broadcaster to be allowed to beam its news programmes into Moscow. Initially it was only available in the exclusive Savoy Hotel for viewing by foreign guests, but amateur Russian engineers found they could rig up an aerial to get the network's signal on their home television screens. In the days before the internet and mobile phone, this had a considerable impact on how Russians saw events in their own country, and made censorship of news almost impossible.

They almost missed out on the drama of the last day of the Soviet Union. Only when CNN executives got wind that ABC's Ted Koppel had secured unique access to the Kremlin to film Gorbachev's last days were they jolted into action. In Atlanta CNN president Tom Johnson decided to throw all the station's resources into battle with their rival. A former publisher of the *Los Angeles Times*, Johnson took over the CNN presidency the previous year and has established a reputation for being ferociously competitive. He set out himself for Moscow on December 18, taking with him Stuart (Stu) Loory, a former CNN Moscow bureau chief who could speak Russian, to lobby for the first interview with

Boris Yeltsin as the new leader of Russia and the final interview with Gorbachev as leader of the USSR, though they were not even absolutely sure a transition would happen.

Johnson called on the Russian information minister to make his case for the Yeltsin interview. He cited to Poltoranin their exclusive coverage from Baghdad, and showed the information minister the latest colour global satellite distribution map, emphasizing that no other news organization on the planet could reach as many nations. Poltoranin snapped, 'I know that!' Taken aback, Johnson proposed that they would link the interview with Yeltsin to Russian television to ensure it got shown across the country. 'The entire spirit of the talks became very friendly after that,' he recalled. Johnson was brought to meet Yeltsin, who agreed to an exclusive interview on the day, though precisely when that would be Yeltsin could not tell him. He gave the Russian president a copy of *Seven Days That Shook the World*, a CNN book on the failed August coup. Poltoranin promised an interview on the day.

It helped that CNN was a known quantity in Moscow, explained bureau chief, Steve Hurst. 'We were in the offices of serious players day and night.'

The company started bringing people to Moscow from all over the world. Charlie Caudill, senior CNN producer in charge of live coverage, flew in from Atlanta to head the biggest crew ever assembled for a single foreign television event up to that time. The group of seventy-five included executives, producers, directors, interviewers, camera operators, sound operators, managers and interpreters. Unit manager Frida Ghitis arrived in Moscow to find that the bureau staff had already spent weeks 'begging for interviews from Yeltsin and Gorbachev', and strategically placing boxes of chocolates and bottles of whisky in the hands of their aides. 'There was great pressure to beat the competition,' she remembered, 'and Koppel's name came up with some frequency.'

The large CNN team then wait for the day of Gorbachev's resignation. 'We were nervous that Gorbachev would resign ahead of schedule or that other networks would outflank us,' said Loory. On the afternoon of December 24 there is a false alarm. Everyone swings into action. 'So now we are rolling to the Kremlin with five or six trucks with cameras and equipment,' recalled Caudill. 'The lights are out at the Kremlin. Tom hands his business card to the guard at the gate. The guard has no idea what is going on.' In fact nothing is happening and the convoy of CNN vehicles and thirty-four staff turns round and goes back the way it came.

With everyone far from home, Johnson decides to host a Christmas Eve party in the hotel. He asks Frida Ghitis to get him a Santa Claus hat. A Russian helper is unable to find the right material in the stores. Even the seamstresses at the Bolshoi Theatre and the Moscow Circus cannot help. Ghitis spots a picture in a newspaper of a Norwegian Santa Claus delivering presents to children in a Moscow orphanage. 'In the end we bought the hat from the Norwegian Mister Claus,' she said. 'The party of course was a bust, in spite of Johnson's lovely hat and matching white beard. Just as it got under way we learned that everything would happen next day, and everyone was much too busy preparing for the two interviews.'

Now that the interview with Yeltsin is about to take place, Charlie Caudill is checking with Russian officials that all the arrangements in the White House are in place and that the simultaneous translation will work smoothly. He asks Yeltsin's aide which ear he would prefer for the earpiece. The aide replies, 'He's deaf in one ear.'

'Which ear?'

'I don't know.'

'Ask him!'

'No, I will not ask the president of Russia which ear!'

Caudill turns to the CNN technician, who can speak Russian, 'When Yeltsin sits down, whisper in his ear, "Nice to meet you." If he smiles, it is the correct ear.'

The moment arrives. Escorted by Johnson, Yeltsin makes a majestic appearance, slowly descending a wide carpeted staircase, immaculate in suit and shiny black shoes, his mane of silver hair perfectly in place, showing no sign that he 'sweats buckets' before going on television. He parades along a red runner on the polished parquet floor to where three upholstered drawing-room chairs with gold brocade are arranged for Steve Hurst and Claire Shipman to conduct the interview. The technician murmurs a greeting as Yeltsin sits and the earpiece is fitted on his left side. He smiles. They have guessed the correct ear. The Russian president lost the hearing on his right side as a result of untreated otitis, an inflammation of the inner ear, when he was a youth.

Johnson, who once worked for President Lyndon B. Johnson, is struck by how Yeltsin resembles his former boss in that he is 'very strong, powerful, forceful, a real giant of a man'. Shipman finds the Russian president in ebullient form. 'He was on his game, really in his prime, very aware of his power and incredibly confident, but not crowing in an obvious way. He had a gleam in his eye, and a mischievous look. I felt he was impatient to get there.' Hurst remembers Yeltsin as being 'very excited, very much on edge, not at all sure of what would happen next'.

Yeltsin uses the interview to reassure viewers abroad that the break-up of the Soviet Union does not mean nuclear weapons falling into the wrong hands. He urges the world not to worry about it. There will not be a single second after Gorbachev makes his resignation announcement that the nuclear codes will go astray, he says. 'We will do all we can to prevent the nuclear button from being used – ever.'

He professes empathy with his defeated rival. 'Today is a difficult day for Mikhail Sergeyevich,' he says graciously, when asked what mistakes Gorbachev made. 'Because I have a lot of respect for him personally and we are trying to be civilized people and we are trying to make it into a civilized state today, I don't want to focus on those mistakes.'

Instead he scolds the international community for not extending more aid to Russia in its hour of need. 'There has been a lot of talk, but there has been no specific assistance,' he says. Perhaps this is because willing nations do not know to what postal address they should send humanitarian assistance. 'Now everything is clear, and the addressees are known.' Living standards will decline for at least another year, he warns, and the world must help Russia to shed its 'nightmarish totalitarian inheritance'.

Yeltsin chides US secretary of state James Baker for waiting until he left Russia after a fact-finding visit the previous week to express pessimism about the survival chances of the Commonwealth of Independent States that will replace the Soviet Union, though everyone, including the Russian president, knows the CIS is little more than a fig leaf for the divorce.

'Mr Baker, when he and I had a four-and-a-half-hour meeting here in Moscow, never told me that, so those who doubt the success of the commonwealth should beware and not be so pessimistic. The people here are weary of pessimism, and the share of pessimism is too much for the people to handle. Now they need some belief, finally.'

He ends the interview beaming and wishing everyone, 'Happy Christmas!'

The proceedings are recorded by a broad-faced man with a short haircut standing at a discreet distance with a heavy film camera on his shoulder. Yeltsin's personal cameraman, Alexander Kuznetsov, has the task of recording the Russian president's daily activities. He sees his role as providing footage of Yeltsin that will be sufficiently flattering so that 'Naina is satisfied and his daughters will not be making faces in front of the television'. He is secretly an admirer of Gorbachev, and was in negotiations with Andrey Grachev to work for the Soviet president until he received a more tempting offer from Yeltsin. He did not mention this when he was being hired as 'Yeltsin couldn't stand Gorbachev'.

The job of recording the colourful Russian president's life and times, he reflects, puts him 'in the front row of the political theatre of the time, enjoying the performance of the best actor at the end of the second millennium'. However, in Kuznetsov's opinion, 'It is Gorbachev's name that will be written in history in gold writing – and Yeltsin's only in capital letters.'

17

Perfidiousness, Lawlessness, Infamy

O N SATURDAY, AUGUST 17, 1991, KGB CHIEF VLADIMIR
Kryuchkov invited a small number of highly
placed party members to join him for a steam bath in a
secret KGB guesthouse at the end of Moscow's Leninsky
Prospekt. They included defence minister Dmitry Yazov,
prime minister Valentin Pavlov, President Gorbachev's
chief of staff Valery Boldin, and two other senior party
officials, Oleg Baklanov and Oleg Shenin.

Wrapped in towels in the sauna they made small talk.
Kryuchkov told them of an intelligence report that
seemed to show Gorbachev kowtowing to America. It
wasn't until they had dressed and were drinking vodka
and Scotch whisky at a trestle table in the garden that
Kryuchkov revealed the reason they had all been
invited.

The country was facing total chaos, he said.
Gorbachev was not acting adequately. He had intelligence that Gorbachev planned to fire the prime minister
and other members of government, including himself,

after the ceremonial signing of the new union treaty on the following Tuesday. The treaty would mean the end of the USSR and could not be tolerated. If Gorbachev would not lead them and if they could not control him, he would have to be forced to leave the scene.

It was time to make a move, he went on. Gorbachev was due to return from his Black Sea vacation on Monday. They would send a delegation to Foros tomorrow, Sunday, and ask the president to join them in declaring a state of emergency. If he refused, they would invite him to resign. They would set up an emergency committee and do what was needed themselves.

They all went along with the plan. Yazov offered to provide a military plane to fly to Foros. In the meantime he would bring troops into Moscow to demonstrate to the populace where power lay. The defence minister smirked at Boldin. He joked that when Gorbachev saw that his chief of staff was involved, he would say, '*Et tu, Brute?*' Boldin was hardly in a mood for humour, however. He was ill with a liver ailment and had been on an IV drip in the hospital for a week, but he had signed himself out because the country was disintegrating and 'I simply had to set my personal considerations aside'.

The plotters were told by Kryuchkov that interior minister Boris Pugo was an instigator of the plan and he was confident that Vice President Gennady Yanayev would cooperate once he was informed. He was also sure they could handle any resistance from the general population. Two hundred and fifty thousand pairs of handcuffs had been ordered from a factory in Pskov, and Lefortovo prison made ready for an influx of detainees.

The coup got under way the next day, Sunday, August 18, with the house arrest of Mikhail Gorbachev. A military plane provided by Yazov landed at the Belbek military base near Foros at 5.00 p.m. after a three-hour flight from Moscow. On board were Baklanov, Shenin, Boldin and another enthusiastic putschist, General Valentin Varennikov. The four men represented the pillars of the Soviet establishment. Baklanov, with a broad earnest face and furrowed brow, was head of the Soviet Union's military-industrial complex. Shenin, prematurely bald with a large domed forehead, was the Politburo member responsible for party organization. Boldin, besides being Gorbachev's chief of staff, was a senior member of the Central Committee. Varennikov, in large rimless glasses with a thin moustache and lank hair combed over in Hitler style, was commander of Soviet land forces.

The delegation was driven by KGB officers in two ZiL limousines to the state dacha with marble walls and orange-tiled roof where the Gorbachevs were spending the last day of their two-week summer vacation. They were joined inside the compound gate by another plotter, General Yury Plekhanov, the stolid unsmiling head of the KGB's Ninth Directorate, who represented a fifth pillar of Soviet power, the security organs. Plekhanov deployed new guards around the perimeter of the dacha, ordered the head of Gorbachev's security to return to Moscow and put men with automatic weapons outside the garage so none of Gorbachev's party could get to the cars or use the radio telephones in the automobiles.

The president was in his second-floor office dressed in shorts and a pullover, reading the text of the speech he would give to launch the new union in Moscow in two days' time. In it he had written a warning: 'If we turn back now, our children will never forgive us such ignorance and irresponsibility . . .'

In a guesthouse on the dacha compound, Colonel Vladimir Kirillov, one of the two plainclothes officers in charge of the nuclear suitcase, was watching television when the screen went blank. An emergency light on the *chemodanchik* started blinking. This was it – a nuclear alert! He picked up his radio telephone with a direct link to government communications. He was told there had been an accident, and not to worry. At 4.32 p.m. he lost contact with his controller in Moscow, KGB General Viktor Boldyrev. General Varennikov appeared at the door. 'How are your communications?' he asked. 'There aren't any,' replied the colonel. 'That's how it should be,' said Varennikov. He assured him that contacts would be restored within twenty-four hours.

At 4.50 p.m. the head of Gorbachev's bodyguard interrupted the president to say that a group of people had arrived to speak with him. Gorbachev was not expecting anyone. Somewhat alarmed he picked up a receiver to call Kryuchkov in Moscow. The line was dead. All four telephones on his desk and the internal phone were no longer working. In an outer office Anatoly Chernyaev suddenly realized that his government line, satellite link and internal telephone were all down.

He guessed immediately what was up.

Gorbachev went to the veranda where Raisa was reading a newspaper in the company of their thirty-four-year-old daughter Irina and son-in-law Anatoly Virgansky, a surgeon. He warned them they might be arrested. 'I will not give in to any kind of blackmail,' he promised Raisa.

He went back and found that Baklanov, Shenin, Boldin, Varennikov and Plekhanov had rudely occupied his office. Baklanov did the talking. The country was facing disaster, he said. A committee of emergency was being set up. Yeltsin was under arrest, or at least soon would be. The president must immediately sign the decree on the declaration of a state of emergency, or resign and hand over powers to Vice President Yanayev. Then he could stay in Foros while 'measures' were taken.

Gorbachev demanded to know who was on the committee and was shocked to hear that Yazov and Kryuchkov were its leaders. He tried to reason with the intruders. They could discuss and decide matters within the framework of the law but martial law and the use of force were unacceptable, he said. With his instinct for manoeuvring and compromise, he suggested a different course for the plotters: 'Since a conflict of opinion has arisen between us, let us immediately convene a Congress of People's Deputies and the Supreme Soviet. And let them decide. If they agree with your proposals by all means let it be done your way, but for my part I reject that and will not support it.'

The conspirators said they would brook no delay. Baklanov suggested, 'You take a rest and while you are away we will do the dirty work and you will return to Moscow.'

At that, Gorbachev blew up. He called the men criminals. 'Go to hell, shitfaces!' he shouted.

The bespectacled Varennikov, who towered over Gorbachev, could hardly disguise his contempt. 'Hand in your resignation!' he barked rudely at the president.

Boldin broke in, 'Mikhail Sergeyevich, perhaps you don't understand the situation—'

Gorbachev cut him off, 'You're an asshole. You should shut up!'

The Soviet president refused to authorize any declaration of martial law. Tempers cooled and he shook the hands of the delegation as they left.

The Gorbachev family, including two grandchildren, Kseniya and Nastya, found themselves isolated by the new KGB guards around the perimeter of the dacha. Gorbachev confided to Chernyaev, 'Yes, this might not end well, but you know, in this case I have faith in Yeltsin, he won't give in to them.' Chernyaev could not help but blurt out, 'These are your people, Mikhail Sergeyevich. You fostered, promoted, trusted them.' Gorbachev cursed himself for having a year before given Shenin the top job of party organizer. He had taken him to be a reformer.

Raisa could not sleep on their first night of house arrest. She was 'tormented by bitterness at the betrayal of people who worked side by side with Mikhail Sergeyevich'. The treachery of Boldin was most hurtful to her. 'We have been soulmates for fifteen years. He was like a family member with whom we trusted everything – our most intimate secrets.' Fearing they might be poisoned, she insisted the family eat only food delivered before the coup started.

Confused, the conspirators returned to Moscow. They had hoped to intimidate the vacillating Gorbachev into signing the decree and giving their putsch legitimacy, or else step down temporarily while they got rid of his awkward rival, Boris Yeltsin. Boldin realized now that they had miscalculated. Without Gorbachev's authority they had no mandate. He later recalled that 'everything went haywire from the start'.

Later on Sunday evening they gathered in Pavlov's office in the Kremlin. Yanayev was summoned to meet them. He was tipsy when he arrived. But he was no pushover. Chain-smoking and downing shots of vodka with a shaking hand, Yanayev had to be cajoled into signing the document declaring himself acting president of the Soviet Union as a result of the 'illness' of President Gorbachev. He finally did so just after the chimes of the Kremlin's Saviour Tower clock sounded eleven o'clock. Kryuchkov and the other conspirators signed a decree to establish martial law for six months. Anatoly Lukyanov, whose closeness to Gorbachev deceived people into thinking he was a democrat, also arrived in Pavlov's office. He needed no persuading to give the coup a veneer of legitimacy as Congress speaker. Foreign minister Alexander Bessmertnykh, summoned back from vacation several hundred miles southwest of Moscow, arrived after midnight. He found his name on the list of committee members and crossed it off. He left for home, not to emerge again until it was all over. But he didn't prevent Soviet embassies taking orders from the committee and disseminating its propaganda. Boldin returned to the hospital where he was heavily sedated.

Meanwhile Yazov issued coded telegram 8825 ordering the top military leadership to move troops into Moscow. Kryuchkov assigned a special KGB unit to place Boris Yeltsin under surveillance in preparation for his arrest.

That Sunday evening Yeltsin was in Alma-Ata, almost two thousand miles from Moscow, meeting Kazakhstan's president Nursultan Nazarbayev. He delayed his scheduled departure to partake of a sumptuous dinner with Kazakh folk music and 'colourfully dressed girls whirling around', during which he amused everyone by playfully performing with wooden spoons on the head of an assistant, Yury Zaiganov. Well fortified, Yeltsin left just after 8.00 p.m. local time for the long flight back to Moscow. When he arrived there he was driven straight to his dacha at Arkhangelskoye. No one stopped him.

Shortly after six o'clock next morning, he was shaken awake by his daughter Tanya who flew into the room shouting, 'Papa! Get up! There's a coup!'

Millions of people in Russia would never forget what they were doing when they heard the dawn proclamation on radio and television that Monday, August 19, 1991, that suddenly reintroduced fear into their lives. Sitting in his vest Yeltsin watched Yury Petrov, state television's star announcer, broadcast a statement by an emergency committee that Gorbachev was ill, that Vice President Yanayev had assumed the duties of the president and that martial law existed in the USSR. The announcer said that the action of political movements was to be halted, illegally held arms were to be handed in, meetings and demonstrations were banned and the mass media was to come under emergency control. After the announcement, Tchaikovsky's *Swan Lake* was broadcast repeatedly.

Most of the Russian leadership lived close to the Yeltsin residence and they began arriving in a panic at his dacha. Alexander Korzhakov turned up, and Ruslan Khasbulatov, the speaker of the Russian Supreme Soviet, came racing across from the dacha next door. They found Yeltsin slumped in an armchair, hung-over and stunned. His top aides, Gennady Burbulis, Ivan Silayev, Mikhail Poltoranin and Viktor Yaroshenko, all came in and congregated around him. Moscow's popular deputy mayor, Yury Luzhkov, showed up, promised to organize resistance and left. Anatoly Sobchak, mayor of the former Leningrad which two months earlier had reverted to the name St Petersburg, who happened to be in Moscow that day, arrived and vowed to rally opposition in Russia's second city. Then he too departed, saying, 'May God help us!'

Yeltsin called Pavel Grachev, commander of the paratroops, whom he had recently befriended, to ask what was going on. The forty-three-year-old general was moving troops around as ordered, but he promised to send a squad to the dacha to ensure Yeltsin's safety. Perhaps the plotters did not have the total loyalty of the military.

By 9.00 a.m. Yeltsin had recovered sufficiently to dictate an appeal to the people of Russia to resist the 'cynical attempt at a right-wing coup'. The fax machine was still working in the dacha and within an hour the appeal was being circulated by leaflet throughout Moscow and broadcast on radio stations around the world. Gorbachev, isolated in Foros, heard about the embryonic resistance on a tiny Sony radio that he listened to while shaving.

The Russian president decided to make a run for the Russian White House. 'Listen, there are tanks out there,' Naina protested. 'What's the point of you going?' He replied, 'They won't stop me.' As always his women made sure Yeltsin was presentable before he left. Tanya straightened his jacket so that his bullet-proof vest was not noticeable. 'Your head is still unprotected, and your head is the main thing,' cried Naina.

Yeltsin and Korzhakov decided to go directly to the White House in a convoy of official vehicles with a Russian flag of white, blue and red fluttering from the bonnet of the black Chaika carrying the Russian president. Their departure was watched by a small KGB surveillance division under Commander Karpukhin that had been ordered to take up position in the woods around. Karpukhin would testify later that he had orders to arrest Yeltsin but that he let him drive away. But Kryuchkov had delayed issuing orders to arrest people on a list of eighty democrats singled out for detention, including Eduard Shevardnadze and Alexander Yakovlev. He preferred to try at first to cow the opposition and not appear heavy-handed. It was one of many misjudgements that doomed the coup from the outset.

With Yeltsin squeezed between bodyguards in the back, the Chaika barrelled unimpeded past tanks churning up Kutuzovsky Prospekt and then raced across Novo-Arbatsky Bridge and into the underground car park of the White House, arriving at around 10.00 a.m. In his office he found that all telephone lines had been cut but one: it had been installed the day before the coup and was not yet registered. Yeltsin was able to call allies in Russia and around the Soviet Union.

Outside the White House armoured vehicles from the Tamanskaya motorized infantry division took up position but without orders of any kind. The division chief of staff Major Yevdokimov said he had no intention of harming any of the young men and middle-aged women who had started milling around outside the White House, furious at the idea that Yeltsin might be arrested.

Shortly after midday, Yeltsin came out flanked by bodyguards armed with Kalashnikov rifles and climbed aboard a T-72 tank. He read his statement to about two hundred supporters, raising his voice over the sound of the heavy military vehicles rumbling past. He called for a general strike and opposition to the 'right-wing, reactionary, unconstitutional coup'.

After he hurried back into the White House, the crowd began to pile up concrete slabs and metal rods to form barricades. By late afternoon the numbers had swelled to several thousand.

The coup had already begun to falter. Around the city, tank crews were fraternizing with pedestrians. Pavlov's nerves were failing him and he started drinking large whiskies. Yazov found him 'absolutely plastered' in the Kremlin and he had to be carried out to his car and driven home. He was in no state to take part in the televised press conference of the emergency committee, held at 5.00 p.m. in the foreign ministry press centre.

That Monday evening television viewers saw the committee for the first time – six men in grey-blue suits, sitting at a table on a stage with a pasty-faced Yanayev in the middle. His nicotine-stained fingers trembling, Yanayev justified their action on the grounds that normal life had become impossible. He lied that Gorbachev was 'undergoing treatment' for illness. There was derisive laughter when an Italian journalist asked if they had consulted General Pinochet on how to stage a coup. The Russian and foreign reporters there managed to inform millions of viewers what state television had been withholding, by asking questions about Yeltsin's strike call and the resistance building up at the White House.

That night the Russian president bedded down in the doctor's surgery on the third floor of the White House, where the windows faced the inner courtyard. His family were spirited from the dacha for safety in an unmarked van with curtained windows to a two-bedroom apartment in the suburb of Kuntsevo belonging to one of his bodyguards.

By Tuesday morning, August 20, George Bush, who initially had stopped short of condemning the coup committee – on Scowcroft's advice he had called their action extra-constitutional rather than illegitimate so as not to burn his bridges with the coup leaders – had got a better idea of what was happening. He managed to get through to Yeltsin.

'Boris, my friend,' cried the US president.

Yeltsin was overwhelmed. 'I am *extremely* glad to hear from you!' he shouted in response. 'We expect an attack, but your call will help us.'

'We're praying for you,' said Bush.

From a balcony at the Russian White House, protected by lead shields held by Korzhakov and another bodyguard, Yeltsin read out a second statement. In it he called on soldiers and police to disobey the orders of Yazov and Pugo, but not to seek confrontation.

In St Petersburg Mayor Sobchak confronted troop commanders and persuaded them not to enter the city. At his side opposing the putsch was his special assistant, KGB officer Vladimir Putin. 'Sobchak and I practically moved into the city council,' Putin recounted years later. 'We drove to the Kirov Factory and to other plants to speak to the workers. But we were nervous. We even passed out pistols, though I left my service revolver in the safe. People everywhere supported us.'

Putin was concerned that his behaviour as a KGB officer could be considered a crime of office if the plotters won. He expressed this fear to his boss and Sobchak called Kryuchkov on his behalf. Astonishingly the mayor was able to get the chief organizer of the putsch on the phone to discuss such a matter of minor consequence given the scale of events –

that Putin was resigning from the KGB forthwith.

Kryuchkov by now seemed to realize his mistake in not securing the arrest of Yeltsin. Public opposition was consolidating around the Russian president. The emergency committee was falling apart. Pavlov and Bessmertnykh had disappeared. Yanayev was drinking himself into a stupor. The defenders of the White House now included many high-profile personalities, including Politburo veteran Alexander Yakovlev, the cellist Mstislav Rostropovich, the poet Yevgeny Yevtushenko and Sakharov's widow, Yelena Bonner. Shevardnadze was also there, asking aloud if Gorbachev himself was implicated in the coup. At five o'clock in the morning Yeltsin remembered it was his daughter Lena's birthday and rang to congratulate her. Later he gave her a spent cartridge as a present.

That afternoon one of the military's youngest commanders, forty-one-year-old General Alexander Lebed, went to the White House and secretly informed Yeltsin's defenders that an attack would begin at 2.00 a.m. the next day. Lebed had been impressed by Yeltsin when the Russian president had visited the headquarters of the 106th Airborne Division in Tula earlier in the summer. He observed him making friends with servicemen, taking off his watch and presenting it to a lieutenant and then pulling an identical one from his pocket to give to a sergeant.

All women were told to leave the White House and the defenders got ready for an assault. Preparations were made to smuggle Yeltsin to the sanctuary of the nearby US embassy.

Meanwhile Yazov found he could not get a single military commander to lead an attack on the White House. Field Marshal Yevgeny Shaposhnikov, the forty-nine-year-old air force commander, quietly tried to persuade the old soldier to quit the coup committee. When Yazov asked him instead to prepare helicopters to land KGB Alpha Group troops on the roof of the White House, Shaposhnikov threatened to send a pair of air-craft to bomb military vehicles in the Kremlin. In Stalin's days Shaposhnikov would have been shot, but under Gorbachev the conflicted military had become a debating society.

The Alpha Group mutinied when ordered to attack the White House. Alexander Yakovlev concluded after-wards that 'they refused to have blood on their hands for the sake of such idiots as Kryuchkov and Yazov'.

The danger passed. In the early hours of Wednesday Yazov ordered all troops to withdraw from Moscow. The operetta-like coup collapsed. Kryuchkov tele-phoned Burbulis in the White House at 3.00 a.m. and told him they could sleep peacefully. Next morning the KGB chief requisitioned a plane to take him and other junta members to Foros to try to come to terms with Gorbachev.

The Gorbachev family had watched the plotters' press conference on television with incredulity. 'What perfidiousness, lawlessness, infamy!' wrote Raisa in her diary. 'Needless to say we are ready for anything, even the worst.' She was terrified that the lie about her husband's illness meant they intended he should actually die.

Gorbachev saw some virtue in Yeltsin's stubborn personality at last. He told Chernyaev he was convinced that Boris Nikolayevich had shown his true nature and nothing would break him.

On the second day the nuclear suitcase and its colonel-guardians had been escorted to the airport, where a plane was waiting to take them to Moscow. By nightfall the three suitcases were in the hands of defence minister Yazov and chief of the general staff General Mikhail Moiseyev. Ruslan Khasbulatov later testified that the colonel-guardians of Gorbachev's *chemodanchik* destroyed the cipher to communicate with strategic command, but the vast nuclear arsenal of the Soviet Union had temporarily come under the sole control of the hardliners.

As the coup was collapsing Raisa suffered a minor stroke. 'I felt a numbness and a limpness in my arm and the words would not come,' recalled Gorbachev's wife. She was put to bed by the family doctor, Igor Borisov, who was with them in the house when it all started. Her power of speech came back shortly afterwards but she would never fully recover.

At three o'clock on Wednesday afternoon they heard on BBC news that Kryuchkov was leading a delegation to Foros in the presidential jumbo. This caused panic at the dacha. Gorbachev feared that with the coup in danger they were coming to do him harm. He ordered the five members of his personal security detachment, which had remained loyal, to block the driveway and deploy with machine guns along the staircase. 'This is it, they are going to make us fit Yanayev's announcement [that Gorbachev is unwell],' thought Raisa.

Shortly after five o'clock two ZiLs arrived from the airport bearing Yazov, Kryuchkov, Baklanov, Lukyanov and two others who wanted to plead with Gorbachev for their safety and negotiate a way out of the crisis. They were, by Kryuchkov's account, hoping to persuade Gorbachev to face down the Russian government and halt its drive towards full sovereignty for the sake of the integrity of the Soviet Union. But the beleaguered president refused to meet either the KGB chief or Yazov.

Gorbachev's telephone lines were restored shortly after 6.30, though only for outgoing calls. He immediately got through to Yeltsin who responded in the most affectionate terms. 'Mikhail Sergeyevich, my dear man, are you alive?'

Thirty minutes later he got a call through to George Bush. 'My God, I'm glad to hear you,' said Bush.

'My dear George. I am so happy to hear your voice again,' cried Gorbachev. 'They asked me to resign but I refused.'

Bush responded, 'Sounds like the same old Mikhail Gorbachev, full of life and confidence!'

The US president then called Yeltsin, whom he had recently described as a 'wild man', and told him, 'My friend, your stock is sky-high over here.'

Soon afterwards a second plane landed at Foros bearing armed members of the Russian government led by Alexander Rutskoy and Ivan Silayev, to escort the Gorbachevs safely back to Moscow. When the ministers arrived at the dacha Raisa saw they were carrying

Kalashnikovs. She cried out, 'What, have you come here to arrest us?' When she learned the truth she broke down in tears.

Past quarrels were forgotten as everyone cried and hugged each other. Gorbachev was almost incoherent with excitement, insisting over and over, 'I made no deals.' Rutskoy thought that Raisa, walking unsteadily to kiss each visitor, looked as if she was 'almost dying' from heart failure.

Fearing that a rogue unit might try to blast the presidential plane out of the air, the Russian vice president used a decoy aircraft to bring the Gorbachevs back to Moscow, with a miserable Kryuchkov sitting alone in the back, not fully aware that he was facing arrest.

At 2.30 on the morning of Thursday, August 22, Mikhail Gorbachev descended from the steps of the plane in a windbreaker and stained pullover. Raisa came behind him on the arm of her ten-year-old granddaughter Kseniya, who was wrapped in a blanket. 'I have come back from Foros to another country, and I myself am a different man now,' said Gorbachev to waiting reporters. In the car on the way to the presidential dacha, their daughter Irina broke down in sobs. Raisa was in a bad way: she had spent the journey lying on the floor of the aircraft. The distressed condition of his family, Gorbachev explained years later, was why he did not go immediately to the Russian White House to thank the defenders still gathered there in large numbers. It was a serious political blunder nevertheless. The affection that had surged through the crowds for the previously unpopular Gorbachev quickly began to ebb.

Gorbachev was diminished by the experience and Yeltsin's stature was enormously enhanced. During the coup Yeltsin had rallied progressive forces within the Soviet Union not only to defeat the putschists but to enable his rival, President Gorbachev, to return to office to continue the peaceful process of reform. The unsuccessful coup demonstrated that the big, awkward, hard-drinking *muzhik* from the Urals was the leader best able and most inclined to offer the Russian people an alternative to the doomed communist experiment.

Many international observers had failed to see that for over a year there had been a steady drift to the Yeltsin camp of young, educated, ambitious men and women who believed in democratic ideals. Never having more than a narrow base of active support in the big cities, they were attracted to Yeltsin because he was popular with the *narod*, the people, he had clout with the military, and he could bring them along to their goal.

Despite this, a few days after the coup Bush's national security adviser Brent Scowcroft was still describing Yeltsin as a demagogue, opportunist and grandstander. When this leaked to the *Washington Post*, the new US ambassador Robert Strauss sent a message to Washington that such Yeltsin-bashing was stupid as it only gave Yeltsin another pretext for disliking Gorbachev, the darling of the West.

Kryuchkov, Yazov and other coup leaders were arrested. The KGB chief wrote a letter to Gorbachev saying he was sorry and in general 'very ashamed' of his role. A weeping Yazov was seen pulling on a cigarette and muttering, 'I'm a damned old fool,' just before he was detained. His decision to bring tanks into Moscow turned out to be a strategic mistake. It forced the military to take sides, and they preferred Yeltsin, a popularly elected president of Russia, to Yanayev, an inebriated, non-elected vice president of the Soviet Union. He begged the Gorbachevs' forgiveness. Pavlov also implored the president to forgive him.

Pugo and his wife committed suicide by gunshot. Field Marshal Sergey Akhromeyev, who rushed to Moscow to join the coup but played no part, was found hanging in an office in the Kremlin, one floor below Gorbachev's cabinet. The sixty-eight-year-old war veteran left a letter for the president, written between two attempts at killing himself, saying, 'I cannot live when my fatherland is dying.'

The Communist Party's chief treasurer Nikolay Kruchina, responsible for party assets reputed to be worth $9 billion, plummeted to his death from his seventh-floor apartment. It was also called a suicide. His predecessor Georgy Pavlov died the same way six weeks later. They took many of the secrets of the fate of the party's enormous wealth with them.

On his first full day back, President Gorbachev stumbled again. He decided not to show up at a large demonstration on Thursday morning outside the White House to which he had been invited to celebrate the defeat of the coup. Shevardnadze despaired at yet another blunder. Chernyaev reminded Gorbachev several times that he was expected outside the White House, but the freed hostage 'spurned the joyful, popular celebration'. The result was that when Gorbachev's name was mentioned at the demonstration, there were boos and calls of 'Resign!'

Gorbachev decided instead to hold a press conference in the foreign ministry press centre, where eight hundred national and foreign journalists and officials gave him a standing ovation. This was more to his liking. Astonishingly he defended the Communist Party as still capable of renewal, despite the complicity of its top cadres in the attempted coup. To Chernyaev this was yet another appalling misjudgement that 'swept away the wave of sympathy and human compassion that you saw among ordinary people, on the street, on the first days after the putsch'. Interpreting for Gorbachev, Pavel Palazchenko thought to himself, 'This will cost him dearly.' He commented to an English-speaking colleague, 'The party's over.' Afterwards Alexander Yakovlev told Gorbachev bluntly: 'The party's dead. Why can't you see that? Talking about its renewal is senseless. It's like offering first-aid to a corpse.'

On Friday, August 23, Gorbachev sought to make amends for failing to acknowledge the role of the White House deputies in defending democracy. At 11.00 a.m. he called the speaker of the Russian Supreme Soviet, Ruslan Khasbulatov, to say he wished to speak to the Russian parliament. He could be there by twelve.

The large auditorium and the balconies filled up instantly. Gorbachev was applauded when he came to the podium, but as he attempted to defend members of the government who had supported the junta, there were roars of indignation. Yeltsin, six inches taller in height, loomed up beside him and with a flourish produced a transcript of a meeting of Gorbachev's cabinet attended by about sixty senior and junior ministers and chaired by Prime Minister Pavlov on the first day of the coup.

Gorbachev protested he had not read it. 'Read it now,' commanded Yeltsin, towering over the red-faced Soviet president. Gorbachev did so obediently. It revealed that almost the entire cabinet had betrayed him, whether through conviction or cowardice. One after another they had backed the emergency committee. Yeltsin produced Decree No. 79 suspending the activities of the Russian Communist Party, which he ostentatiously signed in front of the assembly. As Gorbachev stuttered, 'Boris Nikolayevich, Boris Nikolayevich . . . I don't know what you're signing there . . .' Yeltsin snapped, 'I have signed it.'

The scene of Yeltsin's bullying, relayed throughout the world, revealed that Gorbachev was no longer master in the 'other country' to which he had returned. 'I think he may have had it,' remarked George Bush after he saw Yeltsin 'rubbing Gorbachev's nose in the dirt' on television.

As Yeltsin gloated with what Gorbachev regarded as 'sadistic pleasure', the Soviet president suffered interrogation for over an hour from excited deputies. One rushed to the microphone to declare hysterically that all communists must be swept from the country with a broom. Gorbachev snapped back: 'Even Stalin's sick brain did not breed such ideas!' He saw in their eyes no pity and much hatred.

At 1.30 p.m. Khasbulatov whispered to Yeltsin, 'Time we ended this.'

'Why?' asked the Russian president, no doubt recalling his own humiliations orchestrated by Gorbachev at party meetings.

'I can't help feeling sorry for him,' replied Khasbulatov.

Yeltsin smiled and rose to bring the session to a close. He invited Gorbachev to lunch with Khasbulatov in his office. Though he was seething, Gorbachev still had to show his appreciation to his rival for the defeat of the coup and his safe return to Moscow. With some emotion he related to them how he had heard Khasbulatov on the BBC calling the plotters 'criminals' and had told Raisa that if Russia rose up they would surely regain their freedom.

'What was Raisa Maximovna's reply?' asked Khasbulatov quickly.

'She said she never would have thought that we would be saved by Yeltsin and his associates,' said Gorbachev.

When he left, Gorbachev's limousine was delayed for half an hour by hundreds of Yeltsin supporters blocking the way, booing and jeering. The crowds later besieged Communist Party headquarters on Old Square, from which party *apparatchiks* were frantically taking papers, television sets, fax machines, copiers and telephone handsets. The throng moved to the Lubyanka, where the fourteen-ton statue of the founder of the Bolshevik secret police, Felix Dzerzhinsky, was toppled from its pedestal with the help of a crane supplied by Mayor Popov.

Yeltsin gave a radio interview in which he criticized Gorbachev for surrounding himself with a dirty circle of hardliners in the run-up to the coup. 'You cannot absolve him of any guilt in the plot,' he said. 'Who chose the officials? He did. Who confirmed them? He did. He was betrayed by his closest people.' He asserted his supremacy over Gorbachev by dictating whom he should appoint to replace the arrested comrades. Shaposhnikov, the jovial air force marshal with bushy eyebrows, thick jet-black hair and grey moustache who had threatened to bomb the plotters, replaced Yazov. Former interior minister Vadim Bakatin moved into Kryuchkov's office in KGB headquarters, where he horrified the top brass by giving the Americans a blueprint of the listening devices the KGB had planted in a new US embassy building in Moscow.

Gorbachev would later defend his actions by explaining that if the coup had happened a year earlier it might have succeeded but he had been stringing the hardliners along to camouflage his concessions until there was no turning back. The Soviet president found it more difficult, however, to shake off the charge that he had encouraged the plotters by his behaviour in January, when he claimed to know nothing about the bloody military actions in Vilnius but never sought to punish those responsible. The emergency committee had reason to believe he would have done them the same favour, after it had carried out the dirty work and then brought him back to Moscow.

On Saturday, August 24, 1991, finally facing up to the fact that 'the party's over', Gorbachev resigned as the sixth and last general secretary of the Communist Party of the Soviet Union, the all-powerful organization that had been founded by Lenin and led by Stalin, Khrushchev, Brezhnev, Andropov and Chernenko. Though he remained president of the Soviet Union, he conceded that the party that elevated him to his post could not be reformed. He signed over the party's vast holdings to the USSR Supreme Soviet, which voted to ban all party activities. All across the Soviet Union communist officials frantically burned and shredded documents that might incriminate them.

One important reason for the failure of the coup was the speed with which information spread about what was happening. The coup leaders had summoned television chief Leonid Kravchenko in the early hours of Monday morning to prepare the broadcast of the declaration of the state of emergency and impose tight control on news. But every editor and senior official in television headquarters at Gosteleradio, the state television and radio company, could watch CNN in their office. As the day went on they learned from the American network and from their own reporters on the streets of the mounting resistance at the White House.

People around the country who had rigged up an aerial knew that the putsch was being opposed. Ekaterina Genieva, director of the Library of Foreign Literature, who used the facilities of her building near Taganskaya Square to bring out an anti-coup news-sheet, acknowledged that from the start 'we knew what was happening in our country from the Western media'. 'This was a hugely important story and time for CNN,' said Eason Jordan, then CNN international editor. 'In a sense, CNN was a major factor in ensuring the Soviet coup failed.' CNN's bureau was almost across the street from the Russian White House and when Yeltsin made his dramatic stand on a tank, the pictures were sent via satellite to Atlanta, beamed back to Soviet television at Ostankino and sent by microwave to the network's subscribers in the Kremlin, the foreign ministry and several hotels. Television sets around Moscow centre could pick up the microwave relay. On the morning of the coup, media analyst Lydia Polskaya pushed the button for the fourth channel where she could normally get CNN and was stunned to find the Americans reporting as usual. Nursultan Nazarbayev watched CNN round the clock from his office in Alma-Ata and was able to judge quickly that the junta did not merit his support. US secretary of state James Baker acknowledged that the White House used CNN as the fastest source available to get its message of support for Yeltsin to Moscow. 'Praised be information technology! Praised be CNN,' wrote Eduard Shevardnadze in *Newsweek* after the coup failed. 'Anybody who owned a parabolic antenna able to receive this network's transmissions had a complete picture of what was happening.' The coup plotters were faced with insubordination from within Ostankino itself. News director Elena Pozdnyak refused an order to edit out Yanayev's trembling fingers and the derisive laughter of the journalists from the broadcast of the press conference.

Gorbachev fired Kravchenko as head of state

television, brushing aside his excuse that he had no alternative but to obey the emergency committee as Gosteleradio was under the guns of the KGB. The president asked his one-time friend, Yegor Yakovlev, to whom he had not spoken for nearly a year, to take his place. The progressive former *Moscow News* editor astutely got Yeltsin's blessing before accepting. Yakovlev restored banned programmes, rehired journalists who had been dismissed for refusing to accept censorship, and started getting rid of the KGB spies posing as correspondents for the broadcasting organization in Russia and around the world.

One of Yegor Yakovlev's priorities was to get Gorbachev on to international news broadcasts to demonstrate that he was still in business as Soviet leader. He found willing allies in CNN and ABC, which were competing in the aftermath of the coup to get access to Yeltsin and Gorbachev. Both presidents agreed to a request from ABC to appear at a joint televised 'town hall' meeting in Moscow on Monday, September 2, conducted by Peter Jennings, to be shown in both Russia and the United States.

When ABC News president Roone Arledge boasted publicly that 'this historic live broadcast will provide a forum for Americans from every part of the country to ask questions of these two leaders at this critical period of history', the competitive CNN president Tom Johnson and Eason Jordan took the next flight from Atlanta to Moscow on August 29 to 'snag the interviews'. To their delight, Yegor Yakovlev made Gorbachev available a day before the scheduled ABC programme for an exclusive half-hour interview, conducted by Steve Hurst and also shown on Soviet television.

The interview was an opportunity for Gorbachev to boast of the restoration of his political fortunes. That day he had convened a meeting of the presidents of ten of the fifteen original Soviet republics, including Yeltsin, and they had agreed to form themselves into a state council, with Gorbachev at its head, that would revive talks on a new union treaty.

He was taking control again, he insisted. His new alliance with Yeltsin, he told CNN's Hurst, was 'unbreakable'.

18

December 25: Dusk

WITH LESS THAN SIXTY MINUTES LEFT BEFORE HIS resignation address, Mikhail Gorbachev is at last mentally and physically ready. His speech has been printed out for him in large letters to read on air. He is satisfied that he has found the right tone to express his disappointment and feelings of betrayal by Yeltsin in a dignified manner.

While waiting, he gives Ted Koppel the benefit of a few more of his thoughts. Then as the ABC team goes out into the Kremlin corridor, he signals to Yegor Yakovlev and Andrey Grachev to stay. 'Let's have coffee,' he says.

The three sit at the oval table where Gorbachev likes to chat with visitors. Zhenya, the waiter, brings in a tray with coffee, pastries and small open sandwiches.

Grachev senses that Gorbachev does not want to be left alone 'with his thoughts, his undelivered speech and the nuclear suitcase which he would soon have to give up'.

They discuss whether Gorbachev should sign his decree resigning the presidency of the Soviet Union before giving his televised address, or vice versa. Yakovlev advises him to do it after. He thinks it better that everyone watching television sees him doing it. It would add a moment of drama, and finality. The more formalism there is to the event, the more it will be seen as a dignified exit.

They are all rather disheartened by the fact that no ceremony has been arranged by the incoming authorities for the first peaceful transition of power in Russian history.

As they sip their coffee the conversation of the three men spontaneously turns to their apprehensions about what might happen to them in the future.

The fate of Nicolae Ceauşescu is not far from their minds. Two years ago – to the day – the Romanian communist leader and his wife, Elena, were executed by firing squad after an uprising against his totalitarian rule. Gorbachev regarded Ceauşescu with contempt as the 'Romanian führer', but they had maintained a high-profile relationship. Twenty days before the execution Gorbachev had told Ceauşescu who was visiting Moscow that he had no reason to fear the collapse or the end of socialism, and they had agreed on a meeting of prime ministers on January 9. Gorbachev made a strange remark to the departing Ceauşescu. 'You shall be alive on the ninth of January,' he said. By that date Ceauşescu was dead.

Grachev voices a more realistic fear, that the Yeltsin people will start a process to make Gorbachev the fall guy for the past, as the Germans have done to Erich Honecker. This is something that has been exercising the mind of Anatoly Chernyaev all week. Perhaps nothing will happen, he had written in his diary as the end neared. They are Russians, not Germans, after all, and already people are feeling sorry for Gorbachev. But this is not France either. Unlike de Gaulle, Gorbachev will never be allowed to return. So far everything has been done by civilized standards, but they have no guarantee that some time in the future Yeltsin might not try to discredit them all to justify his destruction of the Union. Grachev asks Gorbachev whether he is concerned that somebody would try to get revenge on him by ferreting around in his past.

'I'm not worried,' replies Gorbachev, though he is aware that there have been attempts before to pin something on him for his lifestyle as first party secretary in Stavropol from 1970 to 1978. Eduard Shevardnadze told him once that in 1984, in the jostling for power in the Politburo before Chernenko died, officials at the interior ministry were instructed by a rival of Gorbachev to dig up compromising material on his Stavropol days.

Gorbachev himself received a jolt two years ago when Andrey Sakharov took him aside to warn him of a plot to besmirch his name. Huddled together on chairs in a corner of the dimly lit stage in the Kremlin Palace of Congresses following a session of the Congress of People's Deputies, the former dissident confided to Gorbachev that he had evidence the *nomenklatura*, the Soviet Union's high-ranking officials, were out to get

Above: August 19, 1991: Boris Yeltsin, flanked by his security chief, Alexander Korzhakov, climbs onto a tank to defy the coup staged by communist hardliners. It is the beginning of the end of the Soviet Union and of Gorbachev's grip on power.

Left: November 1991: Yeltsin begins giving Gorbachev the cold shoulder to emphasize his growing ascendancy over him.

Below: **December 7, 1991**: The clock starts ticking towards December 25 as Boris Yeltsin, Leonid Kravchuk and Stanislau Shushkevich (*three on right*) meet in a state hunting lodge in Belarus and decide to break up the Soviet Union.

Right: How can we survive? Gorbachev discusses the bleak future for the Soviet Union with aides Anatoly Chernyaev and Georgy Shakhnazarov.

Below: **December 21, 1991:** Yeltsin in Alma-Ata with, from left, Kravchuk, Nazarbayev and Shushkevich, as they celebrate creating the Commonwealth of Independent States to replace the Soviet Union.

Below: **December 23, 1991:** Coats off as Gorbachev and Yeltsin come together in the Kremlin for a nine-hour discussion on transfer of power. They will never meet again. Yeltsin's security chief Alexander Korzhakov is behind Gorbachev.

December 25, 1991: Yegor Yakovlev (*on right*) prepares Gorbachev for post-resignation interview.

December 25, 1991: Claire Shipman and Steve Hurst interview a carefully groomed and triumphant Boris Yeltsin shortly before Gorbachev's resignation.

Above: December 25, 1991: Gorbachev walks to his Kremlin office accompanied by Ted Koppel of ABC.

Right: December 25, 1991: Happy Christmas, dear George! Gorbachev calls President Bush for an emotional farewell minutes before his resignation.

Left: December 25, 1991: Pavel Palazchenko interprets during telephone conversation between Gorbachev and George H. W. Bush – who does not realize ABC's Ted Koppel is listening in.

Left: December 25, 1991:
Andrey Grachev leads
Gorbachev from real to
mock presidential office for
resignation speech.

Below: December 25, 1991:
Grachev passes Johnson's
Mont Blanc ballpoint to
Gorbachev when official Soviet
pen runs dry.

Below: December 25, 1991: Gorbachev signs resignation documents before his
speech rather than after, catching television crews unawares.

December 25, 1991: Gorbachev closing the file on his speech and his presidency. Liu Heung Shing's celebrated photograph earns him a thump from a Kremlin security guard and helps AP win the 1992 Pulitzer Prize for Spot News Photography.

December 25, 1991: Muscovites watching broadcast of Gorbachev's resignation speech on railway station television set.

December 25, 1991: Kremlin officials lower red flag from Senate Dome for last time.

December 25, 1991: Kremlin worker takes bundled-up red flag to storage basement.

Yeltsin meets Bush shortly after his triumph over Gorbachev, and at last becomes a member of the club of world leaders.

Barbara Bush with Raisa Gorbachev in happier days.

Senate Building today with new Russian flag flying above Gorbachev's former Kremlin office; it is now the ceremonial residence of the Russian President.

him. The Nobel Prize-winning physicist was quite specific. 'You are vulnerable to pressure, to blackmail, by people who control the channels of information. They threaten to publish certain information unless you do as they wish . . . Even now they are saying you took bribes in Stavropol, 160,000 rubles has been mentioned.' Gorbachev suspected that Yeltsin was behind the rumours but Sakharov may have been referring to hardliners plotting to discredit the president and seize power.

Now that the issue has been raised again by Grachev, Gorbachev insists there is nothing for him to worry about. 'My conscience is clear. Do you really think there could have been any very extraordinary privileges available in Stavropol? There were no special apartments, not even a special store. We bought our food at the canteen of the district party committee. Until recently Raisa Maximovna was keeping all our receipts.'

'And what about Krasnodar?' asks Grachev. 'Krasnodar is right next door to you, and some incredible things went on there at Medunov's.'

There had been a notorious case of corruption in the Krasnodar region next to Stavropol involving the first secretary, Sergey Medunov, a favourite of Brezhnev.

'Medunov, he's something else again,' exclaims Gorbachev. 'I read complaints against him myself, especially from the local Jewish population: bribes, extortion, and what orgies in the official dachas! He wasn't afraid of anything. And for good reason. He had direct access to Brezhnev.'

As general secretary of the Communist Party from

1964 to 1982, Leonid Brezhnev was notorious for his love of expensive gifts and for his failure to investigate allegations of corruption against his most generous donors. After Brezhnev died in 1982, Gorbachev, by then a member of the Politburo, was instrumental in getting Medunov fired, along with corrupt USSR interior minister Nikolay Shchelokov. Gorbachev recalls for his companions that Shchelokov had given the orders to destroy him in retaliation. But it was the interior minister who was destroyed. Shortly after losing his post, Shchelokov was found dead, apparently from self-inflicted gunshot wounds.

The Gorbachevs were, however, not above sending presents to Brezhnev themselves, according to Brezhnev's daughter Galina. Two years earlier she told the Moscow television programme *Vzglyad* that Raisa Gorbacheva gave expensive presents, including a necklace, to the Brezhnev family to win favour for her husband. The episode of the programme containing Galina's allegation was banned by Kremlin officials for 'aesthetic reasons'. An alcoholic who would end up in a psychiatric hospital, Galina was a suspect witness, and had political reasons for discrediting the Gorbachevs. Her husband Yury Churbanov was arrested for taking bribes and jailed for six years after a trial that was widely interpreted as a sign from Gorbachev that political corruption would not be tolerated.

As party boss Gorbachev also received gifts, such as the velvet dressing gowns and sable hats pressed upon him years earlier by the then Kazakh first secretary Dinmukhamed Kunayev, a Brezhnev loyalist whom

Gorbachev subsequently accused of corruption. Some of the most lavish gifts ended up on the third-floor warehouse informally known as Aladdin's Cave in Old Square where top party members were required to deposit expensive gifts, though few did, according to Valery Boldin. Gorbachev's betrayer would later make unverifiable claims in his memoirs about Gorbachev keeping for himself valuable gifts of gold, silver and platinum.

While Grachev knows there is no serious case for Gorbachev to answer about Stavropol, there is potential embarrassment in the populist charge that Yeltsin has constantly made against him, his love of luxury as head of a supposedly egalitarian society. Even the steadfast Shakhnazarov found grossly offensive the sumptuous holiday dacha that Gorbachev commanded to be built at Foros with state funds for his exclusive use.

They suspect, rightly, that this will diminish as a sensitive issue in direct proportion to Yeltsin's embrace of the perquisites of power after Gorbachev is gone.

Gorbachev's aides worry more about what might be found in the files and archives that will fall into the possession of the new authorities. In the last few days they have employed three people, listed in Chernyaev's diary as Weber, Yermonsky and Kuvaldin, to cart sacks of paper to rooms they have rented in Razin Street and sift through them for any time bombs. Fearful that they might be locked out of the Kremlin at any time, Gorbachev has had crates of Politburo documents transferred to General Staff headquarters and Chernyaev has taken some sensitive documents home for safekeeping, despite Grachev's warning that he shouldn't 'exclude the possibility of a search of your place when they come up with a suit against Gorbachev'. Chernyaev does not believe it will come to that, but he is worried that if things do not go well for Yeltsin he will have to look for people to blame. 'I will be the first candidate as a witness,' he notes in his diary. 'However, there is nothing criminal or compromising in my archives. But to find something against Mikhail Sergeyevich is possible, especially as he was so frank in personal conversations.'

Gorbachev was made aware of this danger as far back as August 23, the day the *apparatchiks* were ordered out of the Central Committee building after the collapse of the coup. A distraught senior party official, Valentin Falin, had called Gorbachev to ask him if he was in agreement with the ban just imposed on the Communist Party. When he said he was, Falin asked, 'Are you aware that in the safes of the Central Committee there are documents that are extremely delicate and affect you?' Gorbachev had replied, 'I know. Don't you understand the position I'm in?'

One positive consequence of the fall of the USSR, however, is that there will no longer be any Soviet institutions to bring charges against Gorbachev for violating the Soviet constitution.

Other members of Gorbachev's staff have different concerns about retribution from the new crowd preparing to take over the Kremlin. Pavel Palazchenko worries about a comment he made to Ted Koppel on camera. He told the ABC interviewer that while he might not characterize the seizure of power by Yeltsin today as a coup d'état, it is nevertheless 'something that's being done by democratically elected people in a less than democratic and fair way'. When it was broadcast on ABC television, a friend said, 'only half-jokingly and perhaps quite seriously' that he should perhaps ask the Americans for some kind of protection from Yeltsin.

As the last Soviet president ruminates about his past, a convoy of six white vans rented from Intercar is racing towards the Kremlin accompanied by the sirens and flashing lights of a police escort.

Having finished their televised interview with Boris Yeltsin in the Russian White House, the CNN crew has to get across town and set up transmission equipment in a very short time to broadcast Gorbachev's last public act as president of the collapsing superpower, and to complete the second leg of their exclusive coverage of the two leaders.

Senior CNN producer Charlie Caudill recalled a chaotic scene after the Yeltsin interview. 'We break down all the equipment, load it into six vans, in thirty minutes. This is rush hour. We have to give "donations" to the police and get a full red-light screaming escort through the streets of Moscow. Tom and I are in the lead car. People probably think we are Yeltsin and Gorbachev.'

The interviewers, Steve Hurst and Claire Shipman, find themselves hustled into a police car that races along at the back of the convoy, its emergency lights flashing in the dark streets. 'I never in my life thought that an

American like me would be in a motorcade like that,' said Shipman, who has often seen official cars speeding down the 'ZiL lane' in the centre of the highway, which would 'kill anyone who got in the way'.

The CNN cavalcade comes to a halt at the Borovitsky Gate of the Kremlin. Yeltsin's new guards are unsure of their instructions and several times check by telephone with superior officers as the crew wait impatiently to be admitted. Eventually an official car appears to lead the line of vans into the Kremlin, past the Armoury and the Great Kremlin Palace and across Kremlin Square to the Senate Building.

It is 5.35 p.m. before the army of technicians gets to the third-floor corridor, where they are directed to Room No. 4 in which Gorbachev will make his address. This is a mock presidential office, furnished to look like the real office eighteen metres away along the corridor, and used only for television interviews. It is sometimes called the 'green room' as its walls are sheathed in greenish oyster damask above burr maple panelling.

CNN has an agreement with Gosteleradio that they will join forces to transmit the resignation address together live. The unique arrangement resulted from a meeting Tom Johnson and Stu Loory had with Gorbachev a few days back, when they presented him with the same CNN book on the coup that they had given Yeltsin. They proposed to the Soviet president that they would broadcast his resignation address live around the world and interview him immediately afterwards. Gorbachev had listened politely and asked Johnson about CNN's global reach. He jokingly inquired if the network's 'empire is doing well now – it's not being dismantled, is it?'

'At the present time it is not, Mister President,' replied Johnson.

'Well, it means you have structured your empire quite well,' laughed Gorbachev, 'but be sure to give enough power to your republics!'

Knowing that their rivals from ABC had got a head start, they pleaded that while ABC's American audience was much bigger, their audience levels spike incredibly for major news events. Yegor Yakovlev later called the CNN executives to say that Gorbachev had agreed to the live broadcast of his final address and an interview immediately afterwards.

Caudill is horrified to find Russian TV technicians have brought in three big cameras, 'like in the 1950s', to transmit the pictures to both the Russian and world-wide audiences. He needs higher-quality pictures. 'No way are we going to use these,' he says. His technicians set up a state-of-the-art camera to route the pictures to their truck, and from there to Russian TV and on to a CNN feed, 'an incredibly difficult operation'. Caudill has the extra pressure of having the company's president breathing down his neck. Johnson says to him as they work frantically, 'Caudill, you know this is your ass!'

By ten minutes to seven the room has been transformed into a brightly lit television studio. There are three central television cameras, a CNN camera and audio equipment to provide simultaneous translation. Of ABC there is no sign. The crew from Atlanta is unaware that Koppel and Kaplan are hanging out with

Gorbachev in the president's real office down the corridor, compiling material for their documentary on the final days.

Pavel Palazchenko finds the scene a little unreal. While the president is preparing to resign and hand over control of nuclear weapons to Boris Yeltsin, there are more Americans inside the Kremlin than Russians – television executives in tailored suits, interviewers with pancake make-up, producers, directors, editors, writers, photographers, camera crews, microphone holders, assistants with clipboards, engineers and technicians, all milling around and giving instructions and checking wires and microphones. Gorbachev's interpreter wonders as he listens to the medley of American accents, 'Who could have thought that this – all of this – were possible just a year ago?'

A few hundred yards away, in Red Square, scores of Muscovites have gathered, though they have little interest in witnessing history being made. They are shoppers crushing into the big GUM department store that takes up the side of the vast square opposite the Kremlin, to buy what they can before it closes. Word has got around that some scarce items have appeared on the shelves. They form jostling queues to snap up whatever items of use they can find.

They ignore much of the tawdry goods on display, especially a pile of plastic passport covers. They are stamped 'USSR'. Only tourists will buy these in future.

19

Things Fall Apart

A FTER THE FEARFUL DAYS OF AUGUST 1991, WHEN IT seemed, however briefly, that totalitarianism would return to the Soviet Union, the leaders of the constituent republics one by one announced their intention to form independent states. On Saturday, August 24, even Ukraine declared it would seek independence.

Yeltsin was taken aback. Sovereignty within a new union was one thing. But even he found it difficult to contemplate the outright defection from the Soviet Union of the fifty-two million people in Ukraine whose fate had been linked with Russia's for centuries.

Nevertheless, the Russian president formally recognized the independence of the Baltic republics of Lithuania, Latvia and Estonia, which had always been somewhat semi-detached members of the Soviet Union. Foreign countries followed suit, no longer wary of offending Gorbachev. But both Yeltsin and Gorbachev faced a dilemma. If the rest of the USSR was disintegrating, what should take its place?

The first initiative to resolve the crisis came in late August. Yeltsin's secretary of state Gennady Burbulis called the Kremlin and suggested to Gorbachev's adviser Georgy Shakhnazarov that they should meet in the White House and work on new ideas for the future of the Soviet land mass.

A political scientist with a bald head and thick black eyebrows, Shakhnazarov doubled as a poet and writer of science fiction under the name Georgy Shakh. But many of his original compositions these days were political memos that he delivered to Gorbachev, always urging him towards ever more daring democratic reforms.

Burbulis was an abrasive former professor of Marxist philosophy from Sverdlovsk. He had the zeal of the converted, having evolved in a short time from communist ideologue to ruthless anti-communist. His evolution was so dramatic that on a television quiz show, contestants who listened to a recording of one of his delirious homages to Leninism thought it was the old Stalin-era apologist Mikhail Suslov. With gaunt face and high-pitched voice, Burbulis was known as Yeltsin's 'grey cardinal', though he had distinctly worldly tastes. He was the first of the Russian government officials to order himself a ZiL after the coup, and Yeltsin observed how thrilled he was when the escort car raced ahead of his new limousine, its light blinking and sirens screeching.

The main difference between Shakhnazarov and Burbulis was that the former wanted to maintain the Soviet Union and the latter wanted to destroy it.

Gorbachev's adviser consented to go to the White House, 'though you would think that as I held higher rank as aide to the president of the Soviet Union he would come to my office'. Giving in on this small detail, he realized, symbolized the shift in power.

When he arrived, accompanied by Gorbachev's legal adviser Yury Baturin, they were made to wait half an hour in an anteroom. More small humiliations followed during the day-long negotiations in Burbulis's cavernous office. Several times Yeltsin's secretary of state went off to chat with his aides, and twice he went to a separate table to conduct business with other visitors. Shakhnazarov concluded that he wanted them to know they were not top priority.

The sticking point was whether there would be a single union state with some devolved sovereignty, as Gorbachev wanted, or a less centralized union of states, as the Russians insisted. If the latter idea prevailed, then the USSR was indeed finished. Burbulis made it clear that he envisaged Russia going it alone in the world. But when Shakhnazarov asked him if he were prepared to allow an independent Ukraine to keep the Crimea, Yeltsin's adviser replied, 'Absolutely not!' The Russian-populated peninsula in the Black Sea had been ceded from Russia to Ukraine in 1954 by Khrushchev at a time when the Soviet Union was regarded as a permanent entity and it didn't matter much. Now it did.

Both sides took a break to report to their respective masters. Gorbachev and Yeltsin conferred separately on the telephone. Yeltsin retreated from Burbulis's hard-line position and said he would agree to an all-union army and foreign ministry. Gorbachev was somewhat heartened. He could perhaps salvage a confederation and a common market similar to, or even stronger than, the European Union.

Yeltsin had to capitulate very quickly on Crimea. The Russian president had raised the issue in a conversation with President Nazarbayev of Kazakhstan. He told him an independent Russia might have to redraw its borders with other republics, a reference to Crimea and Russian-speaking areas of northern Kazakhstan. 'Well then, that's war,' said Nazarbayev. 'That's civil war.' Yeltsin's economic adviser Yegor Gaidar was also emphatic about the danger. 'If you start to discuss the problem of the borders,' he said, 'then you have civil war.' Yeltsin quickly closed this Pandora's box. He could see every day on television the bloodshed that border disputes were causing in the former Yugoslavia.

The Russian and Soviet presidents could at least show a common face to the world again. 'After the coup Russia has changed and so has the president,' Yeltsin declared grandly in a television interview. 'He found within himself the courage to change his views. I personally believe in Gorbachev today much more than I did three weeks ago before the putsch.' The two rivals openly consulted each other during a session of the USSR Congress of People's Deputies. Their only altercation occurred when Yeltsin criticized Gorbachev for creating the climate for the coup, to which the Soviet leader retorted, 'Don't spit on me!'

On September 5 Gorbachev cajoled the congress to approve in principle a new union to be called a Union of

Sovereign States, the details of which would be negotiated by the new State Council comprising the leaders of the willing republics. But it would be the last time his famous powers of persuasion would work their magic on a parliamentary assembly.

An anecdote made the rounds. The 'Union of Sovereign States' meant the 'Union to Save Gorbachev'. (The initials were the same in Russian.)

Gorbachev and Yeltsin performed together on ABC News on the morning of September 6. The much heralded programme was postponed twice because of the hectic schedules of the participants. Sitting side by side in the Kremlin's St George's Hall they told viewers they were getting along fine together.

'There were times when President Gorbachev thought I was a political corpse and I thought he ought not to be president,' said Yeltsin. 'Now we are committed to common work – how to deal with a crisis.'

Gorbachev agreed: 'We do have to cooperate now.'

Then Yeltsin went to ground. Physical exhaustion and melancholy followed the intensity and excitement of battle. He spent almost two weeks on the beach at Yurmala on the Baltic coast, then on September 18, citing a minor heart attack, he retreated to Sochi on the Black Sea. He spent most of the time in a state of semi-paralysis or dictating notes for the second volume of his memoirs.

Everyone it seemed was rushing to get books out. On October 4 Gorbachev sold a short text called *The August Coup* to HarperCollins for half a million dollars. It featured seven colour pictures of himself with a smiling George Bush. It was written in such haste that a garbled reference to President François Mitterrand not calling Gorbachev at Foros nearly caused a diplomatic rupture with Paris.

In Sochi Yeltsin had a visit from Burbulis to discuss strategy. As they sat on deckchairs by the warm sea, his grey cardinal presented him with a 'Top Secret' memorandum called 'Russia's Strategy in the Transitional Period'. It was a blueprint for a fully independent Russia. This would be achieved by going along with the new union negotiations until they failed, thereby preserving the appearance of legality. Yeltsin should then make his own arrangements with the other republics and consign the USSR to history.

Yeltsin faced a decision of enormous consequence. He could win full control of Russia, but the price would be high. Russia would lose the steppes of southern Siberia and 'Russian' cities like Kharkov and Odessa, as well as the Crimean peninsula and Sevastopol, where the Russian fleet had been based since the reign of Catherine the Great. On the other hand, Russia would be rid of the centre, and could seek its own destiny without Gorbachev.

In Moscow Gorbachev was also trying to relax after the strain of Foros. He took his wife to see a performance of Thornton Wilder's play, *The Ides of March*, whose theme of betrayal he and Raisa found timely, and 'really enjoyed it'. A stream of foreign dignitaries came to seek his assessment of the situation. He assured them that the centrifugal tendencies had been reversed. He warned one visitor, 'If we fail to preserve the unitary state, we're going to have another Yugoslavia on our hands. I bet my life on it.' Unlike the Serbs, however, who fought to preserve their hegemony in Yugoslavia's provinces, Russians living in the republics were generally passive as the Soviet Union fell apart. Many of them foresaw only further misery and a return to a new era of totalitarianism if the centre prevailed, and they were encouraged to support the process of dis-integration by the most credible Russian figure of the time, Boris Yeltsin.

When at last he returned to Moscow, on Wednesday, October 10, Yeltsin found Russia in political chaos and his parliament a nest of political intrigue. Geared up for a long period of opposition, neither he nor the deputies had a firm idea of how to use the levers of power that were now within reach. Russian ministers were squabbling and Rutskoy was warning of anarchy. The city was full of rumours of a second coup to prevent the USSR's disintegration.

Gorbachev meanwhile was busy trying to seize back the initiative by rallying the leaders of the republics to the cause of a new union treaty. He convened a meeting of the State Council the day after Yeltsin's re-appearance. The Russian president arrived late and remained sullen throughout. Nevertheless, the leaders of the republics agreed to form a new economic union, with discussions to take place later on a political union. A ceremonial signing of a cobbled-together economic treaty took place the following Thursday, October 18, in St George's Hall. Gorbachev fussed over the seating and whether champagne toasts should be televised (they were), and he made sure that the red flag was bigger than the flags of the republics. He personally decided on the types of chairs most suitable for an official dinner that followed in the St Catherine Hall. He convinced himself that there was a momentum again for a single union state with a common defence and foreign policy. He conveyed this to the visiting German foreign minister Hans-Dietrich Genscher, who assured him of German support for the survival of the Soviet Union but had offended Gorbachev by visiting the independent-minded republics without liaising with Moscow. After Genscher left, Gorbachev called him an 'elephant' and complained that he had behaved shabbily.

While seemingly in favour of the economic union, Yeltsin had been calculating his next big move. On Sunday October 28 he delivered a shock. In a rousing speech to the Russian legislature, sitting in the Great Kremlin Palace, he declared that the only way out of the country's crisis was by drastic action. Therefore he planned to free prices, end subsidies and speed up privatization in the territory of Russia.

'The time has come to act decisively, harshly, without hesitation,' he announced. There would be difficult times ahead but the alternative was ruin. 'The period of moving in small steps is over. We need a major economic breakthrough . . . If we don't seize the real chance to break the unfavourable course of events, we shall condemn ourselves to beggary and our centuries-old state to disaster.' Swayed by his powerful oratory, the parliament gave Yeltsin the power to enforce his 'big bang' economic reforms by decree. Even Gorbachev's loyal aide Anatoly Chernyaev was impressed, seeing Yeltsin's drive as a breakthrough to a new country and a new society.

The first Gorbachev knew about this bold initiative was when he glanced at the television in his office and saw that Yeltsin was speaking. The Russian president had not bothered to alert him, although they had spoken on the phone just the night before. He asked for the text of the speech. Next day he read it several times over on the presidential plane en route to Madrid, where he was co-hosting a Middle East conference with US president George Bush. The economic mechanisms were fine, he thought. But it boiled down to one thing. This was a Russian initiative. The centre had no role. Yegor Yakovlev, also on the plane, warned Gorbachev that Yeltsin clearly meant to destroy the Union.

In Madrid Gorbachev found his international colleagues more apprehensive than ever about his survival capacity. He blustered that Yeltsin was 'rather easily influenced' by his entourage and not to take him too seriously. But his own demeanour gave the game away. James Baker found Gorbachev unfocused, acting like a drowning man who is looking for a life preserver. Spanish prime minister Felipe González urged Gorbachev to persist in his efforts, as Europe needed its two secure pillars, the European Community in the west and the Soviet Union in the east.

At a joint appearance of the Soviet and US presidents, interpreter Palazchenko observed the sceptical, cold and indifferent faces of the Americans, who once regarded

Gorbachev as a top-calibre world leader but now thought of him as 'already a goner'. As the conference ended, Bush bade Gorbachev goodbye with a patronizing pat on the back, saying, 'You're still the master!'

In an extraordinary tacit acknowledgement of the influence of the United States, the new Soviet foreign minister, Boris Pankin, travelling with Gorbachev, quietly asked James Baker to encourage the American president to persuade Yeltsin to preserve the Soviet foreign ministry.

On the plane back to Moscow, Gorbachev told Chernyaev, Palazchenko and Grachev of his determination to succeed in forging a new union. The most pessimistic person on the plane, noted Palazchenko, was Raisa, who had 'grave concerns' for the future.

She had every reason to be worried on her husband's behalf. Nothing was certain. After his speech Yeltsin formed a new Russian government with himself as prime minister and two ultra-radical reformers, Gennady Burbulis and Yegor Gaidar, as deputy prime ministers. It began, with breath-taking audacity, to take over central institutions and convert Soviet industry ministries into stock corporations subject to Russia, a process the demoralized Soviet government was too feeble to resist.

Ukraine forced the constitutional crisis to a head. Its leaders organized a plebiscite on independence to be held on December 1, 1991. Gorbachev assured everyone who would listen that Russia and Ukraine would not and could not separate as the two nations were branches of the same tree. But if Ukraine opted for independence, as seemed likely, it would have to be either allowed by Moscow to break free or cajoled into a redesigned union. The alternative was war.

The possibility of war was taken seriously, especially in Kiev, and alarmist rumours appeared in the media. Ukraine's deputy prime minister Konstantin Masik told *Nezavisimaya Gazeta* that 'Yeltsin discussed with military leaders the possibility of a nuclear strike on Ukraine' to prevent the republic becoming a nuclear threat to Russia. The Russian information ministry protested vehemently to the newspaper that this was propaganda fomenting war, but editor Vitaly Tretyakov pointed out that the charge was not disavowed by Masik or his boss, Ukrainian president Leonid Kravchuk. The Russian government sent its legal counsel Sergey Stankevich to tell Tretyakov that the charge was wild and absurd. Yeltsin's military adviser General Konstantin Kobets also dismissed the story as nonsense.

Yegor Gaidar recalled that the leadership did not discuss plans for using nuclear means in the event of territorial disputes but acknowledged that perceptions were as important as facts.

Though the coup had failed, there was still talk of the military taking a role to enforce a new union. The prospect, and even the desirability, of such a drastic step was raised in mid-November by Gorbachev himself in conversation with Shaposhnikov. By the marshal's account he was invited late at night to the Kremlin. Gorbachev revealed that he was worried that the Soviet Union was about to fall apart despite all his efforts, and 'something needs to be done'. The Soviet president outlined options, one of which was, 'You, the military, take power in your hands, put in place the government that is convenient to you, stabilize the situation and then step aside.'

'And then go directly to Matrosskaya Tishina with a song!' retorted the marshal, referring to the Moscow penitentiary whose name meant Seaman's Silence, where some of the coup plotters were incarcerated. 'We have had something similar in August already.'

'What are you talking about, Zhenya,' spluttered Gorbachev. 'I'm not suggesting anything, I am just going through options, thinking aloud.'

The conversation came to an abrupt end. The idea of military intervention could have tragic consequences, wrote Shaposhnikov in his diary. 'Yeltsin's authority was unchallenged and he would have organized ferocious resistance to such a decision. Civil war could not be ruled out. Having imagined mountains of bodies and a sea of blood of my compatriots and my role as an executioner, I naturally did not support thoughts that were suggested by Gorbachev.'

'One can't exclude the possibility that Gorbachev was testing Shaposhnikov,' suggested Andrey Grachev years later, when asked about this encounter. 'He was playing with several ideas. It was his responsibility to see what levers he could use. It was his duty constitutionally to save the Union.' But society was divided and the Soviet president knew well that in the event any leader in his position tried to resort to these methods people would think he was trying to save himself. 'The principal ambition of Gorbachev was to introduce the idea of division of powers, otherwise he would be acting as a typical Soviet leader, Brezhnev or Stalin, and that would be a denial of what he was doing for six years,' said Grachev. He added that Gorbachev had dismissed any notion of force once, saying, 'What should I do – open fire on the parliaments that I constructed?'

Gorbachev would later give some credit for his decision not to ask the military to intervene to his reading of Margaret Mitchell's novel *Gone With the Wind*, with its graphic description of the terrible losses and sacrifices of war.

The prospect of keeping the USSR together diminished during three more meetings of the republics' leaders that the Soviet president convened in November.

The first, on November 4, left Gorbachev hopeful. He had organized the event in such a way that for forty minutes of live television viewers saw him warning the representatives of ten republics that they could 'slide into the devil's abyss' if they split up. They listened respectfully while the cameras were on. But afterwards there was silence. Everyone eyed Gorbachev and Yeltsin. Grachev thought it was like the scene in *The Jungle Book*, in which the pack waits for the confrontation between the two strongest wolves to find out which will be their leader. As it turned out, Yeltsin was in a conciliatory mood. He agreed on keeping an all-union foreign policy and armed forces. Gorbachev was jubilant. That in itself was a victory.

The second meeting on November 14 would, however, confirm his suspicions that the Yeltsin team, steered by Burbulis, had begun the methodical, step-by-step subversion and destruction of the process. And this time only seven republics attended. Ukraine was not among them.

Yeltsin arrived late. This was a tactic the Russian president often used to unsettle Gorbachev. Ordinarily Yeltsin was fastidious about timekeeping, and he had always had the extraordinary ability to tell what the time was, to the minute, without looking at his watch.

He marched into the second-floor conference room and feigned anger about a report that Gorbachev had criticized Russia at a press conference over events in Chechnya, the rebellious Russian province that had declared independence. 'Since you are criticizing Russia let me respond,' Yeltsin thundered. 'Our new relations have lasted all of three months. Now they're over.'

Gorbachev was stunned. The other leaders made excuses to go to the bathroom. Yeltsin gradually cooled down and the meeting got started. They debated all day, discussing confederation models such as Switzerland and Canada. Gorbachev still wanted a union state; Yeltsin, a union of states. The difference was not semantic. The former preserved the country, while the latter meant dividing the USSR into a number of independent entities. Watching on the sidelines, Gorbachev's aides were convinced the Russian leader was only playing for time and manipulating the process.

Before the coup the presidents of the republics had been reasonably respectful to Gorbachev. No longer. Korzhakov watched as 'Gorbachev became very obedient, knowing that his power was ebbing away'.

The draft treaty was watered down until it provided for a confederation in which each republic had the right to conduct foreign relations and create military units.

When walking round the table and gesticulating to make a point, Gorbachev accidentally knocked over the black Samsonite case containing the nuclear codes. It had been placed at arm's length from him as if to remind the company of his status as commander-in-chief of the Soviet armed forces.

They eventually decided to initial a draft treaty for a 'confederative union state' on November 25. When they emerged to meet the media in the lower hallway, Yeltsin and Gorbachev bantered with each other. Looking at his rival, Yeltsin said, 'We don't always understand you.'

Gorbachev replied, 'That's all right, as long as you eventually catch on.'

The third meeting took place at Novo-Ogarevo on November 25, an exceptionally mild late autumn day with no sign yet of the first winter snows. A round table had been trucked to the dacha and the flags of the republics put in place for a solemn initialling ceremony. Again only seven republics turned up and Ukraine was not among them. But Yeltsin still seemed agreeable to a union, albeit with a weakened centre. He told Soviet television beforehand it could have defence, atomic energy and railroads. Two familiar figures were there flanking Gorbachev. The Soviet president had brought back Alexander Yakovlev as his presidential adviser and Eduard Shevardnadze as foreign minister. Their presence was intended to signal that the old firm was back in business.

Before the media was brought in, Yeltsin dropped a bombshell. He announced he could not initial the treaty as the Russian parliament might not accept the wording. He again demanded that the formula 'Union State' be replaced by 'Union of States'.

Stanislau Shushkevich, head of state of Belarus – known as Byelorussia before it voted for independence in September – said he too needed more time, another two weeks, for consideration.

Exasperated at this 'perfidious move', Gorbachev reacted angrily. 'This little game of yours is not just a postponement, you are rejecting what we agreed on,' he fumed. Yeltsin retorted that in any event they should wait until after the Ukrainian referendum, which was only six days away. If Ukraine voted for independence it would change everything.

To no avail Gorbachev argued the opposite: they must initial it now and give Ukraine no choice but to come in. He harangued them in peasant language. 'We're already drowning in shit,' he exclaimed. 'If you reject the concept of a confederal state, you'll be going on without me.' With that he gathered up his papers and, followed by his entourage, stalked out of the room, saying as he left, 'A break!'

In the Fireplace Room downstairs Gorbachev collected himself. Ever resourceful and increasingly desperate, he came up with the idea that the presidents should make a collective appeal to the parliaments to approve the draft. He wrote a new version and sent it up to the conference room. Shortly afterwards Yeltsin and Shushkevich came downstairs. 'Well, here we are,' snorted Yeltsin as they entered the room. 'We have been delegated to kowtow before the tsar, the great khan.' Gorbachev replied in a conciliatory tone, 'Fine, fine, Tsar Boris.'

Nevertheless it was clear, noted Grachev, that the signing of the treaty had moved off again like the ever-receding line of the horizon. The final document they agreed that day was more like an epitaph for the Union than the proclamation of a brave new world. Yeltsin's prediction that Gorbachev's role would be 'like that of the queen of England's' would be made true.

The presidents left Novo-Ogarevo late that night with vague talk about a signing on December 20. They would never return.

What Gorbachev did not know was that during the break, Yeltsin and Shushkevich had quietly discussed the stalemate, and agreed they would meet in the Belarus capital, Minsk, after the Ukrainian referendum, to talk about common economic problems. They would invite Ukrainian president Leonid Kravchuk to join them and spend the weekend in a secluded retreat where they could perhaps talk about a different type of association.

Both would claim later that they had been negotiating with Gorbachev in good faith but that the Soviet president was insisting on conditions they knew Ukraine would not accept and they had to think of something else.

Gorbachev knew differently. Someone had leaked to him a copy of Burbulis's secret memorandum on Russia's strategy. He was convinced that Yeltsin was laying a trap, stringing out talks until Ukraine voted for independence, and using that as the catalyst for the Union's demise.

On Moscow television on November 30 Yeltsin said he could not imagine a union without Ukraine, but that Russia could not sign a union treaty if Ukraine didn't. The die was cast.

The Soviet president could not bring himself to believe that Ukraine would vote for independence. Most Russians felt they and Ukrainians were politically and culturally of the same stock – Slavs descended from the once united Rus people. Classic Russian writers like Anton Chekhov and Mikhail Bulgakov placed their tales in Ukraine. Gogol and Shevchenko were born there. So too was Brezhnev. Gorbachev and his wife both had Ukrainian blood. They believed Ukraine was to Russia what Bavaria was to Germany. It had been part of greater Russia since the 'Eternal Peace' between Russia and Poland three centuries earlier, when Kiev and the Cossack lands east of the Dnieper went over to Russian rule.

Gorbachev made a televised appeal to the 'normal, sane people' of Ukraine to hear him, not just with their heads but with their hearts, and not to listen to 'all those crafty politicians'. Why only the other day, he said, his Ukrainian driver had come back from a funeral and told him that people in his home town of Lugansk had no intention of separating from the Union. It was an unconvincing example – situated in eastern Ukraine, Lugansk had a large Russian population.

The Soviet president was genuinely shocked when

90 per cent of Ukrainians voted for independence on December 1. Fearing another coup in Moscow and weary of the never-ending shortages, even most of the Russians who made up one-fifth of the population voted to split with 'the motherland'. In Lugansk, 84 per cent supported independence.

The Russian government immediately recognized Ukraine as an independent country. Not to be upstaged, the American administration also formally acknowledged Ukrainian independence, causing Gorbachev to moan, 'How could Bush do this!'

On December 2 Gorbachev called Yeltsin to discuss the outcome. The Russian president took the call while in his car, slumped in the back right-hand seat as usual, with his security chief Alexander Korzhakov in front next to the driver. Yeltsin had been drinking heavily.

'Nothing will come out of the Union now – Ukraine is independent,' gloated Yeltsin on the radio telephone.

'And you, what about Russia?' asked Gorbachev.

'So what! I am Russia! We can live without Ukraine. Perhaps we will go back to the idea of a four-member union: Russia plus Ukraine, plus Belarus, plus Kazakhstan.'

Gorbachev retorted, 'And where is the place for me? If so I am resigning. I'm not going to float like a piece of shit in an ice hole. I am not for myself. But you have to understand without the Union all of you are going nowhere . . . You are going to condemn all the reforms. You have to decide. Everything depends on the two of us to a great degree.'

'How can we do without you, Mikhail Sergeyevich?' said Yeltsin, in a mocking tone.

'Well, where is my place if there is no Union?' asked Gorbachev.

'Don't worry, you stay,' said Yeltsin.

Standing behind their outraged president, Chernyaev and Alexander Yakovlev exchanged glances. It was clear to both of them that Yeltsin did not intend that Gorbachev would stay where he was for much longer.

20

December 25: Early Evening

A S THE EVENING OF THE LAST DAY DRAWS IN, BORIS
Yeltsin has one important thing to do before
assuming full power as the undisputed ruler of Russia.
He must go to the Kremlin to take formal possession of
the nuclear suitcase from Mikhail Gorbachev as soon as
the Soviet president resigns. But he can't leave the White
House just yet. Already he is facing the first crisis of the
new era. After saying goodbye to the CNN crew, Yeltsin
finds a grim-faced delegation from the Moscow soviet
waiting in his fifth-floor office. Their leader is the city's
fifty-five-year-old deputy mayor, Yury Luzhkov, a thick-
set, bullet-headed man wearing a short black coat with
fur collar.

Luzhkov has come to ask Yeltsin to dissuade the city's
democratic mayor, Gavriil Popov, from resigning.
Popov is a former ally of the Russian president. The
tousle-haired mayor of Greek origin was a familiar
figure at pro-Yeltsin rallies before the coup, and he
helped defend the White House in August. Afterwards

he hoped to be given a role in Yeltsin's government – he wanted the foreign ministry – but was passed over. He has joined Gorbachev's consultative council instead, and he and Yeltsin are barely on speaking terms.

Popov is also at war with the Moscow soviet, which is stacked with reactionaries and is blocking his emergency plans for managing the economic transition. He worries that he will be blamed if everything falls apart when Yeltsin introduces shock therapy and privatization in the Russian economy next week.

Moscow is on a knife edge. A decree signed by Yeltsin, reported in all the day's papers, orders the freeing of prices nationwide from January 2. This will end seven decades of subsidies for food and basic materials, during which the Politburo itself determined what people should pay for a loaf of bread. It will inevitably raise prices. Under a splash headline, 'How Will We Live?', *Pravda* warns that from January 2 'the price of bread, milk and meat will treble, the price of salt and matches will quadruple, and that of gas and water will increase by five times'. The sense of despair is expressed by a cartoon in *Izvestia*. It shows a baby hijacking its pram by pointing a gun at the mother and saying, 'Take me to Sweden, fast.'

Popov had appealed for help to James Baker. He told the US secretary of state on a recent visit that the city faced hunger and chaos. It could not support itself through the winter, and needed right away fifteen thousand tons of eggs, two hundred thousand tons of milk and ten thousand tons of mashed-potato mix.

'Some of this material is stored by your army which

throws it out after three years,' Popov admonished the American visitor. 'But a three-year shelf life is all right for us.'

Some American supplies are now arriving in Moscow. Three days ago two US military aircraft landed at Sheremetyevo airport with $200,000 worth of year-old surplus army rations left over from the Gulf War, and limited quantities of sugar, flour and rice are being delivered to the city's orphanages and homes for the elderly.

Muscovites will never forget the discontent and shortages of December 1991. University student Olga Perova recalls being sent to queue at 6.00 a.m. to buy milk for her newborn sister. 'There were empty counters everywhere and everything that had to do with everyday life was horrible.' Anna Pruzhiner, a fifty-two-year-old specialist at the metro construction company Metrostroi, is first in line for milk when the doors of the dairy shop are opened each morning and 'there is such a jam that I barely avoid being trampled into the ground'. Tina Kataeva, thirty-two, who works at an art exhibition centre, is unable to get 'soothers, children's food, Pampers or anything of that sort', and when her actor husband returns from a tour abroad he is quizzed by suspicious German customs officers about carrying so many cans of baby food. Yevgeniya Kataeva, a fifty-five-year-old translator living in Zoologicheskaya Street, is driving on the outskirts of Moscow when she sees a middle-aged man walking down the street with rolls of toilet paper strung around his neck like a scarf. She stops the car and runs over to him to ask where he got the toilet paper. 'Naturally I drive there and buy as much as I can. Every time you get something like that, it is a big deal. You feel great, and discuss it over the phone with friends and among your family.'

Things are so bad that even members of the political elite like Yeltsin's deputy prime minister Yegor Gaidar have to scramble to buy food. His wife, Masha, and their ten-year-old son join a queue for bread at a shop in Nikitskaya Street and when the boy gets the last *bulka*, 'a woman tries to snatch this piece of bread', he later related. He recalled a city of near-panic. 'Grim food lines, even without their usual squabbles and scenes. Pristinely empty stores. Women rushing about in search of some food, any food for sale. Dollar prices in the deserted Tishinsky market. Expectations of disaster in the air . . . day and night, the greatest anxiety is bread.' Eduard Shevardnadze confides to a visiting American that his wife Nanuli hoards any foodstuffs she can find in the near-empty supermarkets. The wife of Lev Sukhanov, Yeltsin's closest aide, has had to queue for two days to buy sugar. The city is utterly depressed. Rudeness is so common that in the words of Viktor Loshak in *Moscow News*, 'the counter is like a barricade with enemies on either side'.

Because money has run out, trade officials can no longer pay the shipping charges to bring food to Russian ports. The cargo planes that normally haul supplies to the Russian capital are grounded because of a shortage of aviation fuel. Moscow's airports at Sheremetyevo, Domodedovo and Vnukovo resemble refugee camps, with stranded passengers sleeping on the floors. Ninety airports across the Soviet Union are closed for lack of fuel. Petrol has run out at filling stations along the highways and even the American embassy has trouble finding petrol for the ambassador's official car. With the fragmentation of the Soviet Union, Moscow can no longer command supplies from its neighbouring republics, where hunger is also a reality.

The country is humiliated by having to accept international charity. *Rossiyskaya Gazeta* reports that the residents of Vologodsky Province northeast of Moscow are receiving aid collected by the wives of Sweden's richest businessmen. 'The Americans were helping a little bit, the French a little bit, the Canadians a little bit. But all this compared to the needs was just a drop in the ocean,' recalled Gaidar. Few people can afford the prices at the peasant markets in Moscow, which are mostly controlled by the mafia. One chicken might cost a month's wages. Adding to the intensity of this perfect economic storm, the price of oil, the main source of dollars, has plummeted on world markets and the flow of oil dollars that keeps the Soviet economy on life support has fallen to a trickle. The foreign currency bank has stopped all payments except for freight charges to import grain from Canada, animal feed from the United Kingdom and other foreign food and medicines.

There are, however, no shortages in the handful of shops reserved for holders of foreign currency. These are crammed with everything one might find in Western supermarkets, but are patronized almost exclusively by expatriates, the real elite in the dying Soviet empire.

These are the diplomats, business people and correspondents who live in specially reserved apartment complexes, and whose children wake up this Christmas morning to find stockings crammed with confectionery and toys. They have purchased turkeys, plum pudding and other delicacies for the Christmas dinner from stores such as Stockmann's of Finland, tucked away in a private section of GUM on Red Square. The nine million Muscovites are effectively barred from these hard-currency emporiums, as the ruble is not convertible. The stores discreetly conceal their wares – grapefruits, bananas, flour in several varieties, spaghetti, French wines – behind paint-coated windows, so as not to draw attention to this consumer apartheid, or to agitate the Muscovites hurrying past with empty string bags.

The mayor demanded a week ago that Yeltsin give him special powers to overrule the city soviet so he can take executive action to prevent paralysis. Otherwise he will resign. The Russian president, unwilling to cede any of his powers to rule by decree, has refused. Popov has not yet quit, and has sent Luzhkov to break the stalemate. As deputy mayor and city administrator, Luzhkov is the real chief executive of Moscow. The stocky former engineer facilitated the opening of the first private businesses, the cooperatives, in the city under Gorbachev's reforms, and in August he helped rally ordinary city people against the coup. He tries to persuade Yeltsin that the mayor's office must be free to take its own initiatives to prevent chaos. Moscow needs control over fuel supplies, and the power and gas networks, as well as the independent management of food stocks.

After more than an hour of sometimes heated negotiations, Yeltsin signs a series of ten decrees giving Popov more power. Luzhkov returns with his group to the city hall. Popov decides to stay on as mayor. He notes that the president has given an assurance that the city will receive 'comprehensive assistance' to implement the transition. More importantly, Popov has consolidated mayoral rule. *Pravda* announces the news with the headline 'The Resignation Farce is Over' and accuses Popov of acting as a tool of the democrats and entrepreneurs who want to destroy the elected council.

The shock therapy Yeltsin is applying to the ailing Russian economy was mooted more than a year earlier when Mikhail Gorbachev flirted with, then abandoned, a 500-day plan to convert the floundering command system to a market economy. One of its authors, Grigory Yavlinsky, worked on the reform programme with the help of Harvard experts Graham Allison and Robert Blackwill. They also sought advice from Harvard economics professor Jeffrey Sachs, who had assisted the Polish government with its shock therapy. Sachs's attitude, according to Chernyaev, was, 'If you don't become like us, you'll get no dollars.' Gorbachev vetoed the plan and no dollars were forthcoming.

Having persuaded the Russian parliament to give him special powers, Yeltsin is ready to make the leap to capitalism. He has given the task to a small and radical group of young economists, led by Gaidar, a devotee of the Chicago school of monetarist economics.

Short, chubby, intellectually gifted and nicknamed *Guboshlyop* because of the way his lips flap when he talks, the thirty-five-year-old Gaidar is to be found on the evening of December 25, 1991, in the long, white-washed Hall of Meetings where a drugged and distressed Yeltsin was brought from his hospital bed four years ago to be shamed by party leader Mikhail Gorbachev for daring to challenge his leadership and privileges. He is working there with Jean Foglizzo, who recently arrived in Moscow as representative of the International Monetary Fund.

'I had a lot to do,' Gaidar recalled. 'The state of the economy was catastrophic.'

It is not an exaggeration. Imports of sugar, tea, cereals and soap from the other republics have fallen by more than three-quarters. Machine building and construction have come to a standstill. For some months the Soviet government has been unable to gather taxes. The USSR has exhausted its foreign currency reserves and has debts of $30 billion. 'In other words,' said Gaidar, 'the Soviet Union was bankrupt.' His problem is that while the old system is broken there is as yet nothing to replace it.

Gaidar had converted readily to liberal democratic ideology after a spell as an economics writer for *Pravda*. The son of a celebrated *Pravda* military correspondent and the grandson of a famous children's author, Arkady Gaidar, he is strongly in favour of Russia breaking with the other republics so that he can experiment with the 'free market' libertarianism principles advocated by Milton Friedman. Friedman is known in Russia for his record on engineering a transformation from communism to capitalism on another continent. In the 1970s the economic guru trained a group of Chilean economists in the University of Chicago – who became known as the Chicago Boys – to help President Pinochet undo the Marxist economy of Salvador Allende. A Russian version of the Chicago Boys has now emerged from the ranks of the young radical economists around Boris Yeltsin.

Yeltsin's mandate to Gaidar is to abolish the centralized economy and Gaidar believes the conditions are ideal for what he refers to as major surgery without an anaesthetic. The country is relatively tranquil, the military is demoralized, the hard-line communist oppo sition has been de-fanged. But speed is important. He needs to make the reforms irreversible by wrecking the old system. Then, the reformers assume, goods will quickly appear on the shelves when the market rather than the government sets the prices. His fellow deputy prime minister Anatoly Chubais has been given the task of privatizing state assets – in a country where practically everything, from bread shops to automobile plants, is owned by the government. Chubais predicts to Gaidar that, whatever the result, he will be hated as the person who sold off Russia. Gaidar knows that he too will have to drink from that poisoned chalice. As Burbulis warns, they belong to a kamikaze government whose members will be discarded by the public after they have rammed through necessary but unpopular measures.

The Russian reformers fret that when goods reappear

in the regular stores there will be serious inflation. But the American advisers are sanguine. Thomas Wolf of the IMF assures Russian economics minister Andrey Nechayev, during a meeting on the afternoon of December 25, that prices on most important consumer items will rise by only 70 per cent in the first month of free pricing. Nechayev is sceptical – with good reason: prices will soar in January by 245 per cent and keep rising after that to 2,500 per cent.

A contemporary IMF working paper admits, 'There remains some suspicion of foreign advisers, together with a reluctance, natural in a former superpower, to admit there are things to be learned.'

One of those who has cooled on the American-inspired therapy is Alexander Rutskoy. Even as Yeltsin is trying to work out a deal with Luzhkov to keep Popov on board, his vice president is holding forth to journalists in an office nearby about how 'we now have anarchy instead of democracy'. Rutskoy is in favour of Russian 'sovereignty' within the Union, but is against breaking up the USSR, and he has hung a map of the Soviet Union behind his desk to make the point. The Russian president and vice president are no longer on good terms, partly because Yeltsin refused to make him prime minister, a position he has kept for himself in addition to the Russian presidency.

Rutskoy once told Yeltsin, according to Korzhakov, 'Boris Nikolayevich, I will never let you down. I will be the guard dog at your throne.' To Yeltsin his vice president has become just a 'loud-mouthed soldier'. Rutskoy has a particular aversion to Gaidar and his team, whom he describes as 'boys in pink shorts, red shirts and yellow boots who had decided to run Russia'. He complains that the conditions are not right for the gigantic experiment they are conducting with the country. A free market can only be introduced in a legal, democratic state, he tells the reporters, but 'today, there is neither power nor democracy in Russia'.

The vice president insists he doesn't want confrontation with Yeltsin – 'Why, that's not logical!' – but things must be put in order first and privatization must not be carried out by robbery and cheating. Gaidar for his part has only contempt for Rutskoy, commenting that behind the 'dashing façade of the moustachioed man-at-arms' lies a vacillating and insecure personality intent on avoiding responsibility for unpopular decisions.

The speaker of the Russian parliament, Ruslan Khasbulatov, is also sliding back to the old Soviet way of thinking, in line with many conservative deputies. He feels 'it might be time to propose that the president dismiss his virtually ineffective government'.

Already Yeltsin's hold on power is becoming tenuous and divisions are deepening in the Russian parliament that in less than two years will lead to a bloody showdown.

There are also the first stirrings of a popular revolt against price rises. Demonstrations have already begun. On Sunday between five and ten thousand people carrying portraits of Lenin and Stalin gathered near the Kremlin and banged teaspoons against empty pots and pans as they formed a 'hungry line' to represent a queue at a soup kitchen. Coming across the demonstration, Ted Koppel saw how they were already nostalgic for the iron-fisted control of rigid communism, and that they had contempt for both Gorbachev and Yeltsin. Koppel tells his ABC viewers, 'The teaspoon striking on an empty pot may yet prove to be the most powerful symbol in this new and uneasy commonwealth.'

The leader of the demonstrators is Vladimir Zhirinovsky, head of the neo-fascist Liberal Democratic Party, who tells his followers that the only reason Americans want to come to Russia to give aid is to scan the territory so they know where to drop their bombs. He threatens that when he gains power he will fill outer space with weapons pointed at the United States, make Afghanistan a Russian province, sell off western Ukraine and blow radioactive waste across the Lithuanian border to kill the population with radiation sickness.

There are other sinister characters discussing, on the day the Soviet Union comes to an end, how to capitalize on the country's chaotic state. Just outside Moscow, in a dacha in the hilly Vedentsovo region, several individuals concerned with the country's future financial structures are wrapping up a secret three-day meeting. From December 22 to December 25, some thirty men of different nationalities, mostly Russian, Ukrainian, Georgian, Armenian and Chechen, have been conferring on how they should divide the former Soviet Union into zones of influence. They are members of Vorovskoy Mir (Thieves' World). Each person in attendance is a *vor v zakonye*, a thief-in-law anointed by fellow inmates in the country's prisons as a super criminal and bound by a code of loyalty. They have travelled from all across the disintegrating Soviet Union to discuss the new opportunities opening up for control of a vast black market in commodities, ranging from caviar and gold to automobiles and spare parts. In the vacuum created by the collapse of the command economy, they are already able to operate a crude capitalist form of supply and demand. Their reach is so extensive that they control an estimated 15 per cent of the movement of all goods in Russia. Now they are poised to make vast profits from the sell-off of state assets that will come in the New Year.

Organized crime has become a serious problem in the dying Soviet Union. With the unleashing of state assets into private hands, it is about to become a major phenomenon in post-revolutionary Russia.

Already in the last months of the Gorbachev era there are illicit and semi-legal fortunes to be made. Unregulated privatization is developing rapidly. Former communist directors are leasing each other prime industrial properties in preparation for taking them over and enriching themselves when the law permits. Much of the Communist Party asset base that Yeltsin nationalized has already been transferred into the hands of private owners.

Rampant corruption in the oil industry has resulted in the wholesale issuing of export licences, allowing entrepreneurs to buy oil for rubles and sell it abroad for hard currency. These stamped pieces of paper, Gaidar said later, were 'a sort of philosopher's stone that could almost instantaneously transform increasingly worthless rubles into dollars'. The oilmen and the corrupt members of the *nomenklatura* whom they bribe are shifting money abroad as fast as they can.

As the Russian president assumes command in the Kremlin, commentator Ilya Milshtein issues a warning to him in an article in *Novoye Vremya* (New Times). The country Yeltsin is taking over, he writes, is 'depraved to the core, a state rotten from top to bottom, a great power of fast thieves and bribe-takers'.

He doesn't have to be told by the media. At the end of December two former KGB officers write to Yeltsin alleging that top party officials are siphoning off immense quantities of money and gold and depositing them in foreign bank accounts. Gaidar manages to get $900,000 from state funds to hire the international security and detective agency Kroll Associates to investigate the allegation. It comes up against a wall of non-cooperation from inside the new Russian ministry of security. After a month of frustration, the contract is not renewed.

21

The Centre Cannot Hold

Yeltsin's drunken assurance that Gorbachev would 'stay' in some capacity in the future arrangements for the Soviet Union was soon broken.

On December 6 the Russian president came to Gorbachev's Kremlin office and told him he was going to Minsk, the capital of Belarus, the next day. There, he promised, he and the republic's leader Stanislau Shushkevich would try to persuade Ukrainian president Leonid Kravchuk to stay in a new union.

Yeltsin emerged from the meeting to tell reporters, 'Every effort must be made to convince the Ukrainians to sign the union treaty.' He added: 'If that doesn't work, we'll have to consider other options.' He didn't say what those were.

Knowing the Russian leadership was tired of having any centre at all, Gorbachev sensed that treachery was afoot. He told Chernyaev that he suspected Yeltsin and Kravchuk had decided to collapse the Union from both sides.

Chernyaev had already thrown in the towel in his own mind. He was going through the motions of feeding Gorbachev documents to sign, such as agreements between the USSR and other countries on an Islamic conference in Dakar, but it was all 'bullshit'. As he wrote in his diary, 'It is hard to realize that only Mikhail Sergeyevich needs me, not the country.' Thinking of his wife and mistress, he wondered, 'How will my women react to this?'

Pavel Palazchenko predicted that the outcome of the meeting in Belarus would be determined by the fact that, for reasons of their own, all three participants hated Gorbachev.

Shortly after 3.00 p.m. on December 7, 1991, a Russian government plane carrying Boris Yeltsin touched down at Minsk, four hundred miles southwest of Moscow. Accompanying him were deputy prime ministers Gennady Burbulis and Yegor Gaidar, foreign minister Andrey Kozyrev and legal counsel Sergey Shakhrai. They were guarded by twenty burly members of the Russian security service armed with assault rifles, under the command of his chief guardian, Alexander Korzhakov.

The plane took off again in the same direction, and after thirty minutes landed at a military airport outside Brest. From there, a small convoy of vehicles took the Russians deep into Belovezhskaya Pushcha, one of the last remaining primeval forests in Europe. As a thick soft snow fell, they raced through the town of Pruzhany and continued almost as far as the Polish border. The cars pulled up at Viskuli, a mansion with square pillars framing the entrance, built in the 1970s for Brezhnev's hunting pleasure, with adjacent bathhouses, cottages, hunting lodge and service block.

Everything was done in the utmost secrecy to ensure that the three leaders representing Russia, Belarus and Ukraine could meet without interruption by journalists or other more dangerous forces. Belarusian KGB head Eduard Shidlovsky had deployed heavily armed patrols in the forest from early morning and sealed off approach roads. He assured Shushkevich that 'everything is all right; we are in close connection with the Russian special security service and there will be no problems'. The enemy they feared were reactionary elements of the Soviet forces who might be tempted to prevent what they were about to do.

Shushkevich and Kravchuk and their top officials had already arrived, having flown together from Minsk late that morning. The Ukrainian president and his prime minister, Vladimir Fokin, had immediately gone hunting. The fifty-seven-year-old, white-haired Kravchuk did not want to be seen hanging around waiting for the Russian leader. Nicknamed the Crafty Fox for his political cunning, the former party ideologue turned nationalist once joked that he never carried an umbrella since he could slip between the raindrops. In August he initially cooperated with the coup, then quit the Communist Party and reinvented himself as a democrat and nationalist.

Kozyrev noticed how tense Kravchuk was. He realized that the Ukrainian boss feared Yeltsin would threaten him and argue for a union, which could cause a breakdown and a resort to a 'Yugoslavia-type script'. Yeltsin also remembered Kravchuk as being very tense, even agitated. The overall atmosphere, Gaidar recalled, was one of profound anxiety with Shushkevich the most agitated and emotional of all. The Belarusian leader was out of his depth in the company of his two wily and powerful fellow Slavs. A prominent nuclear scientist with a square face and bald head, he had little experience of politics. He had been in power only ten weeks, since Belarus rejected the old order and gave power to the reformers in the wake of the coup. His claim to fame outside Belarus was that he once supervised Lee Harvey Oswald when Kennedy's future assassin was an engineer at a Minsk electronics factory. Shushkevich wondered if his two neighbours actually knew what they were doing, but he was prepared to go along. He believed the USSR was 'already ungovernable . . . a nuclear monster'. Also he disliked Gorbachev, whom he had once looked to as a 'god', but latterly found impossible to work with 'because he never listened to anybody'.

Kravchuk knew exactly what he wanted. Before leaving Kiev, the Ukrainian president had told American diplomat Thomas Niles that he was going to Belovezh Forest to sign an interstate agreement with Russia and Belarus that would have no centre. He would claim in his memoirs that there had been months of secret talks beforehand with the Russian and Belarusian leaders that led to the deal they were about to do – which could explain Yeltsin's mysterious remark in January that the presidents of Russia, Belarus, Ukraine and Kazakhstan had decided to draw up a treaty to replace the old Soviet Union, adding, 'I think I may now say where – in Minsk.'

But nothing was certain when the three leaders sat down to a dinner of game and pork that snowy evening in the forest.

With a dramatic gesture, Yeltsin produced the text of Gorbachev's union agreement and put it on the table. According to Kravchuk he said, 'Do you agree with this? Will you sign it? Will you discuss which articles to take out? Your answer will determine the position of Russia. If you sign it, I will sign it.' Kravchuk replied '*Nyet!*' to all three questions.

From that moment on, the Russian leader no longer had to pay lip service to the cause of a union containing Ukraine. He had fulfilled his promise to Gorbachev to ask Kravchuk one more time to sign the union treaty. Kravchuk had refused. The Rubicon had been crossed at last. Here among the pine trees his thoughts went back to the Soviet military actions in Tbilisi and Vilnius, and he renewed his determination that they were not going to wait calmly for a new tragedy 'with our paws folded back like timid rabbits'.

They agreed that it was too risky to start negotiations at their level. Instead their support teams should work through the night to find a formula that would meet their aspirations.

The tension eased. According to Kravchuk, 'We drained our glasses, chatted, there was conversation and toasts, joking and laughter. Belovezh vodka [Belarus's herbal vodka] was there. I drank it too.' The Ukrainian president took some pleasure in disclosing that even Ukrainian districts with large Russian populations had voted for independence in the referendum of December 1. 'What? Even the Donbass voted yes?' exclaimed Yeltsin.

Between ten and eleven o'clock the trio retired to the main bathhouse, along with Burbulis, Korzhakov and the Ukrainian · and Belarusian prime ministers, and relaxed there until after midnight in clouds of steam. Shushkevich denied later charges that they got drunk, though there was plenty of alcohol available in the *banya*. Yeltsin did not even get dizzy, he claimed, and Shushkevich himself did not touch alcohol, as 'I considered that drinking on the eve of signing such a fate-changing document would be a crime'.

Yeltsin's team of Gaidar, Kozyrev and Shakhrai meanwhile invited the experts from Ukraine and Belarus to work with them in a chalet where the Russians were billeted. The Belarusians stayed away, however, and the Ukrainian delegates hung around in the dark and snow outside, occasionally sending an emissary into what Kozyrev referred to as 'our creative laboratory'.

Shakhrai proved to be the most imaginative in finding the precise formula that was to spell the end of the Soviet Union. A Cossack lawyer with mournful eyes and a moustache that curled round his full lips, he had drafted many decrees for Yeltsin, including the order banning the Communist Party of the Soviet Union. He suggested that as the USSR was founded on the basis of a 1922 treaty signed by Russia, Belarus and Ukraine (and the Transcaucasian Federation which had ceased to exist), so the three surviving states could legally dismantle it.

In their accounts of the meeting both Kozyrev and Gaidar maintain they were startled at the simplicity of the idea, and quickly agreed. After midnight the Belarusians and Ukrainians came in from the cold. They all nodded as they read the words. They had a formula to take to their masters. It stated: 'We, the Republic of Belarus, the Russian Federation (RSFSR), and Ukraine, as originators of the USSR on the basis of the Union Treaty of 1922, confirm that the USSR, as a subject of international law and a geopolitical reality, ceases its existence.'

In Gaidar's words, this was the knife that would allow them 'to cut the Gordian knot of legal ambiguity and begin the business of state-building in countries that were already de facto independent'.

The drafters drew up proposals for a successor association called a Commonwealth of Independent States, which other Soviet republics would be invited to join. 'They were our initiatives, not those of the presidents,' insisted Gaidar in an interview years later. 'The final proposals were deliberated at the second level.' Burbulis also insisted, 'We came to Minsk without a text and without any carefully weighed idea of a commonwealth. It was born right there.'

There was no copier at the lodge and the officials had to pass papers through two fax machines to make extra copies. Gaidar wrote out the final texts containing fourteen articles in longhand. At 4.00 a.m. Kozyrev trudged off through the snowdrifts to bring the sheets of paper to the typist's room. There was one stenographer at the lodge, Evgeniya Pateychuk, a terrified local woman who worked for the forestry director and who had been fetched by the Belarus KGB at short notice, without even being given enough time, as she recalled, to comb her hair. Unwilling to wake her up, Kozyrev put the documents under the locked door of the business office. There was consternation in the morning when the typist said that she had found no papers. It was some time before they realized a cleaning lady had put them in a trash can. When they were eventually extracted by Korzhakov from a bag of rubbish, Pateychuk found she could not decipher much of Gaidar's handwriting and he had to dictate some of it over again.

While this was going on, Yeltsin, Kravchuk and Shushkevich gathered for a breakfast of fried eggs, black bread, ham and cheese. The Russian president was in fine fettle. Kravchuk found him stone-cold sober. 'I don't exaggerate! He was in good form, vigorous, he had ideas.'

The three leaders received their copies in late morning, typed with one finger on her battered Optima electric typewriter by the bulky Ms Pateychuk, sitting at a tiny desk and wearing a large white fur hat. They agreed to the idea of a commonwealth as a fig leaf for a divorce. Everything was inevitable now. They made some minor amendments to the draft paragraphs, toasted each completed article with a sip of cognac and sent the pages off for re-typing. The documents were passed through the two fax machines and the final versions clipped into three red hard-backed folders.

Meanwhile workers carried a long marble-top table

into the foyer of the Viskuli hunting lodge. Officials placed the folders in front of miniature flags for Ukraine, Belarus and Russia. Five journalists, cold and hungry after having spent the night in a nearby village waiting for they knew not what, were ushered in to report the ceremony.

Kravchuk, Shushkevich and Yeltsin entered and took their places along the table, with their top aides standing behind them. Shushkevich sat in the middle, as the host, with Yeltsin on his left and Kravchuk on his right. They opened the folders, titled 'Agreement on the Creation of a Commonwealth of Independent States'. The contents spelled out the new reality. After seven decades the USSR was finished in all but name, and its 293 million people destined to be separated among the constituent republics. The new entity would have its headquarters in Minsk. It would have no flag, no ministry of foreign affairs, no parliament, no citizenship, no tax-raising powers and no president. There was, however, a commitment to set up a single military control over nuclear weapons. Other republics would be invited to join.

Suddenly a voice was heard, with a swear word: 'Where are the pens?' There were no writing instruments available to sign the Soviet Union's death warrant. Everyone standing around began producing ballpoints, felt tips and fountain pens from their pockets. Valery Drozdov, deputy editor of the Belarus newspaper *Narodnaya Volya* (People's Will), was among those who handed his pen to the trio at the table.

In a profound silence the three leaders signed the

documents in the red folders. Only Drozdov took note of the exact time on his watch, which ironically bore the symbol of the USSR, the hammer and sickle, on its face. It was 2.17 p.m., on Sunday, December 8, 1991.

Waiters brought around champagne. Yeltsin, 'blushing slightly' as journalist Vadim Bitsan noted wryly, lurched towards the journalists. Korzhakov put his hand up, and snapped, 'Cameras off! No filming!' He warned the photographers, 'print one frame compromising President Yeltsin and you will have to deal with me.'

'I well remember how a sensation of freedom and lightness suddenly came over me,' wrote Yeltsin in his account of the moment. 'In signing this agreement Russia . . . was throwing off the traditional image of "potentate of half the world", of armed conflict with Western civilization, and the role of policeman in the resolution of ethnic conflicts.'

Others reacted differently. Shakhrai felt as if they were burying a relative. Gaidar recalled, 'We all had a heavy burden in our hearts.'

Drozdov did not get his pen back. 'One of the three put it in his pocket out of force of habit,' he recalled. 'I believe it was Yeltsin.'

Evgeniya Pateychuk, the typist, stepped out into the fresh air with her boss, forestry official Sergey Balyuk. It was already twilight and a light snow was falling. 'So, Sergey Sergeyivich, what have we done!' she said. Years later she would protest: 'I typed what I was given; understanding came later, in a day or two.' In her village of Kamenyuki twelve miles away, she became known as the woman who destroyed the Union.

* * *

Yeltsin had not invited Nursultan Nazarbayev, president of Kazakhstan, to the meeting of the Slav leaders in the forest. The head of the powerful central Asian republic was a Gorbachev ally and had yet to declare independence. If they could get him to join them now in Belovezhskaya Pushcha they could present him with a fait accompli and ensure the support of the other Asian republics that deferred to him. But it was not so simple. Nazarbayev was at the time en route by air from Alma-Ata to Moscow. Korzhakov called the commander of Vnukovo-2 airport in Moscow and asked to be connected with the plane, identifying himself as 'chief of security of the president of Russia'. The airport commander refused rudely, saying, 'I have a different chief.' This was typical of dual power, thought Korzhakov. Gorbachev wasn't being taken seriously, but Yeltsin didn't have the mechanisms of power. Nazarbayev took the call when he landed in Moscow. All three leaders spoke to him. Yeltsin read him the documents. But the Kazakh leader was deeply offended at being left out. He telephoned Gorbachev at his dacha to tell him what was happening. Furious at the turn of events, Gorbachev persuaded Nazarbayev to join him and confront the conspirators together in Moscow the following morning.

The three men at the hunting lodge were worried that there might be a military response to what they had done. Gaidar admitted to being a little apprehensive that Gorbachev would take this option, 'though I was more or less sure that it would be impossible for him to do because he would not find one regiment to obey his orders'. Shakhrai was unafraid, as 'everybody knew there was no army any more', though he believed that the Belarusian KGB was keeping Gorbachev informed of everything going on in the forest. Years later the president of Belarus, Alexander Lukashenko, bragged that if Gorbachev had given an order to the Belarusian KGB to arrest the threesome, the order would have been fulfilled 'within minutes'. Gorbachev's aide Andrey Grachev claimed that the conspirators had a helicopter standing by so they could flee to Poland if necessary, though Gaidar did not recall seeing any helicopter.

The attitude of Marshal Shaposhnikov, head of the Soviet Union's armed forces, would be critical. Throughout Sunday morning Gorbachev kept phoning him in an agitated state, always with the same question, 'What have you heard from Minsk?' Each time Shaposhnikov replied, 'Nothing yet.'

Yeltsin, with Kravchuk and Shushkevich beside him, eventually telephoned the marshal. 'Today we in Belarus signed an agreement about a three-state union, Russia, Ukraine and Belarus,' he boomed down the line. 'What's your opinion about that?'

Shaposhnikov asked if other republics would join in.

'Yes,' said Yeltsin.

'And one more question, Boris Nikolayevich. Is there a reference to the armed forces in the treaty?'

Yeltsin: 'Yes. Of course.' The Russian president recited the article confirming that the commonwealth would preserve a common military-strategic space, including single control over nuclear weapons. He told

Shaposhnikov that the three presidents had agreed that he should be the commander.

'Does Nazarbayev approve?' asked Shaposhnikov.

'Yes, he has reacted positively,' replied Yeltsin.

The marshal sensed that Nazarbayev was in fact cool towards the plan, but he didn't argue. He realized something like this was inevitable sooner or later, though he believed the leaders were less intent on destroying the Union than getting rid of Gorbachev. He accepted the post offered.

As soon as he replaced the receiver the telephone rang again. 'So, what's happening?' barked Gorbachev. 'What's going on in Belarus?' Shaposhnikov summarized the conversation with Yeltsin, giving the impression that the Russian president had just called for advice. Gorbachev cut him short. 'Don't put your nose into somebody else's business. I'm warning you!' He slammed down the phone. Gorbachev realized Shaposhnikov had signed on to Yeltsin's coup d'état, and would always remember how he 'wriggled and squirmed like a grass snake on a frying pan' as he lied.

Yeltsin was meanwhile trying to get through to President George H. W. Bush. He gave the hunting lodge operator the number of the White House in Washington. She called back flustered to say that the White House switchboard couldn't grasp who was calling. Kozyrev took the receiver and in fluent English explained who Boris Yeltsin was and why it was important to be put through to the president.

Bush came on the line. Yeltsin read the agreement and

told the US president that this was the only way out of the crisis convulsing the Soviet Union. Addressing Bush as 'Dear George', he told him that the union treaty had reached an impasse and that they had decided to create a commonwealth of independent states. 'I must tell you confidentially,' he said, 'President Gorbachev does not know these results. Because of the friendship between us, I couldn't wait even ten minutes to call you.'

'I see,' said the US president hesitantly. He got the impression Yeltsin was reading from a script. It dawned on him that the Russian leader 'had decided to dissolve the Soviet Union'.

Yeltsin assured him that the agreement recognized the five principles that the United States had stated it required for recognition of future independent states: peaceful self-determination, respect for existing borders, respect for democracy and the rule of law, respect for human rights, and respect for international law.

Next day Bush dictated into his personal mini-recorder: 'I find myself on this Monday night wondering, where was the army? They've been silent. What will happen? Can this get out of hand?'

Yeltsin had used the leader of the free world to his advantage. Telling Bush first had further diminished Gorbachev, and his consultation with the president of the United States implied that they had cleared every-thing with the White House.

It fell to Shushkevich, the third-ranking member of the group, to break the news to Gorbachev. It took him some time to get through. Yeltsin and Kravchuk listened as Shushkevich told the Soviet president what they had done.

'What happens to me?' Gorbachev demanded to know. 'Do you understand how this will be received by the world community?'

The Belarusian leader replied, 'I do understand. We have told Bush and he took it well.'

Gorbachev erupted at this gross discourtesy. 'You talk to the president of the United States of America and the president of the country knows nothing. This is a disgrace!' He demanded to speak to Yeltsin.

When the Russian president came on the line, Gorbachev snapped at him in cold fury. 'What you have done behind my back, with the consent of the US president, is a crying shame, a disgrace.' He demanded that all three Slav leaders come and explain themselves to him in the Kremlin the next day. He was convinced now of his rival's duplicity.

The Ukrainian president laughed at the idea of giving an account of himself to Gorbachev. Kravchuk had taken such a dislike to him – the feeling was mutual – that he was offering to sell Gorbachev's dacha at Foros in Crimea, now part of Ukraine, to anyone who would guarantee that Gorbachev would never be permitted to return there. He also wanted to get back to Kiev immediately. These were dangerous times and he was 'afraid that violent methods would be used against Ukraine'.

Kravchuk and Shushkevich returned to their capitals rather than answer Gorbachev's summons to Moscow. They had nothing to say to him and did not want a lecture or to risk arrest. Both would later explain that they had always found him impossible to work with because he was not straightforward and forthright, qualities they found in Yeltsin. They never met Gorbachev again during his presidency.

When Anatoly Chernyaev, who had spent that Sunday with his mistress Lyuda, got word of the Belovezh Agreement he started to prepare, without any conviction, to make the case against it as Gorbachev's loyal servant. 'I didn't believe in the survival of the Union, even before the putsch,' he wrote that evening. 'I continued to work on the arguments for the Union . . . But why? You can only laugh.' When 'low-life Kozyrev', as Chernyaev referred to the Russian foreign minister, announced to the media that there were two solutions for Gorbachev – self-liquidation of the presidency, or an August-type coup – 'we, Gorbachev's team, shit ourselves'. Nevertheless, he didn't see any alternative but to give themselves to Russia, as the Union was dead.

Yeltsin still worried about a 'counter-coup'. When he got back to the Russian capital late that night – Gorbachev would later claim he was so drunk he had to be carried off the plane – there were rumours circulating that members of the former KGB Alpha Group, then under both presidents, were preparing to arrest the three signatories to the agreement, and that concrete blocks had been trucked to the Kremlin to reinforce defences. Russian radio also broadcast reports of illegal gatherings of intelligence and military generals to discuss a possible overthrow of the republic's leaders.

The next morning security at the Russian White

House was reinforced, with extra guards on duty cradling automatic weapons, stamping their feet in the frigid air. It was the coldest day of the winter, with the temperature falling to minus 18 degrees.

Yeltsin called Gorbachev to say that he would not come to the Kremlin as he feared for his personal safety. 'Are you crazy?' retorted Gorbachev.

Yeltsin replied, 'No, I'm not, but somebody else might be.'

Unknown to Yeltsin, that somebody was his estranged vice president. Alexander Rutskoy had raced to the Kremlin that morning when he heard the news of the Belovezh Agreement and begged Gorbachev to arrest the 'drunken threesome' for a state crime committed to please the United States. Gorbachev told him, 'Don't get so het up, it's not that terrible.' The volatile Rutskoy was now bitterly opposed to the break-up of the country in whose name he had risked his life in Afghanistan. He prepared a press statement attacking his president, but friends talked him out of issuing it. Seeing he had little support, he backed down and a few days later renewed his vows of allegiance to Yeltsin in unctuous terms.

According to Grachev the idea of having Yeltsin apprehended never came to Gorbachev's mind, though he had the power to arrest him for high treason. 'That was the reason they were hiding in the woods.' Some in Gorbachev's entourage, like economist Nikolay Shmelev, believed it was only his aversion to bloodshed that stopped him sending a division of paratroopers to the forest to arrest 'those three provincial men of great ambition'. Gorbachev's former speech-writer Alexander Tsipko would later berate the generals and colonels who 'did not stir a finger to stop the outrage'. Gorbachev's former adviser Arkady Volsky, who had become a Yeltsin supporter, believed that the military would have supported Gorbachev if he had declared martial law.

Whether he was tempted or not, Gorbachev did not try. He was not prepared to spark a civil war. Ordering arrests would have meant taking a road that could have become bloody. 'We can't start a fight. We can't. It would be just criminal, taking into account the conditions under which our people are living.'

There was no doubt, however, about how bitter the Kremlin loyalists felt. At an American embassy reception on Sunday evening, Palazchenko denounced the Belovezh Agreement to diplomats as a second coup, a blatantly illegal act, dividing the country up like some inherited estate to get rid of its president.

Yeltsin overcame his reservations and arrived at twelve o'clock on Monday at the Kremlin, with Korzhakov nursing a weapon in the front seat of the Niva. They were accompanied by armed bodyguards in several cars that deployed around the red-brick fortress. Yeltsin's personal security men insisted on escorting him to the door of Gorbachev's third-floor office in the Senate Building, where they stood face to face with Gorbachev's bodyguards as Yeltsin went inside.

Nazarbayev was there already. He thought Yeltsin looked terribly hung-over. He complained immediately that the Belovezh Agreement was an offence to the dignity of the Asiatic republics.

Gorbachev squared up to his nemesis and accused him of 'some kind of a political coup . . . meeting in the woods and shutting down the Soviet Union'. He wanted to know if the independent states would have their own forces.

'Yes, except for strategic forces,' replied Yeltsin.

'So that means Ukraine will have its own army of 470,000, which is 100,000 more than united Germany!' exclaimed Gorbachev. 'You were the first to recognize the Baltic states and signed agreements on human rights and what is the result? Now there are laws on citizenship that discriminate against Russians. That's what democrats do! They say "Russians get out".'

Yeltsin became indignant and snapped, 'Why are you interrogating me? A way had to be found out of the dead end, and we found it!'

The wrangling got nowhere. Yeltsin left after ninety minutes. Gorbachev dictated a statement claiming the end of Soviet law was 'illegal and dangerous'. It was at variance with the will of Russians, Ukrainians and Belarusians in the March referendum on preserving the Union. It would strand millions of Russians living outside Russia's borders. He called for an emergency session of the Congress of People's Deputies to adjudicate on what he dismissed as the 'initiative' of the three leaders.

In Andrey Grachev's opinion, people were too concerned with their daily problems to take action on behalf of the Union. They had lost faith in Gorbachev and his project, and just kept silent. That evening the presidential spokesman went to a piano recital in the Pushkin Museum given by Svyatoslav Richter – a Ukrainian – and had a late-night dinner with the Italian and Dutch ambassadors. The Belovezh accord was not mentioned by the company, on the principle, he guessed, that 'one doesn't speak of rope in the house of a hanged man'.

Gorbachev's military options evaporated two days later. Hoping to make a case for the Soviet armed forces remaining a cohesive force throughout USSR territory, come what may, he asked Shaposhnikov to arrange for him to address an assembly of top commanders from all over the Soviet Union on December 10. Their reaction to his plea was a stony silence. The majority of generals distrusted him and knew that he no longer controlled the purse strings. The next day Yeltsin conducted his own, two-hour, meeting with the same officers, who reacted more positively to his direct style, and to his promise of a 90 per cent pay increase.

To James Baker these moves were the stuff of geo-political nightmare: 'Two Kremlin heavyweights jockeying for power, calling on the army to follow them, and raising the spectre of civil war – with nuclear weapons thrown in.'

Shaposhnikov later told Baker how serious it was. Some hotheads among the generals wanted to give an ultimatum to the president, demanding that he defy Yeltsin, he said. It would be the August coup all over again. Rumours of military adventures continued to circulate in Moscow. Shevardnadze was alarmed to receive a warning from General Konstantin Kobets, who had organized the defence of the White House in

August, that conservative elements in the military were still strong and secretly organizing. On December 11, Vitaly Tretyakov, the editor of *Nezavisimaya Gazeta*, came to tell Gorbachev that Moscow was full of gossip about a new coup. Some newspapers were repeating the rumours about Kremlin barricades. All this is invented, Gorbachev told him.

By December 12 the parliaments of the three Slavic states had endorsed the Belovezh Agreement. In the Russian parliament the vote – one hundred and eighty-eight for, six against, and sixty-nine abstentions – was greeted with applause. In Shakhrai's opinion the deputies realized the agreement had saved the nation from a civil war. And even some hardliners shared Yeltsin's goal to see off the unpopular occupant of the Kremlin. Communist deputy Sevastyanov urged his comrades to vote in favour, 'so that we can get rid of Gorbachev'.

'Such petty people,' stormed Gorbachev when he heard of the remark. 'The era of Gorbachev is only beginning!' At a press conference he waved the secret memo Burbulis had given to Yeltsin in Sochi – a copy had been leaked to him – and said its thrust was that the 'cunning Gorbachev' must be stopped before trapping Yeltsin into a new union. Burbulis denied that the Russian leaders killed off the Soviet Union to get rid of its president. It was already dead, he said. The declaration in the Belarusian forest was a 'medical diagnosis'.

The tone of Yeltsin's accomplices grew insulting. Information chief Poltoranin said condescendingly that the Soviet president need not worry, that he would not suffer the same fate as Erich Honecker. His foreign minister Kozyrev told the German *Das Bild* newspaper, 'Gorbachev is not a leper. We will find plenty of work for him to do.' Grachev encountered Kozyrev after that and told him to get lost.

The clock was nevertheless ticking loudly for Gorbachev. Nazarbayev had no choice but to accept the fait accompli of the deal in the forest. Kazakhstan, the three Slav republics and the seven other republics still nominally in the Soviet Union agreed they would meet to discuss dumping the Union and joining the Commonwealth of Independent States. They set the date and place: December 21, in Alma-Ata.

Gorbachev still found it hard to accept the reality that the USSR was finished, though he took the precaution of having crates of Politburo archives removed from the Kremlin in army trucks to General Staff military head-quarters in Znamenka Street in the Arbat district. He continued to give almost daily interviews and briefings to journalists, ambassadors and foreign politicians, pouring out a torrent of words as if he could somehow conjure up a compromise by talking about con-stitutional propriety and restraining the opportunists. When British ambassador Rodric Braithwaite and visit-ing UK government official Len Appleyard called on Gorbachev in the Walnut Room, Gorbachev stretched out his hand with a grin, saying 'So what – are you here to find out what country you are in and who I am now?' The president was in bouncing form, with his usual tan, bubbling with verbose and hectic charm, observed

Braithwaite. Gorbachev spent half an hour extolling the merits of a union state, while making withering remarks about the 'highwaymen', 'hairy faces' and 'inexperienced populists' who ruled the roost. As Gorbachev built his 'castles in the air', the ambassador noticed Alexander Yakovlev looking on more and more gloomily, and Chernyaev taking notes, 'with deadpan determination'.

On December 13 Gorbachev told George Bush in a telephone call that the agreement between the three presidents was but a draft, a sketch, an improvisation, and the statement that the Soviet Union was dead was facile and bullying.

Bush said after putting down the receiver, 'Yeah, Gorbachev is kind of a pathetic figure at this point.'

The chief 'highwayman' boasted that Gorbachev would be gone soon. Yeltsin told his team in the White House that he had given Mikhail Sergeyevich a deadline, the end of December, or at the latest January, when they would finish with one era and transition to another.

Gorbachev suggested two options to his aides. He could resign, or else continue to offer his services to the republics as commander-in-chief and holder of the nuclear suitcase. Chernyaev and Alexander Yakovlev looked blankly at their leader. 'Why are you sitting like that?' snapped Gorbachev. 'Make notes, you will have to write this up.' Privately Chernyaev thought to himself: 'Nobody today is going to offer him any position. So the second option is an illusion.' Already Gosbank, the Soviet Union's Central Bank, had told Gorbachev that it could no longer make payments to serving members of the Soviet armed forces and Union civil servants. The Russian government stopped all Soviet-sourced payments 'to the [red] army, officials, to us sinners', complained Chernyaev in his diary. 'We are without salaries now.' Historian Roy Medvedev reckoned that by then the power of the president did not extend further than the buildings of the Kremlin.

It was at this point that the Americans got word that Gorbachev and his aides were desperately worried about an attempt to discredit them by Yeltsin's supporters to deflect criticism for what they had done. It came via a circuitous route.

Pavel Palazchenko invited Strobe Talbott of *Time* magazine and historian Michael R. Beschloss to lunch in his Moscow apartment on Saturday, December 14. The two Americans were in Russia working on a book on the end of the Cold War. After asking his wife to leave the room, the Kremlin interpreter told his guests to write down a message and deliver it to the Bush administration, without revealing that he was the source. The message asked that the leaders of the United States impress upon Yeltsin that Gorbachev be treated with dignity. It warned: 'Some people are fabricating a criminal case against him. It is important that Yeltsin not have anything to do with that.'

In his memoirs Palazchenko claimed his information came from an (unnamed) former member of the Communist Party Central Committee who had approached him in a Kremlin corridor to whisper that efforts were afoot to fabricate a case against Gorbachev.

The source alleged that a shadowy team was searching frantically for compromising material to show that Gorbachev was secretly part of the August coup, and insisted that Palazchenko pass this on to the Americans, who might be able to use their influence on Yeltsin to get the effort stopped.

Palazchenko insisted he was not acting at Gorbachev's prompting to secure American protection. 'Nothing could be further from the truth or more out of character for Gorbachev.' His American guests, however, were sceptical. They believed Palazchenko was following a careful script that was intended to preserve the Soviet leader's deniability. Nevertheless, Talbott agreed to pass on the message.

The request was conveniently timed. James Baker and State Department official Dennis Ross arrived the next day in Moscow for talks with the Russian leaders. Talbott went to see them in the Penta Hotel on Olympic Boulevard. He gave the message to Ross, who showed it to Baker.

The US secretary of state met Yeltsin on the following day, December 16, in the St Catherine Hall in the Kremlin. This was the first time Yeltsin had commandeered the sumptuous chamber where Soviet leaders historically welcomed important guests. Marshal Shaposhnikov sat next to him, a strong signal of where the military's loyalty lay. 'Welcome to this Russian building on Russian soil,' trumpeted Yeltsin at the start of a four-hour conversation.

Baker delicately raised the rumours of possible criminal proceedings being taken against Gorbachev.

Such action would be a mistake that would not be understood by the international community, he told the Russian leader. 'Many people will be watching what's going to happen to Gorbachev.' The United States hoped the transfer of power could be done 'in a dignified way – as in the West'.

Yeltsin responded as if he expected the approach. 'Gorbachev has done a lot for this country,' he said. 'He needs to be treated with respect and deserves to be treated with respect. It's about time we became a country where leaders can be retired with honour.'

Baker saw Gorbachev separately, in the same ornate hall and with Alexander Yakovlev and Eduard Shevardnadze at his side. Gorbachev's face was flushed and he had difficulty speaking as if he were having an attack of high blood pressure. Baker sensed, as they chewed Velamints that the secretary of state handed round, that these were three men at the end of their political rope. As with the British, Gorbachev called the Belovezh Agreement 'a kind of coup', carried out by people acting like highway robbers. The conversation trailed off inconclusively. Shevardnadze had nothing positive to say. He knew the game was up. In a telephone call with a contact in the United States, Jim Garrison, he confided, 'The Soviet Union is falling apart. My job is to preside over its collapse.'

Gorbachev went that evening in a heavy snowstorm to a performance of Mahler's Fifth Symphony, his refuge from depression during Russia's darkest hours. The symphony's funereal trumpet solo was like a requiem for his career.

Yeltsin called President Bush the next day and assured him the transfer of power would take place in a friendly manner. Bush reminded him of the high regard in which Gorbachev and Shevardnadze were held for what they had done for peace. 'I do guarantee, and I promise you personally, Mr President, that everything will happen in a good and decent way,' Yeltsin promised. 'We will treat Gorbachev and Shevardnadze with the greatest respect. Everything will be calm and gradual with no radical measures.'

The White House press secretary Marlin Fitzwater would later claim that the US president not only convinced Yeltsin of the need for a peaceful transition but also told him to be good to Gorbachev and to give him a car, give him a house and treat him well. He related that Bush then called Gorbachev and said, 'You've got to be praising Yeltsin, or at least don't be criticizing him in public. Don't be tearing him down and picking a fight.'

Gorbachev's aides were still concerned that something unpleasant was in store for them. Alexander Yakovlev confided to Chernyaev that he thought Yeltsin was fearful of opposition from people like himself and Shevardnadze and would try to liquidate them. They were alone in Gorbachev's office at the time – the president had stepped out to make one of his regular calls to Raisa – and he lowered his voice in case of listening devices. 'I think they will kill me,' he whispered to Chernyaev. 'I will ask Gorbachev to send me somewhere, maybe Finland, as ambassador. Yeltsin will have to agree, I am too dangerous for him here.'

Chernyaev, also wary of surveillance, responded with a complicit smile.

But these worries were set aside when, on Wednesday, December 18, Gorbachev at last conceded to Yeltsin that it was over, and agreed that at the end of the year, on December 31, the Soviet Union and its governing structures would cease to exist. As to when he would resign as president of the Soviet Union, he wrote a note to himself: 'After the twenty-first – probably; after the new year – possibly.'

The first to be told, outside the Kremlin circle, that he would be gone before the end of the year was an American, Shevardnadze's contact Jim Garrison. As head of the International Foreign Policy Association, Garrison was visiting Moscow that day as part of his task to mobilize aid for the children of the Soviet Union. Alexander Yakovlev brought him into Gorbachev's office for a chat. 'Gorbachev was ebullient, upbeat, smiling,' recalled Garrison, who would be the last foreign guest to visit Gorbachev while he was still president. 'Under the circumstances I was surprised he had time for the likes of me.' Garrison told him how he had organized a load of food supplies to be brought to Russia two days earlier on an Antonov transport plane, the biggest plane in the world, and that at a press conference, the American co-pilot had said with tears in his eyes, 'All my life I have practised flying to the Soviet Union, but I thought I would be flying with a payload of warheads.'

As Garrison got up from the table, Yakovlev put an

arm around him and said, 'You should know we are resigning in one week. Tell no one.'

Garrison was shocked. 'Are you serious?' he asked.

'All options are closed,' replied Yakovlev.

'What, is there anything I can do?' asked the American.

'Yes,' replied Gorbachev. 'Can you bring another Antonov? Can you bring some meat? Moscow is running out of meat.'

On leaving the Kremlin, Garrison made a call to Donald Kendall, the former chairman of PepsiCo which then owned Pizza Hut, and arranged for him to send a planeload of canned beef to Russia in a C-5A Galaxy troop carrier.

Otherwise Gorbachev was deliberately coy for days about when he would step down. On December 20, in a telephone conversation with German chancellor Helmut Kohl, he insisted his departure was not imminent, as the transfer of power must be done in a constitutional manner. But the eviction notices were piling up. That afternoon the presidential account in the State Bank was closed on Yeltsin's orders, leaving Gorbachev unable to authorize expenses for himself or his personal staff. Another Yeltsin decree placed the elite KGB Alpha Group under the sole control of the president of Russia.

On Saturday, December 21, in Alma-Ata, Yeltsin and the heads of state from ten other republics of the original fifteen signed up to the Commonwealth of Independent States. They ignored a long letter from

Gorbachev offering to play a unifying role. The eleven presidents signed documents declaring that the commonwealth was not a state or a supra-state entity. *Moscow News* correspondent Viktor Kiyanitsa reported that the figure of Gorbachev loomed over the proceedings like a mute reproach. The other person on their minds was James Baker, 'who had been flying round the country in search of the nuclear button' and who by insisting on his five conditions for international recognition had 'knocked together the new commonwealth, whether he knew it or not'.

Yeltsin arrived back in Moscow the next day and told reporters that they had discussed Gorbachev's future. In the past leaders had been removed from politics and society, consigned to oblivion and then either reburied after death or vilified, he said. But they were above that. They would allow Mikhail Sergeyevich to continue to play an active role in society and they would give him financial security.

Gorbachev was furious when he was told the republic leaders had acted so condescendingly. 'For me, they have poisoned the air, they have humiliated me,' he fumed. The former general secretary of the Communist Party, who once had tsar-like powers over the republics, declared himself 'shocked by the treacherous behaviour of those people, who cut the country in pieces in order to settle accounts and establish themselves as tsars'. Gorbachev's contempt for the republics' leaders was shared by his aides. Alexander Yakovlev growled that their intellectual level was so low that 'you yourself become dumber talking to them'.

Yeltsin called President Bush once more, to inform him that the commonwealth had been created, 'so the centre will simply cease to exist'. Bush immediately telephoned Gorbachev again.

He found the Soviet president in a foul mood, furious at Yeltsin and the way events were rushing past him. Yeltsin had done a deal behind his back to dismantle the Soviet Union, he said bitterly. 'In politics anything can happen, especially when one deals with such politicians.' The American president calmed him down. 'I am thinking of you professionally and personally,' Bush assured him. He thought Gorbachev was 'stunned about what was happening as a person and as the president of the Soviet Union . . . His authority was slipping away.'

Chernyaev was exasperated with Gorbachev for clinging on to the Kremlin and furious with Yeltsin for the way he was treating Gorbachev. 'Nicholas II at least received a delegation from the Duma with a request for him to resign,' he wrote in his diary. 'He had the courage to give up the crown after three hundred years of dynasty. Gorbachev was simply rudely toppled.' Alexander Yakovlev marvelled at how Gorbachev continued to nurse for so long the forlorn hope that he could rescue the Soviet Union. 'The train had left and Gorbachev was running after it, as if he didn't notice that history was going the other way.' Yakovlev himself knew well how happy the republics were to break away from the centre. One president had told him crudely, 'It is better to be the head of a fly than the arse of an elephant.' But Gorbachev couldn't imagine they would think this way. Was he being too critical, Yakovlev asked himself? No. Both felt deep pain at their many unrealized hopes.

'Criticism can only be fair,' he concluded, 'if it recognizes that Gorbachev was at the forefront of one of the biggest events in the history of Russia.'

22

December 25: Evening

WITH TEN MINUTES TO GO BEFORE MIKHAIL Gorbachev's address to the now-almost-extinct empire he inherited more than six years ago, his stylist and make-up artist comes to his office to prepare him for the cameras. She expertly dabs powder on his birthmark, the vascular malformation on his bald dome that is commonly referred to as a port wine stain because of its purplish colour. The first official portraits of Gorbachev were issued with the birthmark airbrushed out. That was before the communist leader introduced *glasnost*.

The Soviet president wonders where the CNN and Russian television cameras are. He assumes he will be making his stepping-down speech at the desk where he works as president. 'Where are they going to be filming?' he inquires. As director of the television coverage, Yegor Yakovlev tells him that everything has been set up in the sham office, Room No. 4. 'Why not in my office?' asks Gorbachev. Yakovlev explains that there are so many technicians, photographers and journalists involved, not to mention equipment, that they would have had to take over the real office for two hours to prepare for the broadcast. It is too late to change anything. CNN has set up its broadcasting operation down the corridor. They must go there.

'CNN broadcasts to one hundred and fifty-three countries,' remarks Yakovlev, emphasizing the importance of the network's worldwide coverage of the resignation.

'And the eleven countries of the CIS as well,' notes Gorbachev. 'Well, let's not take the risk of changing the location.'

He rises abruptly, puts the farewell address and the resignation decrees into his soft-leather document case, and leaves the office for the last time as president of the Soviet Union.

The mock office is already brightly lit with arc lights as Gorbachev and his aides enter. Setting up and connecting the cameras and cables and communications equipment has just been completed. A last-minute change of location would have caused consternation among the television crews.

Milling around the confined space and spilling out into the corridor are twenty-seven CNN staffers, plus a score of Russian technicians and some official photographers. Filmmaker Igor Belyaev is supervising Russian cameras for his own documentary.

The room has been arranged to resemble Gorbachev's as closely as possible. The floor is covered with a green floral carpet similar to that in his office. Beside the desk is a bank of four telephones, though they have never been connected. Behind the chair, on the left from the camera's perspective, the Soviet flag droops from a three-metre pole, in front of a gold-framed painting of the Kremlin. The wall to the right is draped with scalloped white curtains. Overhead hangs a large chandelier identical to the one in the president's office. However, instead of a high-backed leather chair there is a velvet shield-back chair, so that Gorbachev's profile is clearly outlined for the cameras against the soft oyster green of the damask silk background.

Among the still photographers looking for a good position is Liu Heung Shing, a staff member of the Associated Press bureau in Moscow. Hong Kong-born Liu was driving around Moscow looking for picture opportunities when Tom Johnson called him on his portable telephone and told him to get round to the Kremlin as quickly as he could. Johnson, besides being president of CNN, is also a director of AP. No foreign news agencies have been able to get a pass into the Kremlin to see history being made, but Johnson has added the names of Liu and AP reporter Alan Cooperman to his crew so he can smuggle them in.

At first Liu doesn't have a clear idea of what is happening. 'When I entered the ornate chandeliered room, I knew something big was going on. However, I saw there was no presence of any Russian journalists or TASS photographers. Neither were there any other Western journalists. Tom greeted me and said to please hang around as Mikhail Gorbachev would talk to CNN after the televised speech. I soon found out it was going to be his resignation speech.'

Liu squats in front of the tripod supporting a large first-generation Soviet TV camera and prepares to take the definitive picture of Gorbachev giving up power.

Making his way through the mêlée Gorbachev shakes hands with Tom Johnson and takes his seat behind the walnut desk. The room clears quickly apart from a handful of CNN and Russian personnel. Chernyaev, Grachev, Palazchenko and both Yakovlevs, Alexander and Yegor, hang around out of camera shot.

Gorbachev opens the green folder containing his speech and two decrees. One is his resignation as president of the Soviet Union and the other the transfer of command and control of the armed forces to Boris Yeltsin. An aide comes and places a cup of milky coffee on the desktop to his right. Gorbachev straightens his papers and says in a quiet voice, his head down as if talking to himself, 'If you have to go, you have to go. It's that time.'

With two minutes left Gorbachev holds a whispered consultation with Chernyaev and Grachev. He asks again should he sign the texts now, or after the resignation. They decide that after is better.

A solidly built Russian assistant in red blouse and purple knee-length cardigan points to the camera and asks Gorbachev, 'Is that OK for you, are you comfortable with that?'

'All clear, understood,' replies Gorbachev.

As the moment approaches for the live broadcast, a security man in grey suit and blue shirt and tie leans down and orders Liu to leave. He refuses and the guard glares at him furiously. He hisses at him not to take a photograph during the televising of the address. Liu replies, 'OK!' But he doesn't mean it.

A technician fits a microphone to the president's tie and Gorbachev takes a felt pen from inside his suit jacket. He tries it out on the green folder. It doesn't work. 'Andrey, it is too hard,' he says, glancing back at his spokesman who is hovering over his shoulder. 'You wouldn't have a softer one? Give me a good pen to sign these.'

Johnson, standing a few feet away, sees what is happening. He reaches into his pocket and draws out his Mont Blanc ballpoint, a twenty-fifth wedding anniversary present from his wife Edwina. The sudden movement alarms the three security officials in the room. 'They did everything but draw AK47s,' laughs Caudill. 'Gorbachev says to them, "Nyet, nyet!"'

'We were about to go live on Russian television and around the world with the resignation of Mikhail Gorbachev, the dissolution of the Soviet Union and the conveyance of power to Boris Yeltsin,' recalled Johnson. 'And I am standing one person away from Gorbachev within, say, forty-five seconds to a minute before airtime. He takes this green Soviet-made pen out to just test it. . . . And it didn't work. . . . And I just reached in my pocket and I said, "Mr President, you may use mine."'

'Is it American?' asks Gorbachev with a smile as he takes the German-made pen with black resin sheen and gold point.

'No, sir, it is either French or German,' says Johnson.

'In that case I will use it.'

Once again a member of the media provides the instrument for the Soviet Union's liquidation.

Gorbachev tests the pen on the green folder and, satisfied that it works, ends the discussion with his aides and – despite what he has just been advised – signs the five-page decree abdicating as president of the Soviet Union, and the second decree giving up his post as commander-in-chief of the Soviet armed forces. Hardly anyone takes any notice. The historic event is not televised, as the cameras have not gone live. He puts the pen on the edge of the desk beyond the coffee cup and places the decrees on the left side of the folder.

In cities across the world, viewers tune in to watch the first and last resignation of a leader of the Soviet Union, live on CNN.

In the Washington suburbs, a generation of sovietologists, correspondents, academics and economists who had been dealing with the mysterious and closed USSR over the years pause in their preparations for Christmas lunch to watch the news from Moscow. Many are in a state of incomprehension – even a few weeks ago it seemed the Soviet Union would prevail in one form or other. Some are going to have to seek new careers, their analyses and forecasts consigned to the archives.

As Gorbachev is preparing to make his broadcast, another convoy with sirens wailing makes its way to the Kremlin. It is the president of Russia, who has just finished his crisis meeting with Moscow's deputy mayor Yury Luzhkov in the White House. His car pulls up outside Building 14 just before seven o'clock. Accompanied by Gennady Burbulis, Yeltsin takes the lift to the fourth floor where he has his Kremlin office. An assistant has the television switched on.

Yeltsin's office has a more personal feel than Gorbachev's presidential suite in the adjoining building. The walls are decorated with a picture of Yeltsin on the tank during the coup, an ornate religious icon, and a framed painting of his eighty-three-year-old mother Klavdiya Vasilyevna Yeltsina, copied from a photograph by the painter Ilya Glazunov, a well-known purveyor of Russian nationalism. There is a map of the Soviet Union covered with coloured pins signifying hot spots of ethnic and nationalist crises.

The group gathers round the television set to observe Gorbachev doing what Yeltsin publicly first asked him to do in his famous televised interview ten months ago. At that time his call for Gorbachev's resignation had provoked outrage and dismay around the world.

Everything is now in place for the final act of the transition. As soon as Gorbachev has finished speaking, the Russian president is to walk across the narrow courtyard to Gorbachev's office. There, in the presence of Marshal Shaposhnikov and the television cameras, he will take formal possession of the nuclear suitcase and will become the legal successor in Russia of the last president of the USSR.

The world will see the two rivals shake hands and smile as the *chemodanchik* changes ownership and the curtain comes down on seventy-four years of Soviet rule. At least, that is the plan.

23

The Deal in the Walnut Room

THE DETAILS OF THE TRANSITION OF POWER WERE worked out during a nine-hour encounter between Mikhail Gorbachev and Boris Yeltsin two days before the Soviet president gave his resignation address on the evening of December 25, 1991.

After the conspiracy in the Belovezh Forest that killed off his political career, Gorbachev went through the first two stages of grief – denial and anger. After Alma-Ata he moved to the third stage – bargaining. He now had to negotiate his retirement package. He had got his aides to draw up decrees regarding his pension and living conditions and prepare drafts of a resignation address. But he couldn't bring himself to set the final wheels in motion.

Yeltsin forced the issue in typical fashion. In mid-morning on Monday, December 23, six years to the day since Gorbachev promoted him to Moscow party chief, the Russian president sent word that he was on his way to the Senate Building to set the terms for Gorbachev's exit from political life.

The president's aides were furious at the short notice. Grachev perceived Yeltsin to be acting as he always did, capriciously and aggressively. But, as Gorbachev's former deputy spokesman Sergey Grigoryev put it, 'Yeltsin had Gorbachev by the balls.' Now that the republics had signed up to the Commonwealth of Independent States, scheduled to come into existence on January 1, there was no longer a role for a Union president.

The unexpected arrival of Yeltsin was doubly embarrassing for Gorbachev's staff. They had alerted Ted Koppel and his television crew to be in the Kremlin to film something quite different.

'When we picked up our equipment on that Monday morning we were told Gorbachev would be taping his resignation speech in his office in a matter of minutes,' said Koppel. 'He was, we were told, getting a haircut in preparation. Waiting with us was Gorbachev's make-up artist. At one point a member of the president's personal security guard came to the door to tell us that Gorbachev was a minute away. The president's desk with two Soviet flags behind it was fully lit. Two large cameras from Soviet state television were already beaming the signal out for taping.

'But he never showed up. It was just past 11.00 a.m. and Boris Yeltsin was coming to the Kremlin for a meeting.'

With Yeltsin on his way, Gorbachev had to scrap plans to pre-record his speech and make up his mind quickly as to when he would actually announce his departure to the nation. He told Grachev he would most likely broadcast his resignation speech live the following day. 'There's no sense in dragging this out,' he sighed.

'Wouldn't it be better to wait until Wednesday?' Grachev suggested. 'Tomorrow is December 24, Christmas Eve. In many countries this is the biggest holiday of the year. Let people celebrate in peace.'

'All right,' said Gorbachev, who like his press secretary was seemingly unaware that the 'biggest holiday' in much of the West was Christmas Day. 'But Wednesday at the latest.'

Grachev asked Gorbachev if he thought it would be acceptable for the American and Russian television crews to film the two leaders in the act of greeting each other. This would be an important encounter between the two men who had shaped Russia's destiny and it should be recorded for history. Gorbachev gave his OK with a wave of his hand.

Knowing how prickly Yeltsin could be, and worried he might suspect an ambush of some sort, Grachev went to ask Yeltsin too for permission. 'Rather than be satisfied with one president's approval, I decided to ask the other one for his as well.' As Yeltsin emerged from the lift, flanked by his wary and unsmiling bodyguard, Korzhakov, Grachev inquired if the camera crews could record his arrival. 'Out of the question, otherwise I'll cancel the meeting,' snorted Yeltsin. Grachev signalled to the television people to leave. There was no doubting whose wishes must be obeyed, even in the precincts of Gorbachev's own office.

Koppel remembered the Russian leader glowering as

he walked towards the office. He felt that Yeltsin was angry at him. 'I was paying all this attention to Gorbachev. He felt I should be seeking him out. He was the new boy in town. This was his moment, he was absorbing all the power. It was bleeding through Gorbachev's hands minute by minute.'

In an interview not long before, Yeltsin had bluntly told Koppel his opinion of Gorbachev: 'To a large extent, I don't like him.'

Yeltsin waited until the reporters left before he would even cross the threshold into Gorbachev's sanctum.

Zhenya, the Kremlin waiter, brought in a tray with coffee, cups, shot glasses and two bottles, vodka for Yeltsin and Jubilee cognac for Gorbachev, 'to go with the coffee' as Chernyaev observed drily. After some small talk they took their jackets off and in shirtsleeves and ties moved to the adjacent Walnut Room. It was in this same room that on March 11, 1985, the day after the death of Soviet leader Konstantin Chernenko, the Politburo of the Communist Party agreed to make Mikhail Gorbachev general secretary of the party and undisputed leader of the Soviet Union.

Sitting beneath alabaster chandeliers at the end of the long teakwood table with fifteen chairs, the two antagonists discussed the implications of the agreement reached at Alma-Ata. Gorbachev was angry and heavy-hearted but resigned. As Grachev put it, 'there was no way to put the toothpaste back in the tube'.

Gorbachev conceded to Yeltsin that for the sake of peace and order he would publicly accept the CIS as the constitutional successor to the Soviet Union. Yeltsin listened attentively to his warnings about the dangers of Balkanization. He in turn asked Gorbachev to lend him his support for the next six months, or at least not criticize him, while he imposed shock therapy on Russia.

It was inevitably going to be a tense encounter. Gorbachev's aide Georgy Shakhnazarov noted that it was not in Gorbachev's character to be humble, nor in Yeltsin's to be magnanimous. The two agreed to invite Alexander Yakovlev to 'referee' the meeting.

The sixty-eight-year-old father of *glasnost* came limping into the room. He was intrigued to be there. It meant that he would be a witness 'not only to the beginning but also to the end of the lofty career of Mikhail Gorbachev'. Like his mentor, the former ambassador to Canada and cheerleader for *perestroika* did not want to see the Soviet Union broken up, and he was opposed to what Yeltsin had done. Nevertheless, the Russian president respected him for his courageous role during the coup and for his campaign to expose the crimes of Stalin. In October Yeltsin had appointed Yakovlev to chair a commission for the rehabilitation of victims of political repression.

The two presidents agreed on a transition timetable. Gorbachev would abdicate two days later, on December 25. He would broadcast his resignation speech to the nation at seven o'clock in the evening of that day. After finishing his address, he would sign the decrees resigning as president of the Union of Soviet Socialist Republics and giving up his position as commander-in-chief of the Soviet armed forces. Immediately after that

Yeltsin would come to his office with defence minister Shaposhnikov and take possession of the nuclear suitcase. Gorbachev and his staff could continue using their Kremlin offices for a further four days after Gorbachev's resignation, until December 29, to conduct unfinished business and clear out their desks, after which Yeltsin would move in with his staff as president of Russia. The red flag would come down from the Kremlin on December 31. Gorbachev's adviser, Georgy Shakhnazarov, who was called into the meeting briefly, would tell Gorbachev's assembled staff of aides, officials, interpreters, receptionists, typists and researchers the next day that they had to leave the Kremlin on December 29, and that the presidential apparatus would stop functioning on January 2.

In return for all this, Gorbachev would step down gracefully, not challenge Yeltsin's right to succeed him, and stay out of the political fray to give the Russian president a clear run to implement his economic reforms.

Once the basics were settled, the heads of Gorbachev's and Yeltsin's secretariats, Grigory Revenko and Yury Petrov, were brought in to take notes on the nitty-gritty of Gorbachev's future welfare.

'Gorbachev submitted a list of claims – his compensation package – that ran to several pages,' claimed Yeltsin later. 'Almost all the items were purely material demands. He wanted a pension equalling a presidential salary, indexed to inflation; a presidential apartment and dacha; a car for himself and his wife. But more than anything he wanted a foundation, a big building in the centre of Moscow, the former Academy of Social Sciences, and with it car service, office equipment and security guards. Psychologically his reasoning was very simple: if you want to get rid of me so badly, then be so good as to dig deep into your pockets.'

Yeltsin agreed that the Gorbachevs could see out their retirement in a smaller state dacha and apartment, with two official cars and twenty staff, including security, drivers, cooks and service personnel. He declined to authorize a separate ex-president's office and staff, and he cut back the amount of pension requested and the number of bodyguards. He signed a decree giving Gorbachev a pension equivalent to his salary of 4,000 rubles a month – ten times the average Soviet wage but a mere $40 at the official rate of exchange. The arrangement would not leave Gorbachev in penury. He was already wealthy from advance royalties for his memoirs.

Next they settled on provisions for Gorbachev's inner circle. They agreed to set up a bilateral commission headed by Revenko and Petrov to find jobs for Gorbachev's displaced staff. The Soviet president asked Yeltsin to allow his associates Ivan Silayev and Shakhnazarov to buy their state dachas at reasonable prices. Silayev was the last prime minister of the Soviet Union, an office that had been defunct since the coup, and Shakhnazarov had been by Gorbachev's side throughout the last turbulent years. The Russian president agreed. Turning to Yakovlev, he offered him the same deal. Yakovlev declined. He regretted his decision in years to come, as property prices in the Moscow area soared.

The terms Yeltsin agreed with Gorbachev were on a par with legislation passed by the USSR Supreme Soviet over a year earlier. This had provided for a pension and state-owned dacha with the necessary staff, bodyguard and transport for the president on leaving office. They were also remarkably similar to those granted in 1964 to Nikita Khrushchev, the only other Soviet leader to be ousted from power. Khrushchev, another would-be reformer, was sacked by the Politburo for alleged policy failures and erratic behaviour. He was given a pension and was allowed to remain in his general secretary's mansion and his city apartment for a year after his departure, before moving to a smaller state mansion. But Khrushchev was made a non-person. He simply disappeared from public view. His name did not appear again in Moscow newspapers until he died seven years later. This distressed him deeply. He spent days weeping bitterly. Asked once what Khrushchev did in retirement, his grandson replied, 'He cries.' Gorbachev would not become a non-person but he too would shed a tear before the day was out.

The two adversaries, Yakovlev recalled, managed up to this point to conduct a very business-like and mutually respectful meeting. 'They argued sometimes but without any rancour. I was very sorry they did not start cooperating at that level of mutual understanding before.' He thought whisperers on both sides had helped poison the atmosphere between them.

At one o'clock Zhenya delivered lunch to the three men. They helped themselves to salads and salami, potato and cabbage pies, and bottles of fizzy mineral water. When the waiter emerged with his empty trolley, aides to both presidents quizzed him about how they were getting on. He told them the meeting seemed to have got off to a civilized start.

With the material terms of the transition agreed, Revenko and Petrov left. Only Yakovlev would witness what transpired next.

Gorbachev produced a certificate giving Yeltsin control over the Archives of the General Secretary. This was a collection of between one and two thousand files that contained secret documents passed on by Soviet leaders from the time of the founding of the state by Lenin. They were known to senior Soviet officials as the *Stalinskiye Arkhivy*, the Stalin Archives.

Though many of the crimes of past communist leaders had been acknowledged for the first time under Gorbachev's policy of *glasnost*, the top-secret documents still held proof of criminal actions at the highest levels of Soviet power, most of which had never been admitted publicly. They implicated recent Soviet leaders in the cover-up and denials of the Stalin terror and many other bloody episodes, cover-ups which would sustain charges that, in the past, the Communist Party of the Soviet Union was a vast criminal conspiracy and was involved in international terrorism.

Every general secretary received the archives on taking office. They all knew, or could find out, what secrets they concealed.

One of the files handed over by Gorbachev detailed a plan to send a ship with arms to the left-wing Official Irish Republican Army at a time when the illegal group was conducting a campaign of bombing and killings in Northern Ireland. Called 'Operation Splash' it was approved by Politburo member and KGB chief Yury Andropov, in response to a request from Irish Communist Party leader Michael O'Riordan, who claimed he was in secret contact with the Official IRA. A memo signed by Andropov on August 21, 1972, authorized the submerging of a consignment of captured German weapons, including two machine guns, seventy automatic rifles, ten Walther pistols and 41,600 cartridges, in the Irish Sea off the Northern Ireland coast, to be hauled up later by the 'Irish friends' in a fishing boat. A reconnaissance ship, *Reduktor*, had already picked the spot and sounded the depths, Andropov noted. Yeltsin was later unable to say if Operation Splash succeeded but concluded that quite possibly 'our "friends" once again made themselves known with their trademark explosions and murders, causing the whole world to shudder'.

Gorbachev then pushed back his chair and went to his office safe, from which he extracted two large envelopes tied with string and with broken wax seals. There was one document they should inspect first, he said when he resumed his seat. He began reading the contents to his two companions. It was a memo, dated March 5, 1940, from Lavrenty Beria, head of Stalin's secret police, the NKVD, which recommended the execution in Katyn Forest near Smolensk of 25,700 Polish officers, taken prisoner by Soviet forces invading the east of Poland in the early stages of World War Two. Written on it in Stalin's blue pencil were the words,

'Resolution of the Politburo', and the signatures of Stalin, Molotov, Mikoyan and Voroshilov. Gorbachev also read aloud a deposition from Alexander Shelepin, former head of the KGB. In 1959 Shelepin had given the total number of Polish victims shot in 1940 as 21,857, and proposed to Khrushchev the destruction of all incriminating documents.

The file was conclusive evidence that the Politburo ordered the slaughter of the Polish officers. For five years after Gorbachev took office, it had been Soviet practice to continue the post-war fiction of blaming the Germans for carrying out the mass killings after they invaded the USSR in 1941. In April 1990 the exhumation of bodies and other circumstantial evidence had compelled Gorbachev to admit the truth, but only partially. He authorized the Soviet news agency TASS to express profound regret to Poland for Stalin's 'heinous crime', as if Stalin had acted alone.

Gorbachev had never conceded that the evidence existed of full Politburo approval of one of the worst crimes in European history. Here at last was the absolute proof of the complicity not just of Stalin and the notorious Beria, but of the Communist Party of the Soviet Union.

Yakovlev listened with a growing sense of anger. As a historian, he had been seeking these papers everywhere. He concluded at once that Gorbachev knew all along about their existence, but had kept them from him.

'Gorbachev in my presence gave Yeltsin the package with all the documents on Katyn [and] when the envelope was opened it turned out that they were notes about the shooting of Polish military and civilians,' he wrote later. 'Gorbachev was sitting there stone-faced as if nothing was ever discussed on that matter. Time and time again I asked in the General Department of the Central Committee which documents are in the Politburo archives regarding this, and I got the same response each time – there is nothing.' He was bewildered at finding evidence that Gorbachev had withheld such material over the years. 'Gorbachev would have gained politically and morally if he made them public; he didn't have good judgement of people but he was an even worse judge of himself.'

Gorbachev subsequently claimed that he had only received the incriminating documents the previous evening from Revenko, who had his attention drawn to them by the director of the archives and insisted that the president look at them. By Gorbachev's account, it took his breath away to read 'this hellish paper which condemned to death thousands of people at a single stroke'.

His former chief of staff Valery Boldin would claim in his memoir that he had shown the documents in question to Gorbachev more than two years earlier, prior to a visit to Poland, and that his boss told him not to reveal them to anyone else, saying, 'This is a hanging matter.' Archive annotations show that in 1989 Boldin did open the file containing the Politburo order to shoot the Poles and that every Soviet leader since Stalin, and not excluding Gorbachev, had read the secret file and knew the truth. According to Gorbachev, the two sets of documents Boldin showed him simply related to a Stalin-era commission pinning the blame for the massacre on the Nazis.

Chernyaev would later take the charitable view that Boldin was trying to discredit Gorbachev and doubted that Gorbachev ever did see the execution command.

The three men agreed that the 'smoking gun' documents would have to be delivered to the Poles. 'I'm afraid they can lead to international complications. But now this is your mission, Boris Nikolayevich,' said Gorbachev, handing them over. Yeltsin would release the documents to the Russian media the following October.

The rest of the secret files were stuffed into boxes. 'Take it, now it's all yours,' said Gorbachev. Yeltsin signed the receipt. Yakovlev was later 'dumbfounded' to discover that they included secrets that even he, with his research into Bolshevik atrocities, had not imagined. Among them was an order signed by Lenin for the execution of 25,000 Russian Orthodox priests in the civil war of 1918 to 1921, though it is doubtful if this was carried out. All Russians knew that Stalin's hands were bloody but many revered Lenin as the father of the nation and did not associate him with mass killings.

The man who had presided over the Soviet Union for the previous six years asked about his own immunity from prosecution. 'If you are worried about something, confess it now, while you are still president,' said Yeltsin. Gorbachev did not take him up on his offer.

Next Gorbachev turned to the question of the foundation he was setting up in Moscow to give him a public service role after his resignation. He had already told his aides it would be 'a powerful intellectual centre that will initiate the process of establishment in Russia of a really democratic society, and if necessary the centre will take the role of a powerful opposition against those dilettantes and self-satisfied mediocrities.'

Here in the Walnut Room, using less provocative language, he explained that the foundation would be a non-government organization for the study of economics and politics. He needed a suitable building for what he would call The Fund for Social and Political Research. Yeltsin objected to the phrase 'political research'. He did not want a hostile foundation nosing around in Russian government affairs. Gorbachev insisted that it would not be turned into 'a breeding ground for the opposition'. The exchange became heated, until Yakovlev came up with a compromise. 'Let's call it The Fund for Social and Political Studies,' he suggested. They eventually agreed on the title: The International Foundation for Socio-Economic and Political Studies (The Gorbachev Foundation).

Yeltsin was still leery about Gorbachev's intentions. 'You won't create an opposition party on the basis of the foundation, will you?' he asked. Gorbachev replied that he would not, and moreover, 'I will support and defend the leadership of Russia as long as it conducts democratic transformations.' Satisfied, Yeltsin signed over to Gorbachev the deeds of a marble-fronted three-storey building on Leningradsky Prospekt in northwest Moscow. It had once housed the Lenin School, an academic training ground for members of foreign underground movements.

At six o'clock the Soviet president excused himself. He had scheduled a farewell telephone conversation with John Major.

The British prime minister regarded both Gorbachev and Yeltsin as remarkable men, Gorbachev as a communist who believed communism could be reformed, Yeltsin as an anti-communist who believed it had to be destroyed. At a private dinner in London the previous July, Major had found Gorbachev 'a charmer with a self-deprecating wit' who had regaled him with anecdotes, including the story of the man in the vodka queue who went off to shoot the general secretary in the Kremlin. Major concluded, however, that Gorbachev was simply unable to grasp the basic essentials of the free market and the merits of competition, and that his understanding of privatization was negligible. Nevertheless, the prime minister was sad to see him leave the political stage and was calling to wish him well.

Gorbachev's translator was summoned from his office to interpret the conversation. Palazchenko found the security post in the corridor approaching Gorbachev's office manned by an unusually large number of people, who included Yeltsin's bodyguards. One of them asked for his ID before letting him pass. That hadn't happened before.

The interpreter saw immediately that the cognac had had an effect on Gorbachev. There was a whiff of liquor on his breath and he noticed how Gorbachev chose his words carefully, 'perhaps partly because he did not want any slips of the tongue caused by the drinks he had

had'. Grachev also thought his boss looked flushed and a little dazed as he lifted the receiver, and that he struggled to find the tone of familiarity he used with world leaders, though within a minute or two he had recovered. Chernyaev observed his boss then conduct a conversation with Major that he felt must have stunned the British prime minister with its sincerity.

'Today, dear John,' began Gorbachev, 'I am trying to accomplish what is most important: to keep what is happening here from resulting in losses. You know I still feel that the best solution would be a unified state, but there are the republics' positions to consider.' He re-assured Major that the break-up of the Soviet Union would not result in another Yugoslavia. 'That's what matters the most to me – to you too I would imagine.' Yeltsin and he had been talking for six hours, he said, and had reached 'a common understanding of our responsibility to the country and the world'. He added diplomatically, 'I ask you to help the commonwealth and Russia in particular.' Glancing over at Grachev, as if to confirm their earlier agreement about the timing of his resignation, Gorbachev confided, 'Some time in the next two days I will make my position public.'

He added a comment that betrayed his unwillingness, even then, to accept the finality of his situation. 'I don't want to say my farewells yet,' he told Major, 'because any turn of events is still possible, even a reversal.'

Gorbachev became quite emotional when the British prime minister told him that whatever decision he made, 'you will unquestionably occupy a special place in the history of your country and the world'.

'Thank you for everything,' replied Gorbachev, his eyes glistening. 'Raisa and I have grown very fond of you, both you and Norma.'

While Gorbachev was out of the room, the conversation between Yakovlev and Yeltsin continued in a more relaxed fashion, fuelled by more glasses of vodka. The Russian president reproached Yakovlev for publicly criticizing his actions in making Russia independent and Yakovlev retorted that he thought the decision was 'illegitimate and undemocratic'. But there was little personal antagonism. Yeltsin asked him what he would do with himself now that he no longer had a job as presidential adviser. Yakovlev said he would work for Gorbachev in the foundation. 'Why would you? He betrayed you more than once,' said Yeltsin. 'It's not as if you don't have other opportunities.' This sounded to Yakovlev like an invitation to work with the Russian administration, but he didn't take it up. He said he was simply sorry for Gorbachev. 'God forbid that anyone should be in his situation.'

Yakovlev took it upon himself to warn Yeltsin not to let the intelligence service get too powerful or allow it to control information reaching him. He reminded him that information fed to Gorbachev by the KGB had succeeded in frightening the president into adopting a hard line against the democrats. Yeltsin agreed, and said that he was going to set up five or six channels of information – though, as Yakovlev later noted, nothing ever came out of that. In this context the name of Yevgeny Primakov, director of the Foreign Intelligence Service, came up. Yeltsin said that, from what he knew,

Primakov was inclined to drink too much. 'No more nor less than others,' said Yakovlev drily. Yeltsin looked at him suspiciously, but didn't say anything.

Gorbachev seemed in no hurry to return to Yeltsin's company, and kept Major on the phone for half an hour. The less power he had the longer his conversations lasted. Alexander Rutskoy was overheard once, as he rushed from his office late for a meeting, 'Damn, every time Gorbachev calls he blabs on for a half hour.'

After he bid Major goodbye, Gorbachev remarked to Grachev and Chernyaev that he and Yeltsin had worked everything out, and 'I'm going back in to wind things up.'

Glancing into Gorbachev's office where the door had been left open, Grachev noted the red flag standing in the corner, Gorbachev's eyeglass case on the desk and the nuclear suitcase on the table, all visible confirmation that Gorbachev was still, if only nominally, president of the Soviet Union. 'This is the surrealistic tableau that would have presented itself to anyone who could have taken a cross section through the building and looked into the rooms on the third floor,' he thought. 'Atop the dome, the red flag of the Soviet Union was still flying.'

Zhenya brought plates of cold meat and smoked fish and pickles into the Walnut Room. He also managed to rustle up bread and jam and coffee for Grachev and Yegor Yakovlev in the kitchen. As they ate, they saw that Russian television was showing the 'Dance of the Cygnets' from Tchaikovsky's *Swan Lake*, the same ballet broadcast continuously on Soviet television during the three days of the August coup. It was as if someone inside the television studios was subtly signalling that a second coup was being conducted, this time by Yeltsin.

The two Gorbachev associates pestered the waiter as he hurried in and out of the Walnut Room about the mood of the men inside. 'The mood seems to be good,' the diplomatic Zhenya responded.

In the television room next to the kitchen, Ted Koppel and Rick Kaplan waited in vain, with their antenna rigged up, to communicate with New York via satellite link, in the event of dramatic news from down the corridor. Eventually they gave up and left.

The meeting in the Walnut Room went on for another two and a half hours. Around 9.00 p.m., after Gorbachev had downed two more small glasses of cognac, Yakovlev noticed that he was showing signs of strain. Saying that he wasn't feeling very well, the Soviet president excused himself. He left the room and went to lie down in a resting room attached to an adjacent office.

Yeltsin and Yakovlev found themselves alone again. They threw back little shots of alcohol for another hour. In an expansive mood, Yeltsin promised he would draw up a decree directing that special provision be made for Yakovlev, taking into account his exceptional merits in the cause of the democratic movement. Gorbachev's aide thanked him but noted afterwards, 'He by the way forgot about his promise.'

After they said goodbye, Yakovlev watched Yeltsin striding along the narrow Kremlin corridor, as if marching on the parade ground. 'This was the strut of a victor,' he thought, though the Russian president may have been concentrating on keeping himself erect. Yeltsin's aides took the archive files and followed him. 'In the state he was in it would not have been prudent to hand over to him any sensitive documents,' commented Grachev.

Yeltsin made his way out of the Senate Building into the exceptionally mild night air – it was just below freezing – and crossed the narrow courtyard to Building 14. His closest collaborators were there: Kozyrev, Burbulis and Korzhakov, his loyal assistant Lev Sukhanov and spokesman Pavel Voshchanov.

'It's over. That's the last time I will have to go and see him,' Yeltsin announced.

'You mean that from now on, Gorbachev will have to come and see you,' one of his acolytes asked.

'What for? . . . Well, maybe to pick up his pension,' snorted Yeltsin. With a clinking of glasses, they celebrated his final ascendancy over Gorbachev.

'On this whole territory there is now nobody above you,' said Sukhanov, pointing triumphantly to the wall map of Russia.

'And for this, life has been worth living,' Yeltsin replied.

Meanwhile Yakovlev went to check on Gorbachev. He found him in the resting room. He was crying. 'He was lying on the sofa with tears in his eyes.'

Gorbachev looked up at his old friend. 'You see, Sasha, that's it,' he said.

Yakovlev recognized that this was the most difficult moment of Gorbachev's life. 'These words meant nothing but they sounded like a confidence, a repentance, a desperate cry from the heart, as if they illustrated [Russian poet Fyodor] Tyutchev's words: "Life is a broken-winged bird / That cannot fly." '

Doing his best to console his comrade, Yakovlev assured him of a glorious retirement and world renown through his research institute. He was close to tears himself. 'I had a lump in my throat. I was so sorry for him I wanted to cry. I was overcome with the feeling that something unfair had taken place. Here is the person who was yesterday a tsar of cardinal changes in the world and in his own country, the executor of the fate of billions of people in the world, and today he is the lifeless victim of another crisis of history.'

Gorbachev asked his friend to bring him a glass of water and to leave him alone. 'And that,' observed Yakovlev, 'was how the golden years of reform ended.' He sincerely believed that Gorbachev wanted the best for his country but that he couldn't see it through to the end. 'He couldn't understand that if you took a sword to a monster like the system, you have to go all the way . . . but he was an evolutionist . . . He has no blood on his hands; he wanted to start a civilized society.'

Yeltsin would remember the day-long session as 'protracted and difficult'. He told a reporter that the discussion was confidential, as it involved the passing on of state secrets, but 'after that meeting I felt like going and having a shower'.

Looking back after the passage of time Gorbachev remembered the marathon session with Yeltsin as 'informal and seemingly friendly', but he would reflect bitterly that 'Yeltsin's word, like many of his promises, could not always be trusted'.

It was the last occasion when Gorbachev and Yeltsin would ever meet or even speak to each other. There was little left for Gorbachev to do now but to tell the citizens of the mortally wounded superpower he inherited that it was all over.

24

December 25: Late Evening

HISTORY FINALLY CATCHES UP WITH MIKHAIL Sergeyevich Gorbachev. Thirty seconds before 7.00 p.m. Moscow time, 11.00 a.m. Eastern Standard Time, on December 25, 1991, the first and last president of the Soviet Union takes off his large-lens spectacles, checks to see if they are clean and puts them back on. He glances a couple of times at his watch. Then he looks up at the camera and begins reading from a typed sheet of paper, without the benefit of a teleprompter.

'Dear fellow countrymen! Compatriots!' he begins. 'Given the current situation and the formation of the Commonwealth of Independent States, I am ceasing my activities as president of the USSR. I have arrived at this decision for reasons of principle. I have always spoken out firmly in favour of autonomy and the independence of nations and sovereignty for the republics. But at the same time, I support the preservation of a union state and the integrity of the country.'

Even now he has not quite given up. By 'ceasing' his

activities, he leaves open the door to perhaps resuming them at a future date.

'Events have taken a different course,' he continues. 'The trend towards dismembering the country and the disintegration of the state has prevailed, which I cannot accept. My position on this issue has not changed after the Alma-Ata meeting and the decisions made there. Furthermore, I am convinced that decisions of such importance should have been made by popular will. However, I will do everything within my power to ensure that the Alma-Ata agreements bring real unity to our society and pave the way out of the crisis, facilitating a sustained reform process.'

Watching him from behind the cameras, Grachev feels that Gorbachev's voice at first sounds unnatural and hollow. 'It seemed on the verge of trembling, as did his chin.' But the moment passes and Gorbachev proceeds with his emotions under control.

'Addressing you for the last time as president of the USSR, I find it necessary to state my position with regard to the path we have embarked on since 1985 – especially since controversial, superficial and biased judgements abound,' he says.

Having signed the decree giving up his presidency a few minutes ago, Gorbachev is in fact no longer president of the USSR, but he has ignored the advice of his aides and lost the opportunity to complete the broadcast with a touch of ceremony.

Fate has decided that, when I became head of state, it was already obvious there was something wrong in this country. We had plenty of everything: land, oil, gas and other natural resources, and God has also endowed us with intellect and talent – yet we lived much worse than people in other industrialized countries and the gap was constantly widening. The reason was apparent even then – our society was stifled in the grip of a bureaucratic command system. Doomed to serve ideology, and bear the heavy burden of the arms race, it was strained to the utmost. All attempts at implementing half-hearted reforms – and there have been many – failed one after another. The country was losing hope.

We could not go on living like this. We had to change everything radically.

For this reason I never regretted that I did not use my position as general secretary merely to reign for a few years. This would have been irresponsible and immoral. I understood that initiating reforms on such a large scale in a society like ours was a most difficult and risky undertaking. But even now, I am convinced that the democratic reforms started in the spring of 1985 were historically justified. The process of renovating the country and bringing about fundamental change in the international community proved to be much more complex than originally anticipated. However, let us acknowledge what has been achieved so far.

Society has acquired freedom; it has been freed politically and spiritually. And this is the most important achievement, which we have not fully come to grips with, in part because we still have not learned how to use our freedom. However, a historic task has been accomplished.

The totalitarian system, which prevented this country from becoming wealthy and prosperous a long time ago, has been dismantled.

A breakthrough has been made on the road to democratic reforms. Free elections, freedom of the press, freedom of worship, representative legislatures and a multi-party system have all become realities.

We have set out to introduce a pluralistic economy, and the equality of all forms of ownership is being established. In the course of the land reform, peasantry is reviving, individual farmers have appeared, and millions of hectares of land have been allocated to the urban and rural population. Laws were passed on the economic freedom of producers, and free enterprise, shareholding and privatization are under way.

Shifting the course of our economy towards a free market, we must not forget that this is being done for the benefit of the individual. In these times of hardship, everything must be done to ensure the social protection of the individual – particularly old people and children.

We live in a new world. An end has been put to the Cold War, the arms race, and the insane militarization of our country, which crippled our economy, distorted our thinking and undermined our morals. The threat of a world war is no more.

Once again, I should like to stress I have done everything in my power during the transitional period to ensure safe control over nuclear weapons.

We opened ourselves up to the rest of the world, renounced interference in the affairs of others and the use of troops beyond our borders, and we have gained trust, solidarity and respect.

We have become a major stronghold for the re-organization of modern civilization on the basis of peaceful, democratic principles.

The peoples and nations of this country have acquired genuine freedom to choose their own way towards self-determination. The quest for a democratic reform of our multi-national state had led us to the point where we were about to sign a new union treaty.

All these changes demanded utmost exertion and were carried through under conditions of an un-relenting struggle against the growing resistance from the old, obsolete and reactionary forces – the former party and state structures and the economic manage-ment apparatus – as well as our patterns, our ideological prejudices, our egalitarian and parasitic psychology. The changes ran up against our intoler-ance, a low level of political culture and a fear of change. That is why we have wasted so much time. The old system tumbled down even before the new one could begin functioning. And our society slid into even deeper crisis.

I am aware of the dissatisfaction with today's grave situation, the harsh criticism of authority at all levels and of my personal role. But I would like to stress once again; in so vast a country, given its heritage, fundamental changes cannot be carried out without difficulties and pain.

The August coup brought the overall crisis to a breaking point. The most disastrous aspect of this crisis is the collapse of statehood. And today I watch apprehensively the loss of the citizenship of a great country by our citizens – the consequences of this could be grave for all of us.

I consider it vitally important to sustain the democratic achievements of the last few years. We have earned them through the suffering of our entire history and our tragic experience. We must not abandon them under any circumstances, under any pretext. Otherwise, all our hopes for a better future will be buried.

I am speaking of this frankly and honestly. It is my moral duty.

Today I want to express my gratitude to all those citizens who have given their support to the policy of renovating this country and who participated in the democratic reform. I am thankful to statesmen, political and public leaders and millions of ordinary people in other countries – to all those who understood our objectives and gave us their support, meeting us halfway and offering genuine cooperation.

I leave my post with concern – but also with hope, with faith in you, your wisdom and spiritual strength. We are the heirs of a great civilization and its revival and transformation to a modern and dignified life depend on all and everyone.

I would like to express my heartfelt thanks to those who stood by my side, defending the right and good cause over all these years. We certainly could have avoided certain errors and done better in many ways. But I am convinced that, sooner or later, our common efforts will bear fruit and our peoples will live in a prosperous and democratic society.

It is 7.12 p.m. when Gorbachev ends his address. He looks up to the camera, and adds: 'I wish all the best to everyone.'

On Russian television, announcer Yelena Mishina declares, 'A new day in a new state.' Seconds later the television channels revert to their normal schedules. One cuts back to a puppet show, another to a documentary on baby care.

Some of Gorbachev's aides and staff have tears in their eyes, having watched their chief complete the final act of his presidency. Chernyaev perceives him suddenly as a tragic figure, 'even though I who was used to seeing him in everyday life find it difficult to apply this term to him, by which of course he will be known in history'. Grachev feels certain that for many people watching, an unpardonable and irreparable error is being committed, as the country and the world looks on.

For Alexander Yakovlev, standing partly hidden behind one of the cameras, it is a seminal moment, the end of the road on which he embarked with Gorbachev nearly seven years ago. At the same time it is yet another occasion when Gorbachev ignored his advice. Hardly any of his suggestions for the speech appeared in the final draft, which was mostly Chernyaev's work. He feels Gorbachev couldn't find the strength or the courage to analyse critically and understand what has happened, especially in these final days. The speech in the end demonstrates how his comrade lost touch with reality in the four months since the coup. It is a laborious attempt to defend himself, to justify himself and save face. 'This is the typical delusion of someone devoid of self-analysis,' reflects Yakovlev. 'He did not come out of that psychological cul-de-sac where he put himself, having taken offence with the whole world.'

With all eyes on Gorbachev, Palazchenko finds himself thinking that perhaps someone is watching him too, 'wondering where I would be a couple of weeks later'. The next day he and his colleagues will go their own ways, with their labour record books stamped: 'Discharged from his post due to the liquidation of the office of the president of the USSR.'

CNN's Russian interpreter, Yury Somov, is in fact watching his Kremlin counterpart and thinking that 'Gorbachev was the biggest catch of Palazchenko's career and now Gorbachev is going down'.

Somov does not share the teary emotions displayed by Gorbachev's aides. He notes that half of the CNN crew are Russian and believes none of them give a damn. 'There was no feeling among us that it was a momentous event. It was just a power struggle. It wasn't affecting us.' Far from being awed by the downfall of an empire he believes that everything collapsed a long time previously. 'What was emerging was years of chaos and theft,' he explained years later. 'I knew at the time that was what was going to happen.' Somov was not given to empathizing with politicians. He was of the opinion that 'you can't be a good interpreter without being jaded and cynical and you can't be a good interpreter if you are emotional'.

He does, however, feel professional pride in the accomplishment of CNN. 'We were patting ourselves on the back. It had never been done before on the network, getting an interview with the leader of a nation on the same night he resigned!'

CNN producer Charlie Caudill reckons Gorbachev's 'emotional and passionate address' to be the most painful speech he has ever heard. 'The room was full of melancholy and after the broadcast Gorbachev looked beaten, sad – the adrenalin had drained away, gone.' He finds himself thinking back to the day in 1968 when US president Johnson announced he would not run for a second term, an event Caudill witnessed as a White House correspondent. 'President Johnson was conducting a war in Vietnam that had lost popular support and had been, like Gorbachev, clearly repudiated by the people, and, like Gorbachev, he had fought as long as he could and then came to terms with reality.'

Tom Johnson was assistant press secretary in the LBJ White House that same day. He too is keenly aware of the similarities between Gorbachev's resignation and the former US president's decision not to seek re-election. 'I really felt a sense of sadness on both occasions, a sense that each man had tried in his own way to leave the world a better place, but that each had been swept aside by forces each had unleashed.'

Gorbachev waits to make sure the television cameras are no longer rolling. He gives a sigh and sits back. There is a brief silence, then people start moving around again.

Claire Shipman and Steve Hurst pull up chairs in front of the desk for their scheduled CNN interview. Caudill insists that hangers-on leave the room. 'I mean we're doing the world here – we're not just doing local.'

'Can we make this short?' pleads Gorbachev, suddenly drained. He has only a few minutes before the handover of the nuclear suitcase to Boris Yeltsin in his office. Grachev tells CNN there is time for four questions only.

In the interview, which is broadcast live around the world – except for Russia – Gorbachev says he hopes that, as life improves for the people, they will look back at this time as hard, but necessary. 'We had to begin, and it is good that we began. Now I will have to recover a little bit, relax, take a rest.' Asked how Raisa and other members of his family are taking his resignation he answers, 'Bravely.'

Gorbachev seems to Shipman weak, defeated, exhausted and melancholy, as if the energy was sapped out of him and he is still puzzling how it all came to pass. She feels as if they have intruded on a very private moment. 'I almost felt bad being there. It was almost like going to a funeral.' Hurst is struck by how sombre the atmosphere is. 'There was sadness in his eyes and none of the ebullience.'

Central Television in Moscow carries the interview two hours later, after producers at TV headquarters satisfy themselves there is nothing in it that will offend Boris Yeltsin.

As Gorbachev gets up from his desk he picks up the Mont Blanc pen and with a reflex movement slips the shiny black object into his breast pocket. Tom Johnson thinks fast. He must not let Gorbachev disappear into the corridor with his precious writing instrument, which is now of some historical significance. During Gorbachev's address the CNN president had whispered to Caudill, 'What do you think I should do about the pen?' Caudill had muttered, 'Get it back!' When Gorbachev pauses to shake his hand on the way out, the CNN president says, 'Sir, my pen!' Palazchenko translates. 'Oh yes!' says Gorbachev, his face breaking into a smile. He hands over the pen and leaves.

Shipman is taken aback that Gorbachev has no understanding at all of the importance of the instrument. 'I was looking at Tom and Charlie and thinking, this is crazy. We are going to have the pen he signed away the Soviet Union with.'

One of Gorbachev's aides does make a half-hearted attempt to persuade CNN to leave the pen behind. The response is, 'No way!' (In 2008 Johnson donated the pen to the Newseum, a museum of news and journalism in Washington.)

Liu Heung Shing gets the picture he wanted to capture the finality of the occasion for the Associated Press. 'Gorbachev was looking rather grim the whole evening and was coming to his last page of the speech,' he said. 'I picked up my camera, pointed and shot the frame showing him closing the folder containing the speech.'

A few seconds after he pressed the shutter, Liu felt a fist thumping into his kidneys from behind the tripod. Tom Johnson saw the security man hit Liu from behind just as Gorbachev was taking off his glasses and closing his file. He mouthed the question, 'Are you all right?' Liu nodded. He urgently needed to get his picture developed as quickly as possible at the AP bureau across town in Kutuzovsky Prospekt. The same guard was blocking the door. 'All I could do was to plead, "Please! Please! Please!" At last, he opened the tall and thick door, I rushed down the red carpet runner, turned the corner and continued to run as fast as I could at the end of the corridor. All the awaiting Western and Russian journalists and cameramen were startled to see me running out all by myself. Some showed me their middle fingers in the air.

'By the time I came out of the darkroom with the colour negative film, I took a deep breath as I realized the frame of Gorbachev was pin sharp, and the speech folder was blurred as I had wished. Next day, it fronted virtually every newspaper in the world, including the *New York Times*. It reminded me of an earlier experience of Beijing 1989, when I transmitted the frame of a man in front of the tanks by Jeff Widener.' Liu Heung Shing publishes the picture of Gorbachev in his book *USSR: The Collapse of an Empire*, along with other AP photos that earn the agency the 1992 Pulitzer Prize for Spot News Photography.

Many of Gorbachev's supporters are immensely moved by his address on television, though in the British embassy across the river from the Kremlin, Ambassador Rodric Braithwaite considers Gorbachev's address to be 'dignified, adequate but no more'.

Fyodor Burlatsky, editor of *Literaturnaya Gazeta*,

perceives his farewell as a grandiose and tragic exit of Shakespearean dimensions, and thinks of the line from *Hamlet*, 'Thus conscience doth make cowards of us all / And thus the native hue of resolution / Is sicklied o'er with the pale cast of thought.'

Lev Kerbel watches the speech on a small TV screen in the kitchen of his Moscow apartment. The seventy-four-year-old Soviet-realist sculptor, born on the day of the Bolshevik Revolution and famous for his marble statues of Lenin and the enormous Karl Marx monument in Karl-Marx-Stadt in the former East Germany, makes tea, adds cognac and tells John Kampfner who has dropped by to see him, 'We fought fascism, we fought for the Soviet Union, and now we are told it's no longer there.' For Kampfner, correspondent of the *Daily Telegraph*, his biggest frustration this Christmas is that his newspaper, like most of its rivals, does not have a Boxing Day issue and he has to 'witness one of the most momentous days of post-war history without being able to write about it'.

Yegor Gaidar watches Gorbachev's resignation speech in his office in Old Square, where he is working late on a policy statement called the Memorandum of Economic Policies in conjunction with the IMF and the Central Bank. Though he helped engineer his downfall, he is sorry for Gorbachev to some degree. 'I think he was well meaning as a politician. The very good thing about him was that he literally did not want to use force to retain the power of the Soviet empire in Eastern Europe. So his going is not a surprise, but a thing accomplished.' For Gaidar three key dates marked the end of the Soviet Union. 'The first is the twenty-first of August when the coup collapsed. The second is the eighth of December when we had Belovezhskaya Pushcha. The third is the twenty-fifth of December when Gorbachev resigns.'

President Bush follows Gorbachev's address on television at Camp David. It is still only 11.00 a.m. on a balmy winter morning on the East Coast of the United States when the last Soviet president starts speaking. 'The finality of it hit me pretty hard; it was Christmas time, holiday time,' Bush recalls. He feels 'a tremendous charge' watching 'freedom and self-determination prevail as one republic after another gained its independence'. He was always confident that in the end, given the choice, the people of Central and Eastern Europe and the Soviet Union would put communism aside and opt for freedom. But without Gorbachev and Shevardnadze the Cold War would have dragged on and the fear of impending nuclear war would still be with them. 'We all were winners, East and West,' he notes later. 'I think that was what made much of the process possible – that it did not come at the expense of anyone.'

According to Robert Gates, head of the CIA, there is no feeling in the administration on this historic day that the United States has helped destroy the USSR, nor any sense of winning. He does not think that George Bush is about to declare victory in the Cold War. He worries however that this 'cataclysmic' event has unleashed forces pent up for seventy years, and they have yet to see, much less understand, the full consequences.

Brent Scowcroft believes that Gorbachev deserves a less ignominious exit. Bush's national security adviser is stunned that the end of an era of enormous and unrelenting hostility has come in an instant, and most incredibly of all without a single shot being fired. Looking back he takes 'pride in our role in reaching this outcome . . . We had worked very hard to push the Soviet Union in this direction, at a pace which would not provoke an explosion in Moscow, much less a global confrontation.'

Colin Powell, who as chairman of the Joint Chiefs of Staff has made a number of trips to Moscow, reckons Gorbachev hoped to revive a dying patient 'without replacing its Marxist heart'. He believes that the end of the Cold War was made possible because of the bold brand of leadership practised by Mikhail Gorbachev and President Ronald Reagan. 'That Christmas Day, the unimaginable happened,' he wrote. 'The Soviet Union disappeared. Without a fight, without a war, without a revolution. It vanished . . . with the stroke of a pen.'

For many young Muscovites, December 25, 1991, is the day that Radio Maximum 103.7, Russia's first private FM station, goes on the air, with a mandate to play only pop and rock music. All evening it broadcasts the Beatles non-stop, whose numbers include 'Back in the USSR' and 'It's Been a Hard Day's Night'. The American-born owner, Peter Gerwe, reluctantly allows a brief news bulletin to be read on air announcing Gorbachev's resignation. Years later he says, 'That was the first and last piece of news I did in Russia.'

25

December 25: Night

BORIS YELTSIN CAN HARDLY BRING HIMSELF TO LOOK AT the television screen in his office as Gorbachev begins to speak. He has not been provided with a copy of the text and he does not know what the outgoing occupant of the Kremlin is about to say. Within a minute, however, the Russian president has worked himself up into a fury. Gorbachev does not say he is resigning, only ceasing his activities. He implicitly criticizes Yeltsin for 'controversial, superficial and biased judgements', and for the way the Commonwealth of Independent States was created without the 'popular will'. And he promises to do everything in his power 'to ensure that the Alma-Ata agreements bring real unity to our society' – as if he had any role in ensuring anything any more!

As Gorbachev proceeds to justify his actions in office, Yeltsin snaps, 'Switch it off. I don't want to listen any more.' He tells Gennady Burbulis to bring him a transcript. Grachev sends the text over to Burbulis after

Gorbachev has finished. As Yeltsin reads through it he expresses exasperation at what he considers to be a self-serving political manifesto rather than a farewell to politics. Gorbachev is taking credit for all the political and spiritual freedoms Russian people now enjoy. He does not once mention Boris Yeltsin by name or even by title. He gives Yeltsin no credit for the defeat of the attempted coup against him in August. Nor does he wish the Russian president well as his successor. Perhaps he should have ordered Gosteleradio to pull the plug on the broadcast, as he had been tempted to do.

Now, as so often in the past, the touchy Siberian allows pique to dictate his actions. He refuses to go to Gorbachev's office to receive the nuclear suitcase as agreed two days ago. It must be brought to him, he blusters.

Yeltsin picks up the telephone and calls Marshal Shaposhnikov, who is waiting in an office on the second floor of the Senate Building for the summons to proceed to Gorbachev's cabinet for the historic transfer. With him are a number of generals, gathered to witness and facilitate the important and symbolic exchange.

'Yevgeny Ivanovich,' says Yeltsin, 'I can't go to Gorbachev. You go by yourself.'

'Boris Nikolayevich, this is a very delicate matter,' the marshal protests. 'It would be desirable that we go together. What is more, I'm not sure if Gorbachev will transfer all the [nuclear] property to me by myself.'

'If there are complications, call me,' says Yeltsin. 'We will discuss other options for the transfer.'

Shaposhnikov is not altogether surprised. He too is

exasperated by Gorbachev. Watching the farewell address he found himself reflecting that the president has overstayed his welcome, and that he should have resigned after the coup. How much hope there had been for the Soviet Union when Gorbachev became general secretary of the Communist Party in 1985! 'He was young, modern, energetic, with many advantages over his colleagues. He introduced *perestroika*, *glasnost*, democratization, all human values. But the further it went the more doubts there were, and disillusions. The main thing – life was not becoming better. The economy continued to deteriorate and the political situation was developing at such speed that the whole system started to fall apart.' Having defeated the putschists without Gorbachev, the citizens of the USSR simply stopped responding to him, Shaposhnikov knows. Many people don't want the Soviet Union to fall apart, he believes. Shaposhnikov's wife certainly does not want new borders created. She has been worrying that they will have to go abroad in future to visit their daughter who lives in Odessa, now in independent Ukraine. But they are all sick of the Soviet system and they just don't want Gorbachev any more.

The marshal takes his briefcase with the transfer documents, mounts the stairs to the floor above and enters Gorbachev's suite. He waits ten minutes in the cramped reception room, along with the two colonels who are assigned to accompany the nuclear suitcase and who are perched side by side on the sofa, so ubiquitous and inscrutable that some of Gorbachev's staff have stopped noticing them. Their gift for looking inconspicuous has frequently impressed Palazchenko, who remembers them sitting almost always silently, with an oddly inexpressive yet dignified look.

When Gorbachev calls him in, Shaposhnikov sees that the *chemodanchik* is resting on the ex-Soviet president's desk. He finds Gorbachev holding up quite well, but noticeably ill at ease. The marshal relates his instructions, that Yeltsin is not coming and that he is to take the case to Yeltsin.

Gorbachev thinks the situation is 'rather comical, not to say stupid'. In this final confrontation, however, he has the upper hand. He is in possession of the object that the Russian president needs to legitimize his grab for power. Let him come and claim it. Gorbachev no longer has to answer any summons from his rival.

There is an impasse. Yeltsin won't come and Gorbachev won't budge. Both presidents must sign the transfer documents and both must be satisfied that this procedure is done properly, in front of witnesses.

Told that Gorbachev will not hand over the suitcase, Yeltsin still refuses to honour the original agreement on the handover. Let Gorbachev bring it to him then, he growls. Gorbachev must come to his office, or to the neutral territory of the St Catherine Hall, and deliver it to him there. St Catherine Hall with its vaulted ceilings and gold chandeliers is where Gorbachev humiliated him four years ago, prompting Central Committee members to throw a 'bucketful of filth' over him for daring to question the pace of *perestroika*. He instructs Burbulis to convey his demand to Gorbachev.

Gorbachev is indignant. 'I was told he had refused to

come, despite our agreement,' he later recalled in his memoirs. 'It turned out that Yeltsin, together with his entourage, had listened to my televised speech and flown into a rage. After a while I was told that the Russian president proposed to meet on "neutral territory" – in the Catherine Hall, i.e. the part of the Kremlin where talks with foreign leaders were usually held . . . Thus even in the first minutes after stepping down I was faced with impudence and lack of courtesy.' He believes that this derogation from their arrangement is not an isolated backlash of Yeltsin's feelings of revenge, but is part of a policy of harassment he is conducting against him.

Grachev believes the 'preposterous idea' of Gorbachev going to Yeltsin with the suitcase was suggested by one of his more belligerent advisers, when it became clear that Gorbachev was leaving office with dignity and with his head held high rather than as a vanquished foe. 'Yeltsin wanted to show Gorbachev he was no longer superior to him. Yeltsin's fury related to his feeling that it should be his day of triumph. In his presentation, however, Gorbachev made everybody realize the historic shift he had achieved. He was stepping down not as one defeated. Yeltsin felt he remained a secondary figure in the aura of Gorbachev and the success of *perestroika*. He must have realized that never in his life would he match his opponent.'

Shaposhnikov tries to break the deadlock. He suggests that Gorbachev sign the transfer papers and that one of the colonels brings them to the Russian president, and when Yeltsin confirms he has received the documents Gorbachev can transfer the nuclear suitcase to Shaposhnikov who will send it across to Yeltsin.

The marshal calls Yeltsin, who has calmed down after his outburst. He agrees to the compromise. Shaposhnikov witnesses Gorbachev's signature on the transfer agreement. An officer leaves with the papers, along with the decree of the USSR president transferring supreme command over the armed forces to the president of Russia. After a few minutes Yeltsin's office calls to say the Russian president accepts that the documents are in order. The transfer can take place.

One of the colonels unlocks the black metal *chemodanchik*. Gorbachev checks the equipment inside. Everything is in its place. He shakes hands with the two military men who have accompanied him around the globe, thanks them for their work and says goodbye. The colonels leave the office with the communications device. Shaposhnikov stays behind for a final few words with his former commander-in-chief.

In Gorbachev's anteroom, Chernyaev tries to make sense of the military uniforms coming and going. He sees Shaposhnikov leaving, 'smiling as usual and saying "Hello!"' and 'clearly embarrassed' about the whole affair.

He and the two Yakovlevs go in and sit at the oval table with Gorbachev. They find him red-faced and clearly upset over the way Yeltsin has behaved. They help calm him down and prepare him for the television cameras once more.

During the verbal artillery between the two Kremlin buildings, Ted Koppel of ABC has been standing by with his crew to film the ceremonial handover of the nuclear suitcase from the Soviet to the Russian president. Just before 8.00 p.m. he is invited back into the presidential office. Gorbachev has recovered his composure. He greets the ABC personnel with smiles. The nuclear suitcase is already with Yeltsin, he informs them, as if nothing untoward has happened. 'Now it is Yeltsin who holds his finger on the nuclear button.' All that remains for Gorbachev 'is to clear out some personal effects, some papers'.

But Boris Yeltsin has not finished tormenting his rival.

Mikhail Gorbachev, like everyone else, expects that the Soviet flag will continue flying over the Senate dome until December 31. Russian and world media were told specifically by Yeltsin's press secretary Pavel Voshchanov, on December 17: 'On New Year's Eve, the hammer-and-sickle flag of revolutionary red that has flown for seventy-four years over the Kremlin, the medieval brick fortress on the Moscow River, will be lowered, marking the formal end to the Soviet era.' The Russian flag would then be raised triumphantly, in a blaze of fireworks, to herald the new year and a new era, he said.

The red flag is this evening still hanging from the flag-pole above the illuminated green dome as Gorbachev delivers his valedictory address, visible to the usual small crowds of strollers and tourists in Red Square. But twenty minutes after Gorbachev finishes, two workmen emerge from a trapdoor on the roof of the Senate

Building and climb up metal steps on the curved side of the dome to a circular platform with a waist-high railing at the top. From there they pull down the six-metre-by-three-metre flag from the tall mast. As it comes to the bottom of the pole, one of them gathers it up, as a waiter would remove a tablecloth in a restaurant. The men then attach the white, blue and red flag of pre-revolutionary Russia to the rope and hoist it up the mast. They hold the end of the large expanse of fabric until it reaches the top, then release it so that the flag billows out triumphantly in a southwesterly breeze, helped by jets of compressed air hissing from a tube inside the flagpole.

Few people in Red Square notice what is happening. No one has alerted the public or the foreign media to expect such an act of historical significance this evening – the switching of emblems over the building where Lenin and Stalin exercised their power. Only Russian television was tipped off by Yeltsin's aides to have a crew in position to record the event. Serge Schmemann of the *New York Times* recalls, 'I was back in the bureau writing a piece about Gorbachev resigning; I don't think there were any other reporters there.' However, his wife, Mary, and children Anya, Alexander and Natasha were nearby. 'They happened by chance to be in Red Square when the red Soviet flag came down for the last time over the Kremlin and the white, blue and red Russian flag rose in its stead. My children noted the exact time, 7.32 p.m., and called me.'

As the flag with its three broad horizontal stripes of white, blue and red flaps and cracks in the artificial breeze, the bells of the Kremlin's Saviour Tower start ringing, and continue for several minutes. People walking near the Kremlin look up with curiosity and some concern. Though the Saviour Tower clock chimes merrily every fifteen minutes, the heavy bells ring out only rarely to mark profound events. The sound prompts more late evening strollers and tourists to notice the tricolour. Schmemann's family recall cheers from a handful of surprised foreigners and an angry tirade from a lone war veteran. There are a few calls of 'Oh!' 'Oh!' 'Oh!' as Russian strollers see what is happening, and whistles and laughter from some young men craning their necks upwards. One person claps.

The news quickly spreads and foreign correspondents hurry to Red Square. Militiaman Alexander Ivanovich, one of the greatcoated guards at the Lenin Mausoleum, who had marched off to dinner while the red flag was flying and returned to find the flag of the Russian Federation in its place, tells James Clarity of the *New York Times*, 'It was a good surprise.' An inebriated and confused Muscovite asks an onlooker near the Mausoleum, 'Why are you laughing at Lenin?' He is shushed by a passer-by who cautions him that a foreigner is watching. Francis X. Clines, also of the *New York Times*, is noting down the exchange. 'Who cares?' says another Muscovite. 'They're the ones who are feeding us these days.' Uli Klese, a photographer on vacation from Germany, finds the subdued public reaction strange. 'When the Berlin Wall came down, everybody was out in the streets,' he tells Michael Dobbs of the *Washington Post*. 'This was an event of the same kind of magnitude, but no one seemed to care.'

Steve Hurst spots the switching of the flags through a window in the Kremlin from where the dome at the apex of the triangular Senate Building is visible. 'I looked out the window and saw the hammer and sickle coming down. I remember what a strong visual that was.' According to Stu Loory, while the CNN crew is dismantling their equipment someone gets word about what is happening and a window is opened to videotape the event. Gorbachev's security people demand that the window be closed. 'Tell them I will take full responsibility,' shouts Tom Johnson to his interpreter, but the guards shove him away from the window. 'Bodyguards are bodyguards everywhere in the world,' said Loory. 'They couldn't care less about the responsibility of the president of CNN!'

Andrey Grachev sees with dismay the red flag 'hastily torn from the cupola of the Kremlin as if it were the Reichstag', as he is leaving the Russian fortress to give an interview to French television in their office in Gruzinsky Lane. The flagstaff is directly above the presidential office, and 'happily for Gorbachev he cannot observe this heart-breaking moment'.

A foreign television crew that has missed filming the event acquires a videocassette for 200 French francs from an enterprising Muscovite in Red Square who recorded the change of flags.

When Gorbachev learns what has occurred, he perceives it as another affront to his dignity. He believes that Yeltsin 'gave instructions for the lowering of the Soviet flag and the hoisting of the flag of the Russian

Federation and personally saw to it that the procedure be completed according to schedule and filmed by television cameras'.

Meanwhile the CNN crew become the sole witnesses of the exchange of the nuclear suitcase some ten minutes later, after they have dismantled their equipment and are assembling in the Kremlin corridor.

'At 7.56 we were waiting in the hallway outside the green room for all of our party to assemble before we could leave,' said Loory. 'At the other end of the corridor, near the entrance to Gorbachev's working office, a man appeared carrying a cloth-covered suitcase with a protruding antenna. He disappeared into a doorway. We were watching the nuclear codes passing from Gorbachev's control to Yeltsin's.' Charlie Caudill recalled, 'We are being led out by handlers down a very long corridor. All of a sudden a side door opens twenty-five feet in front of us. Armed soldiers come out. They block the way and make us halt. A door on the left opens up. A high-ranking military guy comes up, box under his arm. The opposite door opens, same-looking kind of dude. He snaps to attention. They salute each other. The officers exchange the object.' The television cameras have been packed away and an opportunity is lost to make a video record of the historic moment.

Stu Loory alone witnesses another little piece of history. He goes ahead of the CNN crew to make sure the rental vans are in place outside. 'I walk around closer to where the trucks are. A Kremlin worker comes towards me holding the flag folded up in a rectangle under his arm.' Loory stops the man and takes a photograph, and thereby secures the only picture of the last flag of the USSR to fly over the Kremlin as it is carried away. He immediately regrets not offering to buy it. Tom Johnson later tries to acquire the emblem from a Kremlin official but the offer is politely yet firmly refused. Gorbachev himself wants to secure the red flag as a memento for future display but it disappears into the basement stores of the Kremlin.

As he leaves the Senate Building with the television crew, Johnson waves his Mont Blanc in the air and calls out, 'How much do you think I can get for this?' The technicians and engineers cheer and slap each other on the back. 'We did it! We did it!' cries Johnson.

They have pulled off a remarkable feat. Mikhail Gorbachev abdicated on television with a logo on the lower right-hand corner of the screen informing one hundred and fifty-three countries of the world that they are seeing it courtesy of CNN. 'In the annals of competitive journalism, this was an unprecedented victory,' claimed Loory.

In Washington President Bush's aides show him the text of a statement they have drafted praising Gorbachev for liberating the Soviet people from the smothering embrace of a totalitarian dictatorship. After looking it over, the president holds a conference call with his advisers on whether this is a proper response. Scowcroft suggests that Gorbachev's resignation is too important 'to kiss off with a statement' from the press secretary, Marlin Fitzwater.

Bush decides to take Marine One from Camp David to Washington and address the nation from the Oval Office on the far-reaching consequences of what has just happened in the Kremlin. The networks and cable television companies suspend their scheduled programmes at 9.00 p.m. EST on Christmas Day to allow the president to make his own television address from the Oval Office. While sparing Gorbachev's sensitivities by not declaring outright that the fall of the Soviet Union is a victory for the United States in the Cold War – for two years he prohibited his staff from depicting events in Eastern Europe and the Soviet Union as a triumph for the United States – Bush uses the word 'victory' a number of times, clearly implying that America is the winner. The nuclear threat is receding, he says, Eastern Europe is free, and the Soviet Union itself is no more. 'This is a victory for democracy and freedom. It's a victory for the moral force of our values. Every American can take pride in this victory . . .'

After paying tribute to Gorbachev, the US president acknowledges the new reality. He announces that the United States recognizes and welcomes the emergence of a free, independent and democratic Russia, 'led by its courageous president, Boris Yeltsin'. He declares that the US embassy in Moscow will in future be the embassy to Russia. He says he supports Russia's assumption of the USSR's seat as a permanent member of the United Nations Security Council. And from today America will recognize the independence of Ukraine, Armenia, Kazakhstan, Belarus, Kyrgyzstan, Moldova, Turkmenistan, Azerbaijan, Tajikistan, Georgia and

Uzbekistan. Bush had delayed formal recognition of Russia until after Gorbachev resigned, as a personal courtesy to his deposed friend and his partner in ending the Cold War. His administration has already recognized Estonia, Latvia and Lithuania, the Baltic republics that completed the make-up of the original Soviet Union.

'This is a day of great hope for all Americans,' concludes President Bush. 'May God bless the people of the new nations in the Commonwealth of Independent States. And on this special day of peace on earth, good will toward men, may God continue to bless the United States of America. Good night.'

Now that the Soviet Union is history, White House officials feel free to express the opinion that Gorbachev clung on too long to power. Gorbachev 'is leaving at a level that's a lot lower than he would have had a month ago', an administration official tells the *New York Times*. 'He's taken away from his own currency and cost himself a bit of his place in history by letting events pass him by. It's sad to see a man of such stature and historical importance misjudge events that way.' The anonymous spokesman claims that Bush privately wrote off Gorbachev after the Middle East conference in October in Madrid, at which the penniless Soviet delegation had to ask the Spanish government to pick up their hotel bills.

Current and former world leaders shower Gorbachev with praise. In London John Major notes that it is given to very few people to change the course of history, but that is what Gorbachev has done and, whatever happens today, his place in history is secure. Chancellor Helmut Kohl of Germany, which achieved unity under Gorbachev's watch, expresses the view that his place in the history of the century will not be challenged by anyone. NATO secretary general Manfred Wörner says that Europe is grateful to Gorbachev for his essential contribution towards a Europe whole and free. Ronald Reagan declares that Gorbachev will live for ever in history and Margaret Thatcher expresses gratitude to him for doing 'great things for the world . . . without a shot being fired'.

One of the few discordant notes comes from the People's Republic of China, which is ruled by the Communist Party of China, now the largest single political party in the world. China's communist leaders have dealt with their own people's demands for democracy and the end of corruption by massacring hundreds of students and workers in Tiananmen Square on June 4, 1989. China's foreign ministry acknowledges that the demise of the Soviet Union heralds the end of the East–West conflict and the dawn of a new multipolar age. But seeking to justify the bloody path the Chinese party has taken to remain in power, it complains that Gorbachev got it wrong. Gorbachev's 'new thinking, *glasnost* and political pluralism', states the Chinese government, 'have brought only political chaos, ethnic strife and economic crises'.

In Minsk, Stanislau Shushkevich does not watch Gorbachev's final address on television. He has better things to do. Late in the evening the Belarus leader hears that the red flag has come down and the Soviet Union he helped dismantle has come to an end, almost a week before its official sell-by date of New Year's Eve. Asked twenty years later what his reaction was when he was told, Shushkevich replies with one word: '*Pravilno!*' Translated roughly it means, 'Just right!'

26

December 25: Late Night

I$_{T}$ IS NINE O'CLOCK IN THE EVENING AND A GHOSTLY silence has descended on the Kremlin. Andrey Grachev returns there from his interview in the French television studios in Gruzinsky Lane. He has received a call on his car phone telling him Gorbachev wants him back in the Kremlin as soon as possible. Outside the Senate Building there are only a couple of drivers and guards. Gorbachev's press secretary finds the corridors and offices on the third floor to be deserted. He locates Gorbachev in the Walnut Room, sitting at the oval table with a chosen few of his aides. For once his boss has called him not to work but to socialize. A bottle of Jubilee cognac has been opened and glasses passed around.

Gorbachev is in a melancholy mood. He is despondent about the casual manner in which he has been dispatched from office, without even a farewell ceremony, 'as is the custom in civilized countries'. He is hurt that not a single one of the leaders of the republics

– former communists with whom Gorbachev has had comradely relationships over the years – has called to thank, congratulate or commiserate with him on the termination of his service. He ended repression, gave people freedom of speech and travel, and introduced elections that put them in power, but they stay silent. They are all in a state of euphoria, busily dividing up their inheritance, thinks Gorbachev bitterly. 'Yesterday hardly anyone had heard of them, but tomorrow they will be heads of independent states,' he says. 'What does it matter what fate they are preparing for their nations?'

Chernyaev feels only scorn for the ungracious leaders who owe their political careers to Gorbachev, a number of them highly corrupt satraps who had switched from communism to nationalism solely to retain power. 'Neither Nazarbayev, nor Karimov, nor Niyazov, not to mention Kravchuk or other second-raters, bothered to call Gorbachev to say even official words "appropriate to the occasion",' he notes in his diary, referring to the presidents of Kazakhstan, Uzbekistan, Turkmenistan and Ukraine. 'What can you do! Homo Sovieticus is the biggest, most difficult problem remaining for the fledgling democracy that Gorbachev created.'

Grachev concludes that they are so fearful of incurring Yeltsin's displeasure, that 'not one of them found the moral force to make a personal gesture to Gorbachev, who was becoming a pariah'. (It is more than five years before one of the new leaders in the republics speaks to Gorbachev again. After President Askar Akayev of Kyrgyzstan, an old friend of Yeltsin, welcomes Gorbachev to his capital, Bishkek, in 1996 and fêtes him at a public event, Yeltsin refuses to shake Akayev's hand for a year, and chides him when they next meet, saying, 'Askar, how could you?')

The ex-president toasts his small group of advisers in the half-lit Walnut Room, where Zhenya the Kremlin waiter has left out some salad and meat dishes before going off duty. The gathering includes Gorbachev's most intimate associates and favourites. There is Grachev, who has made the best of a hopeless case in briefing the world's media on his behalf during the final days. Also there are Yegor Yakovlev, head of state television; Alexander Yakovlev, who helped him launch *perestroika*; Anatoly Chernyaev, his loyal aide; and Georgy Shakhnazarov – all of them his most progressive and honest advisers through good times and bad.

Chernyaev is Gorbachev's closest confidant, bluntest critic and most prolific chronicler. The septuagenarian with the complicated private life is also the guarantor of Gorbachev's good name. Having been at Foros during the three days of the coup he has testified to the truth of Gorbachev's account of his temporary imprisonment. His integrity and sterling reputation – even Valery Boldin regards him highly – ensures that no one will ever take too seriously the damaging theory, doing the rounds in Moscow and in some Western academic circles, that Gorbachev was secretly complicit in the conspiracy of the hardliners. However, theirs has not always been an easy relationship. When Gorbachev cracked down on the Baltics, Chernyaev wrote a letter of resignation, though after much agonizing he did not deliver it. He now believes his decision was correct.

Working together as commander and aide-de-camp, Gorbachev and he have been through great campaigns together and there is a devotion, in spite of everything. He has often interpreted events more astutely than Gorbachev. He privately considers that Yeltsin, for all his gaucheness and his mediocrity as a person, is the chieftain Russia requires at this moment in history. Gorbachev, as the product of an impermanent entity created by Lenin, never really understood Russia or its place in history. A year ago Chernyaev confessed in his diary that he was beginning to dislike working for Gorbachev. 'He's never once said that he appreciates me, never said, "Thank you," not even when it would be useful to him to mention my contribution.' Boldin, who has nothing good to say about his former boss, echoes this complaint in his memoir, alleging that Gorbachev's relations with his staff lacked human warmth and mutual respect, and that 'it was galling to see him treat them like servants'.

Gorbachev for his part allowed himself to harbour doubts about Chernyaev in the days when he was under the influence of the conspiratorial Kryuchkov. He confided once to his chief of staff that Chernyaev was not to be trusted as he could be the source of information leaks, and he instructed Boldin that the range of secret information reaching Chernyaev should be limited.

Yegor Yakovlev has been in the Kremlin all day mainly because he feels he should be with the president at this emotional time. He is a member of the 'first generation' of *perestroika*, the intellectuals who believed in Gorbachev from the start and rallied enthusiastically to the cause of reforming the system. The son of Vladimir Yakovlev, the first head of the Cheka, the forerunner of the KGB, he transformed the *Moscow News* from a Communist Party propaganda sheet into a standard bearer for *glasnost*, going as far as he thought Gorbachev was prepared to tolerate. They fell out when Gorbachev temporarily sided with the hardliners a year earlier, but three months ago when everything changed in the aftermath of the coup, Gorbachev appointed him head of state broadcasting and a member of his political consultative council. He is taking a risk aligning himself so closely with Gorbachev. The president of Russia is in control of state television, and Yakovlev will know tomorrow if he will be kept on.

Like Chernyaev, the other Yakovlev in the circle has also been hurt over time by Gorbachev's thoughtlessness. Alexander Yakovlev once confided to Chernyaev that in six years working with Gorbachev he had never heard a single thank you. He complained, 'I don't even feel any gratitude from him for the fact that the idea of *perestroika* was born in our first conversations in Canada back when I was ambassador.' Their relationship was at times quite fraught and is still complicated. Only a year earlier, Gorbachev was told by Kryuchkov that Yakovlev was an agent of the CIA. The president became so paranoid that one day in late summer 1990 he got it into his head that his adviser was planning a coup with other radicals. He tracked Yakovlev's whereabouts to a forest hundreds of miles away, where he was picking mushrooms with his grandchildren. On the telephone he practically charged the flabbergasted

Yakovlev with conspiring against him. In the event the die-hard conservatives were right to suspect the long-term intentions of Gorbachev's ally. Three years after the fall of the Soviet Union Yakovlev asserts that he and Shevardnadze realized full well during the *perestroika* years that their advice to Gorbachev would lead to the destruction of the system, and he boasts that 'We did it before our opponents woke up in time to prevent it.' The coup opened Gorbachev's eyes to the machinations of Kryuchkov but he has never completely got over his mistrust of Yakovlev. He knows that it wasn't only Yeltsin who relished his humiliation in the Russian parliament after the coup. He noticed some of his own associates gloating, Alexander Yakovlev among them.

Georgy Shakhnazarov also helped destroy the system, though he has often been frustrated by Gorbachev's vacillations. The sixty-seven-year-old Armenian regularly urged Gorbachev in the late 1980s to convert to social democracy and move towards multi-party politics, which was unthinkable at the time. 'As often happens in revolutionary systems,' he would observe later, 'there are things which seem banal today but which you couldn't even mention then.' Gorbachev once suspected him too of leaking information – about decisions on the Armenian–Azerbaijani conflict in Nagorno-Karabakh – and asked Kryuchkov to investigate, but nothing came of it. Twenty-one months earlier it was Shakhnazarov alone who was invited to join Mikhail and Raisa for a private glass of champagne to celebrate his leader's elevation to the presidency. Now he is here to bear witness to his abdication. Raisa herself has not come for the obsequies. The Kremlin late nights have always been men-only affairs.

For all the perceived slights and injustices in the service of Gorbachev, however, a warmth and sense of camaraderie has returned to the relationship between the dethroned king and his reform-minded courtiers in these final hours. The small group of aides in the empty Kremlin building is at one in believing they serve a historic figure and a great man. This bond unites them, and draws them to Gorbachev as December 25, 1991, comes to a close.

The lowering of the Soviet flag from the Kremlin has a profound effect on all of them. Even Alexander Yakovlev, the most radical of the *perestroika* reformers, feels it tear at his emotions. He, Chernyaev and Shakhnazarov all fought under the red flag in the Great Patriotic War against Hitler's armies. Just a year ago Yakovlev declared that he would defend the revolutionary emblem, 'as my father defended it during the four years of the civil war and as I defended it during the Great Patriotic War'. It is no longer there to defend.

Andrey Grachev regards the day as both a defeat and a tragedy. It signals the defeat of a statesman forced out of office before completing his mission, and the tragedy of a reformer forced to abandon his plans before they bore fruit. It occurs to the comparatively youthful spokesman (in this company) that some other friends are missing at the table, but at least no one is present who is not wanted. Judas is not at this last supper, but 'even if Judas had been in Gorbachev's entourage, his betrayal would have already taken place'.

The most prominent reformer at Gorbachev's side as the Cold War ended is missing from the gathering. Eduard Shevardnadze watched the resignation speech in his apartment on Plotnikov Lane, off the Old Arbat, preoccupied with news of a civil war that has broken out in his native Georgia. The former Soviet foreign minister, like the two Yakovlevs, rejoined the presidential team after the coup. Recently he and Gorbachev have spent some late evenings alone together in the Kremlin, just to talk, but they never could rediscover the warmth that marked their relationship when they were achieving great things together on the international stage. Shevardnadze cannot forgive Gorbachev for protecting the Soviet army over the 1989 killings of demonstrators in the Georgian capital, Tbilisi, and for not speaking out in his defence when he was under attack from hardliners. He feels that the president never listened to the advice of the people genuinely loyal to him. Moreover he bears a grudge over Gorbachev's failure to mention him when accepting the 1990 Nobel Peace Prize. He believes that had Gorbachev 'done something, said just a couple of words, Shevardnadze would have received the Nobel Prize, too'. He is convinced Gorbachev came to resent his foreign minister's popularity in the West, concluding that 'the world had gotten to know me and trust me and Gorbachev wasn't pleased about it'. During the coup Shevardnadze publicly raised questions about Gorbachev's degree of complicity, and Gorbachev later told a press conference that that statement should be on Shevardnadze's conscience. Shevardnadze would also have liked Gorbachev to acknowledge, in the farewell address, his role in ending the Cold War, but his suggested input was ignored. Now he feels that returning to his old job was a grave personal mistake.

As the men in the Walnut Room make toasts and refill their glasses, Gorbachev reminisces about his early days as a career communist and the importance in his life of Mikhail Suslov, the ascetic grey eminence who shaped communist thinking in the period between the Stalin and Gorbachev eras. The young Stavropol *apparatchik* was at one time so in awe of Suslov he took to sporting the same type of fedora he wore. Suslov groomed Gorbachev for stardom, never imagining that his protégé would one day help destroy the party as a would-be reformer. Alexander Yakovlev by contrast has only contempt for Suslov. In his research he has identified him as one of the ideologues and directors of a programme of mass murders under Stalin. He has established that Suslov took part in organizing arrests, was directly responsible for deporting thousands of people from the Baltic states, and orchestrated the persecution of prominent Soviet artists and scientists. In his opinion, Gorbachev's mentor deserves to be tried for crimes against humanity. But he says nothing.

Gorbachev recalls how terrified he was when he came to work in Moscow and how his eyes were opened as to how policy was made when he became a candidate member of the Politburo. He informs his comrades that after finishing his memoirs he intends to write a book explaining how and why the idea of *perestroika* was born in his head. He asks Chernyaev, by the way, to tell

Horst Telchik, the senior aide to German chancellor Helmut Kohl, that money for his book *The August Coup*, which has just been published in the West, should not be sent to Moscow. In the uncertain economic and political climate it is better to keep hard currency outside the country for now.

Though he is slow to voice his appreciation for loyalty, Gorbachev is moved by the fact that on this evening of his utmost distress, 'together with me were the closest friends and colleagues who shared with me all the great pressures and drama of the last months of the presidency'. These are the people who understand the real meaning of what has taken place. 'Many were on duty in the Kremlin around the clock. They were not motivated by professional interests but by sincere feeling. I felt it very deeply, especially as I had conflicts with some of them in the past.' He believes that only close associates like these could know how great a burden was the historical task he undertook, how hard things were sometimes, and how events often drove him to the point of despair.

The melancholy reformers stay on in the Kremlin until it is approaching midnight, reluctant to accept the fact that the last day of the last Soviet leader has to end – and their careers with it.

'A couple of bottles of cognac were drunk,' recalled Grachev. 'The atmosphere was solemn, sad. There was something of a feeling of a big thing accomplished. There was a kind of feeling of everyone sharing.'

The presidential ZiL is waiting for Gorbachev when he leaves the Senate Building and steps out into Kremlin

Square after bidding emotional farewells to his comrades. The driver takes the exhausted ex-president through the deserted streets of the city centre, across the Moscow River bridge and along Kutuzovsky Prospekt to Rublyov Highway and finally into the driveway of the dacha. It is turning colder and the headlights reflect off ice crystals on the frozen snow piled up by the tarmac. The driver does not park the ZiL in the garage, as he normally does, but turns and heads off into the night.

There is a shock for Gorbachev when he enters the presidential residence. Clothes, shoes, books, framed pictures and personal souvenirs are piled on the floor or crammed into boxes and crates, ready for moving to their new home. It is not a night for a relaxing midnight walk with Raisa around the paths. Besides, he is feeling the symptoms of influenza.

Igor Belyaev brings to his Moscow apartment the tapes he has made of the president holding talks with officials and diplomats during his last days. The documentary-maker has some unique shots of Gorbachev taking care of outstanding business, such as releasing Alexander Solzhenitsyn's KGB file. Belyaev admires his fellow alumnus from Moscow University. He wants him to be loved by the Russian people while he is still alive, and appreciated as a person whom Russia has failed to understand. Knowing of Belyaev's devotion, Yegor Yakovlev had put him in overall charge of the project by ABC and Gosteleradio to record Gorbachev's departure. As he expects, the filmmaker finds that there is extreme sensitivity at the television centre about any attention being paid to Gorbachev. Other than the actual resignation broadcast and the Soviet–American film, hardly anyone in television headquarters in Moscow wants to be involved in a positive programme on Gorbachev's contribution to the world.

Belyaev stores the reels under a sofa, where they remain for a decade before they are retrieved. He is not able to show his documentary on Russian television until the tenth anniversary of Gorbachev's resignation, in December 2001.

In another part of the Kremlin, Yeltsin is also staying late rather than returning home. But as Gorbachev is downing cognac, it is Yeltsin this evening who is the sober one. The Russian president is chastened by his new responsibility as supreme commander-in-chief of the armed forces, with legal control of the nuclear suitcase. When Shaposhnikov comes to his office to complete the business of transferring the *chemodanchik*, he finds Yeltsin in a subdued mood. As has happened before, an outburst of petulance has been followed by self-doubt and feelings of remorse.

An hour ago there were two presidents of two different political entities resident in one city. Now Yeltsin is on his own and must play by new rules. His rapture on seizing absolute power, he admits later, is quickly replaced by 'a bad case of the jitters'.

Yeltsin is intrigued by the communications screen, authorization buttons and telephone system in the case. Shaposhnikov observes how he thoroughly familiarizes himself with the equipment and how it works, talks to the officer-specialists, and resolves all questions of their accommodation, their routine, their personal life and work procedures. 'After that I stayed with Yeltsin for another hour and we talked in detail about the problems of the armed forces.'

The problems are overwhelming. Since 7.00 p.m., when the last Soviet leader signed the decree resigning as commander-in-chief, the 3.8-million-strong Soviet military has ceased to exist. The country to which they all swore an oath of allegiance is no more. Its nuclear forces are in four republics but are now subordinate to the Russian president. As defence minister and commander, on paper, of the armed forces of the Commonwealth of Independent States, Shaposhnikov has new responsibilities. He expresses grave concern to his political chief about the chaos that may follow after the vast military machine is broken up.

The collapse of the communist superpower has left units of the Soviet army, navy and air force in newly independent countries. The marshal must oversee the withdrawal of conventional forces of Russian nationality and all nuclear weapons from Russia's 'near abroad'. Before the fall of the USSR, the operational area of Moscow's armed forces extended across 8.65 million square miles, from the Pacific to Western Europe. It has been reduced to the 6.6 million square miles of Russian territory which shares borders with Norway, Finland, Estonia, Latvia, Lithuania, Belarus, Ukraine, Georgia, Azerbaijan, Kazakhstan, China, Mongolia and North Korea.

All the operational maps are out of date. Moscow has

lost Estonia, Latvia and Lithuania, with their strategic Baltic Sea ports, Moldova, Belarus and Ukraine in the heart of Europe, the Caucasian states of Armenia, Georgia and Azerbaijan, and the once loyal 'stans', Kazakhstan, Kyrgyzstan, Tajikistan, Turkmenistan and Uzbekistan.

The new governments are busy seizing Soviet military assets. There is confusion everywhere. Ships and aircraft are being hurriedly relocated by Russian commanders to prevent them being requisitioned by other republics. On Shaposhnikov's advice Yeltsin this morning ordered the pride of the Soviet fleet, the enormous and sophisticated new aircraft carrier *Admiral Kuznetsov*, still undergoing trials, to set sail from the Crimean port of Sevastopol and relocate to Murmansk in northern Russia, to prevent it from being seized by the new Ukrainian authorities.

Ukraine's position on the Soviet military units on its territory was conveyed to Moscow that day in the form of an interview given by Leonid Kravchuk to *Izvestia*. The Ukrainian president reassures Russia that he does not object to Yeltsin being supreme commander-in-chief of the strategic forces on his territory, but with the mandatory condition that strategic missiles and tactical nuclear weapons be removed from operational status. 'That is, we will have nuclear weapons, but it will be impossible to launch them. In that case the world will know that Ukraine is not responsible for any misfortune, God forbid.'

With respect to conventional forces, Kravchuk promises that Russian officers will not be expelled, and they will not invite Ukrainian officers serving in the Soviet army elsewhere to come and serve in Ukraine. 'If we went ahead with that, we would have to provide for their return and, consequently, expel people who are living here now. That would involve a great resettlement of peoples and would lead to confrontation . . . The quick return of Ukrainians to Ukraine would be unrealistic and would create turmoil in the minds of the 11.5 million Russians living there.'

As for Gorbachev's recent and frequent complaints that Russians are now finding themselves in foreign countries, Kravchuk comments bitterly that there are many Ukrainians living in Russia, but there is not a single Ukrainian school nor a single newspaper in Ukrainian in Russia, whereas half of all Ukrainian children are taught in Russian-speaking schools in Ukraine.

Shaposhnikov leaves the Kremlin as midnight approaches, relieved at the way things have turned out. Ambassadors and correspondents had been plaguing him with questions about who had political control over the nuclear weapons. As he walks to his limousine, a Russian journalist calls out, 'In whose hands is the nuclear button?'

'In safe hands,' he replies, with a smile.

In the Penta Hotel across town CNN executives celebrate their journalistic coup late into the night. The Americans are cock-a-hoop. For the highly combative Johnson it is 'an incredible moment in the lives of all of us'. In the early hours Stu Loory leaves for the Rossiya, the monstrous concrete hotel adjacent to Red Square, where there is a studio with satellite uplink to Los Angeles, so he can appear on CNN's *Larry King Live*. He holds up the Mont Blanc pen for American viewers to see as he tells the story of how it was used to liquidate the Soviet Union. Next morning at breakfast Johnson asks for it back. Loory takes the pen out of his pocket and hands it over. 'You only think it's yours!' he says with a straight face.

The CNN celebrations are interrupted by a call to CNN manager Frida Ghitis from Georgia, where civil war is in full swing. President Zviad Gamsakhurdia is under attack from armed opposition forces in Tbilisi. Christiane Amanpour and Siobhan Darrow and camerawoman Jane Evans have braved gunfire to get to Gamsakhurdia's dugout in the parliament and have interviewed him under fire.

'It was a crackling call over a satellite phone telling us the interview with the Georgian leader in his bunker was ready,' said Ghitis. 'All we had to do now was get the tape back to Moscow so we could show it to the world.'

This would be another global exclusive. As regular flights in and out of Tbilisi are not operating, a CNN producer in Moscow calls a pilot contact in the Russian air force to make the two-and-a-half-hour flight to Tbilisi and return with the tape immediately. The pilot, a small man in a large fur hat, says he will do it for $10,000 cash. Tom Johnson gives him $5,000 and promises the other half when he returns. The pilot does not show up again for twenty-four hours, by which time the BBC has broadcast its own interview with Gamsakhurdia and the CNN Moscow office has broadcast a copy of Amanpour's interview acquired from a courier who came on a flight from another airport in Georgia. When the tardy pilot at last arrives, he demands the other $5,000. CNN staff at first decline, but as he is accompanied by two large, menacing bodyguards, they come to the conclusion it might be unwise to refuse. According to Ghitis, 'We paid the money, received the tape and put it in the trash. The new Russian capitalism was making its way into the old Soviet Union.'

27

December 26: The Day After

THE MORNING OF DECEMBER 26, 1991, IS SUNNY BUT
much colder. The temperature has dropped to
minus 6 degrees and icicles have formed beneath the
snow-covered roof of the presidential dacha. Gorbachev
wakes to find that the ZiL limousine is no longer waiting for him in the driveway. Another Yeltsin promise –
that he can retain his presidential transport until
December 29 – has not been kept. With some difficulty
Gorbachev's guards manage to get a spare ZiL that, as
Chernyaev notes acidly, is 'kindly' provided by Yeltsin,
so that Gorbachev can return to the Kremlin, where he
also has three days' grace, or so he believes, to clear out
his desk and keep last-minute appointments.

The new ruler is making Gorbachev aware of his
dependency on the Russian presidential whim. Yeltsin
has ordered his security chief Korzhakov to single out
Gorbachev's guards and drivers for harassment to make
the family leave the dacha as quickly as possible. His
rationale, he claims later, is that as sole president he

must commandeer the presidential residence right away, no matter what he promised. Barvikha-4 has a military command post and all the communications for the country's top leader. The supreme commander of the country's military forces cannot be somewhere without facilities for the nuclear button and the accompanying colonels.

Notwithstanding his new civilian status, Gorbachev is still conveyed at a terrific pace along the reserved centre lane of Kutuzovsky Prospekt in the borrowed ZiL, with police cars before and behind. When he arrives in the Kremlin, where the Russian flag is fluttering over the Senate cupola, he finds that the attitude of the Kremlin guards, normally deferential, has become distinctly surly. When Andrey Grachev and Anatoly Chernyaev turn up to help Gorbachev with his final duties, they too are made aware that the security people and ancillary staff are under new orders. Grachev observes how they are rudely and deliberately making Gorbachev aware of the change in his status.

The loyal aides are struck by how drawn and out of sorts Gorbachev looks. He is hung-over and fighting the aches and discomfort that accompany a bout of influenza. Aside from the crushing blow of being forced out of office, he has to concern himself with the emotional turmoil affecting Raisa and the physical disruption in their personal life. He broods about the way he is being kicked out of office as 'most uncivilized, in the worst inherited Soviet traditions'.

'They are throwing me out of the dacha and they are taking the car away,' Gorbachev complains angrily as he enters his office, where a brass plaque on the door still proclaims: 'M. S. Gorbachev, President of the Union of Soviet Socialist Republics', and the red flag remains in place behind his desk.

Chernyaev again wonders why Gorbachev still wants to use the presidential office in the Kremlin. It is a temptation for his foes to treat him with disrespect. But he finds it difficult to contradict Gorbachev at such a sensitive time. 'He is stubborn and I'm not comfortable to be sharp with him while arguing. He might think that I am being too cheeky, now that he is not a president any more.'

Gorbachev's farewell address came too late for the deadlines of the Russian morning dailies, leading Chernyaev to conclude that 'not a single newspaper carried the full text as everybody is afraid of Yeltsin'. Much of the coverage is critical of the outgoing president. *Rossiyskaya Gazeta*, the organ of the Russian parliament (which next day does carry the full text), prints a front-page commentary headlined: 'The West Believes Gorbachev: The Russians Believe Yeltsin'. The paper's senior columnist Vladimir Kuznechevsky accuses the United States of wanting to keep the Soviet Union intact and Gorbachev as leader. 'Gorbachev showed convincingly he was at one with major international leaders. With Yeltsin it is a completely different story. He has no interests apart from the interests of Russia, and is satisfying those interests by integrating Russia into the general historical stream.' The paper cites a poll showing that 63 per cent of Russians are happy to see Gorbachev leave office, and 66 per cent are convinced that the Union will be maintained in some form under the commonwealth.

More worrying for Gorbachev and his aides, who are concerned that there will be attempts to discredit them, another commentator in the same daily, Gennady Melkov, calls for an open trial of the main leaders of the Communist Party of the Soviet Union. Under the headline 'Ghost of Nuremberg' he points out that not every German was guilty of crimes under Nazism but that the leadership should take moral responsibility for what they had done. Fifty million people died during the history of the Communist Party, he writes, and no other party in the world killed so many of its own people.

The negative coverage rankles with Gorbachev's accomplices. Alexander Yakovlev tells a reporter, 'I'm really hurt by the ingratitude towards Gorbachev which many people are falling over themselves to express.'

Several newspapers do, however, express sympathy and appreciation for the fallen president. *Izvestia*, the former mouthpiece of the Soviet government, is indignant at the manner in which Gorbachev has been dumped, declaring on its front page, 'He left his high position looking at us directly and frankly in the eyes. He did all he could.' The paper's columnist Gayaz Alimov criticizes the absence of a proper farewell ceremony. 'This is a question of our own dignity as a nation, as a people, and of the honour of the current political leaders. We will be ashamed of this some time later; even now some of us already feel bad about it.' A colleague, Inna Muravyeva, points out that Gorbachev freed the press, removed fear and 'opened the valve' of their self-respect. 'He bequeathed to Russia inflation, beggars in the street, millionaires and 80 per cent of people living on the poverty line, but also Andrey Sakharov and the realization of the value of a person as a proud human being.'

Vitaly Korotich, editor of *Ogonyok*, muses that 'Gorbachev took this country like my wife takes cabbage. He thought that to get rid of the dirt, he could just peel off the top layer of leaves. But he had to keep going until there was nothing left.'

Komsomolskaya Pravda, the radical youth newspaper, acknowledges that while Gorbachev was unable to change the living standards of the people, he changed the people. 'He didn't know how to make sausage, but he did know how to give freedom. And if someone believes that the former is more important than the latter, he is likely never to have either.'

'*Finita la commedia!*' declares *Pravda*, which was shut down after the August coup but has been relaunched by a team of pro-communist journalists, and taken over by a family of Greek entrepreneurs, the Yannikoses. The former organ of the Communist Party, with its trademark masthead of Order of Lenin medals, is daily harassed by Yeltsin's officials. A few days back its electricity supply was cut off, its telephones were disconnected and militiamen loyal to the Russian Federation sealed off the editorial offices on the tenth floor of its office building. Nevertheless *Pravda*'s editor-in-chief, Alexander Ilyin, manages to produce the paper every day. He cautions against the temptation to gloat over Gorbachev's dismissal, saying, 'This is not the time to throw stones at the back of the person who is leaving.'

The retrograde communist newspaper *Sovetskaya Rossiya* declares a plague on both houses. It publishes a cartoon on its front page showing Gorbachev and Yeltsin standing over a pile of smouldering ashes with Gorbachev saying, 'Now I think we can say that *perestroika* has been completed.'

As Gorbachev deals with his morning correspondence, the Italian journalist Giulietto Chiesa arrives in the Kremlin with colleague Enrico Singer, for the first scheduled interview with Gorbachev as a 'simple citizen'. The reporters for *La Stampa* and *La Repubblica* find the atmosphere strange. 'Everything was in disarray, everyone was abandoning their position, and Yeltsin's men were already there, waiting with impatience,' recalled Chiesa. They note that a red flag is still proudly displayed on a pole behind Gorbachev's desk, as if the Soviet Union still exists and he is still president. Gorbachev greets the Italians with his usual elegance but Chiesa perceives his sense of loss.

The former Soviet leader amuses his guests with a story of how, when he holidayed in Sicily with Raisa Maximovna early in his career, he had to show his fist to a French tourist who was coming on too strong to his young wife. 'Perhaps he wasn't French but Italian and Gorbachev simply wants to be courteous to us,' thinks Chiesa. Gorbachev allows some of his bitterness to show when he talks to them about the way the Union was dismantled. He calls the end of the USSR a putsch and the press conference of the regional presidents after their Alma-Ata summit a cockfight.

'I myself changed as the country did, but I also

changed the country,' he boasts. 'After all, it's a rare opportunity to help restore one's homeland to the world community, to universal values. That's why I feel that, whatever happens, my destiny has been fulfilled.'

When the Italians ask how his family feel about his resignation, he replies tellingly, 'I am grateful to my family for having endured all this.' The change in his living conditions doesn't scare him, he says, referring to his move from a grand state dacha to a slightly less grand one, for use during his lifetime, with state-supplied cars, drivers, security and servants. 'My family and I are not spoiled people.'

And how did he feel seeing the red flag being lowered prematurely from the Kremlin? 'The same as all citizens of this country,' he replies. 'The red flag is our life. But I don't want to dramatize this moment out of respect to my compatriots.'

After the Italians leave, Grachev asks his boss to sign a copy of *The August Coup*, the slender volume Gorbachev wrote about his experience at Foros. The former president writes a message of gratitude to his spokesman, ending with the words: 'The most important events are still before us. It is noon on the clock of history.' As he reads the inscription in the anteroom, Grachev glances up and sees to his amazement that the hands of the clock stand at noon. Later he learns that the clock has stopped.

Shortly afterwards José Cuenca, the Spanish ambassador to the Soviet Union who overnight has become ambassador to Russia, arrives with a letter of condolence from his head of state. Chernyaev seizes the opportunity to take the envoy aside and ask for his help in getting a new job for Andrey Grachev. Knowing that Cuenca is friendly with the director of the United Nations Educational, Scientific and Cultural Organization (UNESCO), Chernyaev asks him if he would lobby for a position there for his colleague. The ambassador's expression changes. 'This is not possible, not acceptable,' he splutters. 'OK, it's not acceptable, I know that myself,' replies Chernyaev, 'but what are you afraid of? Are you afraid of Kozyrev? Are you afraid he will throw you out?'

Elsewhere in the Kremlin grounds, the Soviet Union is going through its death throes. The Supreme Soviet, the working parliament of the USSR Congress of People's Deputies, is holding its last session in Building 14 just inside the Spassky Gate. Most of the elected deputies represent communist institutions that are now defunct or republics now independent, and have departed for good. There is a single item on the agenda: a declaration disbanding the USSR and recognizing its successor as the Commonwealth of Independent States.

The deputies are intent mainly on making a gesture of protest at the extinction of the Soviet Union, and availing themselves for one last day of the well-stocked parliamentary buffet. Waiting for proceedings to start they lounge around and read newspapers on the wide rows of orange armchair seats, like the early arrivals for a movie in a big-screen cinema. The chamber was actually once the official Kremlin theatre, but only non-fictional dramas have been played out here for the last thirty years.

The forlorn lawmakers are almost outnumbered by journalists expecting to see history made, though the reporters themselves are not infused with excitement, as the end of the assembly is such an anticlimax.

Just as the session is starting, five Kremlin workers, two in fur hats, two bare-headed and one in a ski cap, appear at the entrance doors to the building. They unscrew the matching brass plates on each side that proclaim 'Presidium of the Supreme Soviet of the USSR' and carry them off to a storeroom.

Anuarbek Alimzhanov, chairman of the Congress's Council of Republics, takes his seat at the large wooden table on the stage, flanked by seven flags representing fewer than half the former Soviet republics. He claims that enough deputies have registered to form a quorum to vote on a resolution winding up the USSR, though the few Russian and Belarusian parliamentarians there are attending only as observers.

Their predecessors 'spoke of great things, of world revolution, of social equality, of socialism, of the dream of advancing to communism,' declares Alimzhanov. 'Now our country is returning to capitalism in its wildest form . . . We understand perfectly well what we have lost. We don't know what we have gained.' He chides journalists for 'dancing around the lion that has not yet been slain', but acknowledges that the red flag has come down, their president has resigned and this is their last meeting.

Hardline communist Vladimir Samarin steps up to

fulminate against Yeltsin's 'coup d'état'. He uses such demagogic and offensive terms that the secretariat stop taking notes for the official record. Samarin complains that events have brought the congress to its knees, an image famously countered by anti-communist deputy Ilya Zaslavsky with the words, 'This congress was never off its knees in the first place.' Zaslavsky argued at a previous session that while the Bolsheviks disbanded the last elected pre-revolutionary assembly in January 1918 on the pretext that deputies should leave as the guards were tired, 'This time it's not the guards who are tired, it's the people who are tired.' Deputy Viktor Giblin from the Archangelsk region announces that he will have to take up a job as a street cleaner. Other deputies exchange views on whether the end of the Soviet Union is a tragedy or a comedy.

Liu Heung Shing, the Associated Press photographer whose picture of Gorbachev's resignation is reproduced today on front pages all over the world, wanders around the near empty chamber with his camera. 'There was only one Soviet lawmaker in the empty hall,' he later recalls. 'He was yawning as a speaker at the podium announced the collapse of the Soviet Union.'

Alimzhanov brings the proceedings to an end after less than an hour. 'Now that the president has resigned and the red flag has been lowered over the Kremlin, it is time for us to take our leave,' he says. The deputies vote to consign the USSR to history. The motion states: 'Relying on the will expressed by the top elected bodies of state power of Azerbaijan, Armenia, Belarus, Kazakhstan, Kyrgyzstan, Moldova, the Russian

Federation, Tajikistan, Turkmenistan, Ukraine and Uzbekistan to form the Commonwealth of Independent States, the House of the Republics announces the dissolution of the USSR', after each republic's assembly has ratified the Alma-Ata agreements. Their final act is to dismiss the chairmen of the USSR Supreme Court, the Prosecutor's Office and the State Bank, institutions that no longer exist.

The deputies leave in Chaika and Volga sedans laden with belongings and files, sparking rumours that they are stripping the building of televisions, computers and other official property. Ivan Boiko, head of the department for the security of property of the government of Russia, later denies that any looting took place, though there was a brazen attempt by an official to take out 127,000 rubles from the Committee of Constitutional Control in a suitcase. It is, however, a last opportunity to remove and destroy files that might prove embarrassing or dangerous in future. Similar action is going on in many official buildings across Moscow. Quoting Russian presidential sources, TASS reports that some of the top brass at the new super-security ministry combining the KGB and the interior ministry are fast destroying files on corrupted senior police officers.

The Soviet deputies elected from Russian districts are allowed to keep half their annual salaries, thanks to a resolution of the Russian parliament in the White House. This concession was not unanimous. Sergey Baburin, a thirty-two-year-old Afghan veteran and extreme nationalist – he is a friend of Serbian leader Radovan Karadžić – recommends bitterly that they should be awarded thirty pieces of silver for their treacherous role in failing to protect the Soviet Union.

Shortly before 5.00 p.m. Gorbachev leaves his Kremlin office. He is driven in his limousine across the Moscow River to the President Hotel, located in the historic Zamoskvorechye District. The five-star hotel built in 1982 was formerly known as the Hotel Oktyabrskaya, the Hotel October, in memory of the Russian Revolution, when it was used exclusively by the Communist Party to house visiting dignitaries and fraternal delegates.

In the absence of an official state send-off, Andrey Grachev has organized a grand reception in the ball-room for three hundred Russian and foreign media representatives to accord Gorbachev a final salute. He billed it in messages to journalists as 'the last briefing by the presidential press service'. Those invited are, in Grachev's opinion, 'the only interlocutors capable of appreciating the true role of Gorbachev, and not embarrassed to express their appreciation'.

The director of the hotel, fearful of incurring the dis-pleasure of the new authorities, has done everything in his power to prevent the event taking place in his establishment. He at first refused to accept the booking, insisting that the presidential account was closed. Even when Grachev got Gorbachev to provide cash from his own pocket, he kept saying no, but his Russian bosses in the end instructed him to take the reservation. Chernyaev notes with some satisfaction that the hotel manager, while no longer answerable to the party, is employed by a joint-venture company with Western capitalists, so he had to give in. After all, 'There are some uses for privatization!'

The ex-president looks so downbeat and exhausted as he arrives that those close to him fear he is in danger of having a heart attack.

But as he begins to climb the wide, carpeted marble stairway to the ballroom, Mikhail Gorbachev is greeted with a sound that washes over him like balm. At the top of the stairs the large assembly of guests starts applauding. His mood brightens immediately. Here are people who still want to listen to what he has to say. The brilliant sparkle comes back to his eyes as he is surrounded by well-wishers, and he joins in making toasts with glasses of lemon vodka. He hugs several of his friends, champions of *glasnost* such as Len Karpinsky of *Moscow News* and Vitaly Tretyakov of *Nezavisimaya Gazeta*, and signs autographs for foreign correspondents who have been covering *perestroika* for years. CNN's Tom Johnson gets him to sign his diary with the Mont Blanc pen with which the president dissolved the Soviet Union. The journalists also besiege Andrey Grachev, Anatoly Chernyaev, Yegor Yakovlev, Grigory Revenko and Georgy Shakhnazarov for insider accounts of the final days.

Everyone wants to know what Gorbachev will do next. As he grabs a few sardines from the banquet table he relates how in his native village of Privolnoye in the North Caucasus, his eighty-year-old mother Maria Panteleyevna Gorbacheva had watched his speech on television and then sent him a message: 'Leave everything and come home.' Gorbachev predicts that when he calls her back, she will say, 'Thank God, take a break and be yourself again.'

He speaks with such bravado about his future participation in the political process that a number of journalists feel he is laying the groundwork for a political comeback. 'My role is changing, but I am not leaving the political scene,' he promises. 'I have big plans.'

As always in the presence of ardent admirers – though several in the gathering have written very critically of Gorbachev – he is voluble, expansive and unfailingly charming, masterfully hiding the corrosive effects of the humiliations he has endured in the previous twenty-four hours. The rancour shows only in brief flashes. He complains that Yeltsin opposed everything he did in the last few months and – in an echo of Richard Nixon's famous remark after an election defeat in 1962 that 'You won't have Nixon to kick around any more' – he comments bitterly, 'It's easy to be against Gorbachev all the time. There is no one for them to oppose now. So, let them do what they can.'

He remarks jokingly that there are so many presidents in what was the Soviet Union that losing one is not such a big thing, but losing a country is much more important. Fred Coleman, the *Newsweek* bureau chief, finds him on top form, relaxed and composed. Over a glass of champagne, Gorbachev tells him, 'A great task fell to my lot, and it was accomplished. Others will come who will perhaps do a better job. I wish them success.'

Chernyaev watches his chief having to 'talk his heart out for two hours . . . and us sinners were also tortured quite a bit!' He tells David Remnick of the *Washington Post* that Yeltsin has insulted and provoked Gorbachev and made it personal, but that Gorbachev feels he has completed his mission, no matter what lies ahead. 'His goals, his strategy and events all bear him out, despite the mistakes in tactics, the hesitations. His greatest mistake was that he always tried to balance things, to unite everyone, and that was absolutely impossible to do.'

While the reception is in progress, the newsreader on the television set in the bar of the hotel is reminding viewers that as a consequence of the demise of the Soviet Union, they all woke up that morning no longer citizens of a great superpower but citizens of one of fifteen independent nations.

As he is driven home after the reception, Gorbachev passes several buildings where the Russian tricolour has been hung to mark the change in government. There are no red flags to be seen anywhere. The lowering of the communist emblem over the Kremlin on December 25 was the signal for Soviet flags to be pulled down from public buildings across the vast country and replaced with the white, blue and red flag of independent Russia.

In St Petersburg as elsewhere the Russian flag is hoisted over public buildings. But a red flag continues to fly from a metal pole on the House of Political Enlightenment, where the communists have been allowed to retain an office since it was turned into an international business centre. It is visible from the

Smolny Institute where Vladimir Putin, future president of Russia, works as the head of the committee for external relations in the office of the mayor, Anatoly Sobchak.

The ex-KGB officer gives the order to workmen to remove the flag. The next day the communists put up another one. Putin gives the order once more, and once again his men remove the flag. Vladimir Churov, an aide to Mayor Sobchak, watches as back and forth it goes. 'The communists began to run out of flags and started using all sorts of things,' he recalled. 'One of their last versions wasn't even red but more of a dark brown. That put Putin over the edge. He found a crane, and under his personal supervision had the flagpole cut down with a blowtorch.'

28

December 27: Triumph of the Plunderers

JUST BEFORE 8.00 A.M. ON FRIDAY, DECEMBER 27, A little over thirty-six hours after Mikhail Gorbachev announced he was ceasing his activities as president of the USSR, Russian president Boris Yeltsin leaves his apartment at 54 Second Tverskaya-Yamskaya Street, as usual groomed and spruced up by the women of his family. He climbs into the back of the presidential ZiL, taken on his orders from Gorbachev's dacha two nights ago, and tells the driver to bring him straight to the Kremlin.

The limousine cuts across the ring road, cruises along Tverskaya Street, and turns right past the Intourist Hotel, then left in through the Borovitsky Gate of the Kremlin, finally stopping at the Senate Building. He is joined there by his deputy prime minister Gennady Burbulis, parliament chairman Ruslan Khasbulatov and his minister for press and information Mikhail Poltoranin.

The four men crowd into the lift and take it to the

third floor. Guards snap to attention as they stride purposefully along the red runner in the corridor and burst into the anteroom of the presidential office to confront the receptionist on duty.

Mikhail Gorbachev has not yet arrived. He has an appointment at 11.00 a.m. in the presidential office with a group of journalists from the Japanese newspaper *Yomiuri Shimbun*. Under the deal worked out with Yeltsin in the Walnut Room, he has the use of the office until Sunday.

However, an unpleasant surprise awaits Gorbachev. In the early hours of this morning, on Yeltsin's personal instructions, a group of workmen came with a bag of tools and unscrewed the plaque on the door of the presidential office with the inscription in brass letters: 'M. S. Gorbachev, President of the Union of Soviet Socialist Republics'. They replaced it with one stating, 'B. N. Yeltsin, President of the Russian Federation'. Gorbachev is no longer welcome.

'Well, show us around!' Yeltsin commands the receptionist. Without waiting for a response, he barges into the room. 'Here on the table there was a marble pen set,' he thunders. 'Where is it?' He is clearly implying that the property of the Kremlin is being pilfered by the outgoing officials. The secretary protests, 'There was no set . . . Mikhail Sergeyevich did not use such pens. We bought for him felt pens.'

'OK, and what's here?' demands Yeltsin, peering into the resting room where Gorbachev took his afternoon naps and seeing only the couch and toilet facilities. The Russian president goes behind the office desk and starts pulling out drawers. He comes upon one that will not open.

'Why is it locked?' he booms. 'Call the commanding officer.' An aide arrives with a key and opens the drawer. It is empty.

After nosing around some more, Yeltsin summons Kremlin staff and orders them to dump Gorbachev's remaining private belongings in the corridor. The group then gathers around the oval table in the office. 'OK! Give us glasses,' calls out Yeltsin. A bottle is produced and whisky splashed into the tumblers, which are raised in a triumphal toast.

The secretary in the reception room nervously telephones Gorbachev and tells him what is happening: Yeltsin, Poltoranin and Burbulis have occupied the office and are holding a party there, emptying a bottle of whisky, the assistant says. And his name is no longer on the door.

After an hour and a half of revelry, Yeltsin announces benevolently to the trembling receptionist that he has no need to inspect the Walnut Room or the State Council office. He has seen them before. He and his companions leave, laughing among themselves. 'Behave yourself!' he calls over his shoulder. 'I'm going to come back today!'

Georgy Shakhnazarov arrives minutes later to check that the office is ready for Gorbachev's interview with the Japanese correspondents. 'I found that all the president's things were taken out of the office and there was an order that by ten o'clock in the morning the office was to be ready for the arrival of the new master.'

Anatoly Chernyaev is horrified. 'What a nightmare!

And Yeltsin gets more and more uncouth. He is trampling on everything . . . He must be paying us back for yesterday's reception with the press!' He once again feels utterly dismayed that his boss would still want to come to the presidential office at all. 'Why should he humiliate himself? Why does he have to go to the Kremlin? The flag has already been brought down over the cupola . . . and he is already not a president.'

Gorbachev is in a fury when he arrives shortly after Yeltsin has left. On December 18 Yeltsin had publicly announced that Gorbachev could wait 'until the end of December or, at a maximum, until the middle of January to make a decision on his resignation'. When he did decide to resign on December 25, Yeltsin had clearly and categorically agreed that he could remain in his office until December 29 to wind up his affairs.

'Yeltsin put off his presidential duties to supervise personally my "expulsion" from the Kremlin,' complained Gorbachev in his memoirs. 'I was informed that Yeltsin, Khasbulatov and Burbulis had occupied my office at 8.30 a.m. and held a party there, emptying a bottle of whisky for their "victory". This was the triumph of plunderers, I can find no other word for it.'

The Russian president has had for some time the use of an office in the adjacent Kremlin building. But Gorbachev's continued presence in the historic seat of power, two days after he stepped down, is a manifestation that a single all-union state still exists. It is an affront to the new ruler. Yeltsin is the sole president of Russia but it is Gorbachev who is being fêted by the foreign media and who still claims the right to occupy the presidential office in the Kremlin, with the red flag of the Soviet Union behind his desk.

Grachev reckons that the door plaque and the red flag are not merely symbols for Yeltsin but 'the very goals of the struggle, the chief trophies of his crusade against Gorbachev'.

Yeltsin does not like the 'rumours' that appear later in the press that they literally threw Gorbachev's things out of the Kremlin office. He makes some backhand charges of his own. 'The old tenants did not unscrew the handles from the doors, of course. But they did remove some furniture and even took some official state gold fountain pens from their inkwells. Well, that kind of thing's a habit in our country . . .' He denies acting imperiously, and blames 'friction among the clerks'. He claims that they warned Gorbachev and his staff a week before the move of their intentions. 'It was a period of time quite sufficient to pack up one's papers. From the outset I did not want Gorbachev and his team, or rather its remnants, either to be thrown out of the Kremlin or allowed to linger an extra month packing. Long farewells make for too many tears.'

The idea of moving into Gorbachev's office crystal-lized in Yeltsin's mind only in the last few weeks, when it became evident that the Soviet Union had no future. Before that, when there was a chance that some form of union would be salvaged, there was no discussion of Gorbachev leaving the Kremlin, as he would have con-tinued to command the centre from there, however weakened.

Up to then Yeltsin also gave the impression to his

family that he would rule Russia from the White House. Since being elected Russian president in June he has made minimal use of his Kremlin office, going there mainly for formal purposes. His daughter Tanya said a few weeks ago, 'The White House is his real office; the Kremlin office is just for show – to receive foreign guests and hold other official ceremonies.'

Yeltsin is aware that to rule from the Kremlin will give the world reason to suspect his 'great power' ambitions, and that many of his colleagues will question whether a democratically elected leader should occupy the centuries-old citadel of imperial and totalitarian rule. Some regard the White House, the scene of Yeltsin's heroic stand in August, as the state symbol of Russia, rather than the fortress of the tsars on Red Square.

The Russian president has no patience, however, for suggestions that the Kremlin should be turned into a museum of history and culture after the departure of the last Soviet ruler. The Kremlin is an artistic gem, he acknowledges, but it is also the most important government compound in Russia. 'The country's entire defence system is hooked up to the Kremlin, the surveillance system, all the coded messages from all over the world are sent here, and there is a security apparatus for the buildings, developed down to the tiniest detail.' The Kremlin is moreover the symbol of 'stability, duration and determination in the political line to be followed'.

It was also Gorbachev's bailiwick and it is now Yeltsin's for the taking.

One drawback for Yeltsin is that by moving to the Kremlin and bequeathing the White House as a kind of independent territory to the elected deputies, he is exacerbating the division between parliament and presidential rule, and has left the White House, with its squabbling parliamentarians, to become a staging post for a future revolt against him.

Unable to use the ransacked presidential office on the third floor, Gorbachev descends to the second floor and proceeds to the office of the head of his apparatus, Grigory Revenko, to keep his appointment with the Japanese journalists.

He tells them, 'You know what, I consider I have fulfilled my task.' He points out that the totalitarian system is no more and society has been transformed. 'The main thing is that the people have changed. Now that they have tasted freedom I hope nothing will force them back to the status of before.'

Another Japanese media company makes contact with his staff to offer $1 million for a televised interview in the Kremlin the next day. Gorbachev at first says he will accept but is talked out of it by Chernyaev who points out that it is shameful to come back to the Kremlin where Yeltsin is having fun, and it would be more shameful to be looking for somewhere else to do the interview. Revenko scolds Chernyaev for turning down such an offer but Gorbachev tells Chernyaev he has influenza and is not really feeling up to it. There will be many more lucrative media opportunities in the future.

Gorbachev leaves the Senate Building at midday,

ducks into his borrowed ZiL and departs from the Kremlin through the Borovitsky Gate, never to return so long as Boris Yeltsin is president of Russia.

Early in the afternoon Yeltsin comes back to the Senate Building to occupy what is now his office, this time accompanied by a Russian camera crew. He instructs them to film his first act as master of the Kremlin. This is the signing of a decree providing for Russian jurisdiction over the Soviet Union State Television and Radio Company, Gosteleradio. Sitting at the desk vacated by Gorbachev, the Russian president puts his signature to an order transforming Soviet television into the Ostankino Russian State Television and Radio Company. He also decrees that Yegor Yakovlev should supervise the changeover and remain at its head, prompting a tongue-in-cheek headline in *Izvestia*: 'Yegor Yakovlev Is Ordered to Turn Over All-Union Television and Radio Company to Yegor Yakovlev.'

The state broadcasting station that smeared him when he led the opposition to Gorbachev, and that tried to gag him nine months ago, is at last fully under Yeltsin's control. Yakovlev announces an increased output of news, with a new current affairs programme called *Itogi* (Wrap-up) to be hosted by popular broadcaster Yevgeny Kiselyov. As his administration still controls the second national channel, the Russian president commands both TV channels beamed out to the Russian public – though he mandates Ostankino to shed its dependency on the state within a year and become independent through the issue of shares.

Yeltsin starts his reign as absolute leader in a flurry of activity. After dealing with the future of television, he issues an order stripping his rebellious vice president Alexander Rutskoy of control over five state committees he had been chairing. He signs a decree for the privatization in the coming weeks of stores, restaurants, workshops, vodka distilleries, pharmaceutical plants and baby-food factories. Banks, railways and airlines will come later. Collective farms must transfer land to their members and end the state monopoly on 637 million acres of territory. The decree repeals a 1918 Bolshevik ruling that all private ownership of land, mines, waters, forests and natural resources 'is abolished for ever'.

While the increasingly conservative Russian parliament cannot do anything to stop Yeltsin issuing decrees, it can thwart the new ruler in other ways. That afternoon it turns down an application from prosecutor Valentin Stepankov for the arrest of General Vladislav Achalov, the deputy minister of defence at the time of the August coup, on a charge that he was actively involved. Among many deputies, outrage against the coup plotters is giving way to sympathy for their motives. Thirteen conspirators arrested in August remain in the Matrosskaya Tishina prison awaiting trial, but their conditions have been improved.

Coincidentally, on this day Valery Boldin is released from jail because of deteriorating health. In his four months in captivity for his part in the coup, Gorbachev's fifty-six-year-old ex-chief of staff has lost none of his contempt for his former master. He is adamant that the junta sought nothing but prosperity and peace for the country, with no desire for power, and that the coup failed because they were too scrupulous and decent to use harsh methods. To Boldin its defeat was not a victory for the United States, as many are saying, but a rout of the disorganized units of a great power by its internal opponents.

Meanwhile some one hundred presidents of large American companies arrive in Moscow for a Kremlin meeting on stimulating trade. They were invited by the Soviet government, which no longer exists. The meeting goes ahead, with Yeltsin's people, two days later, to the relief of the somewhat bewildered executives.

With the end of the Soviet Union, the editors of the *Bulletin of the Atomic Scientists* at the University of Chicago move the hands of the Doomsday Clock back to seventeen minutes before midnight. Six years before, when Gorbachev took office, the big hand stood at three minutes to Armageddon. (In January 2010, with new tensions among the world's nuclear nations and in light of Iran's nuclear ambitions, the hands are moved forward again to six minutes to midnight.)

Freed from presidential responsibilities, Mikhail Gorbachev helps Raisa to put their new homes in order. 'We were forced to move to different lodgings within twenty-four hours,' complained Gorbachev bitterly. Yeltsin's security men left all the family's personal belongings strewn around. These have to be gathered up and packed. For both of them it is a humiliating intrusion on their domestic privacy. Raisa is intensely private and has always been determined to keep personal affairs away from the prying eyes of strangers. One day not long after returning from Foros, Gorbachev came home to find her in tears. She was destroying a bundle of fifty-two letters that the young Gorbachev had written to her when on business trips, and that she had kept carefully all her life. She was terrified of another coup and couldn't bear the thought of someone reading them. 'She said, "We can't have other people poking their noses into our life," and she threw the letters into the fire,' related Gorbachev years later. 'She was crying and throwing them in the fire . . . I burned twenty-five of my notebooks. Not my personal diaries but my working notes, with all the nuances, characteristics and plans. I burned them thinking I was somehow helping her by doing this.'

The Gorbachevs and their daughter Irina sort through all kinds of papers that have accumulated over the years – notes, letters, telegrams, photographs and documents. They insist on packing everything themselves, rather than asking for help. Chernyaev is outraged that not only do Yeltsin's people evict the Gorbachevs so soon, but 'for a long time they refused to send a lorry to take away their things'.

There are hundreds of books to be stored in cardboard boxes: volumes on Russian history by Solovyev, Kluchevsky and Karamzin; a ten-volume edition of Pushkin's works; books of verse by Lermontov, the Romantic poet of the Caucasus, and by Mayakovsky, the lyricist of the Bolshevik Revolution; rows of the leather-bound writings of Vladimir Ilyich Lenin; individual favourites like a well-thumbed copy of

Dostoevsky's *The Possessed* which Gorbachev maintains helped turn him into an opponent of the totalitarian system; a memoir by Sakharov that Gorbachev bought abroad; an antique copy of *Vanity Fair* by Thackeray presented to Raisa by Margaret Thatcher; and a beautifully bound volume of *The Kobza-Player* by the Ukrainian poet Taras Shevchenko, whose lines Raisa likes to quote: 'My thoughts, my thoughts, what pain you bring! / Why do you rise up at me in such gloomy rows?'

As her own librarian and filing clerk, Raisa takes care to arrange the books properly and not get them mixed up. On their bookshelves there was always a note saying, 'Friends – please arrange these alphabetically.'

Raisa also has a large collection of photographs to pack. Among them is one of a deferential party *apparatchik* handing her a bunch of carnations with an elegant and polite bow. It is Boris Yeltsin. The year was 1985.

29

The Integrity of the Quarrel

O N NEW YEAR'S EVE FEWER THAN THREE THOUSAND people turn up in Red Square to lay to rest the corpse of the Soviet Union and welcome the first year of capitalist, independent Russia.

In the crowd there are a considerable number of US citizens, some of them evangelists carrying religious symbols. A line of militiamen stand between a few communists gathered near Lenin's Mausoleum and a group of jeering Americans.

The midnight chimes ring out from the clock on the Saviour Tower, prompting the greatcoated sentinels to goose-step off, jerking their elbows high in the air as always. Fireworks burst in the skies above Red Square and the small crowd applauds. No members of the government are present to mark the occasion, no church leaders, no dignitaries to say goodbye to seven decades of Bolshevik rule. It is mostly foreigners who are cheering. Even the fireworks are not Russian. They are set off by a German television company, to make the occasion a bit more festive for the cameras.

In a New Year message Yeltsin tells the people of Russia that they have inherited a devastated land, but not to despair. 'Life is now hard for all of us,' he says. 'Our citizens are at times overwhelmed by a sense of bitterness towards their country. But it is unfair to speak about Russia only in gloomy, deprecatory tones. It is not Russia that has suffered a defeat, but the communist idea, the experiment to which Russia has been subjected.'

It would be more palatable, thinks Anatoly Chernyaev, if he at least mentions the man to whom he is obliged for being able to speak freely.

Mikhail and Raisa Gorbachev see in the New Year at the two-storey mansion in the village of Usovo outside Moscow to which they moved the day after he resigned. Arriving through the gate and glimpsing the green-roofed house with mustard-coloured walls and a weathervane marking the year it was built, 1956, they must feel a sense of déjà vu. This is the same state dacha, Moskva-reka-5, set in a fine wooded estate of one hundred acres, where the Gorbachevs lived for six years from the time Mikhail Sergeyevich was made candidate member of the Politburo in 1979 until he became general secretary of the Communist Party of the Soviet Union in 1985. When they moved to what is now the presidential mansion later that year he assigned Moskva-reka-5 to the newly promoted Boris Yeltsin, who was overwhelmed at its palatial rooms and 'kitchen big enough to feed an army'.

At first Gorbachev does not go anywhere and hardly

meets anyone. 'Desperation and hopelessness never overcame me,' he recalls, while admitting that the first few days were very emotional for himself and his family. A former speech-writer, the philosopher Alexander Tsipko, suggests that Gorbachev retire to his mother's village in Stavropol and write books. Others recommend that he should become more reserved and transcendental.

President Yeltsin and his family move into Barvikha-4 within hours of the Gorbachevs' departure. Naina sets about giving the presidential dacha a post-revolution atmosphere by hanging religious icons on the walls, along with the Glazunov portrait of Yeltsin's mother. Yeltsin likes the grand new country home so much he takes to staying there on weeknights, rather than at the apartment. He delights in its sports hall, tennis courts, children's playground, dog pound, gardens with ponds and ornamental bridges, and the fenced-off section of the river where he can bathe and fish.

Naina tortures Alexander Korzhakov with complaints that Raisa has taken all the good furniture and replaced it with old stuff, though the contents manager, housekeeper and estate manager all confirm that nothing had been removed.

The Russian president also aspires to Gorbachev's former city apartment on Lenin Hills. Korzhakov drives Boris and Naina Yeltsin there to inspect the six-room living space from which the Gorbachevs were evicted so rudely on December 25. The flat-roofed apartment block was built to Gorbachev's instructions in 1985 and betrays his singular lack of architectural taste. Valery

Boldin compares the 'grim, dirty-grey concrete structure' to a prefabricated school. The location, nevertheless, is prime. It is set back off a wide boulevard, named after former Soviet prime minister Alexey Kosygin, that skirts the top of a curving wooded embankment high above a U-shaped bend in the Moscow River. The fourth-floor penthouse the Gorbachevs occupied offers a wide panorama of Moscow city, with Novodevichy Convent in the foreground and the Kremlin spires in the distance. At two hundred and fifty square metres the living space is big even by the standards of the Soviet elite. Korzhakov professes himself shocked by the splendour of the interior. He notes how 'the refinement and riches of the quarters of a French queen would pale in comparison with Raisa Maximovna's boudoir [and] bathroom with jacuzzi in precious stones, onyx and yashma'. Naina particularly loves the bedroom furniture of fine-grained Karelian birch. She is ready to move in on the spot but Yeltsin feels it is too much like a museum, and that everything is very stiff and formal.

There is something else to consider as well. The Gorbachevs have been moved to a three-room apartment in the same building. The Yeltsins would be living cheek by jowl with them. Unwilling to risk any contact with their despised adversary, the new first family decides not to occupy the apartment. But they take the luxury furniture and the German kitchen units despite the fact that they were built-in and difficult to move.

Yeltsin keeps his old apartment at 54 Second Tverskaya-Yamskaya Street in downtown Moscow for another three years, before he moves his city residence to a new block in Osennyaya Street in the western suburbs. He assigns apartments there to his closest associates, including Yegor Gaidar and Alexander Korzhakov, though these privileged tenants spend most of their time in their own country dachas. They have a collective house-warming in 1994 with music supplied by the presidential orchestra. With the foreign currency royalties from his memoirs, Yeltsin later also builds his own three-storey dacha in the settlement of Gorky in woods nine miles west of Moscow.

There are other wonderful spoils of office. Yeltsin takes over Gorbachev's presidential Ilyushin-62 salon-version jet airliner, which he adorns with the word *Rossiya* (Russia) and the Russian tricolour. Later he trades up to a wide-bodied Ilyushin-96, equipped with an enormous double bed. He also acquires an armour-plated BMW imported from Germany. Where he once denounced the perks of the communist leadership, he demands all the trappings of a member of the club of world leaders to which Gorbachev belonged, insisting that his struggle was not against the privileges of the party; 'it was against the party's unbridled, all-enveloping power'. His logic is simple: under communism no one outside the party leadership could aspire to a ZiL. In a market economy anyone with the money can drive whatever limousine they can afford, and there is no shame in that.

Yeltsin is also anxious to show off his possession of the nuclear suitcase. He is immensely proud of his nuclear responsibilities. He decides that the colonel-guardians should stand out rather than look inconspicuous as in Gorbachev's entourage and has a uniform especially designed for them. Everywhere he goes he is now accompanied by two officers in black submarine blazers with shoulder boards and gold braid and buttons.

Though the power struggle between Russia and the USSR is over, and Gorbachev and Yeltsin will never cross paths again in person, the integrity of their quarrel is undiminished by their new roles in Russian life. Linked for ever by history, they are consumed with bitterness over real and imagined slights. Yeltsin ensures that the former Soviet leader becomes persona non grata in Moscow's official circles. While he is not condemned to the status of non-person like Khrushchev, Gorbachev nevertheless feels that the press and television under Yeltsin's 'baleful influence' are encouraged to produce negative stories about him. While the Gorbachevs are on a two-week vacation in Stavropol after his resignation, *Rabochaya Tribuna* (Workers' Tribune) publishes a claim from the Russian procurator that Gorbachev authorized the KGB to spy on Yeltsin during their power struggle, and that the discovery of documents proving this in Valery Boldin's safe explain Yeltsin's 'dubious treatment' in hustling Gorbachev out of the Kremlin.

On returning to Moscow from Stavropol, Gorbachev begins a campaign to re-establish his reputation as a figure of consequence in the world. Anatoly Chernyaev, Georgy Shakhnazarov and Alexander Yakovlev join him as members of his foundation staff. Palazchenko stays on as his English-language interpreter. Besides establishing his foundation, Gorbachev founds Green Cross, an international organization committed to expediting solutions to environmental problems that transcend national boundaries. One of their first visitors is his old American ally, Jim Garrison. 'Why didn't you guys fight back? Why didn't you have Yeltsin arrested?' Garrison asks Yakovlev. 'Jim, let me tell you something about power,' replies Yakovlev. 'All my life I have dealt with power, real power, Politburo power. You have it for a time and then, like sand, you let it slip through your fingers. You leave and life goes on.'

Yeltsin monitors the *perestroika* veterans in his camp for suspicions of divided loyalties. When the head of television, Yegor Yakovlev, tells Yeltsin out of courtesy that he has dined with the Gorbachevs at their dacha, the Russian president replies, according to Yakovlev, 'Do you think I don't know about that!' Then, almost plaintively, Yeltsin asks, 'Why did he invite you to this dinner but not me?'

'Are you crazy?' replies Yakovlev. 'You are president, he is nothing.'

Yeltsin protests, 'He never calls me, he never rings me, he never phones.'

This bizarre exchange leads the television chief to conclude that there exists a 'savage hatred' of Gorbachev buried deep in Yeltsin's soul. Yeltsin fires Yakovlev ten months later, after the broadcast of a documentary about ethnic conflict in the Caucasus that annoys him.

The rivals rush to bring out self-serving

autobiographies: *Mikhail Gorbachev – Memoirs* and Boris Yeltsin's *Zapiski Prezidenta* (Notes of the President), published in English as *The Struggle for Russia*. Yeltsin gets a $450,000 advance on royalties, just over half as much as Gorbachev's advance of $800,000.

Three weeks after Gorbachev resigns, James Baker travels around the former Soviet Union on an inspection tour. His staff carry thousands of dollars in cash to pay for fuel at each airport. His excursion coincides with a short lived Berlin Airlift-type operation during which, in the space of a week, fifty-four sorties of C-5, C-141 and C-130 transport planes carry a total of seventeen million kilos of food and medicine to the newly independent states of the CIS. The State Department ensures that a mercy flight arrives at each airport at the same time as the secretary of state.

In Moscow Baker finds Yeltsin transformed, no longer vague and glib, but self-assured, well informed, a master of complex issues.

Facing a presidential election, President Bush, who observed on the last day of the Soviet Union that 'We all were winners, East and West,' uses his State of the Union address before both houses of Congress on January 28, 1992, to claim an American victory in the struggle with the Soviet Union. More than five hundred Congress members leap to their feet and give a prolonged standing ovation when he declares, 'By the grace of God, America won the Cold War.'

Mikhail Gorbachev is deeply offended. Bush's triumphalism feeds into the perception, already widespread in Russia, that the former Soviet president is to blame for the loss of their superpower status through kowtowing to the West. If Bush won, then Gorbachev lost. Gorbachev accuses *Dorogoi* George of lapsing into 'the old, confrontational way of thinking'.

Later, at the Republican convention in Houston, Bush proclaims that 'The Cold War is over and freedom finished first,' to roars of 'USA! USA!' His Democratic opponent, Bill Clinton, mocks Bush's boast that he defeated communism, comparing it to a rooster claiming credit for the dawn. Clinton goes on to defeat Bush in the presidential election.

Throughout his retirement Gorbachev consistently argues that the end of the Cold War is not a victory for any one side, as all humankind emerged victorious. The threat of a nuclear holocaust became history; many European nations were given freedom of choice, and the security of Russia was strengthened by the development of more normal international relations. The Western conservative ideologists who claim victory are 'simply puffed up with braggadocio'.

In later years the former Soviet leader becomes further disillusioned by NATO's expansion to Russian borders, and he takes every opportunity to remind Western politicians that, during the negotiations on the unification of Germany, James Baker, Helmut Kohl, Douglas Hurd and François Mitterrand all gave assurances that NATO would not extend to the east. They had agreed when Eduard Shevardnadze insisted during negotiations on Germany's future, 'Membership of a united Germany in NATO is unacceptable to us.'

No longer an insurgent fighting for recognition or a pretender fearful of snubs, Yeltsin bombards Western capitals with messages of goodwill and camaraderie. He makes his international debut as undisputed Russian leader in February, flying to London for lunch with Prime Minister John Major. For years afterwards Major enjoys telling of an exchange that showed Yeltsin's deadpan sense of humour. 'I said to him, "Boris, tell me in one word, what is the state of Russia?" He said, "Good." I was surprised – it was falling to pieces at the time. I said tell me in two words. He said, "Not good."'

From London, Yeltsin flies on to New York to take formal possession of the Soviet Union's old seat on the United Nations Security Council. He proceeds next day to Camp David for talks with his new best friend George Bush. He assures the US president that only he and Marshal Shaposhnikov hold nuclear suitcases and that the control of nuclear weapons has passed into secure hands. Bush gives him a ride in a golf cart and presents him with a pair of hand-stitched cowboy boots with silver engraving for his sixty-first birthday. Yeltsin is so taken with the golf carts that he orders some for his grandchildren to drive around the garden of the presidential dacha outside Moscow.

In May, accompanied by Raisa, their daughter Irina and interpreter Pavel Palazchenko, Gorbachev also travels to the United States, on a trip co-hosted by Ronald Reagan and George Shultz and organized by his American admirer, Jim Garrison, and is once more able to drink in the intoxicating brew of celebrity adulation and peer worship so lacking at home. The wealthy publisher Malcolm Forbes Jr puts his private jet, named *Capitalist Tool*, at Gorbachev's disposal to fly the party around eleven American cities where they are accommodated in five-star hotels and greeted by fawning hosts, among them Donald Trump, Ronald Reagan and David Rockefeller. Twenty thousand people come to hear Gorbachev speak in Fulton, Missouri, the location of Winston Churchill's 'Iron Curtain' speech. In the New York Stock Exchange the former communist leader is cheered by traders as he declares that 'anybody who comes to the Russian market will have the opportunity to extract enormous profits'.

President Bush plans a black-tie dinner for Gorbachev with a triple-A guest list. Word gets back to Yeltsin, and he sends Russian ambassador Vladimir Lukin to the White House to make clear that this will be seen as a personal affront by the Russian president. Bush scraps the formal event in the East Room and instead spirits the Gorbachev party upstairs through the back entrance for a private dinner with the Bush family and James and Susan Baker. Gorbachev doesn't disappoint with his charm and self-appreciation. 'A class act, that guy,' the US president enthuses to Baker after they leave. Gorbachev angers Yeltsin on his return to Moscow by claiming credit for US financial aid that Yeltsin hoped to nail down on a state visit to the United States the following month.

The Russian media largely ignores Gorbachev's American odyssey. Instead they give blanket coverage to the second visit of President Yeltsin to the United States shortly afterwards. Yeltsin once disapproved of a

Russian leader taking a spouse on a foreign trip, but this notion is consigned to a bygone era. He takes Naina with him. Yeltsin earns a tumultuous reception for an address to the Joint Houses of Congress in which he clears the way for American companies to do business in Russia. He concludes his speech on Capitol Hill with the words, 'Today free and democratic Russia is extending the hand of friendship to the American people.'

Yeltsin's entourage is delighted with the new-found enthusiasm for him in the US media. His officials note with glee the comment of Michael Wines in the *New York Times* that Yeltsin had at last 'escaped the long shadow of Mr Gorbachev, a man who had mesmerized average Americans and their presidents alike with his flirtations with democratic rule and his frantic dance atop the Soviet power pyramid'.

Five months after the transition, relations between the unforgiving Gorbachev and the belligerent Yeltsin deteriorate sharply. The former Soviet president starts publicly to criticize the harsh impact of shock therapy, which had sent prices sky-rocketing and made people's hard-earned savings worthless. Yeltsin complains that this breaks a pledge not to interfere in politics. Gorbachev explodes to a reporter from *Komsomolskaya Pravda*. 'Listen, Yeltsin is not Jesus Christ. He is not the kind of a person to whom I should answer. Both the right wing and the democratic press have been simply falling on Gorbachev, trying to discredit me, to cause hate and venom.' In any event, he adds, he only promised not to turn his foundation into a political party. Yeltsin accuses Gorbachev of making dangerous and intolerant statements 'in a school-masterly tone'. In true Soviet style he gets interior minister Viktor Verin to carry out an unannounced financial audit of the Gorbachev Foundation. To no one's surprise, the auditors find 'abuses' in foreign operations. Yeltsin's media allies give Gorbachev the same kind of damaging treatment Yeltsin received from *Pravda* when it was under Communist Party control. *Izvestia* for example reports that Gorbachev is buying a house in Florida for $108,350, though no real estate transaction is ever identified.

Around this time Alexander Yakovlev, installed as vice president of the foundation, warns Gorbachev that some individuals have formed a task force to discredit him. Gorbachev tells *La Stampa*'s correspondent Elzio Mauro, 'Now I see these names coming out in the open to attack me, one after the other. They probably want me to leave the country, to go hide somewhere, because I'm a problem to them.' Particularly hurtful is an accusation by Anatoly Lukyanov, former speaker of the Soviet Congress of People's Deputies who is awaiting trial in Matrosskaya Tishina prison as a putschist, that Gorbachev was complicit in the 1991 August coup.

The Commonwealth of Independent States never amounts to much, as its founders always intended. All the republics create their own armies and currencies. Only Belarus shows any enthusiasm for reintegrating with Russia. In Kiev, President Kravchuk cruelly dismisses a proposal by Gorbachev for greater commonwealth unity, saying, 'That is the misfortune of that man, his sickness. Everybody is laughing at him and he does not understand that.'

The Russian Constitutional Court summons Gorbachev to give evidence to a tribunal on the activities of the Communist Party of the Soviet Union. Labelling this 'bizarre trial' a device for settling political scores, Gorbachev blusters that he will not take part in the proceedings even if hauled into court in handcuffs. The court fines him the maximum 100 rubles, about five US dollars, but takes away his foreign passport. It is returned shortly afterwards when former West German chancellor Willy Brandt dies, and Gorbachev wishes to attend the funeral.

Yeltsin's impatience with Gorbachev comes to breaking point in the autumn when Gorbachev again strongly attacks his 'cavalry charge' approach to the economy. On October 8, 1992, three busloads of police arrive and block the doors of Gorbachev's foundation on Leningradsky Prospekt, preventing the staff from entering. Gorbachev turns up minutes later and fumes to journalists on the steps, 'They are out to get Gorbachev, Gorbachev the devil, Gorbachev the prince of darkness, as they call me.' Yeltsin has issued a decree transferring the ownership of the building to the Russian Academy of Finance. The Gorbachev Foundation is allowed to remain but only as tenants paying rent and service charges to the Russian Academy of Finance. Gorbachev complains that all this is done in a typical Yeltsin fashion – 'noisily, rudely and unskilfully' – in order to humiliate him once more and clip his wings.

The Russian president also withdraws from

Gorbachev the two ZiL limousines and the unit of bodyguards that were part of the resignation deal. The former president has to settle for a standard black Volga V8 sedan.

Gorbachev's relationship with Alexander Yakovlev breaks down after Yakovlev receives a telephone call from Yeltsin to tell him that the 'Stalin Archives' that Gorbachev handed over just before his resignation have yielded up the original of the secret protocols to the notorious 1939 Molotov–Ribbentrop Pact, which divided Europe between the Soviet Union and Nazi Germany before World War II. The file contains maps two metres wide, signed by Stalin in red and Ribbentrop in blue. Yakovlev has long sought the original documents for his research on Bolshevik crimes, but Gorbachev had assured him they were destroyed in 1950. 'Finally, I always believed they would be found,' Yakovlev exclaims. Initials on the file indicate that Gorbachev knew they existed. This is backed by the claim of Gorbachev's former chief of staff Valery Boldin, in a memoir full of bile against his former boss, that he showed the originals to the Soviet leader, who instructed him 'not to say anything about it'. The discovery of the secret protocols stuns Yakovlev and he expresses his reaction to Yeltsin in 'a few choice words'. Other files that Yeltsin releases selectively yield up confirmation that Gorbachev regularly read KGB transcripts of Yakovlev's private telephone conversations. Feeling betrayed one time too often, Yakovlev leaves the Gorbachev Foundation in 1993 and accepts an offer from Yeltsin to direct Ostankino television. He also sets up his own International Democracy Foundation and publishes a devastating account of terror under Lenin and Stalin, *A Century of Violence in Soviet Russia*. From 1996 until his death in 2005 his foundation publishes eighty-eight volumes of documents from the Soviet archives.

Yakovlev's departure creates bad feelings within Gorbachev's close circle. Chernyaev accuses him of using the foundation's resources 'to circulate myths about himself', and then, as the wind shifts, deserting Gorbachev for a job with Yeltsin's government. In Chernyaev's opinion, Yakovlev's ambition might be forgivable, as he played a key role in destroying the 'Marxist-Leninist-Stalinist lies and demagoguery' that permeated Russia for so many decades. 'But what I can't forgive is [Yakovlev's] posturing, at home and abroad, as such a champion of high morality (and) crafting his image as the sole author of *perestroika*.' Boldin stirs the pot by alleging in his memoir that *perestroika* and new thinking was in fact 'mainly the work of Yakovlev'.

The relationship between Gorbachev and Shevardnadze, the joint architects of the new world order, also comes to an end. 'Gorbachev was my friend. We had warm, close relations,' he tells a reporter in Tbilisi in 2008, five years after having served as president of Georgia for a decade. 'We played an important role together to end the Cold War and reunify Europe. Since then, we went our separate ways. Relations between us grew cold. I cannot say we are friends any longer.'

George H. W. Bush visits Moscow in his last month as president in January 1993 to sign a historic treaty reducing nuclear stockpiles, the climax of a process that owed everything to Gorbachev and Reagan. Not once does Bush mention Gorbachev by name at the joint press conference with President Yeltsin to mark the event.

Bill Clinton, who takes office as US president some two weeks later, doesn't know at first what to make of Yeltsin. His advisers warn him that Bush harmed US interests by aligning himself too closely with Gorbachev, and he should avoid making the same mistake with his unpredictable successor. Clinton feels he has no choice but to support Yeltsin, 'a proud beggar among the great nations', as the best hope for democratic reform in Russia.

At their first meeting in Vancouver, Clinton observes Yeltsin downing alcoholic drinks through dinner without touching his food. Stories about the Russian's mammoth drinking bouts begin to circulate at the highest levels. In Washington in 1993 Clinton is notified of a major security alert when Yeltsin, who is staying in Blair House across from the White House, is encountered by secret service agents in his underwear in Pennsylvania Avenue, trying to hail a taxi to go for a pizza. The next evening, again according to Clinton, Yeltsin is mistaken for an intruder as he drunkenly tries to exit through a basement, and comes close to getting himself shot.

As Yeltsin's health and insomnia worsens during his first term he is less able to handle copious quantities of alcohol. On a trip to Germany in 1994 he grabs a baton to conduct drunkenly a brass band in the presence of Chancellor Kohl. During a stopover at Shannon airport in Ireland he fails to get off his plane to meet the waiting Irish prime minister, Albert Reynolds. According to Korzhakov, he is ill, and when not allowed off, he sits in his underwear and cries. Naina on another occasion scolds Korzhakov for 'making my husband a drunk', to which Yeltsin's drinking companion claims he retorted, 'No, you brought him from Sverdlovsk an alcoholic!'

Throughout his first term Yeltsin is tormented by the cruel impact on people of the change from communism to capitalism. After January 2, 1992, when prices are freed, the rise in prices far exceeds the predictions of IMF economists. Hyperinflation wipes out life savings, turning millions of Russians into paupers, and stoking discontent and resentment. Free for the first time in decades to sell what they like, lines of people appear on Moscow streets from every walk of life offering household items from spare shoes to ornamental clocks to make ends meet. With an insufficient money supply to meet everyday needs, conditions deteriorate. Crime increases, salaries go unpaid, and the gap between rich and poor widens. The birth rate falls and the death rate rises.

Every sector of society feels the pain. Farms and factories lose their subsidies and cannot buy raw materials. In the first six months of rampant capitalism national income falls 20 per cent, creating pressure on the Yeltsin team to reverse course. When deputy prime minister Yegor Gaidar brings in a single exchange rate, the result is a collapse of the ruble and a huge demand for US dollars to protect against inflation.

In March 1992, agitated by rumours of a global conspiracy to strangle Russian industry by liberalizing raw-material prices, the Russian parliament blocks a plan to free domestic oil prices. Entrepreneurs who have acquired export licences are able to continue buying Russian oil for next to nothing and sell it abroad for dollars. It is the start of a process that will lead to the emergence of the oligarchs.

Privatization minister Anatoly Chubais ends the state monopoly in property ownership with the largest privatization programme in the history of the world. Ownership shares given to factory workers under privatization laws drawn up in collaboration with the International Finance Corporation in Washington are snapped up by industrial directors, most of them former stalwarts of the Communist Party, who become wealthy capitalists overnight. (E. Wayne Merry, head of the US embassy political section from 1991 to 1994, complains to Washington that America's 'evangelical' attempt to remould Russia in its own image is initiating an era of crime and economic destruction.) Many of the new rich send their money abroad in hard currency for safe-keeping. In the first two years of Russian independence, the Central Bank of Russia estimates that the flow of capital out of the country reaches $100 billion, more than the combined total of inward investment and international aid.

The nouveau riche gain a reputation for throwing their money around, spawning new anecdotes: a 'New Russian' asks another how much he paid for his Rolex. On being told $5,000, he retorts scornfully, 'I know where you can get one for $6,000.' Another anecdote concerns an IMF official who moans that 'Everything the communists told us about communism was a lie. Unfortunately, everything the communists told us about capitalism turned out to be true.' One of the first Russian billionaires is Yelena Baturina, who runs a construction company. She is the wife of Yury Luzhkov, who becomes Moscow's mayor in 1992 and oversees a two-decade building boom.

The common Russian perception of Yeltsin's economic team is expressed by Alexander Solzhenitsyn, who returns from exile in the United States three years after the end of the Soviet Union. The writer and Nobel Laureate says that Gaidar has 'thrown into poverty tens of millions of his compatriots, wrecking their savings' and that Chubais enacted privatization 'with the same blind madness, the same destructive haste as the nationalization of 1917–18 and the collectivization of 1930'. Eight weeks before his death in 2009, in an interview in Moscow for this book, Gaidar said he had no regrets about the decisions he made in December 1991, as they were absolutely necessary. 'People were awaiting food catastrophe and there was a danger of a breakdown in energy supply. Only by freeing prices did food return to the shops.' He admitted some tactical mistakes in the transition from a command economy to a free market, 'but strategically I think we made the right decision to avoid a humanitarian catastrophe in a nuclear country'.

In the post-communist chaos few escape the rapacious demands of the ascendant Russian *mafiya*. A financial report prepared for Yeltsin in his first year finds that four out of five of the banks and large private enterprises in Russian cities are paying more than 10 per cent of their revenues to organized crime. Even small-time street hawkers are victims. 'For some time in 1992 we hang out at Arbat selling stuff,' recalls Olga Perova. 'Local gangsters protect us so that we won't get robbed, and we pay them kickbacks.' Contract killings become common. In 1993, one hundred and twenty-three bank employees are gunned down or blown up. Privatization of state apartments results in a particularly ugly type of crime: pensioners are persuaded to sell their living space and stay on rent free, and then are pushed under a bus.

To Gorbachev all this is confirmation that he was correct to oppose Yeltsin in breaking up the old order so brutally. He complains that the bloody shoot-outs in Moscow are worse than those in Chicago during the prohibition era, and that the outflow of billions of dollars deposited in foreign banks to await the arrival of their gangster owners is made possible with the connivance, or inertia, of Yeltsin's government. 'Having beaten his way to power,' Gorbachev jibes in his 1995 memoir, 'Yeltsin instantly forgot his wrathful speeches against abuses and allowed his associates to indulge in corruption and privileges such as the communist *nomenklatura* had never dreamed of.'

As living standards plummet, deputies in the Russian

Supreme Soviet seethe with discontent. The shock therapy is increasingly seen as a Western imposition. Much anger is directed at the American and European experts who commute to Moscow to peddle their advice to the new government. The speaker, Ruslan Khasbulatov, attacks the 'vile' monetarist policy imposed by the Americans. The demagogue Vladimir Zhirinovsky courts populist support by calling the United States 'an empire of evil, the nucleus of hell' that conspires to rule the world.

Yeltsin resists the domestic clamour to restore subsidies and fix prices, but in December 1992 he is obliged to dismiss Gaidar from his government and replace him with Viktor Chernomyrdin, a politician more sympathetic to the plight of state industry, though Chernomyrdin soon finds that Gaidar's reforms have gone too far for the reintroduction of price controls on food items. In a few months Gaidar has managed to smash the state planning system and establish a market economy in a country where civil society hardly existed and initiative had been crushed for the best part of a century.

The volatile Russian president becomes so depressed at the setbacks that he contemplates suicide. On December 9, 1992, he locks himself inside the over heated bathhouse at Barvikha-4, and is only saved from suffocation by Korzhakov who breaks down the door and pulls him out. On another occasion in his Kremlin office he produces a pistol given to him by his security minister Viktor Barannikov – before Yeltsin sacked him for corruption – and threatens to shoot himself. Aides persuade him not to be foolish. He doesn't pull the trigger. The weapon, however, is not lethal: Korzhakov has taken the precaution of boiling the bullets in water to make them harmless.

In the Supreme Soviet the Russian president's enemies proliferate and the communists make up lost ground. However, a motion to impeach Yeltsin fails by a narrow margin. 'This means that the Russian people do not after all want to go back to the bright communist future,' observes Gaidar. But the parliament continues to pass anti-reform measures and mobilize against Yeltsin. It decks itself out in red flags and anarchist and fascist banners and stockpiles arms. It elects Rutskoy as provisional Russian president and he names a new government. Russia once again faces a showdown between the White House and the Kremlin. The crisis comes to a head on September 21, 1993, when Yeltsin issues a decree dissolving the parliament. Armed White House 'defenders', many of them neo-Stalinists and proto-fascists, begin roaming the streets to show their defiance of the order, some in Cossack high hats and belts. In the following days they attack the television station and other key buildings in the city. On October 4 pro-Yeltsin army units fire several shells into the upper floors of the barricaded White House, forcing the communists and nationalists to surrender. The brief civil war results in the deaths of more than 150 people. The outcome is a more authoritarian style of presidential government.

Gorbachev blames Yeltsin for the crisis and calls the storming of the White House an act of madness. 'The army was ordered to shoot at the people! It was unforgivable!' He charges Yeltsin with laying the groundwork for an absolute monarchy under the guise of a presidential republic.

The Russian constitution is changed in a referendum on December 12, 1993, giving stronger powers to the president. A new and weaker parliament, the Duma, is elected. One of its first acts is to grant an amnesty to the leaders of the White House revolt of October 1993, which Yeltsin endorses for the sake of peace.

The plotters of the August 1991 coup are released from prison, but General Valentin Varennikov insists on standing trial. The case is heard in Moscow in 1994. Gorbachev is called as a witness, and gives vent to his feelings about amnesties for coup plotters. 'If we react to such crimes as nothing more than a farce, we would have one coup after another,' he declares. 'We have already lived through the conspiracy of Belovezh Forest, which finished off the USSR by exploiting the consequences of the August coup. Then we had to live through the bloody events of 3–4 October 1993, when before our very eyes parliament was fired on . . . If our future is to be determined by new coup plotters, we will never become a country in which everyone can feel a citizen.'

Varennikov walks free after all charges are dropped, and claims that his acquittal is proof of Mikhail Gorbachev's guilt. In 2008, a year before he dies, the former general presents the case in favour of Stalin in a popular nationwide television project seeking to identify Russia's greatest historical figures. Stalin wins third place behind Grand Prince Alexander Nevsky of

Novgorod and pre-revolutionary prime minister Pyotr Stolypin. Neither Yeltsin nor Gorbachev figures in the final twelve.

President Yeltsin, whose outrage at the bloodshed in the Baltics in 1991 helped change Russian history, in December 1994 authorizes a full-scale and brutal invasion of the Russian republic of Chechnya to end its independence from Moscow. Russian forces fight an incompetent and savage war with Chechen guerrillas that destroys the capital of Grozny and results in the deaths of between 30,000 and 100,000 civilians. General Grachev, who ordered the storming of Grozny, reputedly when dead drunk, is sacked by Yeltsin when Russia is defeated. A peace treaty is concluded in August 1996.

Yeltsin runs for re-election as president of Russia in 1996, amid widespread expectations that he will lose because of a collapse in his popularity and his poor health. He almost puts the election off because of a vote in the Duma on March 15, 1996, to renounce the decision of the Russian Supreme Soviet of December 12, 1991, approving the Belovezh Agreement – which raises questions about the legitimacy of the new Russia. His daughter Tanya helps talk him out of shutting down the Duma and delaying the election for two years, which could provoke a civil war.

His main opponent is Gennady Zyuganov, the candidate of the Russian Communist Party. Zyuganov campaigns to revive the socialist motherland, lumping Yeltsin and Gorbachev together with a world oligarchy as the destroyers of Russia. Convinced that 'the country needs Gorbachev', the former Soviet leader ignores the sage advice of his loyalists and runs as head of the fledgling Social Democratic Party.

The sixty-five-year-old Yeltsin stops drinking, loses weight and manages to summon up one more great burst of energy to campaign for re-election. American and European leaders troop to Moscow to boost their free-market champion. Yeltsin's campaign is helped by financial donations from the oligarchs, a timely announcement of a $10 billion loan from the IMF, the anti-communist bias of the television networks, and television advertisements produced with the expert advice of the American PR firm of Ogilvy & Mather. The Russian president wins re-election by 54 per cent to Zyuganov's 40 per cent.

Gorbachev is humiliated by his performance in the election. With one section of the population accusing him of betraying socialism in the name of reform, and the other of sabotaging reforms to defend socialism, Gorbachev receives a mere half of one per cent of the vote. In a further snub, Yeltsin removes his name from the guest list for his inauguration.

In his second term, Yeltsin's Kremlin court becomes a hive of intrigue. It is a period of political and economic chaos during which Russia's natural resources are being sold off to favoured insiders at fire-sale prices. Yeltsin grows ever more irascible, yields power arbitrarily and treats his staff abominably. Aides assume that, as head of his security, Alexander Korzhakov is monitoring their phone calls and they communicate with each other only in scribbled notes. Always suspicious of over-familiarity, Yeltsin drops his pre-independence collaborators one by one. He lets Gennady Burbulis go because his grey cardinal is annoyingly appearing every day 'in my office, at meetings and receptions, at the dacha, in the steam bath'. Korzhakov survives for five years but is fired after a scandal over election funding. He writes an unflattering book, *Boris Yeltsin: From Dawn to Dusk*, which angers Yeltsin so much they never speak again.

Yeltsin's first, and only, formal contact with Gorbachev after December 1991 comes seven years later. In 1999 he sends a telegram of sympathy to the sixty-eight-year-old ex-president as Raisa Gorbacheva lies dying of leukaemia in University Hospital in Münster, Germany. 'I want to express my deep concern for the ordeal that your family is going through,' he writes. 'I know well how hard it is to experience the illness of a loved one. More than ever, in moments like these, mutual support, warmth and caring are needed. I wish for you, my esteemed Mikhail Sergeyevich, strength and persever-ance, and, for Raisa Maximovna, courage in her struggle against the disease as well as a speedy recovery.'

Gorbachev shows the telegram to his old friend, the Italian journalist Giulietto Chiesa, as they stroll in a park near the hospital in Münster. 'These are kind words, a very nice gesture,' he remarks.

The illness of Raisa touches a chord in Russia, especially as she is struck down by a disease with which her charitable work is associated. When Gorbachev asks his staff to approach the new prime minister, Vladimir Putin, for help in getting a passport for Raisa's sister, Lyudmila, so that she can be available in Germany to become a bone marrow donor for Raisa, Putin's response is instantaneous.

Gorbachev's eyes fill with tears as he talks to Chiesa about these acts of kindness. He thought it would take a whole generation before they understood, he says, taking a crumpled cutting from *Izvestia* out of his pocket and handing it to the Italian. Under the heading 'Lady of Dignity' it reads: 'Maybe we Russians are becoming people again . . . It may only be on this sad occasion, but we are showing great respect for two people who love each other, Raisa and Mikhail. Diminutive and elegant, with sophisticated tastes, Raisa is not like the others. She has been the symbol of a country that wanted to free itself from its dreary greyness. People didn't understand her, or perhaps they didn't want to understand her. Maybe too much was asked of them when the couple was in power. But it's also true that no one was able to bend their will and subdue them.' Raisa cried when she read the article, says Gorbachev.

The transplant cannot be made and Raisa dies four weeks later, on September 20, 1999, at sixty-seven. She is buried at Novodevichy Cemetery in Moscow. Yeltsin does not go to the funeral but issues a statement commemorating 'a wonderful person, a beautiful woman, a loving wife and mother who is no longer with us'.

Vladimir Polyakov, the ex-president's press secretary,

believes the sympathy for the Gorbachevs has a political as well as a humanitarian side. 'People need a certain amount of time to evaluate the past. He [Gorbachev] entered our lives so unexpectedly and when he left, almost as suddenly, people needed a scapegoat. But if it had not been for Gorbachev, Yeltsin would still be sitting in Sverdlovsk as the regional Communist Party secretary. And if Yeltsin had been elected general secretary of the party in 1985 instead of Gorbachev, no changes would have happened in Russia. Now people are asking for forgiveness for not understanding that before.'

In November 1996 Yeltsin collapses and has a quintuple heart-bypass operation. He is never the same afterwards. On December 31, 1999, he announces that he is leaving the remainder of his presidency in the hands of Vladimir Putin, who has risen from mayor's aide in St Petersburg to a senior position on Yeltsin's staff, then head of the FSB, the successor organization to the KGB, and finally prime minister, in which role he has promoted a second war against Chechnya. Yeltsin tells Russians, 'I want to beg forgiveness for your dreams that never came true. And also I would like to beg forgiveness not to have justified your hopes.'

His departure from the Kremlin is as low-key as was Gorbachev's eight years previously. Yeltsin returns to his office after a farewell lunch at 1.00 p.m. and presents Putin with the squat fountain pen with which he signed decrees. 'Take care of Russia,' he says and leaves the Senate Building for good. Both Yeltsin and Gorbachev are invited to attend Putin's inauguration as acting president but avoid each other.

On the tenth anniversary of his abdication, Gorbachev's contempt for the republic leaders who conspired with Yeltsin to break up the Soviet Union remains undiminished. 'I was shocked by the treacherous behaviour of those people, who cut the country in pieces in order to settle accounts and establish themselves as tsars,' he tells reporters in Moscow on December 25, 2001. He could not oppose them at the time, he says, because that might have led to civil war in a nation brimming with nuclear weapons. 'And what is Russia without the Soviet Union? I don't know. A stump of some sort.'

Asked if he is happy, Gorbachev admits to not knowing what happiness is, but remarks that fate allowed him to lead a process of renewal that involved the whole world. 'God! What other happiness could there be!'

The former Soviet president meanwhile is embarking on a lucrative new profession as a model for advertising agencies. In December 1997 he appears in an advertisement for Pizza Hut, for which he is paid $150,000. It includes a scene at a café table in which customers argue whether Gorbachev brought freedom or chaos to Russia and concludes with an old woman saying that because of him the pizza topping goes all the way to the edge of the crust, at which all cry out, 'Hail, Gorbachev!' Gorbachev cites the need for funds for his foundation as the reason for subjecting himself to this indignity. In 2005 he makes a cameo appearance in the video game *Street Fighter II*. In 2007, the man who once possessed the nuclear suitcase allows himself to be used by French fashion house Louis Vuitton to sell their vanity cases around the world. This advertisement, photographed by Annie Leibovitz, shows a pensive Gorbachev in the back of a limousine, a Louis Vuitton bag on the seat beside him, being driven past the graffiti-covered Berlin Wall. The publication poking out of the bag has a barely readable headline in Russian: 'The Murder of Litvinenko: They Wanted to Give Up the Suspect for $7,000', a reference to the poisoning by radioactive isotope of Russian exile Alexander Litvinenko in London the previous year. On his deathbed Litvinenko blamed agents of Putin's Kremlin. The company's ad agency Ogilvy & Mather denies trying to convey any subliminal message. The magazine *AdWeek* describes the Louis Vuitton image as one of the most successful commercial photographs of the decade.

In 2006, the year when both Gorbachev and Yeltsin celebrate their seventy-fifth birthdays, they still have not mellowed towards each other. Yeltsin accuses Gorbachev, for the first time openly, of having advance knowledge of the August coup and waiting it out to see who would win. 'Yeltsin is a liar, it's sheer nonsense,' responds Gorbachev.

Boris Yeltsin dies of congestive heart failure, on April 23, 2007, aged seventy-six. He is buried in the Novodevichy Cemetery. Putin, then in the second of two four-year terms as president, declares the day of his funeral a national day of mourning. Mikhail Gorbachev goes to the burial and offers faint praise, extending his condolences 'to the family of a man on whose shoulders rested many great deeds for the good of the country and serious mistakes – a tragic fate'. Andrey Kolesnikov, writing in *Kommersant*, describes seeing Gorbachev downcast and suddenly looking much older. 'It was evident that he was suffering in ways that few in the hall were; together with the life of Boris Yeltsin, a piece of his own life had been torn away.'

Two years later, at age seventy-eight, Mikhail Gorbachev announces that he is returning to politics, with the creation of a new political party, the Independent Democratic Party of Russia, which he co-founds with billionaire Alexander Lebedev, part owner of the Russian newspaper *Novaya Gazeta* (New Gazette) and proprietor of three UK newspapers. The party is to be 'social-democratic' and advance an 'anti-crisis initiative' developed by economists at the Gorbachev Foundation.

Gorbachev's ardour for the United States cools further over the years. In 2009, as the US and Europe struggle with economic crises, he chides Americans 'who indulged in the euphoria of victory in the Cold War' for thinking that the West's system did not need any changes. 'So if you insist on me giving advice . . . I do believe that what America needs is its own *perestroika*.'

Apart from a brief period at the end of 1991, surveys show that a majority of Russians consistently regret the break-up of the Soviet Union. A nostalgia for the Soviet era develops, partly prompted by great power nationalism, partly by the desire for a return to the days when there was no threat of terrorism from the Caucasus, and partly by the notion that there were good things about the old Soviet system, such as universal education and peace among the nationalities, and that if there were hardships they were shared by everyone.

Despite his active opposition to the August putsch when he took to the streets to confront the putschists in St Petersburg, Vladimir Putin claims that the events of 1991 tore his life apart. Today he judges Vladimir Kryuchkov, the hardliner who organized the coup attempt and who tried to get the KGB Alpha Group to open fire on the defenders of the Russian White House in August 1991, to be a true believer in communism 'for whom I have the greatest respect'. In an address to the Russian Federal Assembly on April 25, 2005, Putin says, 'Above all, we should acknowledge that the collapse of the Soviet Union was a major geopolitical disaster of the century.' As reasons for saying this, he cites the tens of millions of Russians who find themselves outside Russian territory, the depreciation of individual savings, the destruction of old ideals, the disbanding of institutions, the mass poverty that became the norm and the emergence of the oligarchs. Putin concludes: 'Who could have imagined that it would simply collapse. No one saw that coming – even in their worst nightmares.'

President Putin restores some of the symbols of the lost empire in an effort to revive national pride, pacify the restive empire loyalists and bring stability back to the political system. He allows the Russian army again to fly the red flag, though without the hammer and sickle. He brings back, with new words, the Soviet national anthem that inspired Russians in the struggle against Nazi Germany, replacing the anthem by Mikhail Glinka favoured by Yeltsin. He decrees that Independence Day (June 12, the anniversary of the Russian Supreme Soviet's declaration of sovereignty in 1990) be renamed Russia Day, as the notion of independence places too much emphasis on the break-up of the Kremlin's former empire. The former KGB officer also rehabilitates Felix Dzerzhinsky, whose statue was toppled outside the Lubyanka after the coup. On his orders a bust of the founder of the secret police is placed on a pedestal inside the old KGB headquarters in 2005. Putin becomes prime minister in 2008 when his second term as president expires and he is succeeded by his protégé, Dmitry Medvedev.

In their interaction, Gorbachev and Yeltsin broke the Communist Party's monopoly of power, introduced Russia's first democratic elections, provided a free press, set free the Warsaw Pact states of Eastern Europe, gave independence to once powerless Soviet republics and ended the Cold War. That is their legacy.

Russians today, if they can afford it, are free to live as they please, shop in modern stores, dine in elegant cafés and restaurants, emigrate and travel abroad, send their children to elite foreign schools and freely criticize the regime, in print if not on television. At the same time the move towards Western-style democracy has stalled in the aftermath of the fall of communism, the electronic media reflects Kremlin views, courts are subservient to power, protest rallies are broken up, personal enrichment rather than ideology is the driving force in politics, the electorate is powerless to produce results the leadership doesn't like, and the KGB has returned to the forefront of Russian life as the FSB.

For Mikhail Gorbachev, who turned eighty on March 2, 2011, the nightmare for Russia is far from over. He protests that Russian leaders are steadily rolling back the democratic achievements of his time, and that the first and only free, competitive and honest elections ever held in Russia were those that he initiated before the end of 1991. He observes that there are still many people in society who fear democracy. 'We're only halfway down the road from a totalitarian regime to democracy and freedom,' he says. 'And the battle continues.'

The office in the Senate Building in the Kremlin that Gorbachev was so reluctant to leave and that Yeltsin seized in such triumph is no more. It was ripped out in a major reconstruction that took place from 1994 to 1998. The renovated Senate Building is today the ceremonial residence of the Russian president.

The artefacts from Lenin's former Kremlin office down the corridor have long since been removed and are now on display in his dacha at the village of Gorky Leninskiye on the outskirts of Moscow. The immense picture of *Lenin's Speech at the Third Congress of the Komsomol* which dominated the Great Kremlin Palace for nearly half a century has been replaced by a panorama of Alexander Nevsky of Novgorod fighting Teutonic Knights in 1242.

For two decades the embalmed body of the founder

of the communist system that Gorbachev and Yeltsin in their different ways brought crashing down on December 25, 1991, continues to repose in the Lenin Mausoleum in Red Square, preserved by glycerine and potassium acetate and kept at a temperature of 16 degrees centigrade. Queues of Russians form every day to pay their respects and the jack-booted honour guard still springs to life to march back and forth with the precision of the figures on a Swiss clock, every hour on the hour, at the sound of the chimes from the Saviour Tower, as if nothing has changed.

Bibliography

Alexandrov, Mikhail. *Uneasy Alliance*. Westport, Connecticut: Greenwood Press, 1999.

Andrew, Christopher and Mitrokhin, Vasili. *The Mitrokhin Archive*. London: Penguin, 1999.

Androunas, Elena. 'A Letter from Moscow', *Canadian Journal of Communication*, 1992.

Arbatov, Georgi. *The System*. New York: Random House, 1992.

Aron, Leon. *Boris Yeltsin*. London: HarperCollins, 2000.

Aron, Leon. *Russia's Revolution*. Washington, DC: The AEI Press, 2007.

Baker, III, James A. *The Politics of Diplomacy*. New York: Putnam, 1995.

Berton, Kathleen. *Moscow, an Architectural History*. New York: Macmillan, 1977.

Beschloss, Michael R. and Talbott, Strobe. *At the Highest Levels*. Boston, Toronto, London: Little, Brown and Company, 1993.

Black, J. L. *Inside the Dustbin of History*. Florida: Academic International Press, 1993.

Blasi, Joseph R.; Khroumova, Maya; Kruse, Douglas.

Kremlin Capitalism. Ithaca and London: Cornell University Press, 1997.

Boldin, Valery. *Ten Years that Shook the World*. New York: Basic Books, 1994.

Braithwaite, Rodric. *Across the Moscow River*. New Haven and London: Yale University Press, 2002.

Branch, Taylor. *The Clinton Tapes*. London: Simon & Schuster, 2009.

Breakthrough to Freedom. Compiled by Kuvaldin, Viktor. Moscow: R. Valent Publishers, 2009.

Breslauer, George W. *Gorbachev and Yeltsin as Leaders*. Cambridge University Press, 2002.

Brooke, Peter. 'Alexander Solzhenitsyn and the Battle between Good and Evil'. *Dublin Review of Books*. Issue 14, Summer 2010.

Brown, Archie. *Seven Years That Changed the World*. Oxford University Press, 2007.

Brown, Archie. *The Gorbachev Factor*. Oxford University Press, 1997.

Brown, Archie. *The Rise and Fall of Communism*. New York: Bodley Head, 2009.

Brzezinski, Zbigniew and Sullivan, Paige (editors). *Russia and the Commonwealth of Independent States, Documents, Data and Analysis*. Armonk, New York; London, England: M.E. Sharpe, 1997.

Burlatsky, Fyodor. *Mikhail Gorbachev – Boris Yeltsin: Skhvatka* (Fight). Moscow: Sobraniye, 2008.

Bush, George and Scowcroft, Brent. *A World Transformed*. New York: Vintage Books, 1999.

Chernyaev, Anatoly. *Byl li u Rossii Shans? On Posledny* (Did Russia Have a Chance? It is the Last One). Moscow: Sobraniye, 2003.

Chernyaev, Anatoly. *1991: Dnevnik Pomoshchnika Prezidenta SSSR* (Diary of an Assistant to the President of the USSR). Moscow: Terra, Respublika, 1997.

Chernyaev, Anatoly. *My Six Years with Gorbachev*.

University Park, Pennsylvania: Pennsylvania State University Press, 2000.

Cienciala, Anna M.; Lebedeva, Natalia S.; Materski, Wojciech. *Katyn*. New Haven and London: Yale University Press, 2007.

Cohen, Stephen F. and van den Heuvel, Katrina. *Voices of Glasnost*. New York and London: W. W. Norton & Company, 1989.

Coleman, Fred. *The Decline and Fall of the Soviet Empire*. New York: St. Martin's Press, 1996.

Colton, Timothy J. *Yeltsin, a Life*. New York: Basic Books, 2008.

Conte, Francis. *Great Dates in Russian and Soviet History*. New York: Facts On File, 1994.

Crawshaw, Steve. *Goodbye to the USSR*. London: Bloomsbury, 1992.

Der Spiegel. Transcripts of coup leaders' interrogations. October 7, 1991. JPRS-UPA-91-047.

Dobbs, Michael. *Down With Big Brother*. London: Bloomsbury, 1997.

Dobrynin, Anatoly. *In Confidence*. New York: Times Books, 1995.

Doder, Dusko. *Shadows and Whispers*. New York: Random House, 1986.

Dunlop, John B. *The Rise of Russia and the Fall of the Soviet Empire*. Princeton University Press, 1993.

Elletson, Harold. *The General Against the Kremlin*. London: Warner Books, 1998.

Felshman, Neil. *Gorbachev, Yeltsin and the Last Days of the Soviet Empire*. New York: St. Martin's Press, 1992.

Fishlock, Trevor. *Out of Red Darkness*. London: John Murray, 1992.

Fitzwater, Marlin. *Call the Briefing!* New York: Times Books, 1995.

Foreign Broadcast Information Service (FBIS) Virginia, Daily Reports.

Gaddis, John Lewis. *The Cold War*. London: Penguin, 2005.

Gaidar, Yegor. *Collapse of an Empire*. Washington, DC: Brookings Institution Press, 2007.

Gaidar, Yegor. *Days of Defeat and Victory*. Seattle and London: University of Washington Press, 1999.

Garthoff, Raymond. *The Great Transition*. Washington, DC: Brookings Institution Press, 1994.

Gates, Robert M. *From the Shadows*. New York: Simon & Schuster Paperbacks, 2006.

Gevorkyan, Nataliya; Timakova, Natalya; Kolesnikov, Andrei. *First Person*. New York: PublicAffairs, 2000.

Ghitis, Frida. *The End of Revolution*. New York: Algora Publishing, 2001.

Gorbachev, Mikhail and Mlynář, Zdeněk. *Conversations with Gorbachev*. New York: Columbia University Press, 2002.

Gorbachev, Mikhail. *Dekabr-91: Moya Pozitsiya* (December '91: My Position). Moscow: Novosti, 1991.

Gorbachev, Mikhail. *Memoirs*. London: Bantam Books, 1997.

Gorbachev, Mikhail. *On My Country and the World*. New York: Columbia University Press, 2000.

Gorbachev, Mikhail. *The August Coup*. London: HarperCollins, 1991.

Gorbacheva, Raisa. *I Hope*. New York: HarperCollins Publishers, 1991.

Grachev, Andrei. *Final Days*. Westview, 1995.

Grachev, Andrei. *Gorbachev's Gamble*. Polity, 2008.

Handelman, Stephen. *Comrade Criminal*. New Haven and London: Yale University Press, 1995.

Hoffman, David E. *The Oligarchs*. New York: PublicAffairs, 2002, 2003.

Hough, Jerry F. *Democratization and Revolution in the USSR 1985–1991*. Washington, DC: Brookings Institution Press, 1997.

Ilyin, Alexander. *Gennady Zyuganov: 'Pravda' o Vozhde*

('Truth' about the Leader), Moscow: Algoritm, 2005.

Judt, Tony. *Postwar*. Penguin, 2005.

Kalugin, Oleg with Montaigne, Fen. *The First Directorate*. New York: St. Martin's Press, 1994.

Kelley, Kitty. *Nancy Reagan*. London: Bantam Press, 1991.

Khasbulatov, Ruslan. *The Struggle for Russia*. London and New York: Routledge, 1993.

Korzhakov, Alexander. *Boris Yeltsin: ot rassveta do zakata* [From Dawn to Dusk]. Moscow: Detektivpress, 2004.

Kotkin, Stephen. *Armageddon Averted*. Oxford University Press: 2008.

Kotz, David with Weir, Fred. *Revolution from Above*. London and New York: Routledge, 1997.

Kripal, Jeffrey John. *Esalen: America and the Religion of No Religion*. University of Chicago Press, 2007.

Kuznetsov, Alexander. *Kamera dlya Prezidenta* (Camera for the President). Moscow: ACT, 2007.

Lewis, Ben. *Hammer & Tickle*. London: Weidenfeld & Nicolson, 2008.

Lieven, Anatol. *The Baltic Revolution*. New Haven and London: Yale University Press, 1993.

Ligachev, Yegor. *Inside Gorbachev's Kremlin*. New York: Pantheon Books, 1993.

Liu Heung Shing. *USSR: The Collapse of an Empire*. Hong Kong: Asia 2000 Ltd, 1992.

Loory, Stuart H. *Seven Days that Shook the World*. Atlanta: Turner Publishing, 1991.

Lourie, Richard. *Sakharov*. Hanover and London: Brandeis University Press, 2002.

Lucas, Edward. *The New Cold War*. New York: Bloomsbury, 2008.

Major, John. *Autobiography*. London: HarperCollins, 1999.

Marples, David R. *The Collapse of the Soviet Union 1985–1991*. New York: Pearson Education Limited, 2004.

Matlock, Jack. *Autopsy of an Empire*. New York: Random House, 1995.

Matthews, Tom. 'The Coup Makers' Secrets', *Newsweek*, September 9, 1991.

Maynard, Christopher. *Out of the Shadow*. College Station, Texas: TAMU Press, 2008.

McFaul, Michael. *Russia's Unfinished Revolution*. Ithaca, New York: Cornell University Press, 2001.

McFaul, Michael and Markov, Sergei. *The Troubled Birth of Russian Democracy*. Stanford, California: Hoover Institution Press, 1993.

McGiffert Ekedahl, Carolyn and Goodman, Melvin A. *The Wars of Eduard Shevardnadze*. London: Hurst & Company, 1997.

Medvedev, Roy. *Post-Soviet Russia*. New York: Columbia University Press, 2000.

Medvedev, Roy. *Sovetsky Soyuz* (The Soviet Union). Moscow: Prava Cheloveka, 2003.

Medvedev, Roy. *Sovetsky Soyuz: Posledniye Godi Zhizni* (The Soviet Union: Last Years of Life). Moscow: Prava Cheloveka, 2009.

Medvedev, Roy and Chiesa, Giulietto. *Time of Change*. New York: Penguin, 1989.

Mickiewicz, Ellen. *Changing Channels*. Durham and London: Duke University Press, 1999.

Mlechin, Leonid. *Boris Yeltsin: Poslesloviye* (Afterword). Moscow: Centrpoligraf, 2007.

Moran, John P. *From Garrison State to Nation-State*. Westport, Connecticut and London: Praeger, 2002.

Murray, Donald. *A Democracy of Despots*. Montreal, Kingston, London, Buffalo: McGill-Queen's University Press, 1995.

Murray, John. *Politics and Place-Names*. Birmingham: University of Birmingham Press, 2000.

Nemtsov, Boris. *Ispoved Buntarya* (Confession of a Rebel). Moscow: Partizan, 2007.

Oberdorfer, Don. *The Turn*. London: Jonathan Cape, 1992.

O'Clery, Conor. *Melting Snow*. Belfast: Appletree Press, 1991.

Odling-Smee, John. *The IMF and Russia in the 1990s*. IMF Working Paper, WP/04/155.

Odom, William E. *The Collapse of the Soviet Military*. New Haven and London: Yale University Press, 1998.

Palazchenko, Pavel. *My Years with Gorbachev and Shevardnadze*. University Park, Pennsylvania: Pennsylvania State University Press, 1997.

Pankin, Boris. *The Last Hundred Days of the Soviet Union*. London, New York: I.B. Tauris, 1996.

Politkovskaya, Anna. *Putin's Russia*. London: The Harvill Press, 2004.

Powell, Colin. *My American Journey*. New York: Random House, 1995.

Pozner, Vladimir. *Eyewitness*. New York: Random House, 1992.

Primakov, Yevgeny. *Russian Crossroads*. New Haven and London: Yale University Press, 2004.

Pry, Vincent. *War Scare*. Westport, Connecticut and London: Praeger, 1999.

Pryce-Jones, David. *The War that Never Was*. London: Weidenfeld & Nicolson, 1995.

Putsch. Progress Publishers/IP, 1991.

Radio Free Europe/Radio Liberty Daily Reports: Archives (Budapest).

Raspad SSSR (The Fall of the USSR). Compiled by Shubin, A.B. Moscow: Rossiyskaya Akademiya Nauk, Institut Vseobschei Istorii, 2006.

Reagan, Nancy. *My Turn*. New York: Random House, 1989.

Remnick, David. *Lenin's Tomb*. New York: Random House, 1993.

Roxburgh, Angus. *The Second Russian Revolution*. BBC Books, 1991.

Sakharov, Andrei. *Memoirs*. New York: Knopf, 1990.

Sakharov, Andrei. *Moscow and Beyond 1986 to 1989*. New York: Knopf, 1991.

Sandle, Mark. *Gorbachev, Man of the Twentieth Century?* London: Hodder Education, 2008.

Satter, David. *Age of Delirium*. New York: Knopf, 1996.

Service, Robert. *The Penguin History of Modern Russia*. London: Penguin, 1997.

Shakhnazarov, Georgy. *Tsena Svobody* (The Price of Freedom). Moscow: Rossika Zevs, 1993.

Shane, Scott. *Dismantling Utopia*. Chicago: Ivan R. Dee, 1994.

Shaposhnikov, Yevgeny. *Vybor* (Choice). Nezavisimoe Izdatelstvo PIK, 1995.

Shevardnadze, Eduard. *Moi Vybor* (My Choice). Moscow: Novosti, 1991.

Shevardnadze, Eduard. *The Future Belongs to Freedom*. New York: The Free Press, 1991.

Shevchenko, Iulia. *The Central Government of Russia*. Farnham, Surrey: Ashgate Publishing, 2004.

Shubin, A.B. *Paradoksy Perestroiki* (Perestroika's Paradoxes). Moscow: Veche, 2005.

Shulgan, Christopher. *The Soviet Ambassador*. Toronto: M&S, 2008.

Shultz, George P. *Turmoil and Triumph*. New York: Charles Scribner's Sons, 1993.

Sixsmith, Martin. *Moscow Coup*. London: Simon & Schuster, 1991.

Sixsmith, Martin. *Putin's Oil*. New York: Continuum, 2010.

Solovyov, Vladimir and Klepikova, Elena. *Boris Yeltsin*. London: Weidenfeld & Nicolson, 1992.

Steele, Jonathan. *Eternal Russia*. Cambridge, Massachusetts: Harvard University Press, 1994.

Sukhanov, Lev. *Tri Goda s Yeltsinym* (Three Years with Yeltsin). Riga: Vaga, 1992.

Suraska, Wisla. *How the Soviet Union Disappeared*. Durham and London: Duke University Press, 1998.

Talbott, Strobe. *The Great Experiment*. New York: Simon & Schuster, 2008.

Thatcher, Margaret. *The Downing Street Years*. London: HarperCollins, 1995.

The USSR Today. Eighth Edition. The Current Digest of the Soviet Press, 1991.

Timofeyev, Lev. *Russia's Secret Rulers*. New York: Knopf, 1992.

Turner, Ted. *Call Me Ted*. London: Sphere, 2008.

Urban, Michael. *The Rebirth of Politics in Russia*. Cambridge University Press, 1997.

V Politburo CK KPSS (In the Politburo of the Central Committee of the Communist Party of the Soviet Union). Moscow: Gorbachev Foundation, 2008.

Vaksberg, Arkady. *The Soviet Mafia*. New York: St. Martin's Press, 1992.

Vorotnikov, V.I. *A Bylo Eto Tak . . .* (And That's How It Was . . .). Moscow: Kniga i Biznes, 2003.

Wedel, Janine R. *Collision & Collusion*. New York: Palgrave, 2001.

White, Stephen. *Gorbachev and After*. Cambridge University Press, 1992.

White, Stephen; Gill, Graeme; Slider, Darrell. *The Politics of Transition*. Cambridge University Press, 1993.

Wilson, Andrew. *The Ukrainians*. New Haven and London: Yale University Press, 2009.

Yakovlev, Alexander N. *A Century of Violence in Soviet Russia*. New Haven and London: Yale University Press, 2000.

Yakovlev, Alexander N. *Sumerki* (Dusk). Moscow: Materik, 2003.

Yeltsin, Boris. *Against the Grain*. London: Jonathan Cape, 1990.

Yeltsin, Boris. *The Struggle for Russia*. New York: Times Books, 1994.

Zenkovich, Nikolay. *Boris Yeltsin: Raznye Zhizni* (Different

Lives). Moscow: Olma-Press, 2001.

Zenkovich, Nikolay. *Malchishki v Rozovykh Shtanishkakh* (Boys in Pink Shorts). Moscow: Olma-Press, 1999.

Zlotnik, Marc. 'Yeltsin and Gorbachev'. *Journal of Cold War Studies*. Vol. 5, No. 1, Winter, 2003.

Other Materials

Current Digest of Soviet Press
www.eastview.com/Online/SlavicProducts/CDPSP.aspx
Documentary on Fall of Soviet Union
www.youtube.com/watch?v=j-2kx549Mf0
Making the History of 1989 www.chnm.gmu.edu/1989/

Notes on Sources

Translations from books and newspapers published in Russian are my own. Comments and opinions attributed in the text to dramatis personae are generally from my interviews or from the publications listed in the bibliography, unless otherwise stated. Much of the historical detail from 1987 to 1991 is based on my own reporting.

'Goodbye our Red Flag' is from *Don't Die Before You're Dead* by Yevgeny Yevtushenko. New York: Random House, 1995; London: Robson Books, 1998.

Introduction
Description of the colonels is from Palazchenko, p. 361.
Key written sources on nuclear suitcase throughout are Odom, Pry, and Vladimir Umnov in *Ogonyok*, March 1997.
Details of Soviet nuclear arsenal are from Congressional Research Services, Issue Brief 91144.
James Baker's comment is from Baker, p. 583.
Bush's comment is from Bush and Scowcroft, p. 555.

Visit by Christian evangelists is described in Grachev, *Final Days*, p. 87.

1   December 25: Before the Dawn

Weather details are from *www.tutiempo.net*.

Description of Red Square is from contemporary newspaper accounts.

I visited Church of St Louis before this date and spoke to Sofia Peonkova.

Yulia Massarskaya's comment is from *Boston Globe* account by Elizabeth Neuffer, December 25, 1991.

Rationing details from Gaidar, *Days of Defeat and Victory*, p. 111.

2   December 25: Sunrise

Murashev encounter is from Murray, p. 136.

Gorbachev's dacha and couple's lifestyle are described in Gorbacheva's *I Hope*, and in Gorbachev's *Memoirs*; other details are from Chernyaev, *My Six Years*, Korzhakov and Boldin. I take into account Boldin's antipathy to the Gorbachevs throughout.

Raisa Gorbacheva speaks of her fear of telephones in *I Hope*, p. 174.

Account of dream is from Shakhnazarov, p. 493.

Gorbachev's sense of destiny is also explored in Sandle.

Yeltsin's night-time habits and domestic life are from his autobiographies, and Korzhakov, Colton, Aron, Sukhanov, and Solovyov and Klepikova.

Yeltsin describes Rutskoy buying him shoes in *The Struggle for Russia*, p. 32.

Yeltsin's grooming ritual is well described in Solovyov and Klepikova, p. 91.

Naina's description of Yeltsin as 'stone wall' is from August 1992 supplement to *Izvestia*.

3   Hiring the Bulldozer

Reference to Mayakovsky is in Boldin, p. 279.

Yeltsin playing spoons is from Korzhakov, pp. 78–9.

Gorbachev describes Yeltsin intoxicated in *Memoirs*, p. 235.

Description of Gorbachev's Old Square office is from Boldin, p. 66.

Ryzhkov's warning about Yeltsin is in Gorbachev, *Memoirs*, p. 235.

4   December 25: Morning

Gorbachev's comments to ABC Television are from interviews with Ted Koppel and Rick Kaplan.

Koppel dialogue with Gorbachev is from ABC footage.

'So we're going to fly' is in Gorbachev and Mlynář, p. 92.

Hairdresser ritual is from Boldin, p. 225.

Pestov removal and Aushev incident are from Chernyaev, *1991*, diary entries for December 15 and December 20.

Gorbachev's office is described by Boldin.

5   The Storming of Moscow

Conversation on farm is from Shulgan, pp. 265–7.

Privileges of top party members are listed in Dobrynin, pp. 621–2.

Yeltsin dispensing watches is from Korzhakov, pp. 72–3.

Gorbachev's hospital visit is described by Boldin, p. 68.

Gorbachev's instruction to Afanasyev is in Colton, p. 131.

Scolding of Poltoranin is from Matlock, p. 112.

6   December 25: Mid-morning

Description of interior of White House is from Solovyov and Klepikova, p. 276.

Gaidar's comment on media is from interview.

7   A Bucketful of Filth

Yeltsin's exhaustion is described in Colton, p. 125.

Description of Foros is from Chernyaev, *My Six Years*, p. 167.

Comment to Diane Sawyer is in Aron, *Boris Yeltsin*, p. 191.

Gorbachev's sacking of Yeltsin is mainly from Colton, pp. 138–50, Aron, *Boris Yeltsin*, pp. 202–20, Boldin, Chernyaev, *My Six Years*, Gorbachev and Yeltsin memoirs, and my contemporary notes.

Poltoranin's fabrication is in Colton, p. 153.

Zaikov's boast is from Colton, p. 150.

Gorbachev's vow to ban Yeltsin from politics is in Aron, *Boris Yeltsin*, p. 221.

Yeltsin coming across Nechayev is from Korzhakov, p. 86.

8 December 25: Late Morning

Account of Supreme Soviet proceedings is from *Rossiskaya Gazeta*. December 26, 1991.

Kichikhin's remarks are from *Sovetskaya Rossiya*, December 26, 1991.

9 Back from the Dead

Yeltsin describes his distress in *Against the Grain*, pp. 156–8.

Yeltsin in new job and erratic driving are from Sukhanov, pp. 302–4.

Gorbachev's last-minute resolution on elections is described in Brown, *The Rise and Fall of Communism*, p. 515.

Korotich comments are from my contemporary interview.

Yeltsin v. Brakov is from Yeltsin, *Against the Grain*, p. 142.

Comment on 'the bell tolls' is in Gorbachev, *Memoirs*, p. 365.

Solzhenitsyn's comment is from paper for National Arts Club, NY, in 1987.

Gorbachev's musing about retirement is in Chernyaev, *My Six Years*, p. 245.

10 December 25: Midday

Boldin describes Gorbachev's eating habits.

Gorbachev quoting Pushkin is from Grachev, *Final Days*, p. 186.

Story of the South Korean gift is from Boldin, p. 283.

Discussion on royalties and details of Chernyaev's private life are from Chernyaev, *1991*, diary entries for December 18 and December 27.

Amsterdam trip is in Chernyaev's *My Six Years*, p. 4.

Gerasimov on Chernyaev's private life is from *Sovetskaya Belorussiya*, January 11, 2003.

Conversation with Belyaev is from Gorbachev's *Dekabr-91*, p. 96.

Yakovlev 'no longer master' is from Chernyaev, *1991*, diary entry for December 1.

Grachev's comments on Koppel are from interview.

11 Knee-deep in Kerosene

Details of Yeltsin's visit to the USA are mainly from Sukhanov, pp. 143–50, and interview with Jim Garrison.

Yeltsin's behaviour in Baltimore and in White House is from interview with Jim Garrison.

Scowcroft's behaviour during Yeltsin's visit to White House is from Gates, p. 479.

Nenashev's treatment of Yeltsin footage is from Mickiewicz, p. 93.

Theories on Yeltsin falling into the river are explored by Korzhakov, pp. 92–8, and Solovyov and Klepikova, pp. 178–81.

Boldin describes trappings of Gorbachev's presidency, pp. 251–2.

Gorbachev's contrived tantrum is in Timofeyev, p. 78.

Russia's declaration of sovereignty, Sakharov's funeral, election of Gorbachev as president and May Day parade are mainly from my contemporary notes.

Television treatment of May Day broadcast is in Mickiewicz, p. 6.

Raisa comment is from Palazchenko, p. 289.

Gorbachev's plane journey to USA is from Palazchenko, p. 189.

Gorbachev at Camp David is from Beschloss and Talbott, pp. 224–6.

Narciss and Brevno nicknames are from Burlatsky, p. 41.

'Social democracy' quotation is from Brown's *The Gorbachev Factor*, p. 102.

The 'rabid dog' quotation is in Chernyaev, *My Six Years*, p. 280.

The 'no cheese' anecdote is in Beschloss and Talbott, p. 108.

Gorbachev's warning to newspaper editors is related by Chernyaev in *My Six Years*, p. 201.

12   December 25: Early Afternoon

Work on speech is from Chernyaev, *My Six Years*, p. 339, and Chernyaev, *1991*, diary entries for December 18 and December 20.

Shevardnadze and Yakovlev's comments are from Chernyaev, *1991*, diary entry for December 18.

Difficulty calling Bush is from Palazchenko, pp. 364–5.

Gorbachev comments are from ABC television unedited footage of December 25, 1991.

13   Dictatorship on the Offensive

I visited Moscow pensioners with Red Cross.

Gerasimov comment on Nobel Prize is from my notes of briefing.

Gorbachev told me in Ottawa he had considered a referendum on Ryzhkov's plan.

Hedgehog and snake comment is in Aron, *Boris Yeltsin*, p. 404.

Boldin's secret information department is revealed by Chernyaev in *My Six Years*, p. 339.

Kravchenko's relationship with Gorbachev is explored in Mickiewicz, p. 50.

Pozner describes his sacking in *Eyewitness*, p. 67.

Events in Baltics from my reporting.

I attended Yeltsin meeting with deputies on his return from Estonia.

Chernyaev resignation letter is reproduced in Chernyaev, *My Six Years*, pp. 320–4.

'Gangster' quotation is from Gorbachev and Mlynář, p. 132.

Comment on Gorbachev doing what Americans wanted is from Gates, p. 528.

The 'wild man' and 'drive Gorbachev nuts' quotations, and Yakovlev's remark to Boren, are from Beschloss and Talbott, p. 350.

The incident with Hurd is described in Braithwaite, p. 380.

14 December 25: Mid-afternoon

Grachev on Raisa's phone call is from interview.

Raisa's role is comprehensively analysed in Felshman, pp. 189–206.

Colton describes Yeltsin raising Raisa's role with Gorbachev.

Lyudmila Sobchak's comment is from Zenkovich, *Boris Yeltsin*, p. 58.

Laptiev story is from Braithwaite, p. 254.

Naina on plumbing is from Zenkovich, *Boris Yeltsin*, p. 58.

Television treatment of Raisa by Nenashev and Kravchenko is from Mickiewicz, p. 44.

'Cold war' of first ladies is from Kelley, pp. 400–3 and 443–6.

Gary Hart anecdote is from Bush and Scowcroft, p. 6.

Raisa on her private life and on Yeltsin is from Gorbacheva, pp. 7 and 180.

Gorbachev on Raisa's vulnerability is from 2009 interview with Ginny Dougary on Gorbachev Foundation website.

Gorbachev discloses extent of Raisa's illness in *Novaya Gazeta*, February 17, 2011.

15 Hijacking Barbara Bush

The fight for Channel 2 is described in Mickiewicz, pp. 96–7.

Content of Channel 2 is from Shane, p. 180.

Hannelore Kohl incident is in Colton, p. 298.

The 'two bears' comment is from Grachev, *Final Days*, p. 6.

Sources for the Popov incident are Chernyaev, *My Six Years*, Matlock, Baker, Gates, Palazchenko, Beschloss and Talbott, and Bush and Scowcroft.

Incident in Bolshoi Theatre is described in Chernyaev, *My Six Years*, pp. 365–6.

Yeltsin threat, 'Don't force us' is from Boldin, p. 55.

Delors' advice is in Palazchenko, p. 298.

Comment on 'end of empire' is from Gaidar, *Collapse of an Empire*, p. 219.

KGB surveillance of the Gorbachevs is from Andrew and Mitrokhin, p. 513.

Yeltsin's behaviour during Bush visit is described in Chernyaev, *My Six Years*, p. 360, Matlock, pp. 563–6, Palazchenko, pp. 299–306, Beschloss and Talbott, pp. 411–13, Bush and Scowcroft, pp. 510–13 and Gorbachev, *Memoirs*, pp. 806–7.

Gorbachev on being 'tired as hell' is from Chernyaev, *My Six Years*, p. 369.

Account of KGB tip-off to Yakovlev is from Kalugin, pp. 347–8.

16   December 25: Late Afternoon

Conversation between Gorbachev and Bush is from Bush and Scowcroft, pp. 559–61.

Palazchenko's thoughts on Gorbachev and Bush are in Palazchenko, pp. 365–6.

Palazchenko's talk with Yakovlev is in Palazchenko, p. 358.

CNN's activities here and elsewhere are from interviews with Charlie Caudill, Frida Ghitis, Steve Hurst, Tom Johnson, Stuart Loory and Claire Shipman.

Yeltsin sweating 'buckets' is from Yeltsin, *The Struggle for Russia*, p. 21.

Kuznetsov's forecast is from Kuznetsov, p. 12.

17 Perfidiousness, Lawlessness, Infamy

To describe coup attempt of August 1991 I have drawn on accounts by Aron, Boldin, Chernyaev, Colton, Dobbs, Dunlop, Gorbachev, Remnick, Steele and Yeltsin, and in Russian, Korzhakov and Shaposhnikov.

Bush phone call to Yeltsin is from Beschloss and Talbott, p. 434.

Putin describes his role in Gevorkyan, Timakova and Kolesnikov, p. 93.

Gorbachev includes Raisa's diary of the coup in Gorbachev, *Memoirs*, pp. 817–24.

Removal of nuclear suitcase is in Dobbs, p. 391.

Bush's reactions and his telephone calls are from Beschloss and Talbott, p. 532.

Raisa's distress is disclosed in Gorbachev interview in *Novaya Gazeta*, February 17, 2011.

Strauss reference is from Beschloss and Talbott, pp. 444–5.

Yakovlev's quotation, 'The party's dead', is in Remnick, p. 495.

Account of Gorbachev's ordeal in Russian parliament is in Khasbulatov, pp. 170–84.

CNN's role in the coup is mainly from interview with Tom Johnson.

Role of media during coup is detailed in Mickiewicz, p. 105.

18 December 25: Dusk

Conversation in Gorbachev's office is detailed by Grachev in *Final Days*, p. 188, and in interview.

Gorbachev's comment to Ceausˏescu is from *Making the History of 1989* database, item 692.

Shevardnadze's 1984 warning is from Timofeyev, p. 37.

Conversation with Sakharov is in *Moscow and Beyond*, p. 133.

Galina Brezhnev episode was related by legal writer Arkady Vaksberg in Remnick, p. 193.

Gifts allegedly kept by Gorbachev are detailed by Boldin, p. 129.

Interpreter's comment is from Palazchenko, p. 365.

19 Things Fall Apart

Shakhnazarov and Burbulis meeting is from Shakhnazarov, p. 284.

Mitterrand incident is related in Grachev, *Final Days*, pp. 80–2.

Anarchy in Yeltsin's ranks is described in Solovyov and Klepikova, pp. 273–4.

Genscher meeting is detailed in Grachev, *Final Days*, pp. 51–5.

Attitudes to Gorbachev in Madrid are revealed in Palazchenko, p. 339, and Beschloss and Talbott, p. 447.

Request to USA to save Soviet foreign ministry is in Pankin, p. 236.

Rumours of nuclear threat against Ukraine are discussed in Gaidar's *Collapse of an Empire*, and in Odom, Pry and Shaposhnikov.

Gorbachev on military option to save union is in Shaposhnikov, diary entry for December 24, 1991.

Grachev on Gorbachev 'testing' Shaposhnikov is from interview.

Reference to *Gone With the Wind* is from Gorbachev and Mlynář, p. 129.

Banter between Gorbachev and Yeltsin is from Grachev, *Final Days*, p. 112.

Exchange in Fireplace Room is related in Grachev, *Final Days*, pp. 122–3.

Russian–Ukraine historical ties are detailed in Wilson.

Yeltsin on car phone to Gorbachev is from Chernyaev, *1991*, diary entry for December 3.

20 December 25: Early Evening

Popov's appeal is from Baker, p. 530.

Muscovites recalling hardships were interviewed for this book.

Bread-shop incident is from interview with Gaidar.

Gaidar's recollection of 'grim food lines' is from Gaidar's *Days of Defeat and Victory*.

Influence of Harvard economists is analysed in Wedel, pp. 127–8.

Soviet Union 'bankrupt' is from interview with Gaidar.

Wolf–Nechayev encounter is from Kotz, p. 169.

Koppel's encounter with Zhirinovsky is from ABC footage.

Thieves' World meeting is from Handelman, p. 13.

Milshtein quote is in Aron's *Russia's Revolution*, p. 191.

21 The Centre Cannot Hold

How the Belovezh Agreement was reached is from interview with Gaidar and written sources including Yeltsin's *The Struggle for Russia*, Grachev's *Final Days*, Gaidar's *Days of Defeat and Victory*, Korzhakov, Medvedev, Shushkevich in various newspaper interviews, Shaposhnikov and Wilson.

Comment to Niles is from Brzezinski and Sullivan, p. 43.

Kravchuk's account of his reply to Yeltsin's three questions is in Burlatsky, p. 120.

Details of signing ceremony are from Loginov, pp. 462–3, and *Sovetskaya Byelorussia*, '45 People at the Table, by Lyudmila Maslyukova', December 8, 2001.

Pateychuk describes her role on *Liberty Life Radio* Belarusian Service, December 8, 2006.

Attempt to call Nazarbayev is described in Korzhakov, pp. 160–4.

Shakhrai comments are from *www.vesti.ru*, December 12, 2001.

Claim about the helicopter is from interview with Grachev.

Yeltsin's call to Shaposhnikov is from Shaposhnikov, diary entry for December 8, 1991.

Gorbachev's anger with Shaposhnikov is from his *Memoirs*, pp. 848–9.

Bush thoughts on telephone call from Yeltsin are from Bush and Scowcroft, pp. 554–5.

Gorbachev fury with Yeltsin is from his *Memoirs*, p. 849.

Chernyaev's 'You can only laugh' is from Chernyaev, *1991*, diary entry for December 10.

Rutskoy's reaction is from Medvedev, *Sovetsky Soyuz: Posledniye Godi Zhizni*, pp. 567–8.

Tsipko's and Shmelev's comments are from Gorbachev Foundation's *Breakthrough to Freedom*.

Volsky's comment is in Hough, p. 482.

Gorbachev claim that ending Soviet law was illegal is from his *Dekabr-91*, p. 67.

Grachev dinner anecdote is from Grachev, *Final Days*, p. 146.

Baker's 'geopolitical nightmare' is from Baker, p. 563.

Gorbachev's 'petty people' comment is in Chernyaev, *1991*, diary entry for December 12.

Burbulis's 'medical diagnosis' is related in Steele, p. 232.

Braithwaite and Appleyard encounter is in Braithwaite, p. 268.

'Write this up' is from Chernyaev, *1991*, diary entry for December 14.

Story of the alleged plot to discredit Gorbachev is from Beschloss and Talbott, pp. 455–6, and Palazchenko, pp. 353–4.

Yeltsin's promise to Bush is in Bush and Scowcroft, p. 557.

Garrison described his visit to Gorbachev in interview.

The 'poisoned the air' quotation is in Remnick, p. 499.

Yakovlev on 'dumb' leaders is from Chernyaev, *1991*, entry for December 18.

Yakovlev's comments are from his *Sumerki*, diary entry for December 22.

22 December 25: Evening

Sequence of events in the Kremlin is from Grachev interview.

Liu Heung Shing's experiences here and elsewhere are from interview.

Other details of prelude to speech are from CNN footage and still photographs, and from interviews with Caudill and Johnson.

23   The Deal in the Walnut Room

Meeting between Gorbachev and Yeltsin is described in written accounts by Shulgan, pp. 294–8, and Yakovlev's *Sumerki*, diary entry for December 23.

Koppel and Grachev described to me the prelude to the meeting.

Yeltsin's agreement on Gorbachev vacating Kremlin office is recorded in Gorbachev, *Memoirs*, p. 866.

December 29 deadline is in Shakhnazarov, p. 294.

The IRA arms plot is revealed in Yeltsin, *The Struggle for Russia*, pp. 311–16.

Handing over of archives is described in Dobbs, pp. 310–14.

Comment on 'this hellish paper' is from Gorbachev's *Memoirs*, p. 621.

Opening of Katyn files is described in Cienciala, Lebedeva and Materski, pp. 254–5.

'Confess it now . . .' is from Timofeyev, p. 26.

Verbal exchange on foundation's role is in Sandle, p. 273.

Rutskoy's comment on Gorbachev's long-windedness is from Solovyov and Klepikova, p. 281.

Yeltsin's post-meeting comments are from Coleman, p. 354.

Gorbachev's distress is described by Yakovlev in *Sumerki*, diary entry for December 23.

24   December 25: Late Evening

Text of Gorbachev's address is from his *Memoirs*, pp. xxxii–vii.

Chernyaev's thoughts are from Chernyaev, *1991*, diary entry for December 27.

Yakovlev's opinion is from *Sumerki*, diary entry for December 23.

Other reactions are from interviews with Caudill, Hurst, Johnson, Liu, Shipman and Somov.

Kampfner describes visit to Kerbel in *New Statesman*, December 18, 1998.

Gaidar's comments are from interview.

Bush and Scowcroft comments are from Bush and Scowcroft, pp. 563–4.

Powell comment is in Powell, p. 546.

25 December 25: Night

Yeltsin's second thoughts on allowing Gorbachev's broadcast are from ARD German television, cited in *FBIS Daily Report*, December 30, 1991.

Shaposhnikov's thoughts on Gorbachev are from Shaposhnikov, diary entry for December 25.

Gorbachev on dispute over nuclear suitcase is in his *Memoirs*, pp. 865–6.

Schmemann in interview relates how he established time of lowering of flag. Most Russian accounts follow *Izvestia* which put time at 7.38 p.m.

German photographer's comment is in Dobbs account in *Washington Post*, December 26, 1991.

Loory and Caudill describe suitcase transfer and flag disposal in interviews.

Shushkevich told me of his reaction to Gorbachev's address.

Gerwe comment is from *Financial Times*, December 28, 2011.

26 December 25: Late Night

'Homo Sovieticus' comment is in Chernyaev, *My Six Years*, p. 399.

Akayev incident is in Colton, p. 391.

Gorbachev's suspicions of Yakovlev are detailed by Shulgan, pp. 14–15.

Yakovlev boast about destroying the system is from Odom, p. 439.

Yakovlev's sentiment on red flag is from Dunlop, p. 9.

Grachev on 'Judas' is from Grachev, *Final Days*, p. 191.

Shevardnadze comment on Nobel Prize was made on Radio Free Europe on October 2, 2009.

Gorbachev instruction on his royalties is from Chernyaev, *1991*, diary entry for December 27.

Gorbachev on his gratitude to aides is in *Dekabr-91*, pp. 120–1.

Grachev on atmosphere is from interview.

Meeting of Yeltsin with Shaposhnikov is from Odom, pp. 371–2, and Shaposhnikov, diary entry for December 25.

Tbilisi event is from Ghitis, p. 18, and interview.

27   December 26: The Day After

Chiesa described in interview the atmosphere in the Kremlin.

Grachev writes about stopped clock in Grachev, *Final Days*, p. 194.

Incident with Spanish ambassador is in Chernyaev, *1991*, diary entry for December 27.

Message from his mother is in Gorbachev, *Dekabr-91*, p. 124.

Gorbachev on his big plans is from *Time*, January 6, 1992.

Gorbachev on his great task is in Coleman, p. 355.

Chernyaev on Gorbachev's greatest mistake is from *Washington Post*, December 27, 1991.

Putin campaign against red flag is from Gevorkyan, Timakova and Kolesnikov, pp. 95–6.

28   December 27: Triumph of the Plunderers

Yeltsin's arrival in Gorbachev's office is described in Shakhnazarov, p. 309, and in Chernyaev, *1991*, diary entry for December 28, 1991.

Gorbachev humiliating himself is from Chernyaev, *1991*, diary entry for December 27.

The 'triumph of plunderers' is from Gorbachev, *Memoirs*, p. 866.

Yeltsin on long farewells is from his *The Struggle for Russia*, p. 124.

Tanya's comments are from Solovyov and Klepikova, p. 270.

Gorbachev remarks to Japanese journalists are in Shakhnazarov, p. 309.

Japanese offer of $1 million is from Chernyaev, *1991*, diary entry for December 28.

Takeover of Soviet television is described by Elena Androunas in *Canadian Journal of Communication*, Vol. 17, No. 4, 1992.

Account of Raisa's distress is from Gorbachev interview with Dmitry Muratov in *Novaya Gazeta*, February 17, 2001.

Refusal to send a lorry is from Chernyaev, *1991*, diary entry for December 27.

29 The Integrity of the Quarrel

New Year's Eve in Red Square is from report by Seamus Martin in *The Irish Times*, January 1, 1992.

Gorbachev's apartment is described by Korzhakov, p. 172, and Boldin, pp. 200–1.

Garrison exchange with Yakovlev is from interview with Garrison.

Yakovlev's exchange with Yeltsin about Gorbachev dinner invitation is from his interview with Seamus Martin in *The Irish Times*, May 17, 1995.

James Baker's trip is from Baker, pp. 617–18.

Shevardnadze on German unity is from interview with me on April 28, 1990, in *The Irish Times*.

Gorbachev in USA is detailed in Beschloss and Talbott, pp. 465–8.

Yakovlev's reaction to discovery of secret protocols is from his *Sumerki*, p. 419.

Chernyaev's criticisms of Yakovlev are in *My Six Years*, p. 150.

Shevardnadze's comments about Gorbachev are from his interview with Lara Marlowe in *The Irish Times*, August 18, 2008.

Yeltsin's drunken behaviour in Washington is from Branch, p. 198.

Solzhenitsyn comments are from Peter Brooke in *Dublin Review of Books*, Summer, 2010.

Yeltsin's suicide threats are from Korzhakov, pp. 245–6.

Gorbachev in Münster is from Giulietto Chiesa in *Sunday Telegraph*, August 22, 1999.

Polyakov's comments are from Jonathan Steele in *The Observer*, August 29, 1999.

Yeltsin presenting pen to Putin is in Nemtsov, p. 57.

Gorbachev pizza advertisement is from Sandle, p. 274.

America needing *perestroika* is from Ginny Dougary interview with Gorbachev in *The Times*, September 5, 2009.

Putin on Kryuchkov is from Gevorkyan, Timakova and Kolesnikov, p. 94.

Gorbachev on the battle continuing is from his interview on BBC on October 28, 2010.

Significant USSR/Russia Dramatis Personae

Afanasyev, Viktor, editor of *Pravda*, 1976–1989

Afanasyev, Yury, historian, pro-Gorbachev deputy

Akayev, Askar, elected president of Kyrgyzstan in 1990

Akhromeyev, Sergey, marshal of the Soviet army, putschist

Alksnis, Viktor, army officer, campaigned against Gorbachev

Andreyevna, Nina, author of 1988 letter opposing Gorbachev's reforms

Andropov, Yury, general secretary of the Communist Party of the Soviet Union, 1982–1984

Bakatin, Vadim, pro-reform minister, last chairman of the KGB

Baklanov, Oleg, head of Soviet military-industrial complex, putschist

Belyaev, Igor, documentary-maker, friend of Gorbachev

Bessmertnykh, Alexander, Soviet minister for foreign affairs, fired after August coup

Boldin, Valery, Gorbachev's chief of staff, putschist

Bonner, Yelena, widow of Andrey Sakharov

Bovin, Alexander, USSR/Russian ambassador to Israel

Brezhnev, Leonid, first secretary of the Communist Party of the Soviet Union, 1964–1966, then general secretary, 1966–1982

Burbulis, Gennady, close associate of Yeltsin

Burlatsky, Fyodor, pro-reform editor of *Literaturnaya Gazeta*

Chernenko, Konstantin, general secretary of the Communist Party of the Soviet Union, 1984–1985

Chernomyrdin, Viktor, prime minister of Russia, 1992–1998

Chernyaev, Anatoly, close associate of Gorbachev

Chubais, Anatoly, Yeltsin's deputy prime minister, responsible for privatization

Gaidar, Yegor, Yeltsin's deputy prime minister, responsible for shock therapy

Gamsakhurdia, Zviad, elected president of Georgia in 1991

Gerasimov, Gennady, Soviet foreign affairs spokesman

Gorbachev, Mikhail, general secretary of the Communist Party of the Soviet Union, 1985–1991; president of Soviet Union, 1990–1991

Gorbacheva, Irina, daughter of Mikhail Gorbachev

Gorbacheva, Raisa, wife of Mikhail Gorbachev

Grachev, Andrey, Gorbachev's press secretary

Grachev, Pavel, army general, sided with Yeltsin in August coup

Grishin, Viktor, Moscow party chief, 1967–1985

Kalugin, Oleg, KGB dissident

Karimov, Islam, elected president of Uzbekistan in 1990

Khasbulatov, Ruslan, chairman of the Russian Supreme Soviet, 1991–1993

Khrushchev, Nikita, first secretary of the Communist Party of the Soviet Union, 1953–1964

Komplektov, Viktor, USSR/Russian ambassador to the United States

Korotich, Vitaly, pro-reform editor of *Ogonyok*, 1986–1991

Korzhakov, Alexander, Yeltsin's security chief

Kozyrev, Andrey, Russian minister of foreign affairs

Kravchenko, Leonid, head of central television, fired after August coup

Kravchuk, Leonid, elected president of Ukraine in 1991

Kryuchkov, Vladimir, chairman of KGB, putschist

Kuznetsov, Alexander, Yeltsin's personal cameraman

Lebed, Alexander, army general, sided with Yeltsin in August coup

Lenin, Vladimir Ilyich, founder of Soviet Union

Ligachev, Yegor, conservative member of Politburo

Lukyanov, Anatoly, chairman of USSR Supreme Soviet, 1990–1991, putschist

Luzhkov, Yury, mayor of Moscow, 1992–2010

Moiseyev, Mikhail, army general, supported August coup

Murashev, Arkady, liberal Moscow police chief

Nazarbayev, Nursultan, elected president of Kazakhstan, 1990

Nenashev, Mikhail, head of state television until 1990

Palazchenko, Pavel, interpreter for Gorbachev

Pankin, Boris, Soviet minister for foreign affairs after August coup

Pavlov, Valentin, Soviet prime minister, putschist

Petrov, Yury, aide to Yeltsin

Petrushenko, Nikolay, army officer, campaigned against Gorbachev

Plekhanov, Yury, KGB general who held Gorbachevs prisoner during August coup

Poltoranin, Mikhail, ex-editor, Yeltsin press secretary

Popov, Gavriil, mayor of Moscow, 1990–1992

Primakov, Yevgeny, director of foreign intelligence service after August coup

Pugo, Boris, Soviet interior minister, committed suicide after August coup

Putin, Vladimir, aide to St Petersburg mayor, later president and prime minister of Russia

Redkoborody, Vladimir, KGB officer in charge of presidential security

Revenko, Grigory, aide to Gorbachev

Rostropovich, Mstislav, cellist and supporter of reform

Rutskoy, Alexander, vice president of Russia, 1991–1993

Ryzhkov, Nikolay, Soviet prime minister, 1985–1990

Sakharov, Andrey, physicist and human rights campaigner

Shakhnazarov, Georgy, adviser to Gorbachev

Shakhrai, Sergey, Yeltsin aide, drafter of Belovezh Agreement

Shaposhnikov, Yevgeny, air force general, appointed Soviet defence minister after August coup

Shatalin, Stanislav, radical economist

Shenin, Oleg, Communist Party Central Committee secretary, putschist

Shevardnadze, Eduard, Soviet foreign minister, elected leader of Georgia in 1992

Shushkevich, Stanislau, elected chairman of Belarus parliament 1991

Silayev, Ivan, last Soviet prime minister

Sobchak, Anatoly, pro-reform mayor of St Petersburg

Solzhenitsyn, Alexander, former political prisoner and writer

Stalin, Josef, general secretary of the Communist Party of the Soviet Union, 1922–1952

Sukhanov, Lev, assistant to Yeltsin

Suslov, Mikhail, Soviet ideologist in Brezhnev era

Tarasenko, Sergey, aide to Shevardnadze

Tretyakov, Vitaly, pro-reform editor of *Nezavisimaya Gazeta*

Tsipko, Alexander, Gorbachev speech-writer

Varennikov, Valentin, army general, putschist

Vlasov, Alexander, Communist candidate defeated by Yeltsin in election for chairman of Russian Supreme Soviet

Vorontsov, Yury, USSR/Russian ambassador to UN

Yakovlev, Alexander, diplomat, close adviser to Gorbachev, inspiration for *perestroika*

Yakovlev, Yegor, pro-reform editor of *Moscow News*, later head of state television

Yanayev, Gennady, vice president of Soviet Union, putschist

Yaroshenko, Viktor, aide to Yeltsin

Yavlinsky, Grigory, radical economist

Yazov, Dmitry, Soviet minister of defence, putschist

Yeltsin, Boris, Moscow party boss, 1985–1987; chairman of Russian Supreme Soviet, 1990–1991; president of Russia, 1991–1999

Yeltsina, Naina, wife of Boris Yeltsin

Yeltsina, Tanya, daughter of Boris Yeltsin

Yeltsina, Yelena, daughter of Boris Yeltsin

Zhirinovsky, Vladimir, far-right Russian politician

Picture Acknowledgements

Maps: Michael O'Clery

Yeltsin on tank: courtesy of Jim Forrest; Yeltsin and Gorbachev: © Alain-Pierre Hovasse/AFP/Getty Images; Meeting in the Forest: © Novosti.

Gorbachev, Chernyaev and Shakhnazarov: courtesy of Gorbachev Foundation; Alma-Ata: © Vitaly Armand/AFP/Getty Images; Gorbachev and Yeltsin: courtesy of Gorbachev Foundation; Gorbachev and Yegor Yakovlev: courtesy of Tom Johnson;
Shipman, Hurst and Yeltsin: courtesy of Stuart H. Loory.

Gorbachev and Koppel: © ABC Television; Gorbachev calls Bush: © ABC Television; Palazchenko: © ABC Television; Grachev and Gorbachev: courtesy of Andrey Grachev; Gorbachev takes CNN pen: courtesy of Tom Johnson; Gorbachev ready to sign: © Vitaly Armand/AFP/Getty Images.

Gorbachev ends resignation speech: © Associated Press;

Index

Just Joe:
My Autobiography
Joe Duffy

'Beautifully written, honest and thoroughly
enjoyable. A great read'
Gay Byrne

Joe Duffy is a household name in Ireland. As the presenter of
RTÉ Radio One's *Liveline* programme, he takes the pulse of the
Irish nation every day, often delving into highly controversial
topics. Whenever somebody wants to get something off their
chest, the advice is often: 'Talk to Joe'.

Writing with raw honesty, Joe here recounts his difficult upbringing
in working-class Ballyfermot. He paints a poignant, heart-breaking
picture of family life with a hard-drinking father and hard-
working mother. Joe writes with candour about the death of his
youngest brother Aidan and about his often difficult relationship
with another brother, Brendan.

Joe became one of the first from his area to enter the hallowed
halls of Trinity College Dublin, where he developed a strong
sense of social justice, eventually becoming President of the
Union of Students in Ireland, leading protests on campus
highlighting access to education and spending two weeks in
Mountjoy Prison as a result.

After a stint working in the probation service, Joe eventually
moved into a career in broadcasting, first as producer and then
roving reporter on *The Gay Byrne Show*, before finally finding
his niche on *Liveline*. Here, Joe highlights the major stories
raised by the programme, including child-abuse controversies
and scandals in the Irish health service. Joe also deals with the
shocking death in 2010 of Joe's friend and fellow broadcaster
Gerry Ryan.

This is a riveting, deeply felt and fascinating memoir which
goes behind the public face of Joe Duffy to reveal a complex,
passionate man.

Once Upon a Time in the West:
The Corrib Gas Controversy

Lorna Siggins

'All I want is to stay where I am . . . My heart
and soul are in this place.'
(Willie Corduff, one of The Rossport Five)

In a remote, beautiful part of the west of Ireland, a David and
Goliath struggle rages between multinational oil company,
Shell, and some of the local community of Rossport, County
Mayo.

In 1996, Enterprise Oil, subsequently bought by Shell, found
a major source of valuable gas offshore in the Corrib gas
field. In the attempt to build an onshore pipeline and refinery
the oil giant has come into conflict with a small group of
locals who, anxious about the safety of their families, the
environmental impact of the project and the future of their
community, are resisting Shell's plans. The eyes of the nation
fell on this tiny community when, in 2005, five of the
residents were jailed for refusing to allow Shell onto their
land, in contempt of court orders. These men have become
known as The Rossport Five.

Irish Times correspondent Lorna Siggins has been covering
the controversy from the beginning. No one is better placed to
unravel the twists and turns of this fascinating human drama
and its political, cultural and environmental shockwaves.

In a new Ireland where economic logic goes largely
unchallenged, the Corrib Gas pipeline controversy raises
uncomfortable questions about the ways in which Ireland has
changed.